ISLAMIC FINANCE AND BANKING SYSTEM

Philosophies, Principles & Practices

Sudin Haron

Wan Nursofiza Wan Azmi

Kuala Lumpur • Boston • Burr Ridge, IL • Dubuque, IA • Madison, WI • New York • San Francisco
St. Louis • Bangkok • Bogotá • Caracas • Singapore • Lisbon • London • Madrid
Mexico City • Milan • Montreal • New Delhi • Santiago • Seoul • Sydney • Taipei • Toronto

Perpustakaan Negara Malaysia   Cataloguing-in-Publication Data

Sudin Haron, 1954–
    Islamic Finance and Banking System / Sudin Haron,
    Wan Nursofiza Wan Azmi.
    Includes Index
    ISBN 978-983-3850-61-7
    ISBN 987-983-3850-30-3 (pbk.)
    1. Finance–Religious aspects–Islam. 2. Banks and banking–Religious
    aspects–Islam. I. Wan Nursofiza Wan Azmi. II. Title.
    332.10917671

 **Education**

Copyright © 2009 by McGraw-Hill (Malaysia) Sdn. Bhd.

40, Jalan Pengacara U1/48,
Temasya Industrial Park,
40150 Shah Alam, Selangor, Malaysia.
msia_mhe@mcgraw-hill.com

1 2 3 4 5 6 7 8 9 10 IA IA 15 14 13 12 11 10 09

When ordering this title, use ISBN 978-983-3850-61-7

Printed in Malaysia

The McGraw-Hill Companies

FOREWORD

In an increasingly challenging global financial environment that continues to be punctuated by crisis, Islamic finance has continued to remain robust as a viable form of financial intermediation. The transformation and progressive pace of development of Islamic finance is now gaining an international dimension as it becomes an increasingly important component of the international financial system. These developments have been a catalyst for increased financial innovation and participation in the Islamic financial markets.

Malaysia's experience in developing a comprehensive Islamic financial system has brought the country to the forefront in the development and evolution of the industry. An important aspect of this is that the development by the industry is supported by a sound regulatory structure that is in place to ensure the soundness and stability of the system. This has attracted major Islamic financial services players to the country. The Islamic financial system in Malaysia is now regarded as one of the most comprehensive in the world.

The sustainable growth and competitiveness of the Islamic finance industry however depends essentially on human intellectual capital development and the investment in research. There is an urgent need to produce highly qualified professionals in this area so as to ensure continued innovation of new products and services to meet the diverse needs of the economy. The task before us now is how to meet the challenging demand for world-class professionals in Islamic finance who are proficient in both technical and *Shariah* aspects of the subject matter. Strong focus on human capital development through education is the key. Since, there are still many areas of Islamic finance that have yet to be explored, new research findings could pave the way towards the broadening and deepening of the Islamic financial markets and subsequently strengthening the industry's development.

The publication of this book on *Islamic Finance and Banking System* that focuses on theoretical, conceptual and operational aspects, laws and regulations of Islamic banking, Islamic financial markets, takaful system is indeed an important initiative. The information on the relevant areas related to Islamic finance in this book will be valuable to those who wish to gain a greater understanding on Islamic finance. I sincerely hope that the publication of this book will contribute towards greater understanding in the fundamental aspects of Islamic finance. A better understanding will certainly increase awareness of Islamic finance and the tremendous potential it offers as a form of financial intermediation in our global financial system.

Dr. Zeti Akhtar Aziz
Governor
Bank Negara Malaysia

PREFACE

Islamic banking which began as a theological dream has today become a practical reality and accepted worldwide. Islamic banking and finance has transformed from an infant industry in the 1970s to one of the most viable and efficient alternative models of financial intermediation. The Islamic financial services industry has consistently chalked up double-digit growth with a presence in more than 75 countries. It is estimated that total financial assets of the industry now exceed US$1 trillion.

The integration of Islamic finance into the global economy is marked by the growing awareness of and demand for investing in accordance with *Syariah* principles, progress in developing regulatory framework and enhanced international linkages. However, the success of Islamic banking brings forth new challenges to the industry. These include lack of standard financial contracts and products, illiquidity issues, liquidity risk management concerns, regulatory disparities among regulators at the national level and the need for harmonized regulation.

These successes and challenges facing Islamic financial institutions have been widely documented. Nonetheless, there is still an acute dearth of literature which covers concepts and applications of Islamic banking worldwide as well as provides comprehensive illustration of all major aspects of Islamic finance and banking on a more global scale. Having kept a close watch on developments in Islamic finance and banking over the last two decades and excessive work done on the subject, we wanted to contribute in addressing this gap in the literature.

This book is an effort to provide a comprehensive knowledge on Islamic finance and to highlight current development of the industry worldwide. The first four chapters set the tone for the rest of the book. Readers are introduced to the history and development of Islamic banking and are provided with in-depth discussion on the theoretical and conceptual aspects of Islamic banking. The next four chapters cover Islamic banking, *takaful* and Islamic capital market which have all experienced accelerated growth due to increased diversification in investment. The last chapter features the role and development of special organizations related to the Islamic financial system. We have also attempted to give readers an overview of various Islamic banking and financial models as practised in other countries. However, the primary strength of this book lies in its comprehensive and contemporary approach in discussing Islamic finance and banking by covering all the relevant areas.

The recent financial crisis that has emerged due to global credit woes has broaden the appeal of Islamic finance. The global credit crisis has shown the need for laws enshrined in Islamic finance which prohibit speculation and high levels of debt and promote high level of financial prudence. *Syariah* also prohibits immoral transactions and encourages greater social justice through the sharing of risk and rewards and socially responsible investments. It is these ethical and moral safeguards that are missing in the conventional system. As the world is looking for a new economic order amid the current financial woes, Islamic finance is presented with a great opportunity to step up to the mark and gain traction. It is our sincere hope that this book will contribute to a better understanding of Islamic finance and banking and the role it can play in filling the liquidity gap under the new economic order.

This book is not our venture alone. We extend special thanks to our families and friends for their support and encouragement. We also appreciate the invaluable comments of the reviewers on the draft of the book. Finally, we accept responsibility for any errors, omissions and shortcomings that remain.

Sudin Haron
Wan Nursofiza Wan Azmi

CONTENTS

CHAPTER 1

FUNDAMENTALS OF ISLAMIC ECONOMIC SYSTEM

This chapter gives a brief description of matters relating to existing economic systems practised throughout the world. This basic knowledge is essential for anyone who wishes to learn all aspects of Islamic economics. The chapter then covers the concepts and essence of the development of the Islamic economic system of which Islamic banking is a branch.

INTRODUCTION

Efforts to instil Islamic ideas and values into the field of economics only started not more than three decades ago, that is, in the 1970s (Siddiqi, 1996). If we accept this view, it implies that Islamic economic system did not exist before that time. Certainly this is not true; in fact it is even absurd. This is because Islamic economic system had existed alongside Islam. Perhaps Siddiqi was actually referring to the re-absorption process of Islamic principles into the field of economics. The existence of Islamic economics is proven through *Surah al-Maidah*, where Allah (s.w.t.) says:

1

…This day I have perfected your religion for you, completed my favour upon you, and have chosen for you Islam as your religion…   (Q5: 3)

Based on the above verse, it is clear that Islam encompasses all aspects of the human life. This being so, it follows that Islam has its own unique system of economy (Chapra, 1994). The Prophet Muhammad (p.b.u.h.) in his youth practised and implemented this system of economy through trade based on the concept of *mudharabah* with his wife Siti Khadijah. In fact, He participated in all activities involving the development and implementation of Islamic economics. As an example, one of the early concepts of economics in Islam can be found in the method of distributing wealth obtained from battles won. Such Islamic economic activities continued to be developed after the time of the Prophet (p.b.u.h.). During the era of Caliph Omar al-Khattab (634–644), for instance, a great deal was done in the coordination and introduction of economic activities for the good of the Islamic *ummah*, or Muslims, which was consequently adopted by many other parties. Unfortunately, these concepts of Islamic economics were not really made known and some were even forgotten. Instead, Muslims were exposed to economic systems established and developed by non-Muslim intellectuals. As a result, society was led or forced to learn about the economic systems of the West, and consequently became more familiar with capitalist, socialist and marxist economics.

DEFINITION OF ECONOMICS

Barnhart (1988) defined economy or *yconomye* as management of the household. The word economy was first used in the year 1440 and may have originated from a word in the mid-French era, that is *economie*, or from the Latin *oeconomia*, or from the Greek *oikonomia* (which comes from the word *oikonomos* meaning manager or guard).

The use of this word to mean management of a nation's resources was adopted in the year 1651.

The history of modern economics began in 1776 when Adam Smith published his book called *An Inquiry into the Nature and Causes of the Wealth of Nations* which described the principles in a market economy. In his other book, *The Wealth of Nations*, Smith discussed matters relating to determining the price of a commodity; determining the price of land, labour and capital; and the strengths and weaknesses of the market mechanisms. All the ideas and concepts put forward by Adam Smith are still in use today. However, Smith only offered the concept of microeconomics, which is one of the two branches of economics, the other being macroeconomics. Microeconomics is the analysis of individual behaviour in economics, such as determining the price of a certain commodity in the market, or the behaviour of a particular person or a particular firm.

The concept of macroeconomics was introduced in the year 1936 by John Maynard Keynes. The field of macroeconomics covers aspects related to production, income, price level, international trade, unemployment and the work force as a whole. In his book titled *The General Theory of Employment, Interest, and Money*, Keynes discussed factors which stimulate economic crises, determinants of investment, the role of central banks in managing money and interest rates and why some nations develop rapidly while others remain static. Keynes also explained the importance of the role played by governments in evening out the fluctuations of the business cycle (Samuelson and Nordhaus, 1995). Hence, the concepts introduced by Keynes included banking and financial concepts. The concepts of Islamic finance and banking need to be looked at by making comparisons with the macroeconomic concepts offered by this Western intellectual.

Apart from this, there are various definitions of economics put forward by intellectuals. Low and Toh (1997) listed several definitions given by renowned economics intellectuals as follows:

1. Adam Smith: Economics or political economics is the study of the natural world and the causes of the wealth of nations.

2. Naasau William Sr.: Political economics is the science related to the natural world, and the production and distribution of wealth.

3. Alfred Marshall: Political economics or economics is the study of the everyday lives of people, where a part of it is about wealth, while the other part, which is most important, is about man himself.

4. Lionel Robbins: Economics is the science that studies the behaviour of man as a correlation between objectives and limited capacity of multiple uses.

5. Milton Friedman: Economics is the science that studies the methods used by particular societies to solve their economic problems.

6. Richard Lipsey, Peter Steiner, Douglas Purvis and Paul Courant: Economics is the study of the use of limited resources to meet unlimited demands.

7. Paul Samuelson and William S. Nordhaus: Economics is the study of the use of limited resources to produce valuable commodities and distribute them to different people.

8. Rupert Pennant-Rea and Bill Emmott: Economics is something which is difficult to define, but most people would recognize it when they see it. In general, economics is the study of the ways societies of the world live their lives. In more specific terms, economics is the study of the ways in which limited resources are used to produce and distribute products and services to meet the needs of people.

The various definitions of economics given by the intellectuals were summarized by Samuelson and Nordhaus (1995). They summed up economics as the science that:

1. Studies methods of determining the cost of labour, capital and land and ways in which the costing is used for the purposes of resource distribution.

2. Explores the behaviour of the financial market and analyzes the method of capital distribution to the economy as a whole.

3. Analyzes the existing effects on market efficiency resulting from regulations imposed by governments.

4. Studies income distribution and suggests ways to provide assistance to the poor without harming economic performance.

5. Examines the effects of government expenditure, taxation and budget deficit on economic development.

6. Examines the increase or decline in labour consumption and production which creates the business cycle, and establishes government policies to enhance economic growth.

7. Examines inter-nation forms of trade and analyzes effects of trade embargoes.

8. Studies economic growth in developing nations and suggests methods to promote effective use of resources.

Kamus Ekonomi (1993) defined economics as a field of social science that studies the behaviour of humans in the provision of limited resources to meet unlimited needs and demands, where one competes with the other.

Almost all the above definitions of economics revolve around the problem faced by society in making choices to meet unlimited needs based on limited resources. The limited resources must be used in the most effective way so as to benefit the whole of society, and distribution has to be based on efforts put in. Hence, Niemi (1978) defined economics as a study of ways in which society makes choices when distributing limited resources to meet unlimited demands such that society benefits fully and that the benefit obtained is in accordance with their contribution.

The resources referred to relate to human and physical resources. Human resource, also known as the labour factor, includes management and entrepreneurship elements. Labour is the work force that moves an economy and it can be seen as two groups, one comprising the thinkers and managers and the other comprising the workers who implement the tasks as directed. The physical resource is made up of land and capital factors. These factors are also called factors of production. In this situation, the operator works to produce goods with the hope of receiving returns after the product or service is utilized by the consumer. The operator would put in every effort to fully utilize all factors of production, while the consumer would make choices such that the product he buys would meet his needs as much as possible and is worth the money spent in acquiring it.

WORLD ECONOMIC SYSTEM

According to Gregory and Stuart (1999), the economic system is a set of mechanisms and institutions that makes and implements decisions related to the production, income and consumption in a particular region or area. Hence, an economic system is the interaction among participants involved in an organization, according to the regulations and instructions, in the production, distribution and consumption of products and services. An economic system can also be viewed as a regulation whereby society will determine what will be produced, how the product will be produced (this includes matters relating to the institution or organization, the equipment used, as well as the form of resources that are distributed) and how the income obtained from the sale of the products and services is distributed to the masses (Bronstein, 1994). In order to make comparisons of the different economic systems, a fundamental basis which can be used as a measure of the differences has to be established. Bronstein asserted that there are three factors that influence the formation of an economic system, namely the level of economic development, social and cultural factors, and environment.

Gregory and Stuart (1999) described four main characteristics that distinguish one economic system from another. The first characteristic is associated with the way decisions are made. The second is related to the mechanism for the provision of information and coordination of decisions. The third is about property rights. Finally, the fourth covers mechanism in preparing goals and incentives for the masses to execute a particular action.

The main characteristic, that is the issue of the organization of decision-making arrangements, involves aspects associated with methods and processes of decision making practised by organizations or economic agents including governments. Organizations in a society are normally made up of members who constantly interact among one another in carrying out an activity. An organization would have goals from which information would be developed, while assumptions and behaviour would be formulated. All these have roles to play in arriving at particular decisions. Since an organization comprises many members, contradictions are bound to exist between individual and organizational goals. To overcome this problem, an organization establishes rules related to the formation of small groups, work distribution, coordination and monitoring of activities as well as explanation of the incentives offered. All the rules and regulations which are formulated and established will determine the structure of an organization, which will in turn become the basis that distinguishes one economic system from another. Organizational structure can be viewed from two different perspectives.

The first perspective is based on the way a particular activity is implemented. Organizations in this category fall into two types, one based on hierarchy and the other, association. Under the hierarchy type of organization, decisions are made by the higher-ups, while the rank and file merely implement the decisions and instructions to achieve the goals set. Under the association type of organization, decisions are made collectively by members, there being no relationship between the leaders and the workers. The second perspective involves the way in which distribution of resources is decided upon. Organizations in this category are classed as non-centred and centred organizations. In non-centred organizations decisions are made at the lower levels, while in centred organizations centralized decisions are made at the top levels.

The second characteristic, related to the mechanism of the provision of information and coordination of decisions, refers to two forms of economy, namely planned economy and market economy. In planned economy, all agents are coordinated by way of set instructions which are documented and established by the central agency. The agent is required to implement all instructions alongside incentives and restrictions given by the authorities who prepare the plan. Returns received by implementers will depend on their achievements of given instructions. In market economy, on the other hand, an organization decides on the use of resources based on the forces of supply and demand. This means that the market situation will coordinate the decision-making process of economic units. The main thing that differentiates a planned economic system from a market economy is the decision maker. In market economy, clients can exercise their right to choose, and their right to use whatever they wish. On the other hand, in a planned economic system, it is the planner who determines production activities and the products to be produced. In this case, the priority of the planner overrules priority of the masses.

The third characteristic that differentiates economic systems is property ownership rights in society. Property ownership rights are of three types: first, the right to transfer ownership, which involves giving, transferring or selling property to another party; secondly, the right to use the property; and thirdly, the right to use whatever that is produced from the property held. Property ownership may also be categorized into three main forms: individual or private ownership, public ownership and joint ownership. In private ownership, all three types of ownership rights are provided to the individual. In public ownership, however, those rights are held by the nation.

The fourth characteristic which differentiates economic systems is the way incentives are given to society to regulate economic activities. An incentive is an instrument which can be used to encourage or motivate people to do something. Normally, the authorities may offer two kinds of incentives, that is, material incentive and moral incentive. Material incentive is common in the current economic system, and it can be divided into private incentive and collective incentive. Collective material incentive is given with the intention of promoting a sense of social consciousness and solidarity, while private incentive encourages competition and individualism. Moral incentive motivates the receiver to be more responsible towards society so as to attain a high position. This kind of incentive does not involve tangible gain for the receiver.

Based on the explanation of the four characteristics, the economic systems of the world can be divided into several main clusters. The most frequently used clusters are capitalism and socialism. There are many theories that relate to these economic systems. However, those theories will not be discussed in detail in this book. Capitalism is an economic system characterized by individual ownership of factors of production. The process of decision making lies in the hands of the owner of the factors of production and the decision made is based on or coordinated by market mechanisms. The market becomes the place for owners to obtain information, and material incentives become the motivation for the people. This method was pioneered by Adam Smith in his book, *The Wealth of Nations* in 1776. According to him, the most efficient economic system exists when there are market competition and no government intervention in the economy. There are various kinds of capitalism in the world. Schnitzer (1994) in his book, *Comparative Economic Systems*, divided capitalism into two classes, individual capitalism and social capitalism. Individual capitalism system is commonly called market economic system or open economic system, while social capitalism is normally known as the system of mixed economy.

Individual capitalism is a system practised by Anglo-Saxon nations. In the 19th century, the United Kingdom was the leading nation implementing the system, while in the 20th century it was the United States that led. Social capitalism, meanwhile, has become the practice of European countries like Germany and nations in the East such as Japan and South East Asia. In this system, the government plays an important role in promoting economic development and providing welfare services to the society. Through this system, employers are more loyal to their workplace and the company cooperates in planning strategies for mutual benefit. In other words, in the capitalist system there is smart partnership between the government and the private sectors.

There are various differing concepts and definitions for the socialist system. For instance, there exist differences in the socialist concept as practised in France and several Eastern European nations compared to that in nations like the former Soviet Union, China, Cuba, North Korea and Vietnam. The West is of the opinion that nations under communist regimes, like Russia, China, Cuba, North Korea and Vietnam are not socialist countries, but are instead nations that practise communism. The words socialist and socialism are said to be relatively new and were introduced in England and France in the early 19th century. However, the concept had already been mentioned by philosophers, right from the time of Plato (427–347BC). In fact, a Christian thinker, Thomas Aquinas (1225–1274) held the view that property could be owned by individual but its use should be for all (Schnitzer, 1994). During the Renaissance period (that is, a period of great cultural change in Europe that spanned from the 14th to the 17th century) many intellectuals discussed the kind of society that they would like to see created. The majority of them wanted a utopia kind of society, that is, a society which has a perfect social system, which creates social happiness, whereby the principal entities in this situation are economic and social factors, not religion. Utopic socialism is based on the theory that the existence of the world is meant to provide joy and happiness to the people, and that each human being has a natural right to it (Fly, 1983).

Modern socialist system is a system that was developed as a social reformation due to the brutalities triggered by the industrial revolution which began in England in the middle of the 11th century. The term industrial revolution means changing from traditional society to modern society through economic industrialization. Robert Owen, an English socialist, is said to have started the modern socialist era in 1800 when he created the social change scheme by altering the beliefs of individual. He believed that true happiness is attained by making others happy (Schnitzer, 1994). Socialism began to spread to the political system of England by the middle of the 19th century. Large-scale retrenchment of workers due to an economic depression became the main factor for the development of this ideology. This movement subsequently received support from trade unions and intellectuals who believed that political and economic structures should be changed for the good of the workers. Socialism began to spread as a political movement at the end of the 19th century, whereby political parties based on this ideology were established in France and Germany in 1900. As with the capitalist system, there are many variations of the socialist system.

Gregory and Stuart (1999) divided socialism into two groups, market socialism and planned socialism. Market socialism is characterized by public (national) ownership of factors of production, and decisions are not made centrally, but instead a decentralized process based on market mechanisms is used. Material and moral elements are used as incentives to motivate people. In planned socialism, on the other hand, there is also public ownership of the factors of production, but decisions are made at the central level.

Planners at this level will issue instructions to be followed by those in the system, and both material and moral incentives are used to motivate the people.

There is also classification in socialism, based on the Marxist and non-Marxist ideologies. Marxists believe that revolution is necessary in order to establish the socialist ideology. The non-Marxist group, on the other hand, is of the stand that changes could be made to the existing economic, political and social systems without any revolution. The Marxist socialist system was pioneered by Karl Marx (1818–1883), who viewed that the transformation from capitalism to communism was inevitable. Capitalism exploited workers and caused friction in an organization. Hence, the system should be replaced with socialism in which the concept of common ownership was given importance.

The communist system is at the tail end of the socialist system, and is characterized by the absence of market and money. Distribution of necessities depends on needs. This basic concept of communism was discussed by the Greek philosopher Plato in his book, *Republic*. Plato was of the opinion that a perfect nation is one with communist societies, where everything is collectively owned, at least for the upper classes. The upper classes that rule and control the nation would eat in the same hall and sleep in the same building as the common people, and would even obtain aid from them.

Marx's views on socialism are found in his book, *Das Kapital*. In this book, Marx wrote his economic theory which forms the basis of the communist ideology. Marx's emphasis on the crucial importance of the role played by the government or nation was reinforced by V.I. Lenin (1870–1924). Lenin was one of the greatest revolutionary thinkers of the 20th century. He believed that inequality and capitalist attributes still existed in socialism; hence, stern action on the part of the government was necessary. However, Marx and Lenin merely offered views about the role of the nation and ways to distribute income in socialism. They did not discuss methods of distributing limited resources.

While Karl Marx is regarded as the one who initiated modern communism, Lenin is viewed as the one who developed the ideology. Through the Bolshevick Revolution in 1917, Lenin successfully established the Soviet Union and subsequently the Communist Party in March 1918. The Soviet nation and the communist ideology continued to be upheld by several leaders such as Joseph Stalin who ruled from 1924 to 1953, Nikita Khrushchev from 1953 to 1964 and Leonid Brezhnev from 1964 to 1982. The influence of communism developed further with the end of the Second World War, and began to spread to Eastern Europe, China, North Korea, Cuba and Vietnam. During its peak period, almost one-third of the world population were living in nations that practised this system.

The communist system, whose origin and reference was the Soviet Union, moved into a transition period beginning in 1985 when Mikhail Gorbachev came to power. Gorbachev introduced radical reformations to the economic, political and societal structures. Eventually, it was the reformation itself which caused the disintegration of the Soviet Union and which saw the end of communism in the Soviet Union. Gorbachev introduced the *prestroika* concept (which means restructuring), the *glasnost* concept (which means openness in public affairs) and the *democratization* concept (a concept that takes into account the views of those in the lower ranks).

The break-up of the Soviet Union which consisted of 15 separate republics began when 3 of the republics, namely Estonia, Latvia and Lithuania declared their respective independence in 1990. In 1991, there was an attempt by ardent believers of communism to seize power and overthrow Gorbachev. Although the attempt failed, Gorbachev lost his power and was forced to resign, and as a consequence the structure of the Communist Party crumbled. This opportunity was used by Boris Yeltsin, the President of the Russian Union, to replace Gorbachev as the leader of the Soviet Union. However, during this time the nations in the Soviet Union began to declare their respective independence and took over properties belonging to the Soviet Union in their respective countries. In December 1991, 3 main republics in the Soviet Union, namely Russia, Ukraine and Belarus agreed to establish the Commonwealth of Independent States, and on 21 December 1991 eight former Soviet nations agreed to rejoin the Union. With that came the end of the Soviet Union (Schnitzer, 1994).

The changes executed by the Soviet rulers serve as an example for other communist nations. Political change also occurred in the Eastern European nations which were ruled by communists, such as East Germany, Czechoslovakia, Bulgaria, Poland and Hungary. Such changes normally occurred in two phases. In the first phase, the communist rule was replaced by communist reformists who were prepared to share power with non-communist groups, and eventually eroded the monopoly power of the communist party. In the second phase, non-communists were chosen to replace the government, with the hope that the ruling party would cooperate with the West and establish a market economy. To date, other communist nations like China, Vietnam, North Korea and Cuba have also started the process of business relationships with the West, and in certain cases have allowed the establishment of market economy in their respective nations.

ISLAMIC ECONOMIC SYSTEM

Based on the definitions of economy and economics given in the early part of this chapter, it can be concluded that economics is a branch of knowledge about the ways people use existing resources to create products and services for their use. The Islamic *ummah* or Muslims are people who work to obtain *rezeki* (sustenance) by using the resources made available by Allah (s.w.t.) for their use while living in this world and as preparation for the Hereafter. This fact shows that there must exist knowledge related to economy in

Islam. There are many examples in the verses of the Quran which relate to economy. Apart from that, there are many *Hadith* that carry guidelines, views and lessons on aspects relating to economy given by the Prophet (p.b.u.h.). In fact, Allah (s.w.t.) mentioned economic matters related to the days of the earlier prophets. For example, the following two verses describe economic matters during the time of Abraham and Shu'ayb:

> *And We made them leaders, guiding men by Our command, and We sent them an inspiration to do good deeds, to establish regular prayers, and to practise regular charity; and they constantly served Us (and Us only).*   (Q21: 73)

> *Give just measure, and cause no loss (to others by fraud). And weigh with scales true and upright. And withhold not things justly due to men, nor do evil in the land, working mischief.*   (Q26: 181–183)

Apart from the above verses there are many other verses presented by Allah (s.w.t.) in the Quran that are of relevance to economy. Furthermore, the Prophet Muhammad (p.b.u.h.) in his *Hadith*, frequently discussed issues of economy and business.

From the explanation above, it is clear that the religion of Islam is not merely about the relationship between human beings and their Creator, but it also covers the ways humans are to manage existing resources on earth in line with the reason and intent of them being made available. The following verses explain this:

> *It is He who hath created for you all things that are on earth; moreover His design comprehended the heavens, for He gave order and perfection to the seven firmaments; and of all things He has perfect knowledge.*
> (Q2: 29)

> *It is He who has made the sea subject, that ye may eat thereof flesh that is fresh and tender, and that ye may extract therefrom ornaments to wear, and thou seest the ships therein that plough the waves, that ye may seek (thus) of the bounty of Allah and that ye may be grateful.*
> (Q16: 14; see also Q30: 46; Q35: 12; and Q45: 12)

Say: Who has forbidden the beautiful (gifts) of Allah, which He hath produced for His servants, and the things, clean and pure, (which He hath provided) for sustenance? Say: They are, in the life of this world, for those who believe, (and) purely for them on the Day of Judgement. Thus do We explain the Signs in detail for those who understand.

(Q7: 32)

It is evident that Islam is not a religion that places importance solely on the Hereafter, but also on worldly affairs. However, Islamic economic knowledge was not developed and passed down from generation to generation. In fact, what is even more disheartening is the fact that the fundamental substance of economics claimed to have been developed by intellectuals from the West was in fact stolen from the works of great thinkers of Islamic economics. Islamic scholars who conducted various researches discovered that there are a lot of similarities between the views presented by Western intellectuals and the views of Islamic thinkers who had lived in much earlier times. Listed below are some of such views (Karim, 2002):

(i) The *optima pareto* theory originated from the works of Imam Ali r.a. titled *Nahjul Balagh*.

(ii) Priest Bar Hebraeus from the Syariac Jacobite church copied several chapters from the book *Ihya Ulumuddin* written by Imam Ghazali.

(iii) Priest Raymond Martini from the Spain Ordo Dominican church copied many chapters from the books of *Tahafata al-Falasifa, Maqasida al-Falasifa, Al-Munaqid, Misykat Al-Anwar* and *Ihya Ulumuddin* written by Imam Ghazali.

(iv) St. Thomas Aquinas plagiarized many chapters from the works of al-Farabi.

(v) Writings of Adam Smith in the book *The Wealth of Nations* (1776) shared a lot of similarities with the works of Abu Ubayad (d. 838 A.C.) titled *al-Amwal* or *The Wealth*.

Apart from the works of early Islamic thinkers of economics which were copied by Western intellectuals, there exist many more works related to economics produced by Islamic thinkers and scholars. According to Karim (2002), some of the works on economics by early Islamic thinkers are:

(i) *Risala al-Shahabah* by Abdullah bin al-Muqaffa (109–145 H / 727–762), works on policies and public financial administration.

(ii) *Kitab al-Kharaj* by Abu Yusuf (113–182 H / 731–789), works on financial management.

(iii) *Kitab al-Kharaj* by Yahya bin Adam al-Quraisy (140–203 H / 757–818), a collection of *hadith* about *Fiqha al-Amwal*.

(iv) *Kitab al-Amwal* by Abu Ubaid al-Qasim bin Salam (140–157 H / 774–838), works about policies and public finance.

(v) *Kitab al-Amwal* by Abu Hamid bin Zanjawaih (180–251 H / 796–865).

The state where works of Islamic thinkers on economics were neither given due notice nor developed continued from the middle Islamic period to the time when the Islamic civilization ended and right up to the era of the Uthmaniah rule which was centred in Turkey. As a result, not much was written about Islamic economics and eventually a vacuum was formed and the spread of the knowledge became very much constrained. A contemporary Islamic scholar, Kahf (1989) was of the view that too little effort has been made to review the views and guidelines on economics produced by Islamic thinkers of the past, like Abu Yusuf (d. 182 H), Yahya bin Adam (d. 303 H), al-Ghazali (d. 505 A.H.), Ibn Rushad (d. 595 A.H.), al-Izz bin Abdus-Salam (d. 66 H), al-Farabi (d. 339 H), Ibn Taymiah (d. 728 H) and Ibn Khaldun (d. 808 H). Views and ideas expressed by this group of thinkers could stimulate other Muslim economists to study the development and the paths of knowledge associated with Islamic economy. This way, Muslim economists could reassess the applicability of the Islamic economics that had been developed and increase its scope for the benefit of the present-time man.

Khan (1989) was of the opinion that there currently exist three groups of Muslim intellectuals who have contributed towards the revival of discussions on this knowledge. The first is the group of *ulama* (respected people with in-depth knowledge of Islam) who reinitiated discussions on the concept of Islamic economics. This group pioneered the move and is of the view that teachings of Islam regarding economy and economics are all-encompassing and could solve economic problems faced by man. This group uses past methods whereby research is done based on authentic sources. The second group is the modern group, who performs reinterpretations based on authentic sources and undertakes to modify views of traditional *ulama* in line with current situations. The views of this modern group, however, sometimes fail to receive public support. The third group who discusses Islamic economic matters comprises economists educated in the West. They possess expertise in the field of economics and they perform analysis guided by the views of the *ulama*. This third group has contributed a great deal to the advancement of knowledge in Islamic economics.

To date, although there is already ample writings and research on Islamic economics, there are still gaps to be filled and still many economic issues which have yet to be resolved from the Islamic perspective.

ISLAMIC ECONOMIC METHODOLOGY

According to Kahf (1989), an economic system should be founded on an ideology that provides the system with two main components, the first being fundamentals and objectives, and the other component consisting of principles and concepts associated with it. In other words, to understand Islamic economic system, one must first understand Islamic economic methodology. Blaug (1980) believed that methodology of a particular body of knowledge would examine aspects related to concepts, theories and principles of that body of knowledge. Due to the fact that Islamic economic system is a branch of knowledge which has yet to be fully developed, there are, hence, many differing views about Islamic economic methodology. Even though there is an abundance of writings on Islamic economic system, most of the writings only revolve around concepts, leaving out theory. Khan (1989) felt that the writings are conceptual in nature because they revolve around commentaries and views guided by the teachings of Islam. These writings are not theoretical in nature because they do not take into account actual current situations of mankind. The fact that at present, writings that can be regarded as essential readings on Islamic economic system are still non-existent shows that there is yet a long way to go in the advancement of knowledge in Islamic economics. According to Siddiqi (1982), three areas of similarity that exist between the various economic methodologies of the West are:

(i) The basic assumption that a person places importance on himself and behaves in a rational manner.

(ii) His main goal is material gain.

(iii) Each person has the tendency to maximize his possessions of material goods and also has the knowledge and capacity to determine what is best for him.

The above are assumptions of the Western economic methodologies about man. However, the authenticity of such views has to be validated in developing an Islamic economy. The Quran has outlined several natural attributes of man. The following are some of them:

Allah doth wish to lighten your (difficulties): for man was created weak (in flesh).   (Q4: 28)

Fair in the eyes of men is the love of things they covet: women and sons; heaped up hoards of gold and silver; horses branded (for blood and excellence); and (wealth of) cattle and well-tilled land. Such are the possessions of this world's life; but in nearness to Allah is the best of the goals (to return to).   (Q3: 14)

When trouble toucheth a man, he crieth unto Us (in all postures) – lying down on his side or sitting, or standing. But when We have solved his trouble, he passeth on his way as if he had never cried to Us for a trouble that touched him! Thus do the deeds of transgressors seem fair in their eyes!

(Q10: 12; see also Q39: 49; Q17: 67; and Q17: 83)

But verily thy Lord is full of grace to mankind: yet most of them are ungrateful.   (Q27: 73; see also Q7: 10; Q23: 78; and Q39: 49)

We have explained in detail in this Quran, for the benefit of mankind, every kind of similitude: but man is, in most things, contentious.

(Q18: 54; see also Q17: 89; Q14: 34; Q25: 50; Q30: 8; Q22: 66; and Q96: 6–7)

Truly man was created very impatient.
Fretful when evil touches him.
And niggardly when good reaches him.

(Q70:19–21; see also Q17:100, and Q100: 6–8)

Man does not weary of asking for good (things), but if ill touches him, he gives up all hope (and) is lost in despair.   (Q41: 49)

Man is a creature of haste: soon (enough) I will show you My Signs; then ye will not ask Me to hasten them!   (Q21: 37)

We have not sent thee but as a universal (Messenger) to men, giving them Glad Tidings, and warning them (against sin), but most men understand not.

(Q34: 28; see also Q30: 6; Q34: 36; Q39: 49; and Q45: 26)

From the above verses, it can be seen that some of the attributes of mankind include having a preference for material things, being easily swayed or misled, being unappreciative, argumentative and contentious, stinginess, hopelessness, need for haste and ignorance. Although these may be the natural attributes of mankind, this does not mean that Muslims should perpetuate these attributes. Muslims have been given guidelines that must be adhered to. These guidelines are in contrast to the above mentioned natural attributes of mankind. This is one of the uniqueness of Islam. Allah (s.w.t.) wishes to test how far a believer of Islam is willing to comply with His rules. As an example, Islam forbids its believer to be selfish. Islam not only encourages one to be generous, but also must be willing to sacrifice for others. Many verses in the Quran urge Muslims to do good unto one another and praise those who are unselfish (see Q4: 36; Q5: 93; Q16: 90; Q16: 128; Q17: 23; Q28: 77; Q42: 40; and Q60: 8). Secondly, it is improper for Muslims to set possession of property or wealth as their goal. This is because each and everything on this earth belongs to Allah (s.w.t.). As an example, in *Surah al-Baqarah* verse 107, Allah (s.w.t.) says:

> *Knowest thou not that to Allah belongeth the dominion of the heavens*
> *and the earth? And besides Him ye have neither patron nor helper.*
> (Q2: 107; see also Q2: 284; Q3: 109 and 129; Q4: 126, 131 and 132;
> Q5: 120; Q6: 12; Q9: 116; Q10: 66; Q16: 52 and 77; Q18: 26;
> Q20: 6; Q21: 19; Q22: 64; Q24: 42 and 64; Q25: 2; Q30: 26;
> Q31: 26; Q34: 1; Q39: 44; Q42: 4, 49 and 53; Q45: 27;
> Q48: 4, 7 and 14; Q53: 31; and Q57: 2 and 5)

Besides this, the *sirah* (traditional biographies) of the Prophet (p.b.u.h.) shows that He and his Companions practised a highly moderate lifestyle. Moderation is an important concept in Islam. A person who practises the concept of moderation in his life is able to avoid becoming trapped in extremist groups, or developing greed for wealth and riches, or becoming selfish and unwilling to be charitable. Instead, he is involved in *jihad* (striving with every might for the cause of Allah (s.w.t.)). The following verses and *Hadith* may be used as a guide.

> *And be moderate in thy pace, and lower thy voice; for the harshest of sounds without doubt is the braying of the ass.*   (Q31: 19)

> *O ye who believe! Make not unlawful the good things which Allah hath made lawful for you, but commit no excess: for Allah loveth not those given to excess.*
>
> (Q5: 87; see also Q2: 190; Q6: 141; Q7: 31 and 55; Q17: 29 and 110; Q64: 16; and Q73: 20)

> *It is narrated on the authority of Abu Huraira that the Prophet (p.b.u.h.) said: Faith has over seventy branches or over sixty branches, the most excellent of which is the declaration that there is no god but Allah, and the humblest of which is the removal of what is injurious from the path: and modesty is a branch of faith.*
>
> (Sidiqi, undated, p. 27)

Although Muslims must practise moderation, this does not imply that Islam prevents Muslims from pursuing wealth. In fact, the possession of wealth would enable Muslims to perform commands like *jihad*, the giving of *zakat* (alms) and helping others. Verses 20 and 21 of *Surah at-Taubah* state:

> *Those who believe, and suffer exile and strive with might and main, in Allah's cause, with their goods and their persons, have the highest rank in the sight of Allah: they are the people who will achieve (salvation). Their Lord doth give them Glad Tidings of a Mercy from Himself, of His good pleasure, and of Gardens for them, wherein are delights that endure.*
>
> (Q9: 20 and 21; see also Q2: 43, 110, 177, 195, 277 and 267; Q4: 95 and 162; Q5: 35 and 55; Q9: 41 and 103; Q14: 31; Q22: 78; Q29: 6 and 69; Q34: 39; Q45: 15; Q57: 10; and Q92: 17–18)

Apart from the verses above, there are many more that explain the benefits attained by those who do good unto others (see also Q2: 25,

245, 261 and 265; Q3: 198; Q4: 57, 85, 122, 124 and 173; Q5: 9; Q6: 160; Q10: 26; Q11: 23; Q14: 23; Q15: 45–48; Q16: 30 and 97; Q18: 30–31; Q22: 23 and 50; Q27: 89; Q29: 7 and 58; Q30: 15; Q31: 8; Q32: 19; Q35: 33; Q39: 10 and 20; Q43: 71; Q55: 48–76; Q56: 11–40; Q57: 11 and 18; Q64: 17; Q73: 20; Q76: 5–6 and 12–22; Q78: 31–36; and Q85: 11).

Thirdly, in reality mankind does not know what is best for it (see Q4: 11). Hence, human beings require guidance in living their lives. In Islam, only Allah (s.w.t.) is All-Knowing. Due to the highly limited knowledge that mankind has gathered, it is pertinent that humans look towards the Quran and *Hadith* to guide them in carrying out their responsibilities on this earth. Since there exists a marked difference between the Western perspective of economy and that of Islam, a different platform for economy in Islam is present. According to Khan (1989), Islamic economic methodology must consider the following points:

(i)   The main function of methodology is to help attain truth. Hence, the pillars of Islamic economy consist of the teachings of the Quran and *Hadith*, whereby the source is pure and the truth of it is unquestionable. Methodology and views from man only exist when no clear direction can be obtained from the two sources.

(ii) The field of Islamic economics incorporates Islamic values, analysis of the actual state of the economy and transformation of the methods and ways of the existing economy to an Islamic economy model. The pillars of Islamic economy only provide guidance on a number of small issues. For a major part of the actual state of the economy, therefore, what are needed are views and thoughts of man within the framework of Islamic teachings. The issue of methodology, hence, becomes even more crucial when human thoughts and views are adopted.

(iii) Developing an economic model involves concepts called inductive reasoning and deductive reasoning. What this means is that man will use his mental faculties and logic to arrive at particular decisions or views. Inductive reasoning is not forbidden in Islam. In fact, the Quran urges man to observe the natural world and all aspects of its creation. Deductive reasoning is used by Western economists with the assumption that man has perfect knowledge to predict the future. The development of Islamic economics, however, adopts this concept with its own modification. This follows from the fact that in Islam, even though man has knowledge and skills, he is not capable of making accurate predictions. As such, every model that is to be built must take into account various differing factors and aspects.

(iv) Various assumptions are made when discussing aspects of economics from the perspective of the West. For example, man is said to be a rational being who has self-interest and who wants to maximize his gains, etc. However, in discussing Islamic economics, assumptions made must rightly be based on the Quran and *Hadith*.

(v) Islamic economics had been deliberated upon from era to era by many Islamic experts and thinkers. These thinkers were concerned about the economic issues during their time and attempts were made to offer views and methods of solution. The majority of these Islamic thinkers used multidisciplinary methods of the normative kind, and this tradition should be continued in the advancement of present-day economics. In line with this, various fields of knowledge have to be consolidated and taken into account in the process of developing the knowledge of Islamic economics.

Based on the above elaboration, it may be concluded that several main characteristics are seen in an Islamic economic system. They are as follows:

(i) Islamic economics uses a framework from two principal sources, the Quran and *Hadith*, and these sources are not to be questioned nor their truth doubted. This differs from the basic concept of Western economics which is questionable and changes with time.

(ii) The development of Islamic economics must use the inductive method. This method offers explanation of the correctness or otherwise of assumptions and predictions based on reasonability and empirical evidence.

(iii) Islamic economics is founded on ethical values such as justice, fairness, moderation, cooperation, helpfulness and altruism. These values must exist in the behaviour of all units in Islamic economy.

(iv) Islamic economics is by nature normative, which means it has comprehensive rules that are used by all.

(v)   Islamic economics takes into consideration issues which differ from regular economics. It places importance on the *falah* (ultimate success) of man which will eventually lead to the establishment of the *falah* of society.

In Islam, the development of each body of knowledge should be with a particular purpose. The aim of Islamic economic knowledge is one that would be achieved by taking into consideration in totality all aspects of the Islamic religion.

THE ESSENCE OF ISLAMIC ECONOMICS

Based on the various definitions made by Western intellectuals, the crux of economic issue lies in the existence of limited resources to meet unlimited needs of man. Hence, the important points to consider in discussing basic economic concepts are: what is to be produced, how it will be produced and for whom it is produced.

Therefore, one must deliberate whether the development of knowledge in Islamic economics should go the same path as the epistemology of conventional economics.

The first point which needs to be corrected is the limitedness or scarcity of all resources on the face of the earth as perceived in conventional economics. As such, a Western system which takes into account the methods of distributing these limited resources was established. These limited resources are also known as economic goods. Hence, this discipline of the economics shall not exist if everything that man wants can be made available to him without depleting the resources. If we also accept as a fact that resources created by Allah (s.w.t.) are limited, the basis of the deliberations of Islamic economics would also be on the same platform of assumptions as the Western economics.

However, some Islamic economists are of the view that limited resources are not present from Islamic point of view. According to Ariff (1989), Allah (s.w.t.) has made available sufficient resources to mankind to last till the end of life. Scarcity of resources is not due to their non-existence or depletion or extinction, but instead it is due to weakness on the part of man in exploring and acquiring the resources or other similar resources as substitutes. As an example, Allah (s.w.t.) constantly encourages Muslims to seek His bounty on the face of the earth. This is evident in the following verses:

> *Your Lord is He that maketh the ship go smoothly for you through the sea, in order that ye may seek of His Bounty. For He is unto you Most Merciful.* (Q17: 66)

> *But seek, with the (wealth) which Allah has bestowed on thee, the Home of the Hereafter, nor forget thy portion in this world: but do thou good, as Allah has been good to thee, and seek not (occasions for) mischief in the land: for Allah loves not those who do mischief.*
>
> (Q28: 77; see also Q30: 41)

And when the prayer is finished, then may ye disperse through the land, and seek of the Bounty of Allah: and celebrate the Praises of Allah often (and without stint): that ye may prosper. (Q62: 10)

It is He who has made the earth manageable for you, so traverse ye through its tracts and enjoy of the Sustenance which He furnishes: but unto Him is the Resurrection. (Q67: 15)

It is clear from the above verses that nowhere in the Quran can one find anything that informs Muslims about depletion or extinction of the bounties of Allah (s.w.t.). Nevertheless, the verses do provide instructions and rulings which Muslims have to comply with. Some of the rulings and guidances are:

(i) Wealth or the bounties of Allah (s.w.t.) are not confined to certain areas. In other words, Muslims are encourage to disperse through land and sea to seek the bounties of Allah (s.w.t.). Allah's (s.w.t.) bounties are found in abundance in all places and ought to be sought and discovered.

(ii) In seeking wealth, it must never be forgotten that there is life in the Hereafter. Hence, every effort made by man in seeking the bounties must be made with full consideration of the fact that he is held responsible for all his actions in the Hereafter.

(iii) In exploring to seek the bounties, no destruction must be done to the environment. The meaning here is broad. Generally, man can seek as much of the bounties on earth as he wants, but at the same time he must not damage the environment to the extent of endangering life on earth and depleting non-renewable resources.

The second most important factor that is recognized by the West in developing its knowledge in economics is that man's desires are unlimited. With the insatiability of desires, economy will continue to advance and products will continue to be created in order to meet the unlimited demands. There are many theories put forward by the West in discussing man's desires.

One of the early theories of the West that has been accepted by many is the Hierarchy of Needs put forward by Abraham Maslow. According to this theory, man has five levels of needs, and each person will work towards meeting his needs at the basic level before working on to meet his needs at the next level, and so on until he reaches the highest level (Maslow, 1943). The first level is the level of basic or psychological needs, where man needs food, lodging and freedom from diseases. The second level consists of need for security, freedom from threats and danger. The third level involves social needs, that is needs of love, affection and belongingness. The fourth level is the level of self-esteem, where one wishes to be accepted and valued by others. The final, fifth level involves aesthetic needs. Here, one will work towards fulfilling personal desires based on the ability and capacity that one possesses. Apart from Maslow, many other Western theorists have also presented their views on man's needs and desires.

Zarqa (1989) in his writings on human behaviour from the Islamic perspective, took into consideration the views of al-Gazali and al-Shatibi that the desires of Muslims may be categorized into three main hierarchies, namely necessities, conveniences and refinements. As an example, the term 'needs' involves activities of forming, developing and maintaining the five main aspects necessary to become the best *ummah*, namely religion, living, thought, children and wealth. There exists an abundance of teachings based on the Quran and *Sunnah* which educate man towards that perfection. The same goes for other activities to fulfil the other needs which must be done under the guidance of Islamic teachings.

The third important factor that must be considered when developing Islamic economic knowledge is the reassessment of economic theories developed by the West. This is necessary because the theories may not be suitable and cannot be used as a basis for developing Islamic economics. Ariff (1989) presented a number of Western economic theories which are questionable or which cannot at all be used in Islamic economics. Examples of theories that need to be re-examined are: the theory involving competition, the theory of maximizing gain and the theory associated with interest rates.

Based on the crucial facts discussed above, it can be concluded that the essence of Islamic economics differs very much from that of Western economics. Further, the development of the knowledge in question is closely related to development of the individual and the Islamic society, and this development is in accordance with rulings laid down by the Quran and *Sunnah*. Karim (2002) summed up that the process of the development of Islamic economics must be founded on the five principal bases of *tauhid* (oneness of Allah), *adl* (justice of Allah), *nubuwwah* (prophethood), *khalifah* (representative of Allah on earth) and *ma'ad* (ultimate destiny of humankind).

Tauhid is the framework that positions man's behaviour in line with the purpose of his creation. Because mankind is created to worship Allah (s.w.t.), it follows that humans should behave responsibly in this world. Consequently, all actions in connection with economic development or business should be accompanied by responsibility. Anyone whose action goes against Islamic teachings shall be held responsible for his action. The concept of *adl* or fairness includes the philosophy of not doing wrong unto others and not being wronged. Hence, exploitation and unfaithfulness will not exist. *Nubuwwah* is the concept whereby mankind must be guided by the behaviour and actions of the prophets. Among the qualities associated with this are *siddiq* (truthfulness), *amanah* (responsibility and trustworthiness), *fathanah* (smartness, intelligence and wisdom) and *tabligh* (receptiveness to views of others and the ability to communicate well). The concept of *khalifah* involves man as a leader and caretaker of all things on earth. Through this concept, man carries the responsibility to use resources in ways that benefit not only human beings but also all other creations on earth. The last concept, *ma'ad* is the concept of the existence of the Day of

Judgement. In line with this concept, man is to do good in order to obtain rewards on the Day of Judgement.

Chapra (1971) presented the following as the values and goals of Islamic economics:

(i) Economic well-being within the framework of Islamic moral values.

(ii) Universal brotherhood and justice.

(iii) Fair and just distribution of income or wealth.

(iv) Freedom of the individual in the context of social welfare.

One of the beauty and strength of Islam lies in its teaching on the importance of reaping benefits both for this world and for the Hereafter. Islam encourages Muslims to raise their standard of living by seeking as much of the bounties of Allah (s.w.t.) in this world as possible. This confirms that Islam does not forbid the accumulation of wealth, as is evident from the verses Q17: 66; Q28: 77; Q62: 10; and Q67: 15, where Muslims are urged to seek Allah's (s.w.t.) bounties on this earth. Apart from this, the Quran also states that everything that exists on the face of the earth has been created for Muslims. Examples of such verses are:

> *It is He who hath created for you all things that are on earth; moreover His design comprehended the heavens, for He gave order and perfection to the seven firmaments; and of all things He hath perfect knowledge.*
>
> (Q2: 29)

> *Say: Who hath forbidden the beautiful (gifts) of Allah, which He hath produced for his Servants, and the things, clean and pure, (which He hath provided) for sustenance? Say: They are, in the life of this world, for those who believe, (and) purely for them on the Day of Judgement. Thus do We explain the Signs in detail for those who understand.*
>
> (Q7: 32)

A lot of good can come about if Muslims are able to gather Allah's (s.w.t) bounties by upgrading their economic level. For instance, through his wealth a Muslim could contribute *zakat*, give out alms, provide aid to others and participate in striving in His cause as urged in Islam. The following verses have reference to this fact:

And be steadfast in prayer; practise regular charity; and bow down your heads with those who bow down (in worship).

(Q2: 43; see also Q2: 110, 117 and 277; Q4: 162; Q5: 55; Q9: 103; and Q92: 178)

O ye who believe! Do your duty to Allah, seek the means of approach unto Him, and strive with might and main in His cause; that ye may prosper.

(Q5: 35; see also Q4: 95; Q9: 20–21; Q9: 41; Q22: 78; Q29: 6; Q45: 15; and Q29: 69)

And spend of your substance in the cause of Allah, and make not your own hands contribute to (your) destruction; but do good; for Allah loveth those who do good.

(Q2: 195; see also Q2: 267; Q14: 31; Q34: 39; and Q57: 10)

Besides verses of the Quran quoted above which call for Muslims to seek Allah's (s.w.t.) bounties and to use them in the best way possible to attain returns in this world and the Hereafter, there are a number of *Hadith* which deliver the same message. As an example, the Prophet (p.b.u.h.) recommends that Muslims spend part of their time to perform worldly commitments and part of it to pursue matters of the Hereafter, and urges Muslims to do good and to use their wealth in ways that achieve Allah's (s.w.t.) blessings. The same goes for the issue on profit or gain. In Western economics, the theory related to profit is the theory of profit maximization. In Islamic economics, the matter of profit is not only seen from the perspective of economic enhancement or as monetary gain, but also as an enhancement of faith. In Islam, profit is seen from a long-term perspective as well as gains in this world and in the Hereafter. The definition of people who attain prosperity and the qualities they possess are stated in the Quran (see Q2: 2–5; Q3: 200; Q5: 35, 90 and 100; Q6: 21 and 135; Q7: 8–9; Q8: 45; Q9: 88; Q35: 29; Q41: 35; Q42: 20; Q45: 30; and Q64: 16). In Islam, the people who prosper are those who are faithful and devoted to Allah (s.w.t.) and the Quran has laid down the qualities that are required for people to achieve prosperity.

Secondly, the goal of Islamic economic development is characterized by the concepts of universal brotherhood and socio-economic justice. This means Islamic economic development will not benefit only one group of Muslims while other groups of Muslims are left behind in hardship and suffering. This concept of universal brotherhood is very much emphasized in Islam. In fact, Allah (s.w.t.) created male and female in mankind and in various ethnicity and groups in order for them all to know one another (see Q49: 13). Emphasis on the importance of universal brotherhood can be found in various verses of the Quran and *Hadith* which urge Muslims to do good among themselves. The following may be used as a guide:

> *Narrated by Abdullah bin Umar: The Prophet (p.b.u.h.) said, "A Muslim is a brother of another Muslim, so he should not oppress him, nor should he hand him over to an oppressor. Whoever fulfilled the needs of his brother, Allah will fulfil his needs; whoever brought his (Muslim) brother out of a discomfort, Allah will bring him out of the discomforts of the Day of Resurrection, and whoever screened a Muslim, Allah will screen him on the Day of Resurrection."*
>
> (Khan, 1986, p. 373)

> *Narrated by Anas: The Prophet (p.b.u.h.) said, "Help your brother, whether he is an oppressor or he is an oppressed one." People asked, "O Allah's Apostle! It is all right to help him if he is oppressed, but how should we help him if he is an oppressor?" The Prophet said, "By preventing him from oppressing others."*   (Khan, 1986, p. 373)

Abu Musa reported the Prophet (p.b.u.h.) as saying: "A believer is like a brick for another believer, the one supporting the other."

(*Sidiqi*, undated, p. 1368)

Nu'man bin Bashir reported the Prophet (p.b.u.h.) as saying: "The similitude of believers is that of one body; when the head aches, the whole body aches, because of sleeplessness and fever."

(*Sidiqi*, undated, p. 1368)

The above *Hadith* is clear proof of the concept of universal brotherhood in Islam. Hence, one important guideline in the development of Islamic economy is the concept of the mutual sacrifice and cooperation within the framework of Islamic brotherhood. This concept of universal brotherhood is closely related to the concept of justice, another concept of prime importance in Islam. There are many verses in the Quran that state this fact. Among them is the following:

O ye who believe! Stand out firmly for Allah, as witnesses to fair dealing, and not let the hatred of others to you make you swerve to wrong and depart from justice. Be just: that is next to piety: and fear Allah. For Allah is well-acquainted with all that ye do.

(Q5: 8; see also Q4: 58; Q6: 152; and Q49: 9)

According to Chapra (1994), this concept of justice may be split in two parts, social justice and economic justice. Social justice is closely related to relationships among Muslims regardless of race, colour or creed. This is so because in Islam the only factors that differentiate between individuals are one's faith and piety. In line with this, Muslims are prompted to perform good deeds and be of help to one another, for this would strengthen Islamic brotherhood. This call towards doing good deeds is emphasized in many verses in the Quran, and it covers doing good deeds through words and action (see Q2: 95 and 104; Q4: 36 and 48; and 148–9, Q5: 93; Q16: 90 and 128; Q17: 23 and 153; Q28: 77; Q29: 46; Q42: 40; and Q60: 8). Economic justice means the absence of elements of exploitation and misuse of other people's rights for one's own interest. In other words, the concepts of morals and ethics need to be complied with at all times. As an example, verse 183 from *Surah asy-Syura* states:

> *And withhold not things justly due to men, nor do evil in the land, working mischief.* (Q26: 183)

The above verse indicates that Islam forbids one from taking away the rights of others at one's will for one's self-interest. Hence, in Islamic economics, it is necessary for a producer to know not only his own rights, but also the rights of the workers who are working together to produce goods for him, as well as the rights of those who purchase the products.

The third goal set out by Chapra in the concept of Islamic economics is the fair and equitable distribution of income. This goal is clearly related to the concept of justice in Islam. The basic concept of Islamic economics is the assurance that every Muslim would be able to enjoy Allah's (s.w.t.) bounties on this earth. This is especially so when it is mentioned in the Quran that all resources on earth have been created for man and that man is the master of the resources (see Q2: 30; Q6: 165; and Q35: 39). In connection with this, programmes of wealth or resource distribution to the less fortunate are definitely not overlooked in the development of the Islamic economy.

Distribution of wealth to the less fortunate is divided into three categories. First, Islamic economic development takes into consideration giving aid to those without any occupation and ensures that this group receives payment at an appropriate rate. Secondly, emphasis is given to the collection and payment of *zakat* (compulsory charity), whose distribution will not only help the less fortunate but also aid in the betterment of Muslims. Thirdly, distribution of wealth of a deceased must be done urgently, without having to freeze the assets. The concept of fair and equitable distribution of income does not mean that each Muslim gets an even portion regardless of the contribution made by the individual.

Islam does not forbid the accumulation of wealth, or the attainment of more gains or a higher placement in society by an individual. The verses below clearly show the existence in Islam of inequalities in terms of position, ownership of wealth and status of living:

It is He Who hath made you (His) agents, inheritors of the earth: He hath raised you in ranks, some above others: that He may try you in the gifts He hath given you: for thy Lord is quick in punishment: yet He is indeed Oft-Forgiving, Most Merciful. (Q6: 165)

Verily thy Lord doth provide sustenance in abundance for whom He pleaseth, and He provideth in a just measure. For He doth know and regard all His servants.
(Q17: 30; see also Q17: 21; Q2: 269; Q13: 26; Q16: 15; Q9: 21 and 62; Q30: 37; Q34: 36 and 39; Q39: 52; and Q42: 12)

The ultimate goal of Islamic economic system according to Chapra is the freedom of the individual in the context of social welfare. Freedom is the absolute right of an individual because in Islam, mankind is created solely to worship Allah (s.w.t.). However, even though man has been granted freedom, there are limitations that must be observed. These restrictions are imposed should the action of a person contradict the limitations of the *Syariah* law or has the potential to cause harm to himself or others. Islamic jurists are of the view that individual freedom in the context of Islam is subject to the following principles:

(i) The interest of the majority takes precedence over the interest of the individual.

(ii) Although both lightening burdens and seeking benefits are the main goals of *Syariah*, the concept of lightening burdens is given priority.

(iii) A small loss is tolerated to avoid bigger losses, or a small profit may be sacrificed to obtain bigger profits.

FUNDAMENTALS OF ISLAMIC ECONOMIC LAW

A system cannot be established without laws, rulings and regulations that regulate the operation of the system. In Islam, the regulations that control the lifestyle of Muslims are the *Syariah* laws (a detailed description of this is done in Chapter 5). Islamic economic system, therefore, is bound by the laws and regulations as stipulated by *Syariah*.

Syariah laws are derived from four sources. The first source is the holy book of the Muslims, the Quran. The Quran is the authentic and eternal source of the *Syariah* laws. It contains the words or messages of Allah (s.w.t.) that were passed through the Prophet (p.b.u.h.) to guide all mankind. These words and messages are fundamental, all-encompassing and eternal.

The second source of the *Syariah* laws is the *Hadith*, which is second in importance after the Quran. The *Hadith* comprises extracts of information, accounts, history, anecdotes and records of the *Sunnah* of the Prophet (p.b.u.h.) that have been passed down from generation to generation and adopted by Muslims in maintaining their faith and guiding their actions. The *Sunnah* (*sunan* in plural form) describes the Prophet's (p.b.u.h.) habits, customs and the things he used. It also relates to his behaviour, actions, made of actions and verbal responses or comments in different life situations and conditions.

The third source is called *ijma*. *Ijma* means collective views of *mujtahid* or the collective agreement of Islamic jurists at particular instances on issues of law. A *mujtahid* is an expert on Islamic law and in other branches of the religion. Any person who undertakes *ijtihad*, or who perseveres and thoroughly racks his brain in striving to solve a problem, in particular a religious issue, is also known as a *mujtahid*.

The fourth and final source is called *qiyas*. The original meaning of this word is "to measure" or "to draw similarities between two things" (Ali, 1950). In *Syariah* terms, *qiyas* is the process of reasoning by analogy of the mujtahid with regards to difficult and doubtful questions of doctrine or practice. The process involves comparing the problem with similar issues or cases which have already been solved using the rulings in the Quran and *Hadith*.

Both the Quran and *Hadith* are also known as *al-adillat-al-qatiyyah* or absolute opinions or views, and it is evidence whose truth cannot be disputed. This is so because these two sources contain absolute truth and undoubted fundamental doctrines of Islam. These sources are also sometimes known as the origin or root of *Syariah*. *Ijma* and *qiyas*, on the other hand, are known as *al-adillat-al-ijtihadiyyah* or opinions or views obtained by exertion. These two sources are also commonly called *furu'* or branches of *Syariah* law. The use of these four sources in *Syariah* law bestows a high standing on the *Syariah* laws in facing the complicated world of today and in solving various problems related to modern living.

SUMMARY

Economics is a branch of knowledge that deals with the distribution of resources on the face of the earth to meet man's needs. The existing resources are said to be scarce, while the demands of man are limitless. Hence, the use of these resources must be optimized so that wastage can be prevented and man's needs can be met as best as possible. This conventional economic knowledge can be categorized into two categories, macroeconomics and microeconomics. Macroeconomics covers factors of production, overall income, price levels, funds, unemployment and the labour force as a whole. Apart from that, also included in macroeconomics are causes of economic crises, determination of methods of investment and consumption, management of a nation's finance and interest rates. Microeconomics discusses the individual behaviour of man and firms in order to determine the supply and demand of commodities in the market.

Based on the macroeconomic and microeconomic concepts, thinkers of the West established and implemented systems with the ability to satisfy the needs of every unit in the society including individuals, businesses and governments. Eventually, systems with different characteristics, known as the capitalist and socialist systems emerged. The capitalist system emphasized the individual ownership of all factors of production, with the majority of decisions determined by market mechanisms. The socialist system, on the other hand, focused on public ownership with decisions made at the central level.

Although the capitalist and socialist systems succeeded in developing several races and societies in the world, flaws and weaknesses appeared in the practice of the systems. At the end of the 1980s and 1990s, a number of socialist nations fell. At the same time the capitalist societies were in disarray. Such situation showed that the systems were incapable of solving universal economic issues. In connection with this, Islam as a complete religion certainly has its own unique economic system. The Islamic economic system has fundamentals, essence and qualities which are distinct from systems established by Western economists. Further, the goals of Islamic economic system encompass aspects such as economic development within the framework of Islamic values and morals, universal brotherhood and justice, equitable distribution of wealth and individual freedom subject to social welfare.

In contrast to the conventional economic system where regulations which are to be abided by are subject to man-made rules, Islamic economic system complies with two groups of laws. The first is the *Syariah* legislation, comprising rules derived from four sources, the Quran, *Hadith*, *ijma* and *qiyas*. In principal, Islamic economic system is a system of economy whose development and implementation are governed by *Syariah*. Within this Islamic economic system, knowledge related to Islamic banking has also been developed.

REFERENCES AND FURTHER READING

Ali, Maulana M. *The Religion of Islam*. Lahore (Pakistan): The Ahmadiyyah Anjuman Ishaat Islam, 1950.

Ariff, Mohamed. "Economics and Ethics in Islam." In *Readings in the Concept and Methodology of Islamic Economics,* edited by Aidit Ghazali and Syed Omar, 96–119. Kuala Lumpur (Malaysia): Pelanduk Publications, 1989.

Bahr, Laurens, Bernard Johnston and Louise A. Bloomfield. *Collier's Encyclopedia*. New York (USA): Collier, 1969.

Barnhart, Robert K. *The Barnhart Dictionary of Etymology*. New York (USA): The H.W. Wilson Company, 1988.

Blaug, Mark. *The Methodology of Economics*. Cambridge (USA): Cambridge University Press, 1980.

Bronstein, Morris. *Comparative Economic Systems, Models and Cases*. 7th ed. Illinois (USA): Irwin, 1994.

Chapra, M. Umar. *The Economic System of Islam*. Karachi (Pakistan): Bureau of Composition, Compilation & Translation, University of Karachi, 1971.

Chapra, M. Umar. *Islam and the Economic Challenge*. UK: Leicester Islamic Foundation, 1994.

Fly, Richard T. *French and German Socialists in Modern Times*. New York (USA): Harper, 1983.

Gregory, Paul R. and Robert C. Stuart. *Comparative Economic System.* 6th ed. Boston (USA): Houghton Mifflin Company, 1999.

Grolier Academic Encyclopedia. New York (USA): Grolier International, 1987.

Kahf, Monzer. "Islamic Economics and Its Methodology." In *Readings in the Concept and Methodology of Islamic Economics,* edited by Aidit Ghazali and Syed Omar, 40–48. Kuala Lumpur (Malaysia): Pelanduk Publications, 1989.

Kahf, Monzer. "Islamic Economics System: A Review." In *Readings in the Concept and Methodology of Islamic Economics,* edited by Aidit Ghazali and Syed Omar, 69–89. Kuala Lumpur (Malaysia): Pelanduk Publications, 1989.

Kamus Ekonomi. Kuala Lumpur (Malaysia): Percetakan Dewan Bahasa dan Pustaka, 1993.

Karim, Adiwarman. *Ekonomi Mikro Islam.* Jakarta (Indonesia): The International Institute of Islamic Thought, 2002.

Khan, Muhammad Akram. "Islamic Economics: The State of the Art." In *Readings in the Concept and Methodology of Islamic Economics,* edited by Aidit Ghazali and Syed Omar, 49–68. Kuala Lumpur (Malaysia): Pelanduk Publications, 1989.

Khan, Muhammad Muhsin, trans. *The Translation of the Meanings of Sahih al-Bukhari* Vol. 3. Lahore (Pakistan): Kazi Publications, 1986.

Loucks, William N. and William G. Whitney. *Comparative Economics Systems.* 9th ed. New York (USA): Harper & Row, 1973.

Low, Linda and Toh Mun Heng. *Principles of Economics.* Revised ed. Singapore: Addison Wesley Publishing Company, 1997.

Maslow, Abraham H. "A Theory of Human Motivation." *Psychological Review,* July 1943.

Maslow, Abraham H. *Motivation and Personality*. New York (USA): Harper, 1954.

Niemi, Albert W. Jr. *Understanding Economics*. Chicago (USA): Rand McNally College Publishing Company, 1978.

Nomani, Farhad and Ali Rahnema. *Islamic Economic Systems*. London, UK and New Jersey (USA): Zed Book Ltd., 1994.

Samuelson, Paul A. and William D. Nordhaus. *Economics*. New York (USA): McGraw-Hill, Inc., 1995.

Schnitzer, Martin C. *Comparative Economic Systems*. Ohio (USA): South-Western Publishing Co., 1994.

Siddiqi, Hamid, trans. *Sahih Muslim* Vols 1 and 4. Beirut (Lebanon): Dar al Arabia Publishing, Printing & Distribution, undated.

Siddiqi, M. Nejatullah. "An Islamic Approach to Economics." Working paper presented at the Seminar on Islamization of Knowledge, Islamabad (Pakistan), January 1982.

Siddiqi, M. Nejatullah. *Teaching Economics in Islamic Perspective*. Saudi Arabia: Scientific Publishing Centre, King Abdulaziz University, 1996.

Smith, Adam. *The Wealth of Nations*, edited by Edwin Cannan. New York (USA): Modern Library, 1937.

Zarqa, Anas. "Islamic Economics: An Approach to Human Welfare." In *Readings in the Concept and Methodology of Islamic Economics*, edited by Aidit Ghazali and Syed Omar, 21–39. Kuala Lumpur (Malaysia): Pelanduk Publications, 1989.

CHAPTER 2

HISTORY AND DEVELOPMENT OF THE ISLAMIC BANKING SYSTEM

This chapter discusses the establishment and development of the Islamic banking system which can be traced back to the birth of Islam in Mecca. The Islamic banking concept failed to expand to become a complete banking system in the early years of Islam. Its development only picked up again in the 1960s, before becoming rapid in the 1970s. The development of Islamic banks in certain countries is also discussed for comparison purposes. This is because not all Islamic banks receive full support from their respective governments. Some have to face numerous obstacles. There are some which initially received special privileges, but later had the privileges taken away from them. There are also others which are given special status and are exempted from a number of regulations and laws.

INTRODUCTION

The Islamic banking system (IBS) is defined as a banking system whose principles underlying its operations and activities are founded on Islamic or *Syariah* rules. This means that all operations of the Islamic bank, that is, transactions involving either deposits or financing, must be based on *Syariah* principles. Such principles also cover other banking transactions like money order transaction, letter of guarantee, letter of credit and foreign exchange. The main factor that distinguishes Islamic banks from conventional banks is that all transactions are administered without involving elements of interest or *riba*. This is due to the fact that Islam forbids the giving or receiving of *riba*. A financial institution cannot be regarded as an Islamic banking institution if its operations involve elements of *riba*. Besides this, the principal objective of the establishment of Islamic banks is to cater to the needs of Muslims in banking transactions. The business management of the banks is based on the concepts of justice and fairness in the interests of society as a whole. The banks are also founded on rulings set in the Quran and *Hadith*.

The establishment of Islamic financial institutions whose operations are based on true *Syariah* principles is a fairly recent phenomena compared to conventional banking. Modern conventional banking system came into existence nearly 420 years ago with the establishment of Banco Della Pizza at Rialto in Venice in 1587 (Homoud, 1985). Nevertheless, in England, modern conventional banks were regarded as non-existent before 1640; the Bank of England was only established in 1694 (Sumner, 1971). The establishment of Mit Ghamr Savings Bank in Egypt in 1963 which operated based on *Syariah* principles marked the early history of Islamic banking and became an eye opener for Islamic thinkers and economists around the world. The success of the Islamic bank in catering to deposit and credit needs of clients proved that *Syariah* principles were still applicable and could be adopted by modern-day businesses. From that time onwards, many Islamic banks were established worldwide, particularly in Islamic countries. According to figures released by the International Monetary Fund, there were more than 300 financial institutions with operations based on *Syariah* rules in 75 countries as at end of 2007. The increase in asset value of Islamic banks exceeded 15% per annum, and it was estimated that the asset value of Islamic financial institutions worldwide at the end of 2007 was US$250 billion (www.imf.org). Activities carried out included all transactions of conventional banks, activities of merchant banks, investment activities, insurance services, mortgage, hire purchase, advisory services and other banking transactions. The establishment of Islamic banks has not been limited to Muslim countries. Islamic banking has gained a footing in non-Muslim countries as well. For example, the Islamic Banking System International Holdings established in Luxembourg in 1978 was the first Islamic financial institution set up in a non-Muslim country. This was followed by the establishment of Dar al-Mal al-Islami in Switzerland in 1981. Apart from this, some banks operating in London and other financial centres in Europe have started using Islamic banking techniques and instruments to cater to the needs of their Muslim clients as well as the needs of Islamic banks which have business relationships with them. Most of the joint-venture banks between European and Arabic parties offer international trade transactions based on the principle of *murabahah*.

Banking products based on *Syariah* principles are also offered by foreign conventional banks. Most of the products or services offered are in the form of investment certificates based on *Syariah* principles. As an example, Kleinworth Benson offered Islamic Unit Trust in 1986. The Union Bank of Switzerland also offered Islamic Investment Fund (Wilson, 1990). The existence of Islamic banks in Western countries is nothing out of the ordinary. In fact, various financial institutions that offer Islamic banking products have been set up in many Western countries such as the United States, the United Kingdom and Australia.

In the United States, Islamic banking was introduced not only in financial institutions but in educational institutions as well. There are more than 20 Islamic financial institutions in the United States which offer deposit facilities, financing and fund management. Meanwhile, there are several educational institutions that are offering courses and seminars on Islamic finance. For instance, Harvard University holds annual forums on Islamic finance. The American Finance House – LARIBA, which was established in 1987, has become the most advanced Islamic financial institution and currently operates in 35 states in the United States. It offers housing financing services, small businesses financing and trade financing (www.lariba.com). In the United Kingdom, the first Islamic bank there, Islamic Bank of Britain Plc began operations on 6 August 2004. It is envisaged that the 1.8 million Muslims in the United Kingdom will have the opportunity to do their banking businesses with the bank (www.banking-business-review.com).

Meanwhile, the Muslim Community Co-operative Australia (MCCA) established in 1989, was the first Islamic financial institution in Australia. With an initial capital of A$22,300 and only ten members, its total assets have grown to A$26 million with a membership of 5,619, which represents an increase of about 50 members on average every month (www.mcca.com.au). This institution offers savings and financing facilities using the principles of *murabahah, mudharabah, musyarakah* and *qard hassan*. Besides these facilities, MCCA also offers facilities for the collection and distribution of *zakat*.

The fall of the Soviet Union also opened up opportunities for Islamic banks to operate in regions which were once under Soviet rule. The Albaraka Group began its operations by setting up a bank in Kazakhstan, named Albaraka Kazakhstan Bank as well as establishing joint ventures in Uzbekistan. Moreover, Islamic banking had gained its footing in Albania (Rudnick, 1992). Besides these regions, financial institutions based on *Syariah* are also found in Russia (BADR Bank) and in China (Ningxia Islamic International Trust and Investment).

While there are Islamic banks which have developed rapidly in both Muslim and non-Muslim countries, there are also those which have experienced failure. For example, the Muslim Community Credit Union (MCCU), an Islamic financial institution established in Australia in the year 2000 in the form of a co-operative offering banking products, was closed and suspended in the year 2002. The closure was due to losses as a result of carelessness and unwise financing (Shaban, 2002; www.mcca.com.au/mcca_the_mccu_story.pdf).

HISTORY OF ISLAMIC BANKING

Although the establishment of Islamic banks only became a reality in the 1960s, this does not mean that banking activities did not exist in Islamic history. Activities which are regarded as practices of modern banking, such as receipt of deposits, loans issuance, money exchange and bills of exchange, existed since the early years of Islam and during the spread of Islam.

Before the birth of Islam, Mecca was the centre of trade and was used as a transit point by traders passing through the city from the north and south borders. Hence, deposit and loan activities developed rapidly and transactions involving money exchange became one of the main activities. These activities continued even after Islam became rooted in Mecca and Medina. From the historical point of view, Islamic banking can be divided into three eras. The first era began from the early years of Islam when it was first born in the city of Mecca up until the period of Caliph ar-Rashidin. The second era stretches from the era of the caliphates until the fall of the Uthmaniyah Empire. This is followed by the third era, which is the era of modern Islamic banking.

Early Era of Islamic Banking System

Islam was born in Mecca when the Prophet Muhammad (p.b.u.h.) first received divine revelations of Islam in the year 610 at Mount Hira', and Islam was consequently preached openly in the year 613 at Mount Sara. Before that time, Mecca was a city of trade, and its business activities continued even after Islam became rooted there. Among the banking activities that remained in operation was the safe-keeping of money and valuables. These savings transactions were made by those with wealth, and savings were entrusted to reputedly highly trustworthy persons. The depositors would choose only persons of proven honesty and sincerity in keeping and returning their valuables. Prophet Muhammad (p.b.u.h.) was one person renowned for his honesty and trusted by the people. He remained custodian of other people's deposits until his migration from Mecca to Medina. Before his departure, the Prophet (p.b.u.h.) appointed Sayidina Ali to return all the deposits to their rightful owners (Homoud, 1985).

Both before and after the arrival of Islam in Mecca, deposits were made for safe-keeping. The person entrusted to keep the deposit would pledge to return the amount deposited. However, during the time of the Prophet (p.b.u.h.), one of his Companions, Az-Zubair al-Awwam would refuse money from depositors if it was in the form of savings. Instead, he preferred it to be in the form of a loan or *qard*. Abdullah az-Zubair explained that when people came to his father with money for him to help keep, his father would maintain that the money was a loan and not a deposit, because he feared that if it was in the form of a deposit, it could go missing. Az-Zubair's action was a wise one; it covered two objectives. First, by treating the deposit as a loan, he had the right to use it. Secondly, if the deposit was not used, it would actually be a loss to its owner. On the other hand, as a loan, the deposit was safer, because it represented a secure guarantee to the owners since the borrower was liable to return the deposit to the depositors.

The history of early Islamic banking through the story of Az-Zubair depicts the change in the concept of deposit, which was originally in the form of trust, to that of loan. Moreover, the deposit facility was not for a particular person or group of persons, but instead it was a public facility. The number of depositors was evidently big; because on the death of Az-Zubair, his son, Abdullah Az-Zubair was hesitant about distributing his father's assets among his siblings even after paying back all of his father's dues. Instead, for the duration of four *hajj* seasons Abdullah made announcements urging those who had deposited with Az-Zubair to come forward and reclaim their money from him. Only after the four *hajj* seasons did he distribute his father's assets. The community of Mecca at that time only knew two uses of money: first, to entrust money to someone else for it to be used in business based on the *qirad* or *mudharabah* principle and then to share the profits of the transaction; and secondly, to loan out money in order to obtain interest or *riba*. The practice of *riba* was widespread before the emergence of Islam, both among Arabs and between Arabs and Jews who were then living in the Arabic peninsula.

With the arrival of Islam, the practice of *riba* was no longer permitted. Nevertheless, this prohibition did not pose a hindrance to the conduct of daily life as well as trade development. Besides this, the practice of exchange of items or money also existed during the early years of Islam. The Prophet (p.b.u.h.) on many occasions had to resolve problems pertaining to money exchange. This is evident from one *Hadith* narrated by Abu al-Minhal: *"I asked al-Bara bin Azib and Zaid bin Arqam about practicing money exchange. They replied, 'We are traders in the time of Allah's Apostle (p.b.u.h.) and I asked Allah's Apostle about money exchange. He replied, "If it is from hand to hand, there is no harm in it; otherwise it is not permissible."'"* (Khan, 1989, p. 157).

In addition, transactions involving money exchange during the early days of Islam did not only entail the exchange of one currency for another; there were activities similar to what is known in today's banking system as money order. It has been said that Ibn al-Abbas received the *warik* (a type of currency that originated from silver and melted down to become dirham, which is a 3.0 gram coin of pure silver) and sent an acknowledgement to Kufah, a mediaeval city of Iraq. Similarly, Abdullah Az-Zubair received money from the Mecca community and subsequently wrote a receivable acknowledgement to his brother, Mis'ab bin Az-Zubair in Iraq who repaid the depositors when they arrived in Iraq.

Middle Era of Islamic Banking System

The middle era of Islam began with the end of the reign of Caliph Uthman in the year 661 AC. What followed was the reign of Caliph Umaiyyah (661–750) with Damsyik as the centre, followed by the reign of Caliph Abbasiyyah (750–1258) which was centred in Baghdad, the reign of Caliph Umaiyyah in Spain (756–1031) and the period of the Uthmaniyah Empire (1350–1918).

The middle era of Islam witnessed the continuation of banking activities which were practised in the early era of Islam. For instance, the transfer of money as practised by the sons of Az-Zubair became the norm among money changers. Apart from this, during the middle of the fourth *Hijrah* century a new development emerged in the history of Islamic banking. Homoud (1985) extracted a story from the first part of the book *Zuhr al-Islam* written by Ahmad Amin. According to the book, Saif Dawala al-Hamadani, who was Amir of Aleppo, issued cheques during his visit to Baghdad. While in Baghdad, Saif visited a local shop Bani Khaqan for a drink and upon leaving the shop he asked the owner for a piece of paper on which he wrote the name of the money changer together with the amount that he owed, 1,000 dinar. The paper was then exchanged by the shop owner for the stated amount of money as written by Saif. When asked by the shopkeeper who it was who wrote on the paper, the money changer replied that the person was the Amir of Aleppo, Saif Dawala al-Hamadani.

The usage of cheques for trade purposes was also a norm in the city of Basrah for which regulations had been formulated for matters related to seals and witnesses. Around 400 H or 1010 AC, Basrah flourished with the activities of money changers. During that period, ships and Muslim traders were travelling to and fro between countries to trade. In his book titled *Safarnama*, Naser Khasro, a Persian traveller, recounted his travel experiences between 437 H and 444 H. During his visit to Basrah, he described that markets were set up in three different venues every day. In the morning, trading took place in Khaza, while activities moved to the Uthman market at midday and at nightfall trading shifted to Qaddahin. Trading and business activities carried out in each market were conducted using cheques issued by money changers. These cheques were then used to purchase whatever the buyers needed. Nonetheless, buyers could only use such cheques as long as they resided in the city of Basrah.

The fall of the Roman Empire at the end of AD 400's and the occurrence of the Dark Ages which swept Europe (from the 5th to the 10th century) had a significant adverse impact on the economic activities of Muslim countries. It was not until the revival of the economies of the European countries in the 12th century and the resurrection of the conventional banking system that the conventional banking system expanded beyond the shores of the European continent to make its debut in the Muslim countries. Although Islamic banking failed to expand during this era, development took place in terms of *fatwa* (legal opinions) by Muslim jurists pertaining to issues of *muamalat*, particularly those involving *riba*. This was the era of many renowned jurists or *ulama* such as Imam al-Azam Abu Hanifah (60 H/698–150 H/767), Imam Malik ibn Anas (93 H/712–179 H/795), Imam Ahmad ibn Hanbal (164 H/778–241 H/855) and al-Shafii (150 H/767–204 H/820), who were the founders of the Hanafi, Maliki, Hanbali and Shafii schools of thought. The views of these *ulama,* particularly on the subject of *muamalat,* have become the reference point for *ulama* in the modern era of Islamic banking in giving their opinions and judgements related to Islamic banking activities such as whether the conduct is lawful and in accordance with *Syariah* principles or otherwise.

Era of Modern Islamic Banking

The development of the Islamic banking system may have started with the establishment of Mit Ghamr Savings Bank, but this does not mean that no earlier attempts were made to establish Islamic financial institutions. Some parties believed that the first attempt to establish an interest-free bank was made in Malaysia in the mid-1940s (Erol and El-Bdour, 1989). However, this organization which was founded on *Syariah* principles was unsuccessful. Another such attempt took place in a rural area of Pakistan in the late 1950s. This local institution did not charge interest on its lending (Wilson, 1983).

The establishment of Mit Ghamr Savings Bank in one of the rural regions in the Nile Valley in Egypt marked the dawn of the modern era of the Islamic banking system and paved the way for the establishment of other Islamic banks. This bank provided basic banking services such as deposit accounts, loan accounts, equity participation, direct investment and social services. The services founded on *Syariah* principles provided by the bank were very well received by the local community and the farmers. The number of depositors increased tremendously from 17,560 depositors in its first year of operation (1963/1964) to 251,152 depositors at the end of the 1966/1967 financial year. Similarly, the amount of deposit increased from £E40,944 (Egyptian pound) at the end of its first year of operation to £E1,828,375 at the end of the 1966/1967 financial year. The bank was successful in preventing customers from going to money lenders for financial assistance. Another factor contributing to the success of Mit Ghamr Savings Bank was its ability to instil a sense of belonging among its customers. However, due to political unrest in Egypt, its operation suffered a setback. In mid-1967, its operations were consequently taken over by the National Bank of Egypt and Central Bank of Egypt. As a result of this action, the interest-free concept was abandoned and Mit Ghamr's operations reverted to an interest-based system. However, the interest-free concept was revived in 1971 under the rule of President Anwar al-Sadat and a new financial institution by the name of Nasser Social Bank was established.

Although Mit Ghamr Savings Bank had to cease operations prematurely and before it was able to extend its services to all business sectors, it nevertheless signalled to the Muslim community that Islamic principles were applicable to modern-day business. This phenomenon stimulated many Muslim scholars around the world to embark on studies related to interest-free banking as practised by Mit Ghamr Savings Bank. However, the scarcity of literature and the non-existence of a comprehensive set of guidelines in *Syariah* caused frustration among the Muslim scholars. Nevertheless, these setbacks were not considered hindrances for those who wanted to go back to religion. The revival of the spirit of Islam sparked renewed interest in Islamic banking and inspired Muslim scholars to continue their efforts to establish Islamic banks in their respective countries. Acknowledging the scarcity and unavailability of proper guidelines concerning principles and practices of interest-free banking, they decided that the first task was to formulate guidelines and frameworks on practical aspects of Islamic banking system. This task was rightly vested in the hands of Islamic theologians and economists.

However, it was a daunting task finding Muslim economists who were also well versed in the knowledge of *Syariah* laws. More often than not, those who possessed in-depth knowledge in economics did not have knowledge in *Syariah*, and vice versa.

To make matters worse, most Muslim economists were educated in Western economies and did not possess strong fundamentals in Islamic economics. For example, when President Zia ul-Haq set up a task force to study and formulate a framework for the introduction of Islamic banking system in Pakistan, only 1 out of the 19 appointed members could be regarded as an expert on Islamic economics. Eleven of them had merely received education from the *madrasa* or religious school (Gieraths, 1990).

The need to establish banks founded on *Syariah* principles reached its peak around the 1970s. The first steps in the establishment of Islamic banks were usually taken by private initiatives rather than the government. Moreover, the process of the establishment of such banks varied from one Muslim country to another. The late Saudi Arabian King Faisal bin Abdul Aziz al-Saud was one of the noteworthy individuals who played a significant role and made a major contribution to the development of Islamic economics and Islamic banking. His Majesty initiated the establishment of the Organization of Islamic Conferences (OIC) and urged Muslim countries to set up their own Islamic banking system (Ali, 1988). The establishment of the Islamic Development Bank (IDB) in 1975 was seen as an impetus for the establishment of other Islamic banks in various Muslim countries. For example, Dubai Islamic Bank, which was the first private interest-free bank, was set up in the same year as IDB. In 1977, three more Islamic banks were incorporated, namely Faisal Islamic Bank of Egypt, Faisal Islamic Bank of Sudan and Kuwait Finance House. Islamic banks set up in the 1970s and early 1980s are as shown in Table 2–1. In South East Asia, the establishment of financial institutions that adopted terminologies resembling the operations of Islamic financial institutions commenced in the Philippines. Phillipine Amanah Bank was established in 1973 by *Presidential Decree No. 263* issued by the then President Ferdinand Marcos (www.islamicbank.com.ph).

TABLE 2–1 Islamic Banks Set Up in the 1970s and 1980s

Name	Country	Year of establishment
Nasser Social Bank	Egypt	1972
Islamic Development Bank	Saudi Arabia	1975
Dubai Islamic Bank	United Arab Emirates	1975
Faisal Islamic Bank of Egypt	Egypt	1977
Faisal Islamic Bank of Sudan	Sudan	1977
Kuwait Finance House	Kuwait	1977
Islamic Banking System International Holdings	Luxembourg	1978
Jordan Islamic Bank	Jordan	1978
Bahrain Islamic Bank	Bahrain	1979
Dar al-Mal al-Islami	Switzerland	1981
Bahrain Islamic Inv. Company	Bahrain	1981
Islamic International Bank for Investment & Development	Egypt	1981
Islamic Investment House	Jordan	1981
Albaraka Investment and Development Company	Saudi Arabia	1982
Saudi-Philippine Islamic Development Bank	Saudi Arabia	1982
Bank Islam Malaysia Berhad	Malaysia	1983
International Islamic Bank	Bangladesh	1983
Islamic Bank International	Denmark	1983
Tadamon Islamic Bank	Sudan	1983

TABLE 2–1 (continued)

Name	Country	Year of establishment
Qatar Islamic Bank	Qatar	1983
Bait Ettamouil Saudi Tounsi	Tunisia	1984
West Sudan Islamic Bank	Sudan	1985
Albaraka Turkish Fin. House	Turkey	1985
Faisal Finance Institution Inc.	Turkey	1985
Al-Rajhi Company for Currency Exchange & Commerce	Saudi Arabia	1985
Al-Ameen Islamic & Financial Inv. Corp. India Ltd.	India	1985

Source: Haron and Shanmugam, 1997.

Most of the Islamic banks mentioned in Table 2–1 have now been in operation for more than 30 years. These banks have not only been able to offer facilities similar to that of conventional banks, but they have in fact shown commendable performances with most of them generating profits. Apart from this, Islamic banks have attracted non-Muslims to patronize them. Even though Islamic banks in the Muslim countries were set up on private initiatives, the full support of governments is essential in guaranteeing the success of the banks. Countries such as Pakistan, Iran and Sudan, for example, have completely Islamized their banking systems. Other Muslim countries operate a dual-banking system whereby both Islamic and conventional banks operate parallel to each other. In countries where the government lends full support, development of the Islamic banking system is better planned and progress has been rapid. On the other hand, slow progress is observed in countries where the involvement of the government is limited. In Malaysia, for example, the full support of the government has paved the way for the rapid development of Islamic banking in the country. In early 1993, a total of 21 banking services based on *Syariah* principles were developed by the Central Bank of Malaysia or Bank Negara Malaysia. By the end of the same year, a total of 21 financial institutions had participated in the Interest-free Banking Scheme.

Significant development of the Islamic banking system in Malaysia was achieved when an Islamic inter-bank money market was established in early 1994. This system involves the inter-bank trading of Islamic financial instruments, Islamic inter-bank investments and Islamic inter-bank cheque clearing system (Bank Negara Malaysia, 1994). This Islamic inter-bank money market has facilitated banks in Malaysia to venture into investments or short-term loans among themselves in accordance to *Syariah*. To further spur the growth of the Islamic banking system, the Malaysian government launched the Financial Sector Master Plan 2001–2010 in 2001. The Master Plan contains a strategic blueprint for the development of the country's financial system with the development of Islamic banking as one of its objectives. In an effort to promote active trading and expand the use of Islamic financial instruments to the international level, Malaysia once again took the helm when it cooperated with Bahrain, Brunei, Indonesia and the Islamic Development Bank to establish the International Islamic Financial Market. This institution, which was established under a Royal Decree and headquartered in Bahrain, commenced operations on 1 April 2002. Founding members include the Islamic Development Bank, Bahrain Financial Authorities, Labuan Offshore Financial Services Authority, the Central Bank of Sudan, the Central Bank of Indonesia and Brunei Finance Ministry. Other members of the organization include the Central Bank of Iran, Kuwait Finance House, Abu Dhabi Islamic Bank and Shamil Bank of Bahrain.

Since the objectives and operations of Islamic financial institutions differ from those of their conventional counterparts, consequently their methods of accounting and auditing also differ from the conventional ones. Hence, in line with the aim to create uniformity in the accounting and auditing practices in the Islamic finance industry, the Accounting and Auditing Organization for Islamic Financial Institutions (AAOIFI) was established on 27 February 1990, corresponding to 1 Safar 1410 H, in Algiers, Algeria. This organization was registered in Bahrain on 27 March 1991 corresponding to 11 *Ramadhan* 1411 H. Another development in international-level Islamic banking was the establishment of the Islamic Financial Services Board (IFSB). The IFSB, which is based in Kuala Lumpur, was officially inaugurated on 3 November 2002 and began operations in March 2003. There are three categories of membership, namely full membership, associate membership and observer membership. In 2008, there were 21 full members, 21 associate members and 136 observer members (www.ifsb.org).

Dr. Ahmad Mohamed Ali, President of the Islamic Development Bank, in his working paper presented at the Fifth Forum on Islamic Finance 2002 at Harvard University, USA, divided the development of Islamic banking and financial institutions into six phases. The first phase, which took place in the 1950s, is regarded as the starting point of Islamic finance and banking. During this period, Islamic intellectuals began giving their views on concepts of Islamic banking to replace conventional banking systems. The suggested outline of the Islamic banking organization was based on the concept of twin *mudharabah*. The 1960s saw the emergence of early institutions of Islamic banks like Mit Ghamr Savings Bank in Egypt in 1963 and Lembaga Tabung Haji in Malaysia in 1966. The period of the 1980s was the most active phase in terms of the development of Islamic banking systems. During this decade, many banks were established and new products introduced. Conventional banks also showed interest in providing Islamic banking services through the window concept. In addition, with the aim of extending knowledge, many research programmes, teaching and training related to this branch of knowledge were introduced in institutions of higher learning. The development and growth of Islamic banks worldwide was made even easier when the International Monetary Fund participated in research activities and with the publication of articles on Islamic banking. Trust funds founded on *Syariah* principles were also launched. The 1990s witnessed the development of Islamic banking in the American capital market, where the Dow Jones Islamic Index was launched. In addition, accounting standards on Islamic banking were issued by AAOIFI. Events that occurred in various phases are shown in Table 2–2.

DEVELOPMENT OF ISLAMIC BANKING SYSTEM IN SELECTED COUNTRIES

Currently, Islamic banks are operating in most Islamic countries. However, the experiences of the banks differ from one country to another. Differences are found in aspects such as history of establishment, laws to be abided by, and opportunities and support from the governments concerned. Islamic banks would not be faced with problems if the governments of the countries concerned are truly committed to developing Islamic banking systems. Due to the differences mentioned earlier, a brief description will be given of the establishment of Islamic banks in selected countries. Egypt is chosen because it is where the history of Islamic banks began. In Sudan, Islamic banks received special treatment in the beginning, but later with a change in the ruling government, the special treatment was withdrawn. Turkey has a secular form of constitution and regards religion as separate from politics. Iran and Pakistan have changed their entire banking systems to Islamic banking systems. Malaysia is regarded as a country committed towards establishing the Islamic banking system.

TABLE 2–2 Development of Islamic Financial and Banking Institutes According to Specific Periods

1950s	• Islamic scholars and economists began presenting models of banking and financial systems to replace banking based on interest rates. • A twin *Mudharabah* concept suggested as model for Islamic banking.
1960s	• The practice of Islamic financing principles began. • Operation mechanisms for Islamic financial institutions were recommended. • Rise and fall of Mit Ghamr Savings Bank in Egypt, 1963–1967. • Establishment of Lembaga Tabung Haji in Malaysia, 1966.
1970s	• Islamic banks and Islamic non-bank financial institutions were established. • Academic activities began to be organized. • Academic institutions were set up. • *Mudharabah* financial mechanism began to be established. • Establishment of Islamic Economic Research Centre, Jeddah. • Start of publication of books on Islamic banking. Topics covered were profit-loss sharing, *mudharabah* and leasing. • Establishment of Dubai Islamic Bank, 1975. • Opening of Islamic Development Bank, 1975. • First International Islamic Economics Conference held in Mecca in 1976.

TABLE 2–2 (continued)

1980s	• Government intervention in promoting Islamic banks.
	• Setting up of more private sector banks.
	• A variety of Islamic banking products introduced.
	• Increased interest among academicians and financial groups in the West in Islamic banking.
	• Conventional banks began to make available the window concept that offers Islamic products.
	• Increase in research programmes, teaching and training.
	• Growth of Islamic index and trust funds.
	• Pakistan, Sudan, Iran, Malaysia and other countries attempted to change their banking systems or to use the Islamic system.
	• IMF published working papers and articles on Islamic banking; research and publication on Islamic banking flourished.
	• Establishment of Fiqh Academy of OIC and other Fiqh Boards.
	• Establishment of Islamic trust funds throughout the world.

TABLE 2–2 (continued)

1990s	• Growth in the Islamic window concept.
	• Enhancement in asset-based financial instruments, recognition of the importance of Islamic financial institutions and banks.
	• Establishment of Islamic Index at Dow Jones and the Financial Times.
	• Regulations and supervision given attention.
	• Standards of AAOIFI issued.
	• Start of task of establishing support institutions.
Early 2000s	• Continuous growth and maturity alongside risk challenges.
	• Completion of the architecture of Islamic finance.
	• Attention on risk management and corporate control.
	• Capitalization of Islamic banks through mergers.
	• Creation of an asset-backed securities market.
	• Islamic Financial Services Board, Malaysia formed in 2002.
	• Establishment of the International Islamic Rating Body, Bahrain.

History of Islamic Banking System in Egypt

The history of the establishment of Islamic banks in Egypt started with the establishment of Mit Ghamr Savings Bank in 1963, followed by the establishment of Nasser Social Bank in 1972, Faisal Islamic Bank in 1977 and International Bank for Investment and Development in 1980. The establishment of Mit Ghamr Savings Bank by Ahmed al-Naggar is regarded as the milestone in modern Islamic banking. Mit Ghamr Savings Bank offered five types of banking services based on *Syariah* principles. These services comprised deposit accounts, financing accounts, equity participation, direct investment and social services. The bank offered two types of deposit accounts, savings account and investment account. The savings account did not offer any returns or *riba*, while the investment account was based on the concept of profit and loss sharing. Similarly, there were two types of financing facilities, non-investment financing and investment financing.

Non-investment financing is the type of financing provided to clients who maintain a savings account in the bank. There is no charge incurred on the borrower. The borrower only needs to pay back the amount borrowed. Investment financing, on the other hand, is financing given out particularly to small entrepreneurs, under the concept of profit and loss sharing. Repayment of the financing is done either at the end of the financing period or in instalments. Equity sharing is the concept whereby the bank acts as a business partner and contributes the initial capital for an intended enterprise. Allocation of profit is based on the ratio of the capital issued or on the ratio agreed upon by the bank and the partner concerned. In direct investment, the bank itself issues capital and starts a business. Social services are services provided by the bank in the collection of *zakat* and in channelling the *zakat* to goodwill projects and society.

With the existence of Mit Ghamr Savings Bank, the inhabitants of the interior regions of the Nile Valley no longer needed to rely on financing by lenders who imposed high rates of *riba*. The farmers had the burden of their debts lightened. This success of Mit Ghamr received praise and the recognition from the Ford Foundation. In its report issued in June 1967, the Ford Foundation applauded the success of the bank in winning support from farmers and villagers (El-Ashker, 1990). The growth in the number of depositors and deposit amount is shown in Table 2–3. It can be seen that growth was highly encouraging during the four years of its operations. Total number of depositors increased by 73% for 1964/65 and subsequently by 400% and 65% for 1965/66 and 1966/67, respectively. The total deposits meanwhile increased by 367% for 1964/65, 360% for 1965/66 and 108% for 1966/67.

TABLE 2–3 Number of Depositors and Total Deposits for Mit Ghamr 1963/1964–1966/1967

Year	Total depositors	Total deposits
1963/1964	17,560	40,944
1964/1965	30,404	191,235
1965/1966	151,998	879,570
1966/1967	251,152	1,828,375

Source: El-Ashker, 1990, p. 61.

However, due to changes in the political climate of Egypt, its operation suffered a setback and it was taken over by the National Bank of Egypt and Egypt Central Bank in mid-1967 and subsequently *riba* was introduced into the operations of Mit Ghamr. This change from Islamic banking system to a *riba*-based system reduced the number of depositors substantially. Nevertheless, the concept of Islamic banking was revived in 1971, under the rule of President Anwar al-Sadat when the government established the Nasser Social Bank in 1972. Even though the operations of Nasser Social Bank are similar to those of Mit Ghamr Savings Bank, the former offers a full range of banking services and a wide range of investment activities including foreign exchange services. Unlike Mit Ghamr whose establishment was under private initiative, Nasser Social Bank received full government support as well as government subsidies in maintaining its financing operations.

Apart from Nasser Social Bank, two other Islamic banks were established in Egypt at the end of the 1970s, namely Faisal Islamic Bank of Egypt (FIBE) and Islamic International Bank for Investment and Development. FIBE is a joint venture between Saudi Arabia and Egypt. It was incorporated under a special act, that is, *Law No. 48/1977*. This Law confers on FIBE a special status and provided the bank with special privileges from the government. However, the bank comes under the supervision of the Central Bank of Egypt. The Law also outlines the total capital allowed and has enacted total shares be 51% owned by Egypt and 49% by Saudi Arabia. However, the Law allows Saudi Arabia to sell its allocation to other Arab parties as well as to non-Muslims in Egypt. FIBE is also subject to three other acts, namely *Company Act, Investment of Arab and Foreign Funds Act*, and *Banking and Control Act*.

The Islamic International Bank for Investment and Development (IBID) was established in 1980 through a Ministerial Decree, in line with the requirements of the *Investment Law of Arab and Foreign Funds and Free Zones Law (number 43) of 1974*. Unlike FIBE, IBID which began its operations in October 1981, is wholly owned by the Egyptians.

Both FIBE and IBID offer services which are almost similar to those of commercial banks. FIBE offers current account services without overdraft facilities. Savings account services are not provided, but customers could open investment accounts for specific durations where returns are on a profit-sharing basis. FIBE also provides two types of financing, namely short-term financing, and medium and long-term financing. Short-term financing is normally based on the principle of *murabahah*, while medium and long-term financing are mostly based on the *musyakarah* principle. FIBE is also involved in business, either through equity participation or through its subsidiary companies.

In terms of social services, FIBE contributes towards the advancement of Islamic economy by actively organizing seminars and conferences, financing publications related to Islamic economics and setting up its own library. All these social activities are funded by FIBE through its own fund set up primarily for these purposes or money from *zakat*. Unlike FIBE, IBID provides savings account facility to its customers. In addition, IBID has also introduced a facility known as Investment Savings Accounts to encourage depositors to invest but at the same time they could withdraw part of their savings at any time if required. This differs from the normal investment account where an investor is not allowed to withdraw his money before it is due. However, returns for both types of deposit are on a profit-sharing basis. IBID also provides financing facilities for various projects involving the agricultural, industrial and commercial sectors. These financing facilities may be short-term, medium-term or long-term and are normally based on the principles of *mudharabah* and *musyarakah*.

In June 2006, the Central Bank of Egypt decided to merge IBID with two conventional banks, United Bank of Egypt and Nile Bank, to form the United Bank in an attempt to restructure the banking system. The decision to merge these three banks was made in order to solve their financial problems. For instance, IBID had not only struggled with high debts for a number of years but also failed to increase its paid-up capital to a new minimum of £E500 million under the capital adequacy requirements imposed by the Central Bank of Egypt in 2005.

The United Bank is 99.9% owned by the Central Bank of Egypt and is now the third largest banking entity in the country. The United Bank has 34 branches of which 7 are Islamic branches. This new bank provides traditional banking services as well as Islamic banking products and services. Among the traditional banking products and services offered are investment accounts, savings accounts, postponed deposits, traditional certificates, credit cards, safe deposit boxes, remittances services, brokerage services and crediting employees' salaries to their bank accounts (www.theubeg.com).

The bank's investment account is equivalent to term deposit with variable return and depositors are only allowed to withdraw their deposits after three months. Savings accounts comprise investment savings account, general savings account, savings book of pilgrimage and *umrah* and the US Dollar savings account. In terms of traditional certificates, United Bank offers the diamond certificate (a three-year certificate with a fixed return), the golden certificate (a three-year certificate with cumulative fixed return), the five-year certificate with a fixed return, the three-year certificate in US Dollar with a fixed return and the millionaire certificate (*Syariah*-compliant certificate).

The United Bank also offers Islamic banking services under the name "Rakha'a" which means prosperity. This sector was created as a result of the merger between the branches of IBID and the Islamic *Syariah* transactions branches of the United Egyptian Bank and Nile Bank. Under its Islamic banking sector, the bank applies concepts such as *musyarakah, mudharabah, murabahah, bai salam, istisna, bai ajil* and *ijarah* in its financing and investment portfolio. The bank also offers the "*Dyar*" Islamic Real Estate Financing Services which provide *Syariah*-based financing for purchasing a house, renovating the house or for building a house. Under these financing schemes, the bank applies *murabahah* concept for short- and long-term financing of between 1 and 15 years.

Another Islamic bank in Egypt is the Egyptian Saudi Finance Bank (EFSB) which is a subsidiary unit of the AlBaraka Banking Group. The EFSB has 18 branches and offices throughout Egypt and offers various types of *Syariah*-compliant banking services including retail banking, foreign trade services, letters of credit, savings pools, investment trustees, instrument *umrah* as well as mutual funds, securities and custody. The EFSB also fulfils its social obligation through the operation of its *zakat* funds and social fund for development. The latter fund is used to finance development projects for new and small enterprises. The bank provides medium- and long-term financing for various economic activities involving the telecommunications sector, airports and air transportation sector, public garages sector, medicine and medical requirements sector, exporting industries sector, industry sector, tourism sector and oil sector.

Although Egypt was among the first country to establish an Islamic bank, it has in recent years lagged behind in the development of an Islamic banking system compared to countries like Bahrain and Malaysia. The combined market shares of Islamic banks in Egypt constitute only 5% of the total banking system. One of the main factors cited as to why Egypt has fallen behind in the development of Islamic banking is the high profile scandals of Islamic investment companies in the 1980s. According to El-Gamal (2006), the failure of Islamic Money Management Companies in Egypt in the 1980s has somewhat damaged the public perceptions of Islamic banking in the country. By 2008, there were two *Syariah*-based financial institutions in Egypt (Faisal Islamic Bank of Egypt and Egyptian Saudi Finance Bank) and 13 conventional banks operating Islamic windows. Nonetheless, only 128 branches of the thousands of branches operated by these 13 conventional banks offered Islamic products (www.sukuk.net).

History of Islamic Banking System in Sudan

The development of Islamic banking in Sudan is somewhat unique compared to that in other Muslim countries. This is due to the fact that Islamic banking in Sudan underwent two distinct periods: a period of full government support and a period of distress in the banking sector. During the first period, Islamic banking enjoyed encouragement and full support from the government. This period saw the rapid development of Islamic banking in Sudan and most of the regulations imposed were in support of the rapid growth of the banks. However, when this support was withdrawn, banks in Sudan were faced with obstacles and had to comply with regulations which hindered their growth.

The concept of Islamic banking was introduced in Sudan with the establishment of Faisal Islamic Bank of Sudan (FIBS) in 1977. The FIBS was established under a special law known as the *FIBS Act of the National People's Council* and began operations in May 1978. Initially, FIBS enjoyed a range of facilities and was exempted from various regulations such as regulations on banking services, insurance, auditing and tax on profits. These privileges were however withdrawn when the government Islamized the entire banking system in Sudan in 1984. As with other Islamic banks, the FIBS offers deposit facilities, which include savings account, current account and investment account. These facilities are based on the principle of profit sharing. For financing facilities, the principles practised include *mudharabah, musyarakah* and *murabahah*. The initial success of FIBS spurred the government to support the establishment of more Islamic banks. Consequently, three more Islamic banks were created in 1983, namely Tadamon Islamic Bank, Sudanese Islamic Bank and Islamic Cooperative Development Bank. In 1984, two more banks began operations, Albaraka Bank (Sudan) and Islamic Bank for Western Sudan.

In September 1983, the government of Sudan launched its Islamic laws and the whole banking system was required to convert its operations to be in line with *Syariah* principles. By September 1984, the entire banking system in Sudan was supposed to operate in accordance with *Syariah* principles. In actual fact, however, conventional banks continued to practise interest-based banking activities. This resistance to the Islamization process of the banking system not only came from the conventional banks, but also from the authorities at the Central Bank of Sudan. When the government which wanted to Islamized the banking system was overthrown, all the conventional banks ceased to offer products and services based on *Syariah* principles. Only Islamic banks continued to offer such services. The government made the decision to re-Islamize the entire banking system in Sudan in 1991. It was reported in the media that the transformation process this time was done in a more sincere and organized manner (Ahmad, 1994).

In 2005, a peace agreement called the Comprehensive Peace Agreement (CPA) was signed by the Government of Sudan and the Sudan People's Liberal Movement in the South. The signing of this peace deal ended decades of civil war which erupted in 1983. With the signing of the CPA, the *Central Bank of Sudan Act 2002* was amended in 2006. Under *Section 5* of the Act, the banking system in Sudan consists of a dual banking system with Islamic banking continuing to operate in the North and conventional banking operating in the South. The Bank of Southern Sudan (BOSS), a branch of the Central Bank of Sudan, was established to regulate and supervise the conventional banks as well as branches of Islamic banks in the South. Even though the South is given autonomy on its banking system, both conventional and Islamic banks adopt only one national monetary system (Mohamed Rajab, 2006). By the end of 2007, there were 32 banks operating in Sudan with 8 Islamic banks and 2 conventional banks operating in Southern Sudan (Central Bank of Sudan, 2007).

History of Islamic Banking System in Turkey

Although 99% of the population in Turkey are Muslims, the country does not recognize itself as a Muslim country. Instead, Turkey has chosen to become a secular country. This change started in 1928 when Mustafa Kamal At-Taturk , founder of modern Turkey, held the notion that the advancement of Turkey could only be achieved by emulating Western models and by separating religion from all other things. This situation has perpetuated until today. In *Article 2* of the country's constitution, it is stated that Turkey is a democratic, secular and socialist nation. *Article 24* clearly states that religion must be kept separate from politics, social matters, economy, laws and other matters associated with the country, and religion is only to be used for personal purposes. In the 1960s, the government's view regarding religion began to soften as a result of three main factors. First, the western-educated elite had started to accept the presence of Islam and had allowed the establishment of political parties founded on Islam in Turkey. Secondly, the government consented to education centred on religion. As a result, since 1965, about 10% of secondary schools and 40% of upper secondary schools in Turkey are Islamic religious schools. The third factor was the rise of Islamic movements in the Middle Eastern countries, and it was these Middle Eastern countries which mostly financed the religious activities in Turkey. In addition to this, a number of the Organization of Islamic Conference member countries, as well as the Islamic Development Bank had pressured the Turkish government to open its door to Islamic banks in the country.

As a result of the factors mentioned above, during the 10th general election in 1983, the Turkish government pledged to promulgate special laws to allow the establishment of Islamic banks in Turkey. The Prime Minister of Turkey at that time, Turgut Ozal, was of the view that individuals should be given the choice to patronize their preferred banking institutions. Turgut Ozal's consent for Islamic banks to operate was also the Prime Minister's bonus to his supporters who were faithful followers of Islam (Baldwin, 1990). Even so, this move was met with varying opposition especially from those of hard core secular stand and from prominent figures of the conventional banks.

The decree of a special law, *Decree 83/7506* on 16 December 1983, which was later published as *Official Gazette No. 18256* on December 1983, paved the way for the establishment of Islamic banks in Turkey. This Law consists of 17 articles and describes the methods, rules of establishment, permissible activities and other associated matters that must be complied with by Special Finance Houses (these are financial institutions established to provide only interest-free financial products and services). In addition, comprehensive rules and regulations were issued by the Undersecretariat of the Treasury and Foreign Trade through *Official Gazette No. 18232* dated 25 February 1984. The regulations issued comprise 35 articles and cover various aspects related to the establishment, operations and liquidation related to Islamic banking such as total capital required for establishment, the total number of members of Board of Directors and the types of facilities allowed to be provided. This Law also outlines the methods of administering the facilities provided and the ways to calculate profit.

Another law related to Islamic banking in Turkey was issued by the Central Bank of Turkey. The Law was published in the *Official Gazette 18348* dated 21 March 1984. The Law comprises 18 articles, and covers matters such as regulations concerning licence, the powers of the Central Bank in fixing liquidity ratios and the authority of the Central Bank in regulating and supervising the operations of Islamic banks. Although there exist three separate laws which Islamic banks have to comply with, all three laws do not contain the words "Islam" or "*Syariah*" in them. Islamic banks are only referred to as "Special Finance Houses". Similarly with the concepts used in the facilities provided; there is no mention of the principles of *mudharabah, musyarakah*, etc. in the regulations issued. *Syariah* principles are referred to as "participation accounts" or "profit-sharing and loss-sharing accounts". It is believed that these acts an attempt by the government to avoid an open conflict with the aims and principles contained in the country's constitution (Baldwin, 1990).

At the end of 1994 there were only three Islamic banks operating in Turkey. The first bank, which commenced operation in 1985, was Albaraka Turk Ozel Finans Kurumu. Its biggest shareholder was Albaraka Investment and Development Corporation from

Saudi Arabia. The second bank, which also began its operations in the same year, was Faisal Finans Kurumu or better known as Faisal Finance Institution Incorporation and was established with capital contributions from the Dar al-Maal al-Islami Trust group, also from Saudi Arabia. Turk-Kuveyt Evkaf Finans Kurumu, the third Islamic bank which started operations in 1988, was a joint-venture bank between the Islamic Development Bank, Kuwait Finance House and Vakiflar Bankasi. By the end of 2004, there were seven Islamic banking institutions in Turkey, namely Albarakah Turkish Finance House, Emin Sigorts A.S., Family Finans Karamu (formerly called Faisal Finance Institution), Faisal Islamic Bank of Kibris Ltd., Ihlas Finance House, Kuwait-Turket Evkaf Finance House and Asya Finans Kurumu A.S. (www.islamic-banking.com/banking).

In November 2005, the *Banking Act No. 5411* was enacted. Under this Act, all special finance houses are transformed into "participation banks", thus gaining the bank status. Participation banks operate under the purview of the Banking Supervisory and Regulatory Agency. In accordance with the *Banking Act, 2005*, participation banks are authorized to collect deposit under the "profit-and-loss participation accounts" and the "special current accounts". Participation banks may also offer two types of financing, which is *murabahah* and financial leasing. As at end of 2008, there were four participation banks in Turkey, namely Albaraka Turk, Bank Asya, Kuvyet Türk and Türkiye Finans. Together, these banks held 4.2% and 3.3% share of total deposit and total loans in the Turkey banking system, respectively as at the end of 2007 (www.byegm.gov.tr).

History of Islamic Banking System in Malaysia

As with other Muslim countries, Malaysia was affected by the Islamic resurgence movement among the intellectuals especially around the 1970s. There were calls from individuals and certain groups and agencies for the government to establish Islamic banks to cater to the needs of Muslims in Malaysia. During the Bumiputra Economic Congress in 1980, a resolution which required the government to allow the Pilgrimage Board (commonly known as Lembaga Tabung Haji) to establish an Islamic bank for the purpose of collecting and investing money owned by Muslims was passed. In 1981 at the National Seminar on the Concept of Development in Islam, participants of the seminar urged the government to promulgate a special law which would allow the establishment of banks and financial bodies whose operations would be based on Islamic principles.

In line with these requests, the government appointed a National Steering Committee on Islamic Banking on 30 July 1981. It was chaired by Tan Sri Raja Mohar bin Raja Badiozaman. The secretarial functions were entrusted to the Pilgrimage Board. This committee studied the operations of Faisal Islamic Bank of Egypt and Faisal Islamic Bank of Sudan in preparing its report (Connors, 1988). The final report was submitted to the government on 5 July 1982 and the following recommendations were made by the committee:

(i) An Islamic bank whose operations are in accordance with the *Syariah* principles should be established;

(ii) The Islamic bank shall be incorporated as a company under the auspices of the *Companies Act 1965*;

(iii) Since the *Banking Act of 1973* is not applicable for the operations of Islamic banks, a new banking act, *Islamic Banking Act 1982*, must be introduced to license and supervise Islamic banks. The supervision and administration of this new Act shall be the responsibility of the Central Bank of Malaysia; and

(iv) Islamic banks shall establish their own Syariah Supervisory Board whose function is to ensure that the operations of Islamic banks are in accordance with *Syariah* law.

In order to pave the way for the establishment of Islamic banks, the *Islamic Banking Act 1983* was gazetted and came into effect on 7 April 1983. This Act outlines the rules which must be conformed to by Islamic banks that wish to operate in Malaysia, as well as the powers of the Central Bank of Malaysia in supervising and regulating Islamic banks in Malaysia. At the same time, the government also passed the *Government Investment Act* in 1983 to empower the government to issue Government Investment Certificates based on *Syariah* principles.

The first Islamic bank to operate in Malaysia was Bank Islam Malaysia Berhad (BIMB), which was incorporated under the *Companies Act 1965* on 1 March 1983 and commenced operations on 1 July of the same year. BIMB offers common products and services that are available at conventional banks except that the bank follows *Syariah* principles. BIMB also has subsidiaries whose operations are based on *Syariah* principles. These subsidiary companies comprise Syarikat A-Ijarah Sendirian Berhad (a leasing company), Syarikat Al-Wakalah Nominees Sendirian Berhad (which provides nominee services) and Syarikat Takaful Malaysia Sendirian Berhad, whose main activity is to provide general insurance cover and family insurance. BIMB was listed on the Main Board of the Kuala Lumpur Stock Exchange on 17 January 1992. It was not until 1999 that the establishment of a second Islamic bank was approved by the government.

It is the long-term objective of the Central Bank of Malaysia to create an Islamic banking system parallel to the conventional system. This can only be accomplished through three main components. First, the system must have sufficient number of players; secondly, services and products must cover the whole banking system; and thirdly, inter-bank markets where operations comply with Islamic principles must be created.

In line with the objective to create an Islamic banking system that runs in parallel with the conventional system, a total of 21 Islamic banking products were introduced by the beginning of

1993 and on 4 March 1994 the Central Bank of Malaysia launched a scheme known as the "Interest-free Banking Scheme". Through this scheme, financial institutions are allowed to offer Islamic banking products and services. The pilot phase of this scheme involved the three largest commercial banks in Malaysia and the second phase saw ten more financial institutions joining the scheme.

At the end of 1993, the Islamic banking system in Malaysia comprised 1 Islamic bank, 20 conventional financial institutions made up of 10 commercial banks, 8 finance companies and 2 merchant banks which offer services and products based on Islamic principles. In addition, on 3 January 1994, the Islamic inter-bank market was introduced. This market consists of the following three aspects:

(i) Inter-bank trading in Islamic financial instruments.

(ii) Islamic inter-bank investment.

(iii) Islamic inter-bank cheque clearing system.

In line with the intention to further strengthen the development of the Islamic banking system in Malaysia, the Central Bank of Malaysia established the National Shariah Advisory Council on Islamic Banking and Takaful (NSAC) on 1 May 1997. The NSAC comprises ten members, including one international member. Various decisions were made by this council including allowing compensations to be incurred on borrowers who fail to repay financing, allowing women lawyers and non-Muslim lawyers to be witnesses to financial documents, and allowing for a second guarantee. Use of the term "interest-free banking" was changed to "Islamic banking", and participating banks were required to promote the status of the departments concerned which should be headed by someone of a senior position. On 1 October 1999, the status of monopoly enjoyed by BIMB ended when the government consented to the establishment of a second Islamic bank, Bank Muamalat Malaysia Berhad. This second full-fledged Islamic bank was established as a result of a merger between Bank Bumiputra Malaysia Berhad and Bank of Commerce (M) Berhad. Under the merger arrangement, the Islamic banking assets of Bank Bumiputra, Bank of Commerce and BBMB Kewangan Berhad were transferred to Bank Muamalat Malaysia Berhad. This second Islamic bank began operations with 40 branches and 1,000 staff.

The commitment of the Malaysian government in promoting the Islamic banking system could be seen from its on-going plans to this end. As stated in the Financial Sector Master Plan 2001–2010, by 2010 the Islamic banking industry and *takaful* will have the following features (Bank Negara Malaysia, 2001, p. 79):

(i) Constitute 20% of the banking and insurance market share with an effective contribution to the financial sector of the Malaysian economy.

(ii) Represented by a number of strong and highly capitalized Islamic banking institutions and *takaful* operators offering a comprehensive and complete range of Islamic financial products and services.

(iii) Underpinned by a comprehensive and conducive *Syariah* and regulatory framework.

(iv) Supported by a dedicated institution (*Syariah* commercial court) in the judiciary system that addresses legal issues related to Islamic banking and *takaful*.

(v) Supported by a sufficient number of well-trained, high calibre individuals and management teams with the required expertise.

(vi) Epitomize Malaysia as a regional Islamic financial centre.

Tan Sri Nor Mohd. Yakop, the second Finance Minister, during the officiating of the Non-Islamic Financial Institutions Seminar organized by Islamic Institutions of Banking and Finance Malaysia on 1 March 2004, stated that the Islamic banking system has entered the third wave of its development. The first wave was the introduction of Islamic banking; the second referred to the creation of an Islamic capital market; and this decade represents the third wave. The third wave encompasses the development and expansion of Islamic assets and financial instruments associated with *waqf*, trust, micro credit, *qard hassan* and *zakat*.

In line with the aspiration to make Malaysia the centre for Islamic banking, the Central Bank of Malaysia, Bank Negara Malaysia, approved the applications of three foreign Islamic banking institutions to operate in Malaysia. On 27 May 2004, Kuwait Finance House was granted licence, while Al Rajhi Banking & Investment Corporation, Saudi Arabia and a consortium made up of Qatar Islamic Bank, RUSD Investment Bank Inc. and Global Investment House were granted their respective licences on 14 October 2004. Kuwait Finance House started its operation in August 2005 while the Al Rajhi Bank opened its first branch in Kuala Lumpur in October 2006. At present the bank has some 19 branches throughout the country. In January 2007, Asian Finance Bank commenced operation as the third foreign Islamic bank in Malaysia. The Asian Finance Bank is backed by a consortium of shareholders comprising Qatar Islamic Bank and associates (70%), RUSD Investment Bank Inc. of Saudi Arabia (20%) and Financial Assets Bahrain W.L.L. (10%) (www.asianfinancebank.com).

Concurrent with the progressive liberalization of the Islamic banking industry and the recommendations made under the Financial Sector Master Plan to further strengthen the institutional structure of the banking institutions participating in the Islamic banking system, Bank Negara Malaysia approved the Islamic subsidiary structure to replace the Islamic window institutional structure in 2005. Hence, the seven domestic banking groups were allowed to transform their current Islamic window into an Islamic subsidiary within their respective banking groups. But this transformation was not made mandatory. Under this new structure, Islamic banking subsidiaries are now governed under the *Islamic Banking Act 1983* instead of the *Banking Financial Institutions Act 1992*. The new structure eliminated most of the obstacles that had impeded Islamic windows in participating in non-traditional banking businesses such as wholesale and retail trading; purchase of assets and landed properties; and the purchase of equities via joint-venture and portfolio investments.

The Islamic financial landscape in Malaysia was again transformed in 2006 with the launching of the Malaysia International Islamic Financial Centre (MIFC) in August of that year. The MIFC is the collective efforts of Bank Negara Malaysia, the Securities Commission of Malaysia, Labuan Offshore Financial Services Authority and Bursa Malaysia. It involves the participation of industry players representing the banking, *takaful* and capital market in Malaysia. The main objective of MIFC is to promote Malaysia as the major hub for international Islamic finance through several incentives designed to create a conducive environment for conducting Islamic finance business in Malaysia. As part of its initiatives, domestic and international banks operating in Malaysia may conduct Islamic banking business in foreign currencies through the International Currency Business Units (ICBU) within the institutions. Foreign participation in Islamic subsidiaries was also raised to a ceiling of 49% of total equity, which was later relaxed in 2007 by allowing full foreign equity ownership for Islamic financial institutions established under the MIFC. The MIFC initiatives also allow domestic and financial institutions to conduct a wide range of business in international Islamic banking and *takaful* in international currency by establishing the International Islamic Banks (IBB). The IBB which also falls under the purview of the *Islamic Banking Act 1983* can either be a branch or subsidiary of the parent financial institution. They are accorded the same incentives as the ICBU.

Presently, there are a total of 17 Islamic banking institutions (9 Islamic subsidiaries of the domestic banking groups, 2 domestic

Islamic banks, 6 foreign Islamic banks), 2 International Islamic Banks and 16 Islamic banking operations conducted through windows by commercial banks, investment banks and development financial institutions. As at end of 2008, the Islamic banking assets accounted for 17.4% of the total banking assets of the Malaysian financial system (Bank Negara Malaysia, 2008). Total deposits in the Islamic banking system at the end of 2007 accounted for 11.9% of the total deposits in the domestic banking sector. Meanwhile, the financing issued by the Islamic banking system as at end of 2007 was 13.7% of the total loans issued in the Malaysian banking sector (James, 2009).

History of Islamic Banking System in Iran

As with Pakistan, Iran has also converted its entire financial system to Islamic banking system. The history of the Iranian Islamic banking system began immediately after the Islamic revolution in the country in 1979. The first step taken by the new regime was to take over all commercial banks in Iran. According to Mehdi Barzagan, Prime Minister of Iran at the time, the take-over process was inevitable due to the banks not making profit and the presence of unhealthy elements. It had to be done to protect the country's rights and wealth, and to set the country's economy in motion (Aryan, 1990). As a result of the take-over and reorganization of the banks, the banking system was represented by only 6 commercial banks (there were originally 30) and 3 specialized banks. In addition, the government established 22 provincial banks, one for each province (Hedayati, 1993).

The Islamic banking system in Iran was implemented on a gradual basis. It took six years for the system to be fully implemented. Several factors had caused delay in the implementation, such as the process of nationalizing the banking system, the unpredictable political situation, the freezing of

Iran's overseas assets, depression, and war. The first step taken towards the establishment of an Islamic banking system was the introduction of a service charge into the banking system to replace the *riba* system in 1981. Through this system, banks imposed a 4% service charge on loans issued. For deposits, on the other hand, depositors were given a "guaranteed minimum profit". At the same time, a comprehensive legislation to Islamize the operations of the entire banking system was prepared by a committee comprising bankers, academicians, businessmen and *ulama*. Eventually in March 1982, the committee submitted the proposed legislation to the Revolutionary Council. The law was passed in August 1983 as the *Law for Usury-Free Banking*.

The Law required banks in Iran to fully convert their operations in accordance with *Syariah* principles within three years and convert their outstanding interest-based deposits to interest-free deposits within one year from the date the Law was passed (Aryan, 1990). With effect 21 March 1984, depositors are not allowed to place their money into *riba*-based accounts while banks are not allowed to provide interest-based credit facilities. From March 1985, the entire banking system in Iran had been fully converted into an Islamic banking system. Meanwhile, Bank Markazi (Central Bank of Iran) is the sole authority in monitoring and supervising the entire Islamic banking system in Iran. However, interest is still allowed in all international trading transactions. Foreign banks were at first allowed to operate in free trade zones. But starting from 2004, foreign banks are permitted to open branches throughout Iran provided that the loans offered are based on the profit-loss sharing principle (*Tehran Times*, 1 May 2004). In 2007, three foreign banks received permits to conduct banking activities in Iran whereas six more foreign banks are reported to have opened branches in the country (*Tehran Times*, 29 April 2008). As at end of 2008, there were seven commercial banks, four specialized banks, six private banks and one near-bank (www.cbi.ir).

History of Islamic Banking System in Pakistan

The history of Islamic banking system in Pakistan started immediately after the coup d'etat executed by General Zia-ul-Haq ended in July 1977. On 29 September 1977, General Zia appointed the Council of Islamic Ideology (CII) to study and prepare a report on the elimination of *riba* in the country's economic system. In November 1977, CII appointed 15 experts in banking to assist the council in the preparation of the report. Subsequently in February 1980 this panel of experts submitted to CII the report titled "Report on the Elimination of Interest from the Economy". After making certain amendments to the report, the final report was then submitted by CII to General Zia in June 1980.

The report presented by the council was very comprehensive and covered specific topics. Among the topics covered include issues, problems and strategies that would be used in the process of elimination of the interest system in economy, necessary steps in the implementation of Islamic banking system, matters related to the operation of commercial banks, which cover aspects of financing and receiving deposits, and operations associated with specific financial institutions such as Pakistan Industrial Credit and Investment Corporation, Industrial Development Bank of Pakistan, National Development Finance Corporation, Agricultural Development Bank of Pakistan, Small Business Finance Corporation, Equity Participation Fund and insurance companies. In addition, this council listed in its report the responsibilities and functions of the State Bank of Pakistan (the central bank) in controlling and formulating financial policies based on the Islamic banking system that was to be introduced.

Apart from CII, there were groups formed by other agencies to study the process of elimination of *riba* from the country's economic system. For instance, the Finance Minister of Pakistan appointed a committee known as the Committee on Islamization to conduct one such study. A report, titled "Agenda on Islamic Economic Reform", was submitted by the committee to the Minister of Finance in April 1980. The State Bank of Pakistan also formed six working groups to examine and make recommendations for the elimination of *riba* from the various sectors in the economy. This group submitted its report in November 1979. Similarly, the Pakistan Banking Council formed a Superior Task Force with the responsibility to formulate the necessary regulations and procedures for the implementation of the Islamic banking system. The Task Force submitted their report on 4 August 1980.

Even though there were various groups that conducted studies and prepared reports on ways to eliminate the *riba* system in Pakistan, a number of financial institutions in Pakistan were in fact already offering services based on *Syariah* principles before the reports were presented. In July 1979, three financial institutions, namely, House Building Finance Corporation, National Investment Trust and Investment Corporation of Pakistan had converted their entire operations to *Syariah*-compliant ones. Another financial institution, Bankers Equity Limited, which began its operations in October 1979, also practised *Syariah* principles in all its operations.

As in Iran, the Islamic banking system in Pakistan was implemented in phases. The phases involved are as follows:

(i)   The first phase began on 1 January 1981 when all banks in Pakistan accepted deposits in the form of profit-sharing deposits.

(ii) In the same year, the government announced the *Mudharabah Companies and Mudharabah Rules 1981*. Commercial banks were allowed to use money deposited for the purpose of transactions as listed by the State Bank of Pakistan. However, where methods of investment were concerned, banks were still free to choose between *Syariah*-based or *riba*-based methods.

(iii) On 14 June 1984, the Finance Minister, in his budget speech, announced that all interest-based transactions, whether new or existing, were to cease in six months.

(iv) Beginning January 1985, all financial transactions involving government and government agencies were conducted based on *Syariah* principles.

(v) In April 1985, the same ruling was imposed on all individual entities and companies.

(vi) From 15 July 1985, all deposits placed with the financial institutions became interest-free.

Although in principal all deposits and financing received and given out by commercial banks in Pakistan were free from all elements of interest, deposits and financing in foreign currencies continued to be based on interest rates. In November 1991, the Federal Shariat Court ruled that all procedures practised by banks in Pakistan did not conform to Islamic principles. The government and financial institutions appealed to the Shariat Appellate Bench of the Supreme Court of Pakistan. On 29 December 1999, the Shariat Appellate Bench rejected the appeal and ordered that all laws involving interest be revoked.

In line with the Court's decision, the government set up a number of committees and task force to consider the best way to implement the decision by the Court. It was eventually decided that the transformation of the financial system as a whole was not possible within a short period of time. Instead, the Malaysian concept whereby the Islamic banking system exists side-by-side with the conventional system was adopted. In relation to this, the State Bank of Pakistan took several measures, including the formulation of policies to promote Islamic banking on a more gradual basis. In December 2001, detailed criteria for setting up Islamic banks were issued by the Central Bank of Pakistan. Pursuant to this, Al-Meezan Bank Limited applied to convert into an Islamic bank. The bank received its license in January 2002 and commenced operations in March of the same year. It became the first full-fledged Islamic bank in the country operating under the name Meezan Bank. Three existing banks, Muslim Commercial Bank, Bank Alfalah and Bank of Kashmir were allowed to set up 7 branches whose operations were based on the Islamic principles. Habib Bank Limited was also allowed to open a *Syariah* branch. In 2004, the State Bank of Pakistan received applications from commercial banks to set up 24 *Syariah* branches (Husain, 2004).

In order to allow commercial banks in Pakistan to open Islamic banking subsidiaries, amendment to the *Banking Companies Ordinance (BCO) 1962* was made under *Section 23* of the *BCO* in November 2002. The following year, the Central Bank of Pakistan developed guidelines for the establishment of full-fledged Islamic banks, Islamic banking subsidiaries as well as guidelines for the establishment of stand-alone Islamic banking branches in Pakistan. The guidelines were issued vide *BPD Circular No. 1* dated January 2003. A circular on the minimum *Syariah* regulatory standards for Islamic banks, Islamic banking subsidiaries and Islamic banking branches, *IBD Circular No. 2* dated April 2004, was issued (Islamic Banking Department, 2008). In 2003, the Islamic Banking Department was established by the Central Bank and is responsible for all matters related to Islamic banking. The same year saw the creation of the Syariah Council comprising two *Syariah* experts and three experts on banking, accounting and law.

As at the end of 2007, total deposits and total assets of Islamic banks were Rs147 billion and Rs206 billion, respectively (Pakistan's official currency is the Rupee). Currently, there are 6 full-fledged Islamic banks and 506 Islamic branches of 12 conventional banks operating in Pakistan. Under the strategic planning for Islamic banking industry as set out by the Central Bank of Pakistan following the re-launch of Islamic banking in the country in 2002, the industry is expected to capture 12% share of the total banking industry by the year 2012. At end of June 2008, the market share of deposits and market share of assets of the Islamic banking industry stood at 4.5% and 4.2%, respectively of the total banking industry (www.sbp.org.spk).

SUMMARY

The history of modern Islamic banking started with the establishment of Mit Ghamr Savings Bank in Egypt in 1963. However, the history of Islamic banking activities can be traced back to the early days of Islam. Banking activities such as deposit taking, travellers cheques issuance, money order and money exchange services, had existed during the time of the Prophet (p.b.u.h.) and his Companions. Unfortunately, the activities were not developed and there was no effort to establish a special organization that consolidated all these activities. The first organization whose activity was related to the collection and distribution of money was the Baitulmal. However, the concept and goal of this institution did not include provision of services to the public in terms of deposits or financing.

The rise of Europe in the 12th century saw the emergence of the conventional banking system. The system eventually spread to Muslim countries. As Muslim countries began to adopt conventional banking, Islamic banking activities ceased to exist. As a result, the Islamic banking system which was introduced during the early years of Islam failed to expand. When Islam was revived in the late 1800s and early 1900s, the practice of *riba* among Muslims became the focal point of discussions among Muslims. Discussions and feelings of uneasiness among the *ulama* and Muslim intellectuals continued up until the establishment of Islamic banking institutions during the modern era. Economist Dr. Ahmed al-Naggar took the brave step of pioneering a *riba*-free system by setting up Mit Ghamr Savings Bank in Egypt and proved that an Islamic banking system could in fact be a substitute for the practice of *riba* by conventional banks.

Mit Ghamr's first modern experiment with Islamic banking inspired other Muslim countries to set up their own Islamic banks, which eventually led to the establishment of a number of Islamic banks in Muslim countries. However, the development of Islamic banks differed from one country to another. Iran, Pakistan and Sudan chose to Islamized their entire banking systems, while in other countries, Islamic banking operates side-by-side with conventional banking. The contributions of certain bodies such as the Islamic Development Bank and International Association of Islamic Banks also boosted the development of Islamic banking in the world.

Up until the end of 2008, there were more than 300 Islamic banks operating in both the Muslim and Western countries. Western conventional banks have also started offering products and services based on *Syariah*. Apart from Islamic banks, there are also fund management companies which implement *riba*-free activities and these companies are reported to be managing more than US$800 billion of Islamic funds. Other financial activities such as insurance and mortgage are now also managed in accordance with *Syariah* principles. In addition, the financial market has begun to use financial instruments based on *Syariah*. In some countries, such as Malaysia, an Islamic financial market has also been established to complement the Islamic banking system. The Islamic banking system has a bright prospect ahead. Even if it is not used as a substitute for the conventional banking system, the Islamic banking system can at least move ahead in parallel with the conventional system in meeting global banking needs.

REFERENCES AND FURTHER READING

Ahmad, Ziauddin. "Islamic Banking: State of the Art." Jeddah (Saudi Arabia): Islamic Development Bank, 1994.

Ahmed, Osman. "The Role of the Faisal Islamic Bank." In *Islamic Financial Markets*, edited by Rodney Wilson, 76–99. London and New York: Routledge, 1990.

Ali, Muazzam. "A Framework of Islamic Banking." In *Directory of Islamic Financial Institutions*, edited by John R. Presley, 3–13. London: Croom Helm, 1988.

Aryan, Hossein. "Iran: The Impact of Islamization on the Financial System." In *Islamic Financial Markets*, edited by Rodney Wilson, 155–170. London and New York: Routledge, 1990.

Baldwin, David. "Turkey: Islamic Banking in a Secularist Context." In *Islamic Financial Markets*, edited by Rodney Wilson, 33–58. London and New York: Routledge, 1990.

Bank Islam Malaysia Berhad. *Bank Islam, Penubuhan dan Operasi*. 2nd ed. Kuala Lumpur, 1989.

Bank Negara Malaysia. *Money and Banking in Malaysia*. Kuala Lumpur: Economic Department BNM, 1994.

Bank Negara Malaysia. *Financial Sector Master Plan*. Kuala Lumpur, 2001.

Bank Negara Malaysia. *Financial Stability and Payment Systems Report*. Kuala Lumpur, 2008.

Central Bank of Sudan. *Annual Report 2007*.

Connors, Jane. "Towards a System of Islamic Finance in Malaysia." In *Islamic Law and Finance*, edited by Chibli Mallat, 57–67. London: Graham & Trotman, 1988.

De Belder, Richard T. and Mansor Hassan Khan. "The Changing Face of Islamic Banking." *International Financial Law Review*. Vol. 12, Iss. 11 (Nov. 1993): 23–26.

El-Ashker, Ahmed. *The Islamic Business Enterprise*. London (UK): Croom Helm, 1987.

El-Ashker, Ahmed. "An Evaluation of the Major Islamic Banks." In *Islamic Financial Markets*, edited by Rodney Wilson, 59–75. London and New York: Routledge, 1990.

El-Gamal, Mahmoud Amin. "Overview of Islamic Finance." Occasional Paper No. 4 (August 2006): 1–13.

Erol, Cengiz and Radi El-Bdour. "Attitudes, Behaviour and Patronage Factors of Bank Customers Towards Islamic Banks." *International Journal of Bank Marketing*. Vol. 7, No. 6 (1989): 31–39.

Gieraths, Christine. "Pakistan: Main Participants and Final Financial Products of the Islamization Process." In *Islamic Financial Markets*, edited by Rodney Wilson, 171–195. London and New York: Routledge, 1990.

Haron, Sudin and Bala Shanmugam. *Islamic Banking System – Concepts and Applications*. Selangor Darul Ehsan (Malaysia): Pelanduk Publications, 1997.

Hedayati, Seyed A.A. "Islamic Banking, as Experienced in the Islamic Republic of Iran." Working paper presented at the International Seminar of Islamic Banks, Sydney (Australia), 9–10 November 1993.

Homoud, Sami Hassan. *Islamic Banking*. London (UK): Arabian Information Ltd., 1985.

Husain, Ishrat. "Evolution of Islamic Banking." Speech given during the opening ceremony of the seminar on Islamic Banking organized by Meezan Bank, Pakistan, February 2004.

Islamic Banking Department, State Bank of Pakistan. "Pakistan's Islamic Banking Sector Review." http://www.sbp.org.pk/ibd/ Islamic-Banking-Review-03-07.pdf

Islamic Development Bank. *Annual Report* (various issues). Jeddah (Saudi Arabia).

James, S. "Good Prospects for Islamic Banking." *Malaysian Business*. FindArticles.com.http://findarticles.com/p/articles/mi_qn6207/ is_200080301/ai_n24977546

Khan, Muhammad M. The Translation of the Meanings of Sahil Al-Bukhari, Vol. 3. Lahore (Pakistan): Kazi Publications, 1989.

Mannan, Muhammad Abdul. *Islamic Economics: Theory and Practice.* Cambridge (UK): Hodder and Stoughton, 1986.

Mohamad Rajab, Dalal. "Naivasha Peace Agreement Analysis and Evaluation Part 1." *Sudanese Journal for Human Rights' Culture and Issues of Cultural Diversity.* Iss. 2 (March 2006): 1–31.

Rudnick, David. "Islamic Banking: Praying for Profit." *Euromoney* (Nov. 1992): 23–25.

Shaban, Mohamed Abu. "The MCCU Story." www.mcca.com.au/ mcca_the_mccu_story.pdf

Siddique, Muhammad. *Islamic Banking System: Principles and Practices.* Islamabad (Pakistan): Research Associates, 1985.

Sumner, William Graham (ed.). *A History of Banking in All the Leading Nations.* Vol. II. New York (USA): Augustus M. Kelly-Publishers, 1971.

Syedain, Hashi. "Counting the Quran." *Management Today* (Mar. 1989): 104–108.

Tehran Times. "Iran Approves Foreign Bank Branches." 1 May 2004.

Tehran Times. "6 Foreign Banks to Open Branches in Iran." 29 April 2008.

Wheeler, Skye. "South Sudan Orders Islamic Banks to Leave." http://www.reuters.com

Wilson, Rodney. *Banking and Finance in the Arab Middle East.* London (UK): MacMillan, 1983.

Wilson, Rodney (ed.). *Islamic Financial Markets.* London and New York: Routledge, 1990.

www.asianfinancebank.com

www.banking-business-review.com

www.byeqm.gov.tr

www.cbi.ir

www.imf.org

www.islamicbank.com.ph

www.Lariba.com

www.mcca.com.au

www.sbp.org.spk

www.sukuk.net

www.theubeg.com

CHAPTER **3**

OBJECTIVES, PHILOSOPHY AND PRINCIPLES OF ISLAMIC BANKING

This chapter describes the objectives and philosophy of business that an Islamic business entity should conform to. In addition, there will be a discussion on the Syariah principles which underlie the operations of Islamic banks the world over. This is so that the reader can have an idea of the line of thought and essence of conviction of those who lead and manage Islamic banks. This chapter also explains how funding resources are obtained and how these resources are used by Islamic banks. Finally, it will describe in detail the fundamentals on which the relationship between the Islamic bank and its customer are secured.

INTRODUCTION

When the governments of Iran, Pakistan and Sudan opted to "Islamize" their entire economic systems, the transformation of the economy to a new order raised several theoretical and conceptual considerations, in particular what type of new economic system to implement. At that time, only three forms of systems existed, namely the socialist, socio-capitalist and capitalist systems. The absence of an appropriate model prompted the three countries to choose the banking sector as the starting point for their Islamization process. The Islamization of the economy involved one principal point, that is, the elimination of interest in all deposits and financing transactions. Many have questioned the appropriateness of a bank to be called an Islamic bank for the mere fact that its transactions do not involve interest although they appear similar to those of a conventional bank. It is obvious that the establishment of Islamic banks in most Muslim countries is to cater to the banking needs of Muslims, and the businesses of these Islamic banks run alongside conventional banks. Since the goal of the establishment of Islamic banks is to meet the banking needs of Muslims, the functions and activities of both Islamic and conventional banks display several similarities.

Basically, the conventional bank performs two primary functions, namely, to accept savings deposits and to lend money. Customers are usually classed into four categories: individuals, businesses, the public sector and other groups. As a place for depositing money, conventional commercial banks normally provide four types of deposit facilities, namely savings account, current account, fixed deposit and negotiable savings certificate. The type of services may vary depending on the type of customers as mentioned earlier. Conventional commercial banks normally offer loans to individuals, businesses, governments and their agencies, and other groups such as cooperatives and organizations. Facilities provided are also of various kinds, which include overdraft, letters of credit, letters of guarantee and others. In addition, conventional banks provide additional services like money order transactions, money exchange and advisory services. The roles played by the commercial banks may change, subject to situation and time. Currently, commercial banks have started to offer services which in the past were offered only by certain financial institutions. Similarly, other financial institutions have also begun to offer services which in the past were only available through commercial banks.

Just like conventional banks, Islamic banks offer deposits as well as financing facilities. As a place for depositing money, Islamic banks offer services almost similar to those of commercial banks, such as savings account, current account and fixed deposit. Islamic banks also offer financing facilities to their customers, comprising individuals, businesses, governments and other groups needing financial aid. Other services offered include money order transactions, money exchange and advisory services. All activities, however, do not involve the element of *riba* or interest.

Although the functions and activities of Islamic banks and conventional banks appear to be identical, this does not imply that they are based on the same conceptual and theoretical grounds. Both Islamic and conventional banks differ in terms of their basis for establishment. Differences exist due to the difference in the platforms used for their establishment. Islamic banks are organizations which are established to administer banking activities based on religious doctrines. Conventional banks, on the other hand, are established solely for business purposes and do not involve any religious aspect.

OBJECTIVES OF ESTABLISHMENT AND BUSINESS PHILOSOPHY OF ISLAMIC BANKS

In principle, business institutions place profit maximization as their prime motive. The amount of profit that an organization sets to achieve would depend on the philosophy adhered to by the owner and the management. Economic theories state that the objective of a business is profit maximization. This profit-making motive becomes even more apparent if the organization established is privately owned; where the owner will work hard to attain high profits since the profits would be solely his. Similarly with businesses established on a partnership basis; each business partner would strive hard for the success of the venture. The same goes for private limited companies, where the shareholder (owner) acts as the manager.

An organization established as a public limited company requires additional support staff in management and administration. Here, the shareholders may not take part in the management of the company. Hence, the management are not the shareholders and they are paid salaries for their work. The appointments and dismissals of the management are carried out by the shareholders, who are normally represented by the Board of Directors. This encourages managers to adopt whatever strategy they deem suitable in order to generate maximum profit to fulfil shareholders' aspirations. Large profits are important in a big business organization for two main reasons. First, large profits would give the impression that the organization is being run effectively, and this would enhance the image of the management. Secondly, shareholders normally would want high returns from the capital invested. Profits would be distributed to the shareholders in the form of dividends. Hence, shareholders will be kept happy if the company succeeds in giving them high yearly returns. The dividends and capital profits (if any) are regarded as compensation for the risk undertaken by the shareholders on making the investment concerned. This fact becomes the principal reason why the ultimate goal of commercial banks is the achievement of maximum returns for their shareholders (Elstone, 1987).

Unlike conventional banks where profit is the sole consideration, the objectives of Islamic banks are founded on two key factors, namely the factors of religion and profit. When an organization is established on the platform of religion, it has to internalize the teachings of that religion which are related to its establishment and operations. Since Islamic banks are founded on the religion of Islam, the banks would have to conform to and comply with Islamic principles. The teachings of Islam would mould Islamic banks into organizations that place more importance on moral elements as compared to conventional banks. The moral elements exist by virtue of the factor of *iman* (faith and belief) and Islamic principles regarding business. Notwithstanding their moral obligations, Islamic banks are expected to make a profit from their operations. This is because as business organizations, Islamic banks need to make profits in order to continue their operations.

According to Ali (1988), the Islamic financial system cannot be introduced merely by eliminating the practice of *riba*; rather, it is done by adopting and fusing the Islamic principles of social justice into its rules, practices, regulations, procedures and instruments to help realize the maintenance and dispensation of justice, equity and fairness. The concept of justice should be based on the Quranic concept of justice. Hence, in its objectives of establishment, the Islamic bank must consolidate and find a proper equilibrium between religion which emphasizes *tauhid* (oneness of God) and moral dimension, and business dimension which places importance on profit. If the moral factor alone is given importance, there is the possibility that the bank would experience losses and be forced to cease operations. If this happens, not only will the depositors lose their deposits, but it would bring about a loss to Muslims as a whole.

Similarly, if the profit factor alone is given priority, the bank would deviate from the actual Islamic platform centred on the concepts of justice and equality, upon which it is established. Society would then regard Islamic banks to be no different from conventional banks. In such circumstances, society would choose to patronize conventional banks over Islamic banks given their longer exposure to the conventional system, and that they are deemed to be more stable and efficient in providing banking services to society.

Khan (1983) stated that the objective of the Islamic bank is to develop, foster and promote the use of Islamic principles, laws and traditions in all banking transactions, financial, business and other related areas. Apart from promoting the "Islamization" of all banking activities, Islamic banks also have the responsibility to promote the establishment of investment companies or other business enterprises so long as these companies are not involved in activities that are forbidden by Islam. The establishment of Islamic banks is not merely for the attainment of profits. Consequently, most Islamic banks have set their business goals and objectives by incorporating moral and social elements. For instance, Bank Islam Malaysia Berhad in the initial period of its establishment had set its goal as follows (Bank Islam Malaysia, 1985):

> *The corporate goal of this bank is to provide banking facilities and services founded on Islamic principles, regulations and practices to all ethnic groups and citizens of this country. These principles, regulations and practices are in truth Islamic mualamah rules (ahkam al-muamalat al-Islamiah) related to banking and financial transactions. The bank's effort to provide these facilities and services are undertaken within the framework of its viability and capability to continuously grow and expand.*

Due to changes that have occurred in the business demands of today and the increasingly globalized Islamic banking landscape, Bank Islam Malaysia has renewed its vision and mission following the launch of the bank's new corporate identity in August 2007. The bank's new vision and mission are as follows (www.bankislam.com.my):

Vision:

> *To be the global leader in Islamic banking.*

Mission:

(i) *To continually develop and innovate accepted financial solutions in line with Syariah principles.*

(ii) *To provide a reasonable and sustainable return to shareholders.*

(iii) *To provide for a conducive working environment and to become an Employer of Choice for top talents in the market.*

(iv) *To deliver comprehensive financial solutions of global standards using state-of-the-art technology.*

(v) *To be a responsible and prudent corporate citizen.*

A close examination of the bank's new goals and mission will reveal that emphasis is now placed on it becoming a global player in Islamic banking products and looking after the interest of its shareholders.

Bank Muamalat Malaysia Berhad, the second Islamic bank to be established in Malaysia, currently have the following as its vision and mission (www.muamalat.com.my):

Vision:

To deliver best value to stakeholders.

Mission:

To become the preferred Islamic financial service provider regionally.

Dubai Islamic Bank, established in 1975, is one of the world's first Islamic banks. It had in the early part of its establishment aimed to prevent Muslims from dealing with transactions involving *riba* as one of its principal objectives because such practice is forbidden by Allah (s.w.t.). Hence, Muslims would be protected from falling into one of the big sins in Islam. Due to changing times, Dubai Islamic Bank, similar to Bank Islam Malaysia, has amended its vision in order to better reflect the significant development and growth that the bank has achieved. It now aspires to be the most advanced bank in providing innovative banking services according to rules stipulated by Allah (s.w.t.). Since 1999, Dubai Islamic Bank has set its vision and mission as follows (Dubai Islamic Bank, 1999):

Vision:

> *To be the leading provider of innovative financial services guided by the teachings of Allah.*

Mission:

> *To be the first Islamic bank worldwide, that has translated true Islamic economic principles into practice, out of firm belief in the need of mankind for an economic system based on the Final Revelation. By partnering with our customers in halal earnings, employing the best business practices, the latest financial services technologies and placing our trust in Allah, we are confident of our success.*

The bank has also specified its values as follows:

(i) **Lifestyle**: We believe in a life that conforms to the values and principles of Islam.

(ii) **Clients**: We value our clients and their satisfaction is our priority. Our clients are our close friends and most valuable asset.

(iii) **Accuracy and efficiency**: We understand that our clients value their time. Hence, we strive to provide services which are accurate, efficient and fast.

(iv) **Strong relationship**: We seek clients' loyalty and work towards strengthening their relationship with us.

(v) **Innovation**: We place importance on the differences in experience undergone by our clients and constantly perform innovations and improve our services for them.

(vi) **Group cooperation**: Group cooperation is essential to what we undertake. We value and respect all ideas and opinions which contribute towards the overall enhancement of the performance of the organization.

(vii) **Social**: We contribute actively to society by developing resources and promoting economic growth.

In line with these values, Dubai Islamic Bank has outlined its goals to cover aspects of quality services, profitability and social responsibility. Its comprehensive goals are as follows:

- To provide banking services with the highest standard according to *Syariah* without involving *riba* and applying the latest technology, using computers, telecommunications and information systems.

- To undertake investments wisely, to obtain optimum returns, not maximum profit, for the mutual benefit of the bank and its clients.

- To coordinate, cooperate and act together with other financial institutions which practise *Syariah* in their transactions in order to support efforts to establish a foundation and regulation for the Islamic financial system.

- To develop the society of Muslims in all areas of economy by investing in the areas of industry, agriculture, trade and real estate to create more job opportunities.

- To promote within society the attitude of helping one another for goodwill through Islamic methods, particularly through *zakat*.

- To contribute to the welfare of society in line with the five essential aspects in Islam: protection of life, authenticity of the mind, property, honour and social justice.

- To encourage the habit of saving and wise investment according to *Syariah* rules, using financial and investment instruments suited to individual needs.

- To provide relevant capital to entrepreneurs to create economic projects and to make available financing methods which conform to *Syariah*.

However, since 2000, the bank no longer reports its values and goals in its annual report.

One of the largest private commercial banks in Bangladesh, Islami Bank Bangladesh Limited (IBBL), has also outlined its special features. These special features revolve around aspects of fulfilling social responsibility and the aspiration to develop the economy of Muslims based on *Syariah*. The poor and the less fortunate are the target groups of this bank. The goals initially were as follows (Islami Bank Bangladesh, 1999):

(i) All activities are performed in accordance with methods of the interest-free system based on *Syariah*.

(ii) The range of investments undertaken is those permitted by *Syariah*.

(iii) Income from investment is shared with depositors under the *mudharabah* principle according to ratios which are regarded reasonable in terms of the deposits they made.

(iv) To introduce a welfare-oriented banking system and to establish equity and justice in the field of trade and commerce.

(v) To encourage socio-economic uplift and provide financial services to the low-income community particularly in the rural areas.

(vi) To play a vital role in human resource development and employment generation particularly for the unemployed youths.

(vii) To achieve balanced growth and equitable development through diversified investment operations particularly in the priority sectors and less developed areas of the country.

However, in line with current developments and globalization demands, Islami Bank Bangladesh later revised its targets and goals as follows (www.islamibankbd.com):

- To conduct interest-free banking businesses.

- To establish participatory banking instead of banking based on creditor-debtor relationship.

- To invest on profit-and-risk sharing basis.

- To receive deposits based on *mudharabah* and *wadiah* principles.

- To establish a welfare-oriented banking system.

- To extend cooperation to the poor, the helpless and the low-income group for their economic upliftment.

- To play a significant role in human development and employment generation.

- To contribute towards the balanced growth and development of the country through investment operations, particularly in the less developed areas.

- To contribute in achieving the ultimate goal of the Islamic economic system.

Meanwhile, Bank Muamalat Indonesia's original vision is as given below (Bank Muamalat Indonesia, 1998):

To make Bank Muamalat Indonesia a bank that is the pride of the *ummah*, that is, one of the best banks in its class. It aims to:

(i) Stay healthy or in good financial condition, and this is to be measured whether in terms of rules and regulations of Bank Indonesia or in terms of *Syariah*.

(ii) Acquire profits.

(iii) Make its shares attractive to society.

(iv) Possess a wide working network with global business capacity.

(v) Provide a productive place for the advancement of career for every staff member.

The original mission of Bank Muamalat Indonesia was:

(i) To play a role in the economic development of the Indonesian race, particularly through efforts to uplift the role of Muslim entrepreneurs and to act as catalyst to the expansion of the Syariah Financial Council

(ii) To deliver appropriate profits to shareholders.

(iii) To work towards optimum operational growth.

(iv) To provide positive contribution to the Muslim society.

(v) To maintain and enhance the quality of working life.

The original vision and mission were later revised in 1999 and applied until 2005. Bank Muamalat Indonesia's new vision is:

(i) To be the principal *Syariah* bank in Indonesia.

(ii) To be a dominant player in the *Syariah* market.

(iii) To be a bank that is respected in the rational market.

The mission was revised as follows:

(i) To become a *Syariah* bank that is managed professionally, emphasizing excellence in management, market orientedness and the spirit of entrepreneurship.

(ii) To become a model for the organization of *Syariah* banks.

(iii) To become the most innovative bank in investment activities.

However, Bank Muamalat Indonesia again made improvements to its mission in 2006. The change was deemed necessary in the light of changes in the Islamic banking system in Indonesia. A number of *Syariah* banks have been established in Indonesia. Among them is Bank Perkreditan Rakyat (BPR) which is active in providing *Syariah* banking products. This has created strong competition in Indonesia's Islamic banking system. At the end of 2008, the Islamic banking system in Indonesia comprised 5 full-fledged *Syariah* commercial banks, 13 Islamic Banking Units which are branches of private national banks, 15 Islamic Banking Units which are branches of regional government banks and 128 Islamic rural credit banks (www.bi.go.id). To meet the challenges to the Islamic banking scene where competition is expected to intensify, Bank Muamalat Indonesia, the leading Islamic bank in Indonesia up until year-end 2007, has the following new vision and mission (www.muamalatbank.com):

Vision:

> *To become the premier Syariah bank in Indonesia, dominant in the spiritual market, admired in the rational market.*

Mission:

> *To become a role model for Syariah financial institutions the world over, emphasizing on entrepreneurial spirit, managerial excellence, and innovative investment orientation, to maximise value to stakeholders.*

This concept of a balance between profit and social obligations is also the stand of other Islamic banks in South East Asia. For example, Al-Amanah Islamic Investment in the Philippines, which was established on 26 January 1990 and commenced operations on 11 February 1991, has stated clearly in its establishment statute that its corporate mission is (www.islambank.com.ph):

> *To promote and expedite the socioeconomic development in the Autonomy Region by implementing banking, finance and investment operations, and to participate in the areas of agriculture, trade and industry, using the concepts of the Islamic banking system.*

The Islamic Bank of Thailand is the only commercial bank in the country that complies with *Syariah*. This bank was established in 2002 and its vision is as follows (www.isbt.co.th):

> *First and foremost, this bank operates businesses based on Islamic rules. This bank should by right become strong and stable with excellent services under efficient management and good supervision.*

Meanwhile, the Islamic Bank of Thailand's mission is:

(i) To maintain the bank's role of non-involvement in interest (*riba*).

(ii) To reinforce the stability of the organization.

(iii) To provide excellent services.

(iv) To provide complete business instructions and supervision.

(v) To implement social and societal development.

Dar al-Maal al-Islamic Trust, an Islamic organization established in 1981 as a holding company for 21 financial and business companies operating Islamic banking businesses and insurance in four continents, outlined the following objectives in 1992 for its group companies (Faysal Islamic Bank of Bahrain, 1992):

(i) To offer to all Muslims, contemporary Islamic financial services that serve to execute their financial dealings in strict respect of the ethical, individual and social values of the *Syariah* without contravening the heavenly imposed prohibition of dealing in *riba*.

(ii) To serve all Muslim communities in mobilising and utilising the financial *resources* needed for their true economic development and prosperity within the principles of Islamic justice, and assuring the right and obligations of both the individual and the community.

(iii) To serve the "Ummat al-Islam" (Islamic communities) and other developing nations by strengthening the brotherhood bonds through mutually beneficial financial relationships for economic development, and an enhanced environment for peace.

To be in line with the changing times, Dar al-Maal also changed its objectives and added values such as the following (Dar al-Maal al-Islami Trust, 1998):

(i) To create an Islamic banking and financial institution in a modern and competitive environment.

(ii) To be known as the front-most Group among Islamic financial institutes, providing services and products of quality and high standards.

(iii) To increase the income capacity of the Group and to maintain continuous value-added benefits for equity participants, investors and workers.

(iv) To contribute to economic development in countries where the Group is based, has investments or has business partners.

(v) To play a principal role in enhancing cooperation among financial institutes.

(vi) To develop good relationships with conventional financial institutes.

The values of Dar al-Maal are:

(i) To abide by Islamic *Syariah* principles which form the legislation for the business being implemented.

(ii) To persevere to obtain *halal* profits and sturdy development, and to increase efficiency.

(iii) To work as a group to protect the interest of the organization.

(iv) To focus attention on the services provided to participants and clients, and to foster relationships based on trust, unity and mutual benefit.

Since the year 2000, however, Dar al-Maal no longer displays the group's goals and values in its annual reports.

Besides Dar al-Maal, another giant company which is involved in the Islamic financial sector is Dallah Albaraka. This group was founded in 1969 and has interests in 300 companies in 44 countries. The total assets of Dallah Albaraka exceed US$7 billion. In the finance industry, this group has interests in 23 *Syariah*-based banks and financial institutions. The goal and philosophy held by its banking institutions at group level are as follows (www.albaraka.com):

Vision:

> *To serve the communities where we live and operate, through responsible social and environmental activities. To meet the long term interest of our clients, providing them with quality products and services. For prospective shareholders, a high return on investment through the selection and implementation of products which are low risk, detailed, and diverse with high future potential. We are committed to providing a professional, creative work environment, for our employees, characterized by transparency, openness, accountability and respect for all.*

Mission:

> *As a multi-purpose investment group; we seek to provide quality Sharia compliant investments and financial services. We will continue to improve and develop the diverse range of our business products – specifically in the areas of recreation, health, environment, food production, and real estate – throughout the Middle East and the rest of the world. We are dedicated to providing high standards of ethics and integrity in everything we do.*

The goal and philosophy of Dallah Albaraka are the tenets of all of its companies up to the level of the subsidiary companies and this can be seen through the vision and mission statement of one of the subsidiary companies, Albaraka Islamic Bank, Bahrain. It reads as follows (www.barakaonline.com):

Vision:

> *To be a leading and diversified international Islamic bank, offering a wide range of quality products and services and forming strategic alliances for a competitive edge.*

Mission:

> *We strive to be a premier regional Islamic bank, dedicated to the economic and social development of our target markets, maximizing our clients' and shareholders' value, and focusing on the human resources development in an environment of creativity and innovation.*

On examination of all the goals and objectives of Islamic banks, it can be concluded that the majority of Islamic banks place emphasis on fulfilling social responsibility. This is what distinguishes Islamic banks from conventional ones. However, even though conventional banks have no religious obligation to fulfil, this does not stop them from performing their social responsibility. In fact, there are instances when conventional banks give greater prominence to social programmes. These programmes encompass aspects of education, lightening the burden of the disabled and raising the standard of living of the poor. By right, Muslims should feel slighted if Islamic banks were to place importance on profit maximization while neglecting their social responsibility. But then they also do not wish for Islamic banks to be overly concerned with social responsibility as to disregard aspects of efficiency and profitability.

SOCIAL PRACTICES OF THE WORLD'S ISLAMIC BANKS

The majority of Islamic banks worldwide are sensitive to social responsibility, and this is in line with the goal of their establishment as institutions with moral and profit-making motives. Whether or not an Islamic bank performs its responsibility or plays its role in enhancing the socio-economic welfare of Muslims can be seen from the social activities conducted. Some banks do not clearly state their social responsibility, yet many of their activities are in fact moving in that direction. Also, there are some which do not mention in detail the social activities conducted.

Among the Islamic banks renowned for their social activities are Jordan Islamic Bank, Islami Bank Bangladesh and Social Investment Bank. In Malaysia, Bank Muamalat Malaysia is also active in fulfilling its social responsibility.

Jordan Islamic Bank (JIB) has been involved in the supply and installation of equipment in educational institutions in Jordan since its establishment. Every year, this bank allocates a part of its profits for the use of universities, scientific research and vocational training. At the end of the 2007 financial year, for example, as much as JD189,320 was given out to universities in Jordan, and the same amount was allotted to finance vocational and scientific training (Jordan's official currency is Jordanian Dinar or JOD). Apart from this, JIB also makes contributions and donations to mosques, *zakat* organizations and associations. An amount of JD201,500 was used for this purpose in the 2007 financial year. In addition, financing structured along the *Syariah* principles of *qard hassan*, *musyarakah* and *mudharabah*, was awarded to individuals facing financial difficulties. Financing was also allocated to youths who wished to be married, and to handicraft makers. By the end of 2007, a total of 71 projects under the craftsmen programme were financed by the bank. The total balance for the said programme was JD1.6 million at the end of 2007 (Jordan Islamic Bank, 2007).

Islami Bank Bangladesh conducts various social activities through a specially created body, The Islamic Bank Foundation. By the end of 1998, this Foundation had built two modern hospitals, service centres, sales centres and started several Bangladesh socio-economic development projects. The Foundation also established two types of training centres, namely vocational institutions providing vocational training to unemployed youths, and colleges that offer religious and moral education. In line with the objective to increase the level of income of the poor, the Foundation set up a sales centre where the public can purchase products produced by the poor and women facing difficulties. In addition, the Foundation has special funds to help those in difficulty as a result of floods or other disasters.

Just like Islami Bank Bangladesh, Social Investment Bank, Bangladesh is highly concerned with its moral responsibility. Not only does this bank implement this responsibility through its range of activities, but it also aids the public or its customers in carrying out activities for the development of *ummah* in the Muslim world. This assistance is given through facilities created to activate public funds which are intended to be channelled for welfare purposes. Collection of funds is done through two ways, that is, either in the form of *wakaf* certificates, whereby the fund contributed will not be returned to the donor but instead is used for the purpose mentioned, or in the form of bonds. In the case of funds collected in the form of bonds, the face value is returned to the owner at the end of the stipulated period, but the yield obtained through the transaction will be channelled to goodwill activities as chosen by the purchaser of the bond. The following are among the financial instruments created for this type of funds for socially useful purposes such as welfare or goodwill (www.siblbd.com):

- Development Bonds of Wakaf Property (general and specific).

- Certificate of Wakaf Cash Deposit (general and specific).

- Family Wakaf Certificate.

- Development Bonds of Mosque Property (general and specific).

- Mosque Community Shares.

- Certificate of Qard Hassan (general and specific).

- Certificate of Payment of Zakat and Taxes.

- Certificate of Hajj Savings.

- Development Bonds of Non-Muslim Trust Properties (general and specific).

- Development Bonds of Local Council Property (general and specific).

In addition to consolidating funds for goodwill purposes, Social Investment Bank has established a savings fund known as the Social Fund. The money channelled to this fund comes from the business profits obtained by the bank. Public contributions in the form of donations, alms and *zakat* are also channelled into this savings fund. The funds collected are used for the poor and needy, as well as for educational support in the form of scholarships and health financing.

Bank Muamalat Indonesia (BMI) has also not neglected its functions as an organization that grants positive contributions to the Muslim society in Indonesia. The following are among the activities on its social agenda:

(i) To develop small businesses.

(ii) To create economic development projects for the society.

(iii) To create a savings fund for the collection of *zakat* and alms from the public.

(iv) To distribute the funds of the International Development Foundation.

(v) To establish a financial institution retirement fund.

BMI has created profit-loss sharing scheme. At the end of 2007, 38.6% of the total amount of financing issued by BMI was financing of this form. Through its partner, Baitumaal Muamalat (BMM), the bank has implemented various corporate social responsibility programmes including the distribution of Rp9.6 million in 2007 in relief aids to areas that were stricken by natural disasters and managing a scholarship programme for tsunami orphans from Acheh on behalf of the Islamic Development Bank. In 2007, a total of 1,600 scholarships were given out to students under this programme (Bank Muamalat Indonesia, 2007).

Bank Muamalat Malaysia also has social and society-related programmes. Apart from issuing *zakat,* this bank conducts a special programme called *Masih Ada Yang Sayang* (There Are Still Those Who Care). Through this programme, the bank conducts activities to collect funds for distribution to students who need financial assistance.

In addition to conducting social activities, Islamic banks have a role in creating awareness among their customers that Islamic banks are in fact different from conventional banks. This awareness is important because without it, customers may perceive there to be no difference between these two types of banks. Such thinking is unhealthy, especially when a client's purpose to patronize an Islamic bank is merely to obtain profits from his savings or investments and not based on religious factor.

Several researches have shown that there are customers who perform transactions with Islamic banks solely for profit purposes (Erol and El-Bdour, 1989; Haron and Planisek, 1994). Efforts to educate society on Islamic banking should be made in an all-encompassing and integrated way. There should be cooperation between Islamic banks and educational institutions. Students should be exposed to knowledge about Islamic banking starting from school level.

FACTORS THAT INFLUENCE THE FORMATION OF THE PHILOSOPHY OF ISLAMIC BANKS

Factors that influence the formation of the philosophy of an organization may be divided into two, namely external and internal factors. External factors are normally beyond the control of the organization. Examples of external factors are laws of the country in which the organization operates, the environment, clients' thoughts and views, competitors' behaviour, changes in the economy and changes as a result of acts of the Almighty. Internal factors, on the other hand, are those that may be shaped or changed by the organization itself.

When there is intention to establish an Islamic bank, the philosophy of the bank will be influenced by external and internal factors. For example, an Islamic bank that is to be established should consider social issues, if any of the following situations prevails:

(i) The law requires that a bank allocate part of its profit for education, research or development of the *ummah*.

(ii) The law requires that a bank provide some funding for loans in the form of *qard hassan*, or channel aids to the needy or the low-income groups.

(iii) There are many competitors conducting social programmes. Hence, the bank must also conduct similar activities to demonstrate its social responsibilities.

(iv) The bank exists in the midst of a caring community. Hence, its social programmes would always obtain the full support of its customers. For instance, if a fund for social causes is launched, customers would give their full support.

Internal factors play a role in the initial stage of the bank's establishment. For example, when a group of investors use their money to set up an Islamic bank, they would normally want high returns, thus resulting in the practice of profit maximization. However, in reality, due to the high capital needed to set up the bank, the owners and managers would often consist of different types of groups. This implies that the formulation of the bank's philosophy will be influenced by two main factors, that is, the extent of the involvement of the owners in influencing the thinking of the management, and the beliefs and practices of the management itself in managing the bank.

Under normal circumstances, the management would be influenced by three conceptions. The first concept is that shareholders would definitely want high returns on their investment. If this belief exists, then the management would be working hard towards gaining profits to deliver to the shareholders with the expectations that they will be entrusted to continue running the bank. High profits also indicate excellent performance and effectiveness in management. The second conception is related to rewards received. If the management believes that rewards are largely dependent on profits attained, they would strive to maximize profits. This is based on the notion that the bigger the profit, the bigger the rewards they would receive in the form of bonuses and annual increments on their salaries. The third belief is that depositors must be rewarded with high returns; otherwise they may switch to other banks. This switching of banks by depositors would give the bank a bad image. In such situations, management would again be striving hard to maximize profits in order to reward high returns to depositors.

Hence, the three key motivators, namely, the desire to attain high returns to allot to the shareholders for the sake of the future of their career; the desire to attain high profits in order for them to obtain maximum salaries, annual bonuses and other forms of rewards; and the desire to give out high returns to depositors to prevent them from switching banks; would all influence the bank's top management to subscribe to the profit maximization philosophy and disregard the social element and welfare of the *ummah*. Social activities such as provision of *qard hassan* loans, financing for small businesses and others, would probably be given the lowest priority.

Although there are hundreds of Islamic banking institutions in the world, they may be classed into three categories as follows:

(i) Ordinary financial institutions offering Islamic banking products and services.

(ii) Islamic financial institutions operating banking businesses.

(iii) Islamic financial institutions offering Islamic banking products and services.

An Islamic banking institution is classed based on the practices and philosophy that it proclaims. A financial institution in the first category merely offers services which are not prohibited in Islam, but does not adhere to other business principles as required by Islam. The second category comprises financial institutions which regard themselves as Islamic financial institutions, but in reality the products and services they offer are similar to those offered by ordinary financial institutions. The third category is considered the best in the sense that not only do these financial institutions offer Islamic banking services, but in fact all their business operations are founded on Islamic business principles. Views that an Islamic bank or an Islamic financial institution should place importance solely on profits are due to conventional banking. Within the context of profit maximization, it must be reiterated that while profit is important, in an Islamic paradigm, it must be balanced with the requirement of social justice.

It follows then that the objective of the establishment of Islamic banks is a blend of the religious and business dimensions. Hence, all business activities related to financial transactions and banking must be conducted in accordance with Islamic principles and laws. These banks are also forbidden from engaging in business activities that are prohibited by Islam. Islam encourages its followers to engage in trade activities as stated in *Surah al-Baqarah*, verse 275, where Allah (s.w.t.) allows Muslims to do business but forbids *riba*. The Prophet (p.b.u.h.) was a trader and businessman in his early life, and so were most of his Companions. The most important aspect of Islamic banking is that its operations must be conducted without any elements of *riba*. The act of giving and receiving *riba* is forbidden, as stated in both the Quran and *Hadith* (a detailed discussion on *riba* is found in Chapter 4 of this book).

Siddiqi (1986) believed that *riba* is considered not only as detrimental to morals, but also destructive to society and is an obstruction to the overall development of the *ummah*. Siddiqi referred to the view of Iman Razi (543 H/1149–606 H/1209), a Muslim scholar who condemned *riba* because it eroded other people's property, gave rise to conflicts in society since only a handful would be rich while the poor would become poorer, and consequently such a situation would tarnish the reputation of the creditor. Regardless of the form of business carried out, elements of uncertainties are bound to exist. Each business executed is not assured of success and the business may at any time be exposed to losses. Since the success of the business is uncertain, it is therefore unfair if the creditor requires the businessman to pay him a fixed amount and the payment must be made regardless of whether or not the business makes a profit. In other words, the creditor would always receive returns from what he has loaned out even when the businessman faces a loss. The businessman, on the other hand, would have to make payments even when his business is not profitable.

Nonetheless, a bank whose operations are free from elements of *riba* does not qualify to be a truly Islamic organization because prohibition of *riba* is only one of the Islamic principles of business. Islam has outlined a range of principles for its followers to conform to when undertaking business. Apart from complying with clear guidelines on methods of handling a business, Islamic banks must also adhere to the rules and laws affecting individual Muslims. When all these rules have been complied with, only then can the bank be regarded as an Islamic organization. Once an Islamic bank understands the position and the rules that an institution or organization needs to adhere to, developing its business philosophy is effortless.

The business philosophy covers a large area and includes a variety of issues such as beliefs, practices and guidelines that must be adhered to by the Islamic bank in its operations. Business philosophy also includes patterns and forms of relationships practised by the bank with its depositors, investors and other parties who require its assistance and services. Further, the business philosophy must be upheld not only by the policy makers but also by the implementers. The parties involved normally include the Board of Directors, managers and staff of the bank. The business philosophy is sometimes different from the mission of the company and at times may even differ from the objective that the company strives to achieve.

Al-Azuhaily (2003) was of the opinion that a financial institution may be regarded as an Islamic financial institution as follows:

> *The function of an Islamic financial institution is to collect funds and to invest them on behalf of its participants (clients who put in deposits using the principle of profit-loss sharing). The goal of this institution is to restore the society of Muslims and to achieve cooperation among Muslims, at the same time complying with the fundamentals of Islamic legislation. This legislation requires that there be no involvement in riba and other prohibited contracts, besides the distribution of profit based on ratios which are unbiased, without any injustice. It also aims to help those in need through interest-free loans in addition to supporting the socio-economic growth of the Muslim society.*

Al-Azuhaily also highlighted the importance for the Islamic bank to display its distinctiveness compared to conventional banks.

Besides complying with Islamic rules and laws, Islamic banks must also be capable of competing with conventional banks as well as have the capability to fulfil the banking and economic needs of Muslims. Among the main characteristics which differentiate between Islamic and conventional banks are:

(i) Islamic financial institutions must comply fully with the requirements of *akidah* by not being involved in any transaction that contains elements of *riba* and other businesses forbidden by Islam.

(ii) Islamic financial institutions must be caring and more understanding when their customers face financial difficulties.

(iii) Islamic financial institutions should not have profit maximization as the principal goal; rather, they should have goals towards socio-economic development and poverty eradication.

(iv) Islamic financial institutions need to be more transparent in each of their transactions. In this way, depositors are made aware of how their money is being used and the returns they would be receiving. Similarly, transparency in the issuance of financing would ensure that there would be no elements of exploitation.

(v) Operations of Islamic financial institutions differ from those of conventional banks, and these include aspects of deposit taking and financing.

(vi) Islamic financial institutions must provide services to all communities in the society regardless of the types of customers and their status.

(vii) Islamic financial institutions must only impose charges on customers in accordance with the actual cost incurred in providing the service concerned.

SOURCES OF ISLAMIC BANKING PHILOSOPHY

Generally, conventional financial institutions do not have a preset source of reference when drawing up their philosophy. Frequently, the philosophy created and chosen is developed based on past experiences and future directions. Management thoughts also have an influence on the type of philosophy to be upheld by the organization. However, this problem is not present in Islamic-based institutions. This is because as a business entity established within the ambit of Islamic principles, the foundations of the philosophy of Islamic business are those principles which have been revealed in the pure and absolute source of Islam, that is, the Quran. Allah (s.w.t.) in *Surah Ali-Imran*, verse 132, says:

> And obey Allah and the Messenger; that ye may obtain mercy.
>
> (Q3: 132)

In *Surah an-Nisaa*, verse 59, Allah (s.w.t.) says:

> O ye who believe! Obey Allah, and obey the Messenger, and those charged with authority among you. If ye differ in anything among yourselves, refer it to Allah and His Messenger, if ye do believe in Allah and the Last Day: that is best, and most suitable for final determination.(Q4: 59)

Further, Allah (s.w.t.) says in *Surah al-Maidah*, verse 92:

> Obey Allah, and obey the Messenger, and beware (of evil): if ye do turn back, know ye that it is Our Messenger's duty to proclaim (the Message) in the clearest manner.   (Q5: 92)

Besides the verses above, other related verses are verses 64 and 80 to 81 *Surah an-Nisaa* (Q4: 64, 80–81), verse 12 *Surah Ibrahim* (Q14: 12), verses 20 to 25 and verse 46 *Surah al-Anfaal* (Q8: 20–25 and 46), verses 51 to 52 and verse 54 *Surah an-Nur* (Q24: 51–52 and 54), verse 33 *Surah*

Muhammad (Q47: 33), and verses 11 to 12 *Surah at-Taghaabun* (Q64: 11–12). Hence, the core philosophy of Islamic banks should be in line with the revelations in the Quran and *Hadith*. Revelations and *Hadith* which require Muslims to uphold justice and virtue, serve as guiding principles for Islamic banks in managing their business affairs. Apart from these two sources, two other *Syariah* sources are *qiyas* and *ijma*. As an institution founded on Islam and mostly led by Muslims, these are the sources that should be strongly referred to. It is considered unwise if Islamic banks disregard these *Syariah* sources and in their place use Western sources as their guide and reference when formulating their philosophy and incorporating it into their corporate objectives and policies.

THE ESSENCE OF THE BUSINESS PHILOSOPHY OF ISLAMIC BANKS

Islam regards business as an endeavour which requires honesty and as a source of sustenance for Muslims. The Prophet (p.b.u.h.) in his early life before he was appointed a Messenger and similar with many of his Companions, was a businessman. It must be remembered, though, that Islam advocates the implementation of business by Muslims according to the principles as stipulated by the religion. The meaning of righteous trade in Islam is best explained in *Surah Fatir*, verse 29, which says:

> *Those who rehearse the Book of Allah, establish regular prayer, and pend (in Charity) out of what We have provided for them, secretly and openly, hope for commerce that will never fail.* (Q35: 29)

The above verse asserts that those who constantly adhere to the teachings of the Quran, never neglect prayer and give to charity are those who will succeed in their business. This verse also expresses that business in terms of charity from the Believers does not come from uncertain sources, but from what Allah (s.w.t.) has bestowed upon them. Hence, a Muslim involved in business should recognize two points: first, that he does not have absolute ownership of the property he possesses, and secondly, that he cannot use all of his property as would a trader who separates part of his property to reinvest in his business as added capital. This is due to the fact that he has the obligation to allocate part of the property to paying *zakat* and offering charity. The business undertaken by the Believers will neither fail nor fluctuate as Allah (s.w.t.) has assured them the return and even added something to the return out of his own bounty (Ali, 1989). Business carried out with honesty and trustworthiness will lead to the earning of profits in this world as well as in the Hereafter. This is in accordance with a *Hadith* narrated by Tirmizie (d. 279H/893), who reported the Prophet (p.b.u.h.) as having said:

> The truthful, honest merchant is with the Prophet, truthful and martyrs. (Narrated by Tirmizie)

Besides the concept of honesty, Islam also emphasizes trustworthiness. This concept is a message conveyed by Allah (s.w.t.) in *Surah an-Nisaa*, verse 58:

> Allah doth command you to render back your trusts to those to whom they are due; and when ye judge between man and man, that ye judge with justice: verily how excellent is the teaching which He giveth you! For Allah is He Who heareth and seeth all things. (Q4: 58)

Apart from the above verse, verse 27 of *Surah al-Anfaal* also touches on trustworthiness. In this verse, Allah (s.w.t.) says:

> O ye that believe! Betray not the trust of Allah and the Messenger, nor misappropriate knowingly things entrusted to you. (Q8: 27)

In the process of conducting business, Islamic banks should by right pay careful attention to the resources involved and the way the banks attain their income. This is of paramount importance because

Islam has always emphasized lawful earnings of livelihood. *Surah an-Nisaa*, verses 29 to 30 of the Quran, state:

> *O ye who believe! eat not up your property among yourself in vanities: but let there be amongst you traffic and trade by mutual goodwill: Nor kill (or destroy) yourself: for verily Allah hath been to you most merciful! If any do that in rancour and injustice – soon shall We cast them into fire: and easy it is for Allah.*   (Q4: 29–30)

Based on the requirements of the religion, Islamic banks are required to have control over their spending. The amount spent should be according to what is required and necessary. This means that expenditure should not exceed benefits to be acquired. Wastage, which occurs when expenditure does not match potential returns, is forbidden in Islam. Islamic banks are also obligated to contribute to the benefits of the Muslim *ummah* but contributions need not necessarily be in the form of cash. The command to avoid wastage and to spend in beneficial ways is found in *Surah al-Baqarah*, verse 219:

> *They ask thee concerning wine and gambling. Say: "In them is great sin, and some profit, for men; but the sin is greater than the profit." They ask thee how much they are to spend; say: "What is beyond your needs." Thus doth Allah makes clear to you His signs: in order ye may consider.*   (Q2: 219)

Surah an-Nisaa, verse 36 also outlines the right conduct for Muslims and which is applicable for Islamic banks in conducting their business and seeking potential clients. It says:

> *Serve Allah, and join not any partners with Him; and do good to parents, kinsfolk, orphans, those in need, neighbours who are near, neighbours who are strangers, the companion by your side, the wayfarer (ye meet), and what your right hands possess; for Allah loveth not the arrogant, the vain glorious.*   (Q4: 36)

The above verse points out that the Islamic bank must be sensitive to those in need of help and should aspire to help them. A similar command is found in *Surah al-Baqarah*, verse 215:

> *They ask thee what they should spend (in charity). Say: Whatever ye spend that is good, for parents and kindred and orphans and those in want and for wayfarers. And whatever you do that is good – Allah knoweth it well.* (Q2: 215)

Surah an-Nisaa, verse 36 and *Surah al-Baqarah*, verse 215 accord a big responsibility to Islamic banks to help those in need. The assistance may be required by two parties, that is, the party that uses the bank as a place to deposit their money, and the other being the individual or trader who acquires financial assistance from the bank in the form of financing facility. It is therefore the responsibility of the bank to render help to both groups. A command related to this is found in *Surah al-Maidah*, verse 1:

> *O ye who believe! Fulfil (all) obligations...* (Q5: 1)

The term *"uqud"* or "obligation" in this verse carries a wide meaning. It can include obligations which are explicit or implicit. An explicit obligation refers to the declaration given by an Islamic bank to certain parties, whether government or public. This obligation may be in the form of the establishment of goals and functions set forth in the article and memorandum of association of its establishment. An implicit obligation, on the other hand, refers to all the responsibilities that the bank must fulfil as an institution using the name of Islam and managed and handled by Muslims, encompassing man's responsibility to Allah (s.w.t.), to the Prophet (p.b.u.h.), towards himself, towards other people, towards society and towards the real world.

Although an Islamic bank has the responsibility to render assistance to those in need, its help can be quite limited. This is because Islamic banks are at the same time responsible for ensuring the security of the money entrusted to them by investors and depositors. Thus, they have to carefully prioritize their contribution and assistance.

There are also verses that command Islamic banks to be just in all their activities. Apart from *Surah an-Nisaa*, verse 29 (Q4: 29), verse 135 in the same *Surah* also touches on this issue. It says:

> *O ye who believe! Stand out firmly for justice, as witnesses to Allah, even as against yourself, or your parents, or your kin, and whether it be (against) rich or poor: for Allah can best protect both. Follow not the lusts (of your hearts), lest ye swerve, and if ye distort or decline to do justice, verily Allah is well-acquainted with all that ye do.*
>
> (Q4: 135)

The command to do justice is also stated in *Surah an-Nahl*, verse 90:

> *Allah commands justice, the doing of good, and liberality to kith and kin, and He forbids all shameful deeds, and injustice and rebellion: He instructs you, that ye may receive admonition.*   (Q16: 90)

When this concept of justice is extended into the banking sphere, in actuality there would be no discrimination issues among customers as Islamic banks must treat their customers equally. Further, when Islamic banks ascertain the profit ratio or impose charges on either their investors or their business partners, justice should be the underlying guide. The Islamic bank is forbidden from taking extra payments from its customers as stated in *Surah al-Maidah*, verse 87:

> *O ye who believe! make not unlawful the good things which Allah hath made lawful for you, but commit no excess: for Allah loveth not those given to excess.*   (Q5: 87)

Mannan (1986) was of the opinion that in an Islamic social system, welfare is maximized only if economic resources are allocated such that it is impossible to make one individual better off without making someone worse off within the context of the Quran and *Hadith*. Hence, anything which is not expressively forbidden in the Quran and *Hadith* but which is consistent with the spirit may be deemed Islamic. Mannan therefore concluded that it is not harmful for Islamic banks to undertake such activities so long as they are not prohibited in the Quran and *Hadith*. In Islam, the absolute ownership of everything belongs to Allah (s.w.t.) as stated in *Surah Ali Imran*, verse 189:

> To Allah belongeth the dominion of the heavens and the earth; and Allah hath power over all things. (Q3: 189)

This absolute ownership does not reflect that Allah (s.w.t.) has created everything for Himself. On the contrary, it is stated in *Surah al-Baqarah*, verse 29 that,

> It is He who hath created for you all things that are on earth; then He turned to the heaven and made them into seven firmaments. And of all things He hath perfect knowledge. (Q2: 29)

Mannan (1986) stressed that everything which Allah (s.w.t.) has created belongs collectively to the whole of human society. Apart from this, Islam acknowledges and recognizes the legal ownership by the individual, that is, the right of possession, enjoyment and transfer of property. However, all ownership is subject to moral obligations. As a matter of fact, even animals have the right to share. This moral obligation is stated in *Surah az-Dhariyat*, verse 19, which says:

> And in their wealth and possessions (was remembered) the rights of the (needy,) him who asked, and him who (for some reason) was prevented (from asking). (Q51: 19)

Good deeds or kindness in the real sense is not only rendered to the poor and needy, but also to those in need who are unable to present their request due to particular reasons. Those who are truly charitable will help this latter group. There are several reasons why people in need of assistance do not request for it (Ali, 1989):

(i) They are ashamed to ask for fear of losing their self-esteem.

(ii) They are influenced by idealistic patterns of thought, so much so that requesting for help does not cross their minds.

(iii) They have no knowledge that they actually need help, particularly when to them it is spiritual wealth that matters.

(iv) They are not aware that there are others who possess something which could fulfil their needs.

(v) They are ignorant and weak. Here, welfare is in terms of assistance accorded by the able to the less able.

As for Islamic banks, while making profit is acceptable, the accumulation of profit without utilization for the betterment of the community is forbidden. Based on this revelation, Islamic banks are expected to be more sensitive towards the needs of the Muslim society, promote more social welfare programmes and activities, and make more contributions to the poor and needy. Islam forbids the accumulation of wealth or the unrestricted possession by individuals exclusively for their self-interest. In fact, Islam commands that property or wealth acquired by lawful means not be hoarded in selfish interest because it could hinder economic growth and result in social imbalances.

In *Surah Ali Imran*, verse 180, Allah (s.w.t.) says:

> And not let those who covetously withhold of the gifts which Allah hath given them of His Grace, think that it is good for them: na, it will be worse for them; soon shall the things which they covetously withheld be tied to their necks like a twisted collar, on the Day of Judgement. To Allah belongs the heritage of the heavens and the earth; and Allah is well-acquainted with all that ye do. (Q3: 180)

It is repeated in verses 1 to 4 of *Surah al-Humazah*:

> *Woe to every (kind of) scandal-monger and backbiter, who pileth up*
> *wealth and layeth it by, thinking that his wealth would make him last*
> *forever! By no means, he will be sure to be thrown into that which*
> *breaks to pieces.*   (Q104: 1–4)

The above revelations serve as a reminder to those who manage Islamic banks to be more cautious in managing assets. The banks are prohibited from accumulating assets without appropriate grounds. Wealth of Islamic banks should be spent on the needy and for the betterment of the society. The failure to do so may result in the destruction of the wealth accumulated by the banks. The destruction may be in the form of failure to smoothly manage the banks, untrustworthy workers, clients not clearing their debts, investments faced with losses, and so on. These are the factors which can lead to great losses to a bank, and may ultimately force it to cease operations.

OPERATIONAL PRINCIPLES OF ISLAMIC BANKS

As with conventional financial institutions, the primary function of the Islamic bank is to channel savings to those who have the need and capability to use it for beneficial causes. Due to the fact that Islam forbids the giving and receiving of *riba*, the Islamic bank must provide its potential customers with banking services which are permissible in Islam. The first step that should be taken before offering any service is to refer to the authentic and fundamental sources in Islamic law, namely the Quran and *Hadith*. All forms of principles and prohibitions related to business must be studied closely. In the Quran, there are many verses related to trustworthiness, justice, prohibition against bribery, giving truthful evidence, ensuring accurate weights and measures and other such matters. In addition, there are verses which say that contracts must be in written form and executed in the presence of witnesses, and warranties must be provided and every responsibility fulfilled.

There are also guidelines provided by the *Hadith*, particularly on matters related to sale and purchase. Some of the relevant *Hadith* are those regarding *salam* (sale and purchase whereby payment is made earlier and the item is delivered later), hire, *al-hawala* (the transfer of debts from one person to another), loans, repayment of loans, freezing of assets, bankruptcy, partnerships, lease, witnesses and terms of business. However, although there is a whole range of verses in the Quran as well as many *Hadith* related to the basics of business, the principles outlined sometimes do not seem to have direct relevance to the world of modern banking. Hence, it is up to scholars and jurists (experts in Islamic legislation) to take up the responsibility to establish principles in business which do not violate rules of *Syariah* and at the same time are applicable and relevant to the banking system.

Various terminologies are used by Islamic banks worldwide to describe *Syariah* principles for particular services offered by the banks concerned. Some banks use Arabic terminologies, some use a mixture of Arabic and English, while others use the local language of the country where the Islamic bank operates. A discussion on the *Syariah* principles used by Islamic banks in particular countries is presented in Chapter 6. Whatever the terminologies used, *Syariah* principles in Islamic banking system can be classed into five categories. The first category is profit-loss sharing principles; the second is sale and purchase principles; the third is principles on which fees or charges are based. The fourth category comprises free services principles and the fifth category is ancillary principles.

Some of the principles generally used by most Islamic banks are *mudharabah, musyarakah, murabahah, ijarah, ijara wa-iqtina, bai muazzal, istisna, qard hassan, wadiah* and *rahn*. Besides these, there are other principles which are used by Islamic banks in certain countries only. For instance, Malaysia has additional principles such as *bai al-dayn, al-ijarah, thumma al-bai, al-wakalah, al-hiwalah, al-ujr* and *al-wadiah yad dhamanah*. Meanwhile, Iran has additional principles such as *jo'alah, muza'arah* and *masaqat*. The use of this range of *Syariah* principles can sometimes cause doubt and confusion, and raises the question of whether the principles used are in fact adopted by *Syariah* or whether they are merely *hila* (plural: *hiyal*). *Hiyal* are instruments created to achieve certain objectives which are basically in conflict with *Syariah*. Not all Islamic jurists take the same stand on the question of recognizing the concept of *hiyal* in creating *Syariah* principles. The Hanafi School of Law supports the use of this concept; most of the writings in support of this concept are by the Hanafi jurists. In the case of the scholars of Shafiis, support is given by later jurists, and their stand is actually against that of the Shafiis.

Two other schools of law have objected to the use of the *hiyal* concept. This objection was more significant when the Malikis established the *saddadah-dhara'i* principle which is essentially a principle that impedes any usage of methods permitted by legislation to achieve objectives which were initially *haram* (unlawful). There has also been massive outcry from the Hanbali jurists who strongly oppose and condemn the use of the concept.

The *Musyarakah* Principle

Musyarakah or *syarika* means partnership in English. *Syariah* divides *syarika* into two categories, that is, *syarikat mulk* and *syarikat 'aqd*. Another form of partnership is termed *mudharabah*, but this principle is normally discussed separately in most Islamic law books. In general, *syarikat mulk* only involves joint ownership of certain properties and it does not involve any joint venture to develop or amalgamate the properties concerned. *Syarikat 'aqd*, on the other hand, emphasizes the concept of joint exploitation of capital and the joint participation in profits and losses (Saleh, 1986).

There are three methods of establishing *syarikat 'aqd*. If money in the form of cash is the main criterion used to establish the partnership, then the partnership is called *syarikat mal* or financial partnership. If the partnership depends on the experience or expertise of partners, the partnership is termed work force partnership or *syarikat a'mal*. If, instead, the partnership is established by virtue of the credit or investment made in the company concerned, then the partnership is termed investment partnership or *syarikat wujuh*. Partnership may be established either as unlimited partnership, equal partnership (termed *mufawada* among the Hanafis), or as limited investment partnership or *syarikat 'inan*.

In the context of Islamic banking, the *musyarakah* principle which is of relevance is *inan syarikat mal* or limited financial investment partnership. This principle is also better known as financing participation, because money in the form of cash is the main criterion that must be met for this partnership to exist. In simple terms, *musyarakah* means a joint-venture agreement between two parties to engage in a specific business activity or specific project with the aim of making profit. The termination of the agreement may be based on time or after fulfilment of certain conditions. Under this principle, both parties will provide the capital and the investor or lender may also participate in the management. Allocation of profit or loss is determined in advance and is not necessarily based on the total capital contributed by the partners involved.

The *Mudharabah* Principle

Mudharabah is the terminology most frequently used by Islamic banks. This principle is also known as *qirad* or *muqaradah*. Scholars have produced various translations for this word. Among the translations are trust finance, profit sharing among trustees, equity sharing and profit sharing. Basically, under this concept, those with capital or money (investor) would assign their money to another party (entrepreneur) to carry out a venture or business. The investor would not be involved in the business and at the end of a stipulated period, the entrepreneur would return to the investor the principal and the proportion of profits made. This principle of *mudharabah* had actually been in use by the Arabs before the revelation of Islam and it continues to be used today (Saleh, 1986). A renowned Islamic jurist, Iman Saraksi, in his book *al-Mabsut*, offered the definition of *mudharabah* and explained how the term was acquired. According to him:

> *The word mudharabah was taken from the word darb which means "(toil) on the face of the earth". The word was termed such because the mudarib (the user of other people's capital) has the right to a share in the profit by virtue of his hard work. Apart from receiving profit, he also has the right to use the capital and work towards fulfilling his own objective. The people of Madinah called this kind of contract muqaradah. This word is taken from the word qard meaning "to submit". In this case, the owner of the capital submits the right on his capital to the amil (the user of the capital).*   (Uzair, 1980, p. 45)

Ibn Rushad, in his book *Bidayat al-Mujtahid*, wrote:

> *There are no differences in opinion among the Muslims regarding the validity of the qirad principle. This principle had been practised before the revelation of Islam and Islam permits it. All agree that this principle is where a person hands over capital to another party for the latter to use in business. The user of the capital would acquire, according to certain conditions, a portion of the profit, that is the portion as agreed by both parties, whether a third, a quarter or perhaps even half.*
> (Uzair, 1980, pp. 45–46)

Based on the above explanation, the *mudharabah* principle may be defined as an agreement between at least two parties, that is, *rabb al-mal* or investor and *mudarib* or entrepreneur or agent-manager.

Under the agreement, the investor agrees to finance the venture or to entrust his money to the entrepreneur who is to trade in an agreed manner and then to return to the investor the principal and pre-agreed proportion of the profits. The profit ratios are based on the agreement made at the beginning of the contract, and there is no guarantee to the investor that the investment would make profit. In the event of loss as a result of circumstances beyond the control of the *mudarib*, the investor will bear all the loss. The *mudarib* loses the time and his efforts only.

There is no uniformity in opinion among the *mazaahib* or schools of law on the use of this principle in business transactions. The *mazhab* of Maliki and Shafii are of the view that *mudharabah* is limited to trade transactions and other trade-related activities. *Mudharabah* cannot include manufacturing functions on the part of the *mudarib*, because such action is regarded as a contract for manufacturing and is termed *istisna*.

Istisna from the perspective of *Syariah* is a contract whereby the buyer requests or asks the seller to manufacture or construct a specified item using the seller's own raw materials at a mutually agreed price. This concept is almost similar to the concept of *bai salam*, in that it involves items not yet in existence at the time of the agreement. However, in *bai salam*, payment is made at the time of the agreement, while in *istisna*, payment is made later on the delivery or completion of the item.

The Hanafis do not object to the application of this principle to manufacturing activities. The Hanbali *mazhab*, on the other hand, allows both the investor and entrepreneur to have two separate agreements, namely an agreement for manufacturing, using the *istisna* principle, and another agreement which uses the *mudharabah* principle, as long as these two agreements do not impose condition upon each other (Saleh, 1986).

The *mudharabah* principle may be used in the Islamic banking system for two different situations, namely between the bank and the supplier of funds, and between the bank and the user of funds.

In the first situation, the bank acts as *mudarib* and the depositor as *rabb al-mal*. In the other instance, the bank acts as *rabb al-mal* and the entrepreneur as *mudarib*. This principle is regarded as a noble principle in the Islamic banking system because it unites two fundamental elements, finance and human labour, in the context which is permitted by *Syariah*. Even though the investor who provides the capital does not in fact contribute any effort to obtain returns from his investment, he at the same time is prepared to bear the risk of losses. If the venture makes profit, then the investor would get back his capital and his share of the profit. However, in the event that the venture suffers a loss, not only would the investor fail to get any returns, but there is also a big possibility that he would lose his initial capital.

The *Murabahah* Principle

Basically, *murabahah* refers to the sale of goods at a price covering the purchase price plus a profit margin agreed upon by both parties concerned. This concept transforms the traditional lending activity into a sale and purchase agreement under which the lender buys goods whether in the form of raw materials, machines or other equipment as required by the borrower for resale to the borrower at a higher price agreed upon by both parties. This concept is also known as the mark-up price concept. If this concept is adopted, Islamic banks would no longer use the profit-loss sharing concept but instead would act as an ordinary business entity involved in the sale and purchase transactions of traded goods.

All the schools of law accept the *mudharabah* principle as an instrument which is permitted to be used in business transactions. However, there are differences in the method of implementation. The first difference is in terms of the amount of mark-up allowed, or the amount of profit the bank is allowed to make when the goods are resold to the customers. The second is in terms of the rights or choices that can be made by the buyers when they find the price to be too high or unreasonable. For purposes of determining the price of the goods sold under the *mudharabah* principle, the Hanbalis are of the view that all the expenditure incurred related to the goods may be totalled to arrive at the selling price. However, the buyers need to be informed of this total amount and the sources of the extra expenditure incurred. Although the same concept is held by the Shafiis an additional requirement is included whereby the payment to a third party by the seller cannot be included in the *murabahah* price unless agreed upon by the buyer. The Hanafis are more flexible in that they allow for the inclusion of all expenditure involved in the business which is related to the *murabahah* goods.

The Malikis, meanwhile, divide expenditure into three categories. The first category is expenditure which can be added to the capital (the selling price of the goods) and this becomes the basis for calculating profit. The second category is expenditure that can be added to the capital but cannot be made the basis for calculating profit. The third category is expenditure that cannot be added to calculate profit.

According to the Shafiis, when a buyer under the principle of *murabahah* finds that the selling price is too high or has been raised by the seller without acceptable grounds and the goods are still with him, then he has the right to return the goods and get a refund. Another choice that the buyer has is to keep the goods and submit a claim on the amount raised. Similarly with the Malikis, the buyer has a choice to buy the goods at a reasonable price or return it. The Hanafis opine that the buyer has to decide whether to go ahead with the purchase at the price given or to return the goods and get a refund. However, if the goods are no longer in the buyer's possession, then the buyer has no other option but to accept the purchase (Saleh, 1986).

The *Ijarah* Principle

Ijarah means a contract to lease or rent or hire. The actual meaning of *ijarah* is therefore a contract or sale involving the use of property owned by a different party. Under *Syariah* perspective, a number of rules apply here. The first rule is *khiyar al-ru'ya*, which is the right to revoke the contract at the time the goods are seen by the buyer. The second is *khiyar al-'ayb*, which is the right to revoke the contract due to the goods being of an inferior quality. The third is *khiyar al-shart*, the right of revocation. The fourth is *fasakh*, which is revocation or nullification, and the last is *ikala*, which is compensation or replacement.

The Malikis consider *ijarah* to be similar to a sale contract where price is exchanged with *munafa'a* or use of a good. The contract must determine whether the *munafa'a* is based on time (period the goods are used) or based on goods. According to the Malikis, the *ijarah* contract may be invalid in two situations. First, it is not valid if the goods rented or leased are used for purposes forbidden by *Syariah* such as using a property as a place for immoral activities or gambling, or to produce liquor and other forbidden goods. Secondly, the contract is considered invalid if it is mandatory in nature such as hiring a mother to breastfeed her own child.

The Hanafis define *ijarah* as a contract for tangible goods or *'ayn*, for purposes that are permitted by *Syariah* and for a fixed period. Meanwhile, the Shafiis regard *ijarah* as a contract on leased or rented goods which can be determined from the onset. The goods must be permissible by *Syariah*, can be transferred and provide fixed return or fixed rent payment. The Hanafis, on the other hand, regard *ijarah* as a contract whereby the owner of the goods grants the lessee the right to use them in return for a payment. The goods must possess *'ayn* and their use is permissible in Islam.

All *mazaahib* or schools of law agree *ijarah* is a binding contract or *lazim*. There are, however, conflicting views regarding the revocation of an *ijarah* contract. The Malikis and Shafiis are of the view that *ijarah* can only be revoked if there are major defects on rented or leased goods. In addition, if the rented or leased goods no longer serve their purpose, then the contract shall be revoked. The Hanafis are of the view that *ijarah* may be revoked if there are acceptable reasons to do so, while the Hanbalis opine that *ijarah* may be revoked if the rented goods are destroyed or have major defects. *Ijarah* may be seen as based either on the period of time or on the task intended to be implemented. If the *ijarah* is based on time, then the time must be stated clearly and the time frame is reasonable. There are several conditions which should be complied with if the rental involves agricultural land. The conditions of rental which may cause losses to the tenant are forbidden; for instance, the tenant being required to dig canals to drain water away when the crops are still in need of water. In the event that the crops are not yet harvested even though the rental period has expired, the contract will be valid until the crops are harvested, and the tenant will have to pay the rental accordingly.

There are also *Syariah* principles on rent which involve the agricultural sector. These are the principles of *mozaraah* and *masaqat*. Under these principles, payment of rent is based on the ratio of the crop production. Both these principles are used in the Iranian Islamic banking system. *Mozaraah* is the contract between the landowner or *mozare*, who would grant his land for a certain period to another party, the entrepreneur or *amel*, for agricultural purposes. In return, both parties would share the yield based on the ratio agreed. *Masaqat*, on the other hand, is a contract between the owner of the crops and the *amel*, for the purpose of reaping the harvest. The yields can be in the form of fruits, leaves or flowers, and will be jointly shared between both parties (Hedayati, 1993).

Another concept is the *ijarah wa-iqtina* concept. This concept involves the renting of a property, whether moveable or permanent, with the choice to own it. In the event that the tenant wishes to own the property, the rental payments prior to it would be regarded as part of the purchasing price. In Malaysia, the *ijarah wa-iqtina* concept is similar to the *al-ijarah thumma al-bai* concept in which rental is followed by sale and purchase. This concept involves two separate contracts, a rent/lease contract and a sale/purchase contract. In the first contract, the customer agrees to rent within the agreed time period. At the end of the rental period, the customer then agrees to purchase the property from its owner at a mutually agreed price (Bank Negara Malaysia, 1994). There is another *ijarah* concept practised in Malaysia, namely the *al-ijarah al-muntahiah bit-tamlik* concept. This concept refers to leasing ending with ownership to the lessee.

The *Qard Hassan* Principle

In Malaysia this principle is termed *al-qardhul hasan*, in Iran as *qard al-hasanah* and in Pakistan as *qarz-e-hasna*. It is a benevolent loan that obliges a borrower to repay the lender the principal sum borrowed. The borrower, however, has the discretion to reward the lender by paying any sum over and above the principal amount borrowed. This principle is the only form of loan permitted by *Syariah*, and is meant for social and economic justice. Allah (s.w.t.) says in *Surah al Hadid*, verse 11, that:

> *Who is he that will loan to Allah a beautiful Loan? For (Allah) will increase it manifold to his credit, and he will have (besides) a liberal Reward.*   (Q57: 11)

As suggested by Saleh (1986), Islamic banks are recommended to offer such loans in the following situations:

(i) This facility may be provided if the banks' loans are mostly based on *musyarakah*. If all financing given is based on *musyarakah*, there is a high possibility that the banks would receive a greater percentage of profit compared to the customers. Loans in the form of *qard hassan* can be used to finance working capital.

(ii) Facilities under this principle may be offered to customers with cash flow problems. This type of facility can be offered to customers whom the banks have investment interest or where the customer is trustworthy and has high creditworthiness.

(iii) This facility may be provided to customers that have large deposits with the banks. Faced with financial difficulties, these customers would normally choose to either withdraw their savings or request for financial assistance from the banks. Hence, in order to avoid possible problems and to safeguard the image of the banks, the *qard hassan* facility may be offered to them.

The *qard hassan* principle has indeed been used widely by Islamic banks in fulfilling their social responsibility. For instance, Jordan Islamic Bank uses this principle to help clients who are faced with financial difficulties. This type of financing is also used to promote and aid micro enterprises.

The *Wadiah* Principle

Wadiah or "trusteeship" refers to an agreement between the owner of assets and another party, whereby the owner gives consent to the custodian to make use of the assets as long as these assets remain in the custodian's hands. Under this principle, the owner would appoint another person as the keeper or custodian of his property which implies a trusting bond between the owner and the custodian. The appointment of the custodian must be done by the property owner or members of his family. Should the custodian fail to return the property or if he denies that he has been entrusted with the safekeeping of it, he would be considered as to have taken the property illegally and would be held responsible for his action. The same applies if the custodian mixes his own property with the property entrusted to him.

In Islamic banking system, *wadiah* is an agreement whereby a customer deposits his money or other items with the bank for safekeeping and the bank must seek permission from the customer to use the deposit at the bank's own risk as long as the funds remain with the bank. The customer may withdraw in part or in whole the deposit at any time he desires and the bank guarantees to honour such requests. In Malaysia, this principle has been extended and is termed *al-wadiah yad dhamanah*, which means safekeeping with guarantee. This concept refers to deposit made by an owner for safekeeping by someone else. *Wadiah* involves the safekeeping of money, among other items where the custodian acts as a guarantor and thus, guarantees to pay or return the full amount of the deposit or part of it when requested. The depositor will not receive any profit, but the Islamic bank may provide gifts or *hibah* to the depositor as a token of appreciation and gratitude for his deposit.

The *Rahn* Principle

Rahn means pledge or pawn. *Rahn* is a contract of security. Under this contract, the creditor secures a loan through a pledge of personal property. The contract becomes binding when possession of the pledge has taken place. Ownership of the security remains with the original owner (the creditor) and is not transferred to the pledgee or pawnee. The transfer of ownership occurs only under certain conditions as stipulated in the contract. The pawnee or pledge is held responsible for the pledged asset according to whichever is lower between the value of the property and the credit provided. But in the event that the asset is lost due to his fault, then he is held responsible for its actual value and he has the responsibility to return the whole amount when the debtor has fully paid his debts. If the debtor fails to pay the debt when it reaches maturity, then the pawnee or creditor is entitled to demand the sale of the pledged asset in order to recover the debt from the sale proceeds. Where the proceeds are insufficient to cover the debt, the debtor is still obligated to repay the remaining amount. On the other hand, any surplus proceeds must be returned to the debtor or owner of the asset.

Other Principles

Apart from the principles already mentioned, there are other principles being used by Islamic banks worldwide. It needs to be reminded here that the use of these principles is not all-encompassing; some principles are used by Islamic banks in only a few countries, while others are used only by particular countries. In addition, a number of principles have only just recently received approval from the Syariah Supervisory Council of certain countries. The following are some of the principles found in the Islamic banking system:

Bai bithaman ajil

The *bai bithaman ajil* principle or formerly known as *al-bai bithaman ajil*, refers to sale with deferred payment. It is used widely in Malaysia and is similar to the *murabahah* principle, except that under the *murabahah* principle, payment is made immediately while in this case payment is deferred. This principle is sometimes termed *bai muajjal*.

Bai al-dayn

Bai al-dayn means debt trading and it refers to the financing of debts. Under this principle, financing is made based on sale and purchase of trade documents. Financial resources are provided for the purpose of production, trade and services. Transactions can only be done on documents which authentically show that trade does exist.

Bai al-inah

This principle involves a sale contract whereby the seller sells his assets to a buyer and at the same time agrees to repurchase the assets from the buyer. The seller sells his assets on credit to the buyer and later repurchases it at a cash price. The repurchase price is normally lower than the agreed selling price. Some *mazhab* do not approve the use of this principle in the Islamic banking system.

Bai istijar

This is a sale and purchase contract whereby an agreement is made between two parties, the seller and buyer. Under the contract, the buyer agrees to buy on a continuous basis, and there will not be any more bargaining between the buyer and seller after the initial agreement is finalized.

Bai salam

This principle involves a sale and purchase contract made between two parties, the seller and buyer. Under the contract, the buyer agrees to make an advance payment but the asset is delivered at a later date.

Hiwalah

The *hiwalah* refers to a transfer of funds or debt from the depositor's or debtor's account to the receiver's or creditor's account. The bank charges commissions for the services rendered.

Istisna

This is a sale and purchase principle whereby an agreement is made between two parties, the seller and buyer. Under the contract, the buyer agrees to buy non-existent goods which are to be manufactured or constructed by specification or order.

The buyer can pay either at the beginning of the contract or when the goods ordered are ready to be delivered. Hence, this principle is also sometimes known as a contract to manufacture or produce. This is in contrast to the *salam* principle whereby the goods intended to be bought need not necessarily exist nor be produced. Also, under *salam*, the buyer has to provide full payment at the initial stage of the agreement. Under an *istisna* contract, the goods intended to be bought must be produced by the manufacturer. The *istisna* contract cannot be terminated when the goods are in the process of production.

Jo'alah

Jo'alah refers to service charge. This principle is practised in Iran. A person called *ja'el* or employer pledges to pay a specified amount of money to another party, the *jo'al*, who will offer certain services according to set terms. The party who will provide the services is called the *amel* or contractor.

Kafalah

Kafalah means guarantee. According to this principle, guarantee is provided by a person to the owner of a property, who has placed or deposited his property with a third party. In the event that a claim is made by the property owner on the property submitted to the third party, and the third party fails to fulfil the claim, the guarantor will have to take over the responsibility of fulfilling the claim.

Musawamah

This principle involves sale and purchase transactions and is similar to *mudharabah*, except that no reference is made to the buyer as to the cost price and there is no need for the seller to disclose the cost price.

Sarf

Sarf is a contract involving the buying and selling of foreign currencies, that is, the exchange of one currency for another. However, some *mazhab* do not allow money exchange if it involves forward contract transactions, that is, transactions at a specified future date at a price (exchange rate) that is fixed on the purchase date.

Ujr

This principle refers to fees and commissions charged for services rendered.

Urbun

This is taken from the concept of *bai al-urbun* which means to pay or receive in advance. Under this principle, the buyer buys a commodity and pays a deposit for it. In the Islamic banking system, the deposit may be used by the bank to carry out certain responsibilities on behalf of its customers. It is also used in the capital market, involving the options to buy or sell a security. Those given the right to the options are required to pay for that right, and that payment is based on the principle of *urbun*.

Wakalah

Wakalah means representative. The principle refers to the situation where a person appoints another person to represent him in a transaction.

Tawarruq

This is a reverse *murabahah* line of credit. This principle involves two levels of transaction. First, a buyer buys on credit from the original seller. Then the buyer resells the commodity for cash to a third person.

PRIORITIES IN THE USE OF *SYARIAH* PRINCIPLES

It is the consensus among Muslim scholars that the various principles adopted by Islamic banks can be classed into two categories, namely principles which are advocated, or strongly Islamic, and principles which are not advocated, or weakly Islamic (Mirakhor, 1987). Strongly Islamic principles are those that conform to Islamic objectives both in form and substance. The weakly Islamic principles refer to practices which conform to Islamic norms in form but not in substance. The basis for judgement as to the strength or weakness of a given principle is the extent to which that mode contributes towards achievement of the objectives of Islamic economics. Hence, only those principles which permit risk-return sharing between providers and users of funds can be considered strongly Islamic. Muslim scholars consider only two principles, that is, *musyarakah* and *mudharabah,* as strongly Islamic. However, most scholars recommend that the remaining principles be applied in cases where risk-return sharing cannot be implemented.

Nevertheless, most Islamic banks apply the recommended *Syariah* principles for deposit facilities only, particularly the investment account facilities. With regard to uses of funds, the principle of profit-sharing is not applied much at all. For example, the percentages of *musyarakah* and *mudharabah* for Bank Islam Malaysia at the end of June 2007 and end of June 2006 were 0.6% and 0.7% of the total financing, respectively. The percentage of fund devoted to this mode of financing for Qatar Islamic Bank was 4.2% for the period ending 2006, and the percentage increased significantly to 10.7% at the end of 2007. Dubai Islamic Bank has the highest percentage of financing in this category whereby the total financing was 19% and 16.7% of the total financing for the periods ending 2007 and 2006, respectively.

While Muslim scholars are constantly suggesting that profit-sharing principles are the preferable principles, Islamic banks seem to prefer the non-advocated principles. According to them, this may be because of their simplicity, the risk aversion of Islamic banks and the fact that the rate of returns can be determined at the beginning of the financing period. The *murabahah* and *ijarah* principles, for example, are implemented based on percentages in determining the mark-up price of goods. Some principles practised by Islamic banks are similar to those of their conventional counterparts, particularly the emphasis on the creditworthiness of customers and the upholding of the creditor-debtor relationship. There is a danger that some of these principles could be misused as means for opening a backdoor for *riba* (Ahmed et al., 1983).

The views expressed by the Muslim scholars are, however, not shared by financial authorities in Islamic countries. The latter believe that solely applying the concept of profit-loss sharing in the Islamic banking system implies that the banking system is headed for an unclear course. Furthermore, the Islamic banking system has to be implemented in a vigilant manner so as to ensure the success of the endeavour. Bank Markazi Jomhouri Islami Iran, the Central Bank of Iran, in its *1984 Annual Report* stressed:

> *Money in the bank is owned by depositors who are of various shapes and sizes; there are rich people there as well as the ordinary person with a deposit of as little as IRR 1,000 in his account. The bank, which acts as the trustee, will then channel this money to debtors. Hence, the system must be capable of protecting the depositors and providing them with sufficient returns. If the depositors are not protected, then the system is considered unjust because of the absence of the concept of 'adl or justice, whereas concept is important in any Islamic system (Mirakhor, 1987, p. 186).*

Based on the above statement, it is clear that even though the majority of Muslim scholars recommend the wide use of the profit-sharing principles, Islamic banks do otherwise. They believe that Islamic banks, acting as trustees, should be concerned about the security and soundness of the banks which in turn are dependent on the degree of risk taken. This is why the profit-loss principle is less used compared to other principles.

SOURCES AND USES OF FUNDS

Besides their own capital, Islamic banks are dependent on depositors' money, which is a major source of funds. Conventional banks offer deposit facilities on the assumption that a person has money to hold or keep. According to the Keynesian approach, people hold money for three reasons, namely transactions, precautionary and speculative purposes. Hence, the first deposit facility provided is the current account. This type of deposit facility is for those who need money for transaction purposes. This facility offers the convenience of withdrawing funds by cheques. Hence, depositors do not place importance on returns or interest. When offering the current account facility, the bank would normally impose a service charge and other mandatory charges like stamp duty, tax and others where applicable. However, due to increasingly strong competition, some banks have started to provide returns on current accounts. There are, however, certain conditions to be fulfilled before the account holders are entitled to receive interest.

Since this account can be devoid of the interest element, Islamic banks are permitted by *Syariah* to offer similar facilities. The *qard hassan* or *wadiah* principles are among the *Syariah* principles which are used by Islamic banks in providing this facility. The depositor is allowed to withdraw his money any time he wishes to do so. This is intended to instil confidence in the depositor that Islamic banks guarantee the deposits made.

The second deposit facility is termed savings account. In conventional banks, savings accounts cater to the needs of those who wish to save money but at the same time want to earn an income. Depositors of savings accounts hold money for precautionary motives. At the same time, they are also induced by their investment motives. These depositors are usually from the low-income group and those with salaries. The same facility is provided by Islamic banks using the principles of *wadiah*, *mudharabah* and *qard hassan*. However, if the *mudharabah* principle is used, customers may not be allowed to withdraw their money any time they desire since the bank uses the deposited money for investment purposes and depositors will be rewarded based on the profit made.

The third type of deposit is fixed deposit. Such facility is offered by banks to cater for the investment motives of customers. These depositors normally have idle funds and are looking for better returns on their money. In Islamic banking, this facility is known as investment account or sometimes also called profit-loss sharing account and is governed by the principle of *mudharabah*. Within this context, the Islamic bank acts as the *mudarib* and the depositor as the *rabb al-mal*. Customers are free to choose the period they want to place their funds with the bank. The bank provides neither guarantee nor fixed return on the amount deposited. Under the principle of *mudharabah*, the customer get a share of the profit made by the bank based on a pre-agreed ratio. The agreement on how the profit or loss will be distributed between the bank and the depositor is made at the beginning of the deposit tenure and cannot be amended during the tenure of the deposits, except with the consent of both parties.

Apart from deposit facilities, Islamic banks may also raise funds by way of issuing investment certificates. Unlike normal investment certificates which have interest rate elements, the certificate issued by the Islamic bank carries no fixed return. The principles of *mudharabah* and *qard hassan* are applicable for this kind of facility. In applying the principle of *mudharabah*, the reward for the depositors is based on the bank's annual profit, whereas under the principle of *qard hassan*, the reward is entirely dependent upon the bank's discretion.

In Malaysia, Islamic banks may also obtain funding from the inter-bank money market, where they may trade Islamic financial instruments. Similar to conventional banks, Islamic banks offer financing facilities to individual as well as corporate customers. However, the mechanism used by Islamic banks differs from that of conventional banks. As entities established on religious foundations, Islamic banks are expected to abide by whatever rules and regulations imposed by the Quran and *Hadith*. On account of their religious obligations or persuasion, Islamic banks are not guided by profit-maximizing goals. Instead, the principal goal is for the betterment of the Muslim *ummah* and their overall business philosophy is based on justice and equity. Hence, Islamic banks have the duty to help those in need, whether they are individual or corporate customers. Non-commodity trading is strictly prohibited by *Syariah*. Since *Syariah* considers money as a non-commodity item, granting loans to customers for profit is therefore unlawful (Siddiqi, 1986). Hence, funds accumulated by Islamic banks will mostly be channelled through equity participation and profit-sharing. The principles of *mudharabah, musyarakah* and *murabahah* are commonly applied by Islamic banks in assisting their commercial customers who face inadequate capital. The financial assistance rendered is used either to start a venture or as working capital. The *ijarah* principle, meanwhile, is applied for leasing facilities as well as hire purchase.

Islamic banks also offer a variety of facilities to individual customers, whether to ease their financial burden or to help them purchase assets such as homes or consumer goods. The *qard hassan* principle normally forms the base of the facilities that are rendered to ease the financial burden of customers, while in the purchase of property and goods, the principles used are *mudharabah* as well as *bai muazzal* (in Malaysia this principle is known as *bai bithaman ajil*).

The above discussion proves that Islamic banks are capable of fulfilling the financial needs of customers in terms of both types and forms of financing required. This does not necessarily imply that Islamic banks are content with their existing products and services. The banks are constantly developing new products to suit the needs of the customers and the market. Other banking services provided by Islamic banks such as letters of guarantee, money order, travellers cheques, safe deposits and remittance services are fee-based services. In Malaysia, these facilities are provided based on the principles of *al-wakalah*, *al-hiwalah*, *al-kafalah* and *al-ujr*.

RELATIONSHIP BETWEEN ISLAMIC BANKS AND THEIR CUSTOMERS

The basic banking functions of Islamic banks, namely, deposit savings and channelling of funds, are similar to those of the conventional banks. Services offered are also fundamentally similar to that of their conventional counterparts. As such, the question arises as to whether the bank-customer relationship for both Islamic and conventional banks is similar. For conventional banks, the relationship is that of creditor and debtor. This relationship was decided upon in 1948, in the case of Foley vs. Hill and others. For example, in Foley vs. Hill, it was held that when a customer deposits money into his account, the bank becomes a debtor and the customer a creditor. In this instance, the money now becomes the property of the bank since the bank is considered to have borrowed it from the customer.

In general, the bank has the right to use the money deposited by customers according to its preferred method. However, the bank has the responsibility to return or pay the money deposited upon the request of the customers, along with interest, if any. This relationship may be terminated with the consent of both parties.

However, under normal circumstances, the decision to terminate the relationship may be made by any party in accordance with the conditions stipulated at the initial stage prior to the inception of the relationship. Developments in the world of banking have changed the relationship between the bank and its customers. It is no longer merely that of creditor and debtor but has been extended to include relationships between trustee and beneficiary, lessee and lessor, and others, depending on the services provided by the bank. When conventional banks extend debt facility to their customers, the relationship established is that between creditor and debtor, whereby each party has rights as creditor and debtor, respectively. Very few cases of disputes between Islamic banks and their customers have achieved resolutions in court. In Malaysia, such disputes are brought to the civil court and not the *Syariah* court. Given that the *Syariah* court is considered not fully ready to resolve matters regarding *muamalat*, it is envisaged that the civil court will continue to play its role for quite some time yet.

Relationship with Suppliers of Funds

The relationship between the Islamic bank and its depositors is not always that of creditor and debtor. The status of the relationship is dependent on the principles of *Syariah* used in creating that relationship. The relationship of creditor and debtor exists if the deposit service applies the *qard hassan* principle. If the *wadiah* principle is applied, then the relationship would be that of trustee and beneficiary, and in the case where the *mudharabah* principle is used, it would be that of an investor-entrepreneur relationship. When the *qard hassan* principle is used, it means the depositor lends his money to the Islamic bank without expecting any rewards or returns. Similarly under the *wadiah* principle which is based on trust; the depositor places his money in the bank for safekeeping based on the belief and confidence that the Islamic bank is a safe place. Hence, there is no profit-making motive on the part of the depositors of current and savings accounts of the Islamic bank. The desire to make profit may be present in customers who choose to deposit their money under the *mudharabah* principle. Nevertheless, even if the profit factor does exist in Islamic banking, it should by no means be the main attraction for customers to patronize Islamic banks. Islamic banks are business institutions founded on religion; hence, relationships that exist should also be based on religious grounds.

Just as Islamic bank does not place profit as its principal goal, so too should not the customers. This means that Muslims should not go to an Islamic bank for the higher returns offered compared to a conventional bank, and vice versa. This point relates to the fundamental principles that influence the economic decisions of Muslims. These fundamental principles are the belief in the Day of Judgement and life in the Hereafter, the Islamic concept of richness, and lastly the Islamic concept of success (Kahf, 1980). These three principles are expected to have a significant impact on the decision-making process of Muslims that is related to economic matters. The first principle has an effect on the depositors' behaviour and decision-making process of those who strongly believe in the Day of Judgement and life in the Hereafter. Hence, their choice of action is based not only on the immediate financial return but also on those returns in the Hereafter. As such, their decision to have a banking relationship with Islamic banks is not to make profit but rather to gain the blessings of Allah (s.w.t.).

Since Islamic bank is an Islamic institution that operates in accordance with *Syariah*, the depositors' action would gain Allah's (s.w.t.) blessings. Moreover, the decision to patronize Islamic bank demonstrates their support for the Islamic bank's goal and philosophy towards enhancing the welfare of the Muslim *ummah*. Such action is also in line with *Surah at-Taubah*, verse 20, which says:

Those who believe, and suffer exile and strive with might and main, in Allah's cause, with their goods and their persons, have the highest rank in the sight of Allah: they are the people who will achieve (salvation).

(Q9: 20)

Therefore, having *jihad* (to strive in the cause of Allah (s.w.t.)) as a motive for establishing a relationship with the Islamic bank ensures that customers do not place profit above other aspects. Apart from the above principle, the concept of wealth in the Islamic perspective could also be taken as a basis in establishing the relationship between the bank and the customer, as found in *Surah Ali Imran*, verse 189 (Q3: 189) which states that everything belongs to Allah (s.w.t.). Wealth is a bounty from Allah (s.w.t.) and man is encouraged to strive for wealth, as stated in *Surah al-Jumu'ah*, verse 10:

And when the Prayer is finished, then may ye disperse through the land, and seek of the Bounty of Allah: and celebrate the Praises of Allah often (and without stint): that ye may prosper. (Q62: 10)

Wealth itself is considered an important means by which man can pave the way for the attainment of his ultimate objective. All persons are exhorted to work to earn a living and accumulate wealth. However, in Islam, the methods of earning, possessing and disposing of wealth must be in line with *Syariah*. There are many *Hadith* which urge Muslims to strive on one's own and not from the income generated from other people's effort. The following is a *Hadith* collected by Al-Bukhari and narrated by Aishah (the Prophet's (p.b.u.h.) wife):

The companions of Allah's Apostle used to practise manual labour, so their sweat used to smell, and they were advised to take a bath.

(Khan, 1989, p. 162)

Similarly with the *Hadith* narrated by al-Miqdam who reported the Prophet (p.b.u.h.) as having said:

Nobody has ever eaten a better meal than that which one has earned by working with one's own hands. The Prophet of Allah, David used to eat from the earnings of his manual labour.

(Khan, 1989, pp. 162–163)

In a *Hadith* narrated by Abu Hurairah, the Prophet (p.b.u.h.) said:

No doubt, you had better gather a bundle of wood and carry it on your back (and earn your living thereby) rather than ask somebody who may give you or not. (Khan, 1989, p. 163)

In addition to this, Islam does not define the concept of richness on the basis of riches or property owned. Instead, Islam defines success as the level of obedience to Allah (s.w.t.) and not the accumulation of wealth. Service and obedience may be rendered by the positive use of capabilities and resources given by Allah (s.w.t.). This is mentioned in the following two *Hadith* collected by the Prophet (p.b.u.h.) and narrated by Abu Hurairah:

Verily Allah does not look to your faces and your wealth but He looks to your heart and to your deeds. (Siddiqi, Vol. 4, p. 1362)

Richness does not lie in the abundance of (worldly) goods but richness is the richness of the soul (heart, self). (Siddiqi, Vol. 2, p. 501)

According to Islamic teachings, if a man really wants to serve Allah (s.w.t.), the utilization of the natural resources, property and riches, or status and position made available to him, must not be regarded as his privileged right but instead regarded as a duty and obligation prescribed by Allah (s.w.t.) for him to fulfil to the best of his ability. This is in line with verse 27 of *Surah al-Anfaal* (Q8: 27) which commands Muslims to fulfil the responsibility entrusted to them by Allah (s.w.t.) and the Prophet (p.b.u.h.).

With the above three principles as a guide, Islamic banks' customers are expected not to be influenced by the profit motive when placing their money in Islamic banks. Instead, they should regard the reason for placing their monies with the Islamic banks as getting blessings from Allah (s.w.t.) and this action is considered as the best way of managing the resources entrusted by Allah (s.w.t.). Hence, the best method of accumulating wealth is by striving on one's own and not from the income generated by other people's efforts. Whatever returns or gains acquired should be regarded as a gift from Allah (s.w.t.) and should be responded to by a feeling of deep gratitude (*syukur*) to Allah (s.w.t.). By instilling such philosophy, customers would not compare returns given by Islamic and conventional banks. Nevertheless, we have yet to reach the point where customers do not regard economic returns as a factor when deciding to patronize Islamic banks. Researches have shown that many still choose to do their banking business with Islamic banks due to return and costs factors.

Relationship with Users of Funds

The relationship between the Islamic bank and the users of its funds depends on the principle used in rendering a particular facility, that is, whether the facility is based on profit-sharing, sale and purchase, fees and fixed payments, or services provided free of charge. If the profit-sharing (*mudharabah* or *musyarakah*) principle is used, then the relationship is that of partners or investor-entrepreneur. If the sale and purchase principle is used, then the relationship is of a trader and his customer. For facilities based on the principle of charges and fees, the relationship is that of employer and employee or employer and his representative. In the case of free-of-charge services, the relationship is of a party who possesses something which he wishes to give out and a party who wishes to receive it. As with the relationship between the Islamic bank and supplier of funds, here the relationship must be founded on relevant religious beliefs.

Both the Islamic bank and users of funds must place the fundamentals of the religion as the core in building the relationship.

Surah al-Maidah, verse 1 (Q5: 1) which calls for all Muslims to fulfil their responsibilities should be upheld by both parties. The bank has the responsibility to help those in need, regardless of the status of the person or the size of the customer's business. The customers who receive funds from Islamic banks, meanwhile, are expected to discharge their liability accordingly. It is surely unjust and unacceptable when a Muslim who receives financial assistance from an Islamic bank refuses to settle his financial liability with the bank. Although in principle, Muslims are obligated to settle their debts, in reality, Islamic banks too face bad debt problems. If one examines the annual reports of Islamic banks, one can see that a big part of funds is allocated for bad debts. This goes to prove that Islamic banks do have default customers. The relationship built with the Islamic bank should be founded on a sense of responsibility and honesty. Islamic banks, on their part, are expected to be more supportive towards their customers. Customers who face difficulties in meeting loan repayments should not be treated harshly. This is in line with *Surah al-Baqarah*, verse 280, which says:

> *If the debtor is in difficulty, grant him time till it is easy for him to repay. But if ye remit it by way of charity, that is best for you if ye only knew.* (Q2: 280)

It is also hoped that Islamic banks would be more receptive and pro-active in the process of creating, moulding and developing entrepreneurs. The *mudharabah* principle, for instance, serves as an incentive for creating new entrepreneurs. Muslims who possess business expertise but who are without capital can approach Islamic banks for financing. The *mudharabah* principle not only encourages existing entrepreneurs to explore potential business areas and opportunities but also inspires new entrepreneurs. Entrepreneurs who enjoy this facility will benefit in two ways. First, they need not worry about repayment. The Islamic bank will only receive its share from the ex-post profit from the business. In the case of losses, entrepreneurs go unrewarded for their time and effort while the risk of loss is completely borne by the bank. Secondly, since the Islamic bank acts as a partner, it will provide full moral and financial support in attaining profit. This is in contrast to the conventional bank, where the interest factor is fixed at the beginning of the loan period, and where the bank is not concerned about the progress of customers' businesses. This is because the conventional bank continues to receive payments even if projects fail or face losses.

Another role played by the Islamic bank is in moulding the entrepreneur towards a more religious and ethical life. This is effectively done in two ways. First, as an investor or partner, the Islamic bank is bound by the limitations of *Syariah*. Hence, the available funds can only be invested in productive and permissible investments. Investments that are associated with immoral activities, gambling, liquor, fortune telling, making of idols and activities involving *riba* are considered unlawful. Secondly, Islam has prescribed principles relating to trade and commerce which must be followed. As a trader, the business transactions must be conducted honestly, faithfully and in a beneficial manner. Islamic banks should ensure effective supervision and monitoring of the funds disbursed, as entrepreneurs are bound to face challenges and obstacles. Without effective supervision and monitoring, the entrepreneur may misuse the funds and conduct unlawful business practices which would eventually bring about losses to both the entrepreneur and the bank.

SUMMARY

The initial objective of the establishment of the conventional bank was to provide a place for people to keep their valuables and to offer debt facilities to those faced with financial problems. As an ordinary business entity, profit maximization is the principal objective of the conventional bank. Interest rates are used to determine returns to be rewarded to the depositors and returns the bank should receive from the users of funds. Consequently, the conventional bank would impose a low interest rate on the depositors and a high interest rate on its debtors. The bigger the gap between these two rates, the bigger the profit gained by the bank, and vice versa. Based on this concept, the actual profit is partial towards the bank and not the customers using the service.

In contrast to the conventional bank, Islamic bank is founded on both profit and religious factors. Hence, while performing its banking businesses in accordance with *Syariah*, Islamic bank is also expected to make profits from its operations and channel this profit to fulfil its moral or social obligations. However, Islamic banks differ in the way they discharge their social responsibilities and obligations. Some banks have clear written statements of their social objectives and implement various activities towards achieving them.

As entities based on religious doctrines, Islamic banks must conform to the philosophies and business principles as highlighted in the Quran and *Hadith*. Banking operations must be in consonance with Islamic teachings. Factors such as justice, equality, trust, honesty, non-prejudice, mutual gain, non-wastage and fulfilling of responsibility are matters that must be adhered to by Islamic banks.

Since the giving and receiving of *riba* is forbidden, Islamic banks operate on principles that are permissible in Islam. These principles are grouped into five main categories: profit-loss sharing principles, sale and purchase principles, fees-based or charges-based principles, free services principles and ancillary principles.

Two main principles practised in the category of profit-loss sharing are *mudharabah* and *musyarakah*. Principles involved in the sale and purchase category are *murabahah, bai muajjal, bai bithaman ajil, bai murabahah, musawamah, istisna* and *bai salam*. The principles followed under the fees or charges category comprise the principles of *ijarah, jo'alah, wakalah, kafalah, ujr* and *hiwalah.* The principle of *qard hassan* is observed in the free services category, while *wadiah* and *rahn* are ancillary principles which support Islamic banking activities. The use of the profit-loss sharing principles is greatly advocated, because of its high benefits in enhancing the economy of Muslims as a whole. The free services principles are used for implementing social activities.

The existence of a variety of applicable *Syariah* principles enables Islamic banks to offer total banking products and services. Hence, customers in most Islamic countries have the choice of whether to obtain Islamic banking services or otherwise. The status and type of relationship between the customer and the Islamic bank, however, depends on the *Syariah* principle applied in the service concerned. Since Islamic banks apply *Syariah* principles in conducting their banking business, Muslims are expected to response favourably and support the establishment of Islamic banks.

The belief in the Hereafter, and the Islamic concepts of wealth and success should instil in Muslims the spirit of loyalty towards the Islamic bank. Moreover, with the qualities of responsibility and honesty embedded in both the bank staff and customers, there is every likelihood that the financing operations implemented by Islamic banks would expand the business of their customers. At the same time, they would succeed in shaping Muslim clients to become entrepreneurs who in turn will also practise Islamic principles of entrepreneurship.

REFERENCES AND FURTHER READING

Ahmed, Ziauddin, Iqbal, M. and Khan, M.F. *Money and Banking in Islam*. Pakistan: Institute of Policy Studies, 1983.

Ali, Abdullah Y. *The Holy Quran, Text, Translation and Commentary*. Maryland: Amana Corporation, 1989.

Ali, Muazzam. "A Framework of Islamic Banking." In *Directory of Islamic Financial Institutions*, edited by John R. Presley. London (UK): Croom Helm, 1988.

Al-Zuhaili, Wahbah. *Financial Transactions in Islamic Jurisprudence*. Vol. 1. Translated by Mahmoud A. El-Gamal. Beirut (Lebanon): Dar al-Fikr, 2003.

Bank Islam Malaysia Berhad. *Annual Report* (various issues).

Bank Muamalat Indonesia. *Annual Report* (various issues).

Bank Muamalat Malaysia. *Annual Report* (various issues).

Bank Negara Malaysia. *Money and Banking in Malaysia*. Kuala Lumpur (Malaysia): BNM, 1994.

Departemen Agama Republik Indonesia. *Al-Quran dan Terjemahannya*. Jakarta (Indonesia), 1974.

Dubai Islamic Bank. *Annual Report* (various issues).

Elstone, R.G. "Objective of Profit-making Intermediaries and of Co-operative Institution." In *The Economics and Management of Financial Institutions*, edited by D. Johannes Jutter and Tom Valentine, 11–21. Melbourne (Australia): Longman Cheshire, 1987.

Erol, C. and El-Bdour, R. "Attitudes, Behaviour and Patronage Factors of Bank Customers Towards Islamic Banks." *International Journal of Bank Marketing*, Vol. 7. No. 6 (1989): 31–39.

Faysal Islamic Bank of Bahrain. *Annual Report* (various issues).

Haron, S., Ahmad, N. and Planisek, S. "Bank Patronage Factors of Muslim and Non-Muslim Customers." *International Journal of Bank Marketing*, Vol. 12, No. 1 (1994): 32–40.

Hedayati, S.A.A. "Islamic Banking as Experienced in the Islamic Republic of Iran." Working paper presented at the International Conference on Islamic Banking, Sydney (Australia), 9–10 November 1993.

Islami Bank Bangladesh Limited. *Annual Report* (various issues).

Jordan Islamic Bank for Finance and Investment. *Annual Report* (various issues).

Kahf, Monzer. "A Contribution to the Theory of Consumer Behaviour in Islamic Society." In *Studies in Islamic Economics*, edited by Khurshid Ahmad, 19–36. Leicester (UK): The Islamic Foundation, 1980.

Khan, M. Fahim. "Islamic Banking as Practised Now in the World." In *Money and Banking in Islam*, edited by Ziauddin Ahmed, Munawar Iqbal and M. Fahim Khan, 259–276. Jeddah (Saudi Arabia), International Centre for Research in Islamic Economics, King Abdul Aziz University, 1983.

Khan, Muhammad M. *The Translation of the Meanings of Sahih Al-Bukhari*, Vol. 3. Lahore (Pakistan): Kazi Publications, 1989.

Mannan, Muhammad Abdul. *Islamic Economics: Theory and Practice (Foundations of Islamic Economics)*. London: Hodder and Stoughton, 1986.

Mirakhor, Abbas. "Short-term Asset Concentration and Islamic Banking." In *Theoretical Studies in Islamic Banking and Finance*, edited by Mohsin S. Khan and Abbas Mirakhor, 185–199. Houston (Texas, USA): Institute for Research and Islamic Studies, 1987.

Qatar Islamic Bank. *Annual Report* (various issues).

Sadeq, A.H.M. *Islamic Banking and Economic Development*. Working paper presented at the International Conference on Islamic Banking, Sydney (Australia), 9–10 November 1993.

Saleh, Nabil A. *Unlawful Gain and Legitimate Profit in Islamic Law: Riba, Gharar and Islamic Banking.* London: Cambridge University Press, 1986.

Siddiqi, Hamid, trans. *Sahih Muslim.* Vols 2 and 4. Beirut (Lebanon): Dar al Arabia Publishing, Printing & Distribution, undated.

Siddiqi, Muhammad Iqbal. *Model of an Islamic Bank.* Lahore (Pakistan): Kazi Publications, 1986.

Uzair, Muhammad. "Some Conceptual and Practical Aspects of Interest-Free Banking." In *Studies in Islamic Economics*, edited by Khursid Ahmad, 37–58. Leicester (UK): The Islamic Foundation, 1980.

www.albaraka.com

www.alislami.co.ae

www.bankislam.com.my

www.barakaonline.com

www.bi.go.id

www.isbt.co.th

www.islamibankbd.com

www.muamalatbank.com

www.siblbd.com

CHAPTER 4

THE CONCEPTS OF INTEREST, USURY AND *RIBA*

This chapter discusses in detail the meaning of interest, usury and riba. This is necessary because there are many definitions given for the word "interest". Apart from the views of Muslims, those of the Jews, Christians, Romans and Greeks will be presented for comparison purposes. Differences of opinions among Muslims regarding riba will also be discussed.

INTRODUCTION

Islam prohibits the acceptance and payment of *riba* or charged interest. Therefore, all operations of Islamic banking must be conducted without any element of *riba*. A great majority of Muslim intellectuals are of the opinion that not only is the practice of *riba* immoral, but that it also hinders the growth of society. *Riba* is seen to cause one's wealth to erode, to be the source of immoralities and to create classes in society, thus creating friction. *Riba* may also bring about a situation where the rich become richer and the poor poorer.

Why does Islam prohibit Muslims from accepting and giving *riba*? Islam is not the only religion which prohibits its followers from taking *riba*. Judaism and Christianity, during their early years, never condoned their followers' acceptance of interest. In fact, the Christian Church regarded the acceptance of interest as a serious sin. In conjunction with the trade and commercial revival in the 12th century, the discussion of interest among Christian scholars and theologians was conducted on a more scientific basis. Finally, in 1836 after a series of discussions, the Christian Holy Office in Rome issued a decree that interest was allowed by law and may be taken by everyone.

The practice of accepting and giving interest has existed since 3000 BC, during the Sumerian civilization. During the Sumerian period (3000 BC–1900 BC) there was evidence of a systematic credit system with loans using two standards of value, grain based on quantity and silver based on weight. These loans contained elements of interest; the interest rate was 33.33% and 20% per year for wheat loans and silver loans, respectively. During the Babylonian period (1900 BC–732 BC), King Hammurabi issued a regulation (around 1800 BC) known as the *Code of Hammurabi*. This *Code* recognized the interest rate established during the Sumerian period and adopted it as the legal rate. This rate was used for almost 1,200 years (Homer, 1977).

This practice of taking interest continued through to the Assyrian (732 BC–625 BC), Neo Babylonian (625 BC–539 BC), Persian (539 BC–333 BC), Greek (500 BC–100 BC) and Roman (500 BC–400 BC) periods. Christianity, during its early years, that is, in the 3rd century, never condoned the practice of taking interest by its followers. Although there was strong opposition from the priests and their churches, merchants continued to practise it. There is evidence to show that during the reigns of kings in the European countries, loans issued were also based on interest (Homer, 1977).

DEFINITIONS OF INTEREST, USURY AND *RIBA*

According to *Kamus Dwibahasa* (1985), interest is money that has to be paid or that is paid for the use of money. This sum, which is expressed as a percentage of money borrowed, is added to the loan. Usury is the practice of lending money at an exorbitant or illegally high interest rate. The *Oxford Dictionary* (1989, p. 1099) defined interest as:

> *Money paid for the use of money lent (the principal), or for forbearance of a debt, according to a fixed ratio (rate per cent).*

This dictionary (p. 365) gives two definitions for usury, the first one being:

> *The fact or practice of lending money at interest; especially in later use, the practice of charging, taking or contracting to receive, excessive or illegal rates of interest for money on loan.*

The second definition of usury according to this dictionary is:

> *Premium or interest on money (or goods) given or received on loan; gain made by lending money.*

The definitions given by *Oxford Dictionary* and *Kamus Dwibahasa* do not fit the meanings of interest and usury as held in the earlier periods. The word "interest" originates from the language of the mid-Latin period, that is, *interesse*, which means compensation for loss, or payment of compensation (*Barnhart Dictionary of Etymology*, 1988). According to Divine (1959), in Roman law, interest, or in Latin *id quod interest*, means compensation for damages or loss suffered by the creditor resulting from the failure of the debtor to settle the loan at the specified date set in the contract. Noonan (1957) asserted that the Latin word *intero* means something that is lost. In this case, interest does not mean a gain; instead it means a loss, that is, compensation given to the creditor as a result of loss incurred through lending. In other words, interest really means damages or loss in a broad context, including possible loss of profit on the part of the creditor through the money lent (Homer, 1977). The definition of interest as loss to the creditor continued to be used until the mediaeval period (the 12th and 13th centuries) (Divine, 1959).

The word "usury" originates from the Latin word *usura*, which during the middle Latin period was referred to as *usuria* (*Barnhart Dictionary of Etymology*, 1988). In the Greek language, usury is termed *tokos*, meaning to "bring forth". Hence, when used in the context of loans, usury is the price paid for the use of loan money. In a wider context, usury covers whatever charge or payment imposed as a result of borrowing either goods or money, including what is termed in Latin as *mutuum*. *Mutuum* is a loan of things meant for immediate comsumption. It involves the transfer of possession and right from lender to borrower. It can be in the form of food products or money used to buy food, as well as loan of items to be used, such as houses and equipment. Due to the fact that most loans are in the form of money, usury therefore means the charge for the use of money. The Christian religion actually strictly forbids its followers from taking usury. But the word usury was rarely interpreted by the Christian priests at that time even though it was generally regarded to be present in loans. St. Ambrose (339–397), one of the early Christian priests, regarded usury as whatever payment made that exceeded the principal borrowed, where the item borrowed may be in the form of money, food, clothing, equipment or other items. St. Augustine (354–430), a contemporary of St. Ambrose, said:

> *The usurer is he who expects to receive more than he has given, whether of money, or of corn, or of wine, or of oil, or of anything else.*
>
> (Divine, 1959, p. 30)

This means that St. Augustine defined usury as the sum received by the creditor beyond the exact amount lent, where the additional amount may be in the form of money, corn, wine, oil or anything else. The first definition of usury issued in the Middle Ages

(1000–1500) by Pope Leo the Great (440–61) in his capitulary of Nynweger of 806 was:

> ...*where more is asked than is given.*   (Noonan, 1957, p. 15)

In other words, usury exists when a person asks for more than what he has provided earlier. Fifth Lateran Council in the year 1515 gave this definition of usury:

> *When gain is sought to be acquired from the use of a thing not fruitful in itself, without labor, expense or risk on the part of the lender.*
>
> (Divine, 1959, p. 64)

Cardinal de Lugo (1593–1623), a Christian reformist, defined usury as follows:

> *Usury is gain immediately arising as an obligation from a loan of mutuum...if the gain does not arise from a mutuum but from purchase and sale, however unjust, it is not usury; and likewise if it is not paid as an obligation due but from goodwill, gratitude, or friendship, it is not usury.*   (Dempsey, 1948, pp. 164–165)

Based on the definition provided by Fifth Lateran Council, usury is the profit expected by the loan giver on the loan of an item which does not by itself produce any return, while the loan giver in turn is not involved in any effort or expenses and neither is he exposed to any risk of loss. Meanwhile, de Lugo interpreted usury as emerging from the process of borrowing and not from sale and purchase. The trade and commercial revival in the 12th century intensified the practice of borrowing or the practice of giving loans. As a result, Christian scholars and theologians began to conduct discussions on interest on an increasingly scientific basis. This period is better known as the Age of Scholasticism (which spanned from the 12th to the 16th century).

This philosophy was made the basis for discussion by 16th to 18th century reformists who recognized the right of the creditor to receive returns from the money he had lent. The money or returns from the borrower or debtor was not regarded as usury but instead as excessive interest incurred on the loan. The meaning of the word interest was given by the Christian Holy Office in the year 1836 when the office issued a public decree that allowed interest to be taken by its followers. Interest is the price for the loan of money and is regarded as the premium for the price of present money in terms of future money (Divine, 1959). It is from this date that the word "usury" is taken to mean excessive interest rate, while "interest" is taken to mean the legal rate.

Modern economists have also offered other meanings to the word "interest". Bohm-Bawerk (1851–1914), a famous Austrian economist, described the origins of the word "interest" in his book *Capital and Interest*. Bohm-Bawerk believed in the influence of time on the value of goods where the present value of the same item is much higher compared to its value in the future.

The public, on the other hand, prefers present goods to future goods. Nevertheless, there are people who are prepared to wait or to postpone consumption and to put to use the goods at a later time. This willingness to postpone consumption is called *exchange value*. This value, according to Bohm-Bawerk, is the relationship between the present and future goods, and is the root for the word "interest" (Bohm-Bawerk, 1959). Fisher (1954), in his book *The Theory of Interest*, defined interest as the percentage of premium charged on money at a certain date in the form of money which is required to be repaid within the next one year. Meanwhile, Keynes (1939) in his book *The General Theory of Employment, Interest and Money*, defined interest rate as a reward for willing to part with money or giving up liquidity. Interest rate depends on the preference that people have about holding onto money.

Riba is an Arabic word which literally means "increase" (*al-ziyada*), "grow" (*al-numuw*), "to rise" and "to become lofty" (*al-irtifa* and *al-uluw*) (Ahmad, 1992). Ibn Manzur (630 H/1223–711 H/1311–2) in his book, *Lissanul Arab*, stated, "The root of it is the increase, of the *riba* of money where it has increased" (Homoud, 1985).

According to several *ulama* such as Al-Khatib Al-Sirbini and Al-Ramli (Shafiis) and Ibn Abidin (Hanafis), an "increase" in the number or amount is considered as *riba*. Meanwhile, the Hanbalis have ruled that the word *riba* is restricted to increases in specific goods only (Al-Zuhayli, 2003).

Al-Tabiri or al-Tabari (d. 310 H/923), an interpreter, was of the view that the word *riba* is related to the word *rabia* or hill and it was thus called because it was greater in height and overlooked the level of the surrounding ground. The word *riba* can be applied in two different contexts. First, it can mean an increase to the item itself, and secondly, it can be an increase resulting from a comparison or a differential between two items (Homoud, 1985).

The word *riba* was also used by the pre-Islamic Arabs. According to them, *riba* was what they dealt in on the basis of increase of money in consideration of extension of the terms of maturity, either from the date of maturity or from the actual date of debt (Homoud, 1985). Thus, in many instances, contemporary Muslim scholars often link the word *riba* with loan, and use this pre-Islamic meaning in their elaboration of the word *riba*.

Khan and Mirakhor (1987) defined *riba* as an addition to the amount of the principal loan on the basis of time for which it is loaned or of the time which the payment is deferred. Salleh (1986) in his commentary on *riba* said:

> *Riba in its Syariah context, can be defined, as generally agreed, as an unlawful gain derived from the quantitative inequality of the countervalues in any transaction purporting to effect the exchange of two or more species (anwa', singular naw'), which belong to the same genus (jins) and are governed by the same efficient cause ('illa, plural: 'ilal). Deferred completion of the exchange of such species, or even species which belong to different genera but are governed by the same 'illa, is also riba, whether or not the deferment is accompanied by an increase in any one of the exchanged countervalues.*
>
> (Saleh, 1986, p. 13)

CONCEPTS OF INTEREST AND USURY FROM THE NON-MUSLIM PERSPECTIVE

Among the non-Muslims, too, there are varied views on interest and usury. However, discussion in this book is limited to particular groups only. The first group is the group in the pre-Christian civilization, that is comprising the Jews, Greeks and Romans. The second group comprises the Christians. There are three reasons why these groups are chosen. First, Islam recognizes the prophets of the Jews namely Abraham, Isaac, Moses, and the prophet for the Christians, Jesus. The names of these prophets are frequently mentioned in the Quran; for example, in *Surah al-An'aam*, verses 84 and 85:

> *We gave him Isaac and Jacob: all (three) We guided: and before him, We guided Noah, and among his progeny, David, Solomon, Job, Joseph, Moses, and Aaron: thus do We reward those who do good:*

> *And Zakariyya and John, and Jesus and Elias: all in the ranks of the Righteous:*   (Q6: 84 and 85)

Similarly in *Surah al-Baqarah*, verse 87, Allah (s.w.t.) says:

> *We gave Moses the Book and followed him up with a succession of Messengers; We gave Jesus the son of Mary Clear (Signs) and strengthened him with the holy spirit. Is it that whenever there comes to you a Messenger with what you yourselves desire not, ye are puffed up with pride? – some ye called imposters, and others ye slay!*
>   (Q2: 87)

Islam recognizes these two groups as "the people of the Book" because the Jews have the book *Taurat*, and the Christians have the book *Injil*. The Quran frequently refers to these people as "the people of the Book" and there are many verses regarding them. For example, Allah (s.w.t.) says in *Surah al-Baqarah*, verses 145 and 146:

*Even if thou wert to bring to the people of the Book all the Signs
(together), they would not follow thy Qiblah, nor art thou going to
follow their Qiblah; nor indeed will they follow each other's Qiblah. If
thou after the knowledge hath reached thee, wert to follow their (vain)
desires – then wert thou indeed (clearly) in the wrong.*

*The people of the Book know this as they know their own sons; but
some of them conceal the truth which they themselves know.*

(Q2: 145 and 146)

The second reason the Jews and Christians are chosen for
discussion is the relative abundance of literature by their great
priests on interest and usury. It is important to lend attention to
these writings, from which comparisons could be made with the
views of some Muslims who contend that interest is not forbidden
by Islam. Thirdly, the views of the Greeks and Romans also need to
be examined because of their contributions to human civilization.
Their views have exerted a great deal of influence on the thinking
of Muslims and non-Muslims on interest and usury.

In the following discussions, the word "interest" will be used
instead of usury. Before 1836, the word usury had the same meaning
as the word interest as used today, that is the sum in excess of the
principal amount of a loan. The definition of usury as exorbitant
or excessive interest was used after the Christian Church legalized
usury at a permissible rate, and this permissible rate was termed
"interest".

This does not, however, mean that other groups are not associated
with interest and usury. For instance, in Hinduism, references to
usury are to be found in ancient Indian religious manuscripts, *Vedic*
(2000–1400 SM) and *Sutra* (700–100 SM). In the *Vedic* text, the usurer or
kusidin, that is the one who gives out interest-rate loans, is mentioned
several times. More detailed references to interest payment can be
found in the book, *Sutra*. Vasishtha, a well-known Hindu lawmaker
of that time, drew up a special law which forbade the highest castes,
Brahmanas and *Kshatriyas* from giving out loans based on interest. In

the Buddhist's holy book of Jakatas (600–400 SM), usury is referred to in a demeaning manner (www.americanfinance.com). By the 2nd century, usury had become a more relative term, as inferred in the *Laws of Menu*, which stated that any interest exceeding the legal rate, which cannot be recovered is called usury-based loan (Jain, 1929). The concept of usury among the Indian society eventually ceased to be a topic of discussion. While it is still condemned, the practice of usury is no longer prohibited or controlled in any substantial way.

The Concept of Interest Among the Jews

The Jews are also forbidden from taking interest. This prohibition is found in two of their holy books, the *Ibrani* book and *Talmud*. This book will only discuss the prohibitions found in the *Ibrani* book. Among the Jews, the *Ibrani* book is known as *Tanak* and among the Christians it is known as the *Old Testament* (Gottwald, 1985). The word *Tanak* is an abbreviation of the three parts of the book, namely *Torah* (laws or *Pentateuch*), *Nevi'im* (prophets) and *Kethuvim* (writing). The *Ibrani* Bible through verse 22: 25 in the chapter *Exodus* and verses 25: 35–37 in the chapter *Leviticus* forbids the Jews from taking interest through loans granted to the poor, and among Jews or among strangers who have been accepted into their community.

Exodus 22: 25, states:

If you lend money to one of my people among you who is needy, do not be like a moneylender: charge him no interest.   (Holy Bible, p. 58)

Leviticus 25: 35–37, state:

If one of your countrymen becomes poor and is unable to support himself among you, help him as you would an alien or a temporary resident, so he can continue to live among you.

Do not take interest of any kind from him, but fear your God, so that your countryman may continue to live among you.

You must not lend him money at interest or sell him food at profit.

(*Holy Bible*, p. 93)

The verses above require Jews not to demand more in return than what they had lend. Seeking profit from the poor is not showing charity or mercy but acting as an extortioner and oppressor, devouring the needy borrower (Divine, 1959). The verses also show that all kinds of interest, moderate or exorbitant, are forbidden and regarded as a form of extortion. The Jews are forbidden from taking interest not only from the poor, but also from those among them regardless of financial position. However, the Jews are allowed to take interest from foreigners from outside the Jewish community. This is illustrated by the chapter *Deuteronomy*, verses 19 and 20.

Deuteronomy 23: 19–20, state:

Do not charge your brother interest, whether on money or food or anything else that may earn interest.

You may charge a foreigner interest, but not a brother Israelite, so that the LORD your God, may bless you in everything you put your hand to in the land you are entering to possess.   (*Holy Bible*, p. 147)

The group of the two verses above is a collection of verses which clearly forbids the Jews from taking interest. In addition, there are verses from other chapters in the *Ibrani* book which praise those who abstain from taking interest and condemn those who do. There are several other verses in the book which touch on this matter. Among them:

Verse 18: 8 in chapter *Ezekiel*:

He does not lend at usury or take excessive interest. He withholds his hand from doing wrong and judges fairly between man and man.

Verse 15: 5 in chapter *Psalms*:

Who lends his money without usury and does not accept a bribe against the innocent. He who does these things will never be shaken.

Verse 18: 17 in chapter *Ezekiel*:

He withholds his hand from sin and takes no usury or excessive interest. He keeps my laws and follows my decrees.

Verse 18: 13 in chapter *Ezekiel*:

He lends at usury and takes excessive interest. Will such man live? He will not! Because he has done all these detestable things, he will surely be put to death and his blood will be on his own head.

The Concept of Interest Among the Greeks and Romans

In contrast to the Jews who are forbidden from taking interest through several verses in the *Old Testament*, there is no single provision in the Grecian law that prohibits the taking of interest. The Mesopotamian civilization considered the taking of interest as legal; so too did the Greeks and Romans.

During the Greek civilization (6 BC till AD 1) there were several types of interest rates for loan repayment and investment repayment. The interest rate was called the "customary interest rate". The interest rate for loans was divided into interest for, namely, normal loans (6%–18%), loans on real estate (6.67%–12%), loans to cities (7%–12%) and loans to industry and commerce (12%–18%). Meanwhile, the interest rate for investment was the rate paid to those who undertook particular investments (6%–10%) (Homer, 1977). In the Roman civilization, payment of interest began in 5 BC and ended in AD 4. *The Law of Twelve Tables* (450 BC) was the first Roman law which permitted the taking of interest within a graduated maximum legal rate. Although the taking of interest was allowed, the interest rate could not be compounded (Thomas, 1976). During the period of Lex Genucia (342 BC), the taking of interest was made illegal. However, the illegal status was revoked during the period of Lex Unciaria (88 BC) and the practice of maximum interest rate was reintroduced. There were four types of interest rates during the Roman period, namely the Roman maximum rate allowed (8.33%–12.5%), the normal interest rate in Rome (4%–12.5%), provincal interest rate (6%–100%) and Byzantine interest rate (4%–12.5%) (Homer, 1977).

This practice of taking interest was, however, condemned by Greek philosophers. Renowned Greek philosophers, Plato (427 BC–347 BC) and Aristotle (384 BC–322 BC) condemned such practice and abolished it from the communities that they established. Similarly, the Roman philosophers such as Cato (234 BC–149 BC) and Cicero (106 BC–43 BC) also condemned the practice of taking interest by the Romans. While all these philosophers were quick to disapprove the practice of taking interest, they failed to develop philosophical bases for their objections. Apart from that, their prohibition of interest raised doubts as to whether interest was regarded as undesirable or because they disapproved of wealth acquired through interest (Bohm-Bawerk, 1959).

Plato's views on interest are found in two of his books, *The Republic* and *The Law*. In *The Republic*, Plato contended that the insatiable desire for wealth was destructive to the state. A government that believed power depended on wealth and that it benefited from the over-spending of squanderers, was likely to encourage their extravagant behaviour, giving them loans at interest and acquiring their properties in the event of default. Individuals who lost their property this way would eventually rebel, become hateful and take vengeance against those who had robbed them of their property. Thus, Plato suggested that everyone should enter into a contract voluntarily and at their own risk, thus reducing disgraceful money-making practices. In *The Law*, Plato asserted that land be made a public property but it should be apportioned to individuals for private use. Furthermore, no opportunity should be presented for people to make excessive money and facilities must not be granted to malicious money-making business. The people may not hold gold or silver except for daily exchange.

Regarding loans, Plato was of the opinion that no one should deposit his money with someone he did not trust and lend it at interest. This is because should anything undesirable occur, the debtor was allowed to not pay back the principal money and interest. Hence, Plato disapproved the creating of wealth by means of trade, of borrowing and lending, and of possession of gold and silver. This is because the fundamental purpose of laws of the state is for the happiness of the people and unity for mutual benefit. Happiness and goodness go hand in hand, but people cannot be both good and exceedingly wealthy at the same time. Although interest was prohibited at that time, if a person failed to fulfil the responsibility agreed upon earlier, or failed to pay after using a service, then the person was bound to pay a fine, where the fine imposed was in the form of interest of 200% per annum (Divine, 1959).

Plato deplored interest on two counts. First, because interest caused strife and feelings of dissension among people within the same community, and secondly because interest was regarded as a tool of exploitation of the poor by the rich. Aristotle was not only in agreement with Plato, but in fact further regarded the concept of interest as truly unjust since money obtained in this manner was employed for a function different from what was originally intended and thus, contrary to the natural purpose of money itself. According to Aristotle, money was devised to facilitate exchange. He condemned interest as the unnatural breeding of money by money. Since interest (*tokos* in the Greek language which means to expand or produce) is money borne out of money and it is contrary to mercy and humanity to demand interest from the poor and needy, taking interest on money lent was considered the most unnatural and unjust of all trade by Plato and Aristotle. The condemnation of interest by these two Greek philosophers was based on the grounds as summarized below:

(i) This type of money-making practice is regarded as a demeaning profession, and it hampers the true economic enterprise function, which is to satisfy wants rather than to seek profit. This money-making method hinders people from carrying out their main duty of practising righteousness.

(ii) The practise of taking interest by the rich is contrary to the charity and benevolence that should be practised by them towards the poor.

(iii) Interest has adverse effect on the welfare of the nation, destroying peace and harmony because it tends to set one class against another.

(iv) Interest, by its very nature, is a violation of justice.

As with the Greeks, the Roman philosophers were unanimous in their condemnation of the practice of taking interest. The reasons they presented were almost the same as those given by the Greeks. Cicero, for instance, warned his son that the two occupations to be avoided were collecting taxes and money lending. However, Cicero did not completely reject the concept of interest; he agreed to the taking of interest within reasonable bounds. Cato held the view that it is at times more profitable to use money in trade or in lending. Nevertheless, he forwarded two analogies for the two occupations as follows:

(i) Trade is a very risky occupation while lending is dishonourable.

(ii) His ancestors regarded the usurer as less desirable than a thief; usurers were fined four times the amount taken whereas robbers were penalized only twice the amount taken.

The views presented by the Greek and Roman philosophers who regarded interest as something low and offensive were also ingrained in the public opinion at that time. These views can be indubitably attributed to the presence of an unhealthy situation associated not only with the practice of taking interest but with the heavy debt burden contracted by the poor as a result of unwise use of money.

The Concept of Interest Among Christians

Initially, Christians were forbidden from taking interest. While the Jews are prohibited by the *Old Testament* from taking interest, nowhere in the book of the Christians, the *New Testament*, do we explicitly find direct evidence on the prohibition of interest. However, some interpret verses 6: 34–35 in the chapter *Luke* as a condemnation of the practice of taking interest, a practice which extorted money from the public and did not bring any benefits (*The Catholic Encyclopedia*, Vol. 15, 1912).

Luke 6: 34–35, state:

And if you lend to those from whom you expect repayment, what credit is that to you? Even sinners lend to sinners, expecting to be repaid in full.

But love your enemies, do good to them, and lend to them without expecting to get anything back. Then your reward will be great, and you will be sons of the Most High, because he is kind to the ungrateful and wicked. (Holy Bible, p. 767)

Due to the absence of explicit prohibition, there emerged various conceptions and interpretations by the Christian high priests, intellectuals and scholars as to whether or not it was permissible for Christians to charge or collect interest. This book will discuss the conceptions of three major groups, namely the 1st to 12th century Christian priests, the 12th to 16th century scholars and the 16th to 19th century reformists.

Each of these selected groups had differing views on interest loans and the way in which these groups described and discussed the concept of interest also differed. The first group prohibited the taking of interest and made such practice illegal. The second group wanted legalized interest to be permitted and the third group legalized interest in Christianity. Soon after the Church legalized the taking of interest in 1836, discussions on the legality of interest discontinued. Nevertheless, certain groups still strived to make it illegal. The last priest who wanted interest illegalized was Father Jeremiah O'Callaghan (1780–1861), whose career began in Ross Carberry (South Ireland) and ended in Vermont (United States). However, Father O'Callaghan did not succeed in his efforts and his fight was considered an individual battle since he did not receive support from other Catholic missionaries or the Church (Nelson, 1949).

Views of the Early Christian Priests

Early Christianity – 12th Century

Since there was no provision in the *New Testament* regarding the taking of interest, the teachings and views on the prohibition against lending on interest as found in the *Old Testament* were taken as a guide in the early period of Christianity. The use of the *New Testament* for reference on the practice of taking interest only began around the year 1050 (Noonan, 1957). Most explanations and declarations on usury and interest were delivered by priests of Early Christianity in their homilies and sermons, in which they explained the detriments associated with interest. They clarified that involvement in the practice of lending money at interest was evil and unworthy because it violated the teachings of Christianity which stressed the quality of benevolence. The practice of taking interest had emerged as a result of extreme greed in the hearts of the usurers (Divine, 1959).

St. Basil (329–379), one of the priests of Early Christianity regarded the sin of interest as an act of inhumanity. The lenders procured profit from the adversities of the needy and accumulated gold and wealth from the tears and hardship of the poor. He tried to coax the rich and the poor from engaging in loan transactions. St. Gregory of Nyssa (335–395) condemned the practice of taking interest on the grounds that the apparent kindness shown by the creditor through rendering help in the form of a loan was actually ingenuine, for the loans rendered to the poor would in reality bring the poor to ruin. Those rendering the loans merely wished to accumulate gold for themselves, without contributing any benefit to others. St. Gregory also likened usury to attacks made on victims who were already wounded. St. John Chrysostom (344–407) was convinced that the prohibitions on the practice of taking interest on loans found in the *Old Testament* for the Jews encompassed the universal prohibitions in the *New Testament*. St. Ambrose labelled the consumer of interest as a fraud and a traitor, and also as tidal waves that caused shipwreck. St. Augustine asserted that imposing interest on the poor was more cruel compared with the crime of a robber who stole from the rich (Divine, 1959). St. Anselm of Canterbury (1033–1109), a skilful Italian trader, was the first person in the Middle Ages to equate the practice of taking interest on loans with robbery (Noonan, 1957).

The opinions and views of the priests towards interest during Early Christianity were reflected in several pieces of legislation, known as *Canon*, formulated and implemented during that period. *Canon 20* which was issued by the Council of Elvira in Spain in the year 306 was the first law passed prohibiting interest by all clerics. Those found practising it would be demoted (*The Catholic Encyclopedia*, 1912). However, the *Canon* did not clearly state whether the prohibition also applied to laymen. Similarly with *Apostolic Canon no. 44* issued by the Council of Arles in the year 314 which forbade clerics, under penalty, from practising interest. *Canon 17* issued by the First Council of Nicaea in the year 325 threatened to dismiss clerics found to practise interest (Tanner, 1990). The prohibition was first extended to the public in *Canon 12* by the Council of Carthage in the year 345 and *Canon 36* by the Council of Aix-la-Chapelle in the year 789.

The condemnation of interest by the Christian Church gained momentum during the 9th century. All priests were required to forbid Christians from taking interest and to punish those who disobeyed. In fact, the *Canon* issued in the third conference of the Council of Lateran in the year 1179 denied Christian burial to all manifest usurers. The Council of Lyons II in 1274 ordained that no society, companies, organizations or individuals should allow foreigners who practised interest to rent their houses. The peak of the protest occurred in 1311 when the Council of Vienne declared that civil laws had no influence, and those who did not consider interest as sinful were regarded as people who had deviated from the Christian faith (Hasting, 1921). The views of the priests of Early Christianity may be summarized as such:

   (i) Interest is anything asked for in return, which exceeds the amount of the item lent or loaned out earlier.

  (ii) The taking of interest is a sin and it is prohibited by the *Old Testament* and the *New Testament*.

 (iii) The hope or intention to receive returns which are more than what has been loaned out is a sin.

 (iv) Interest must be given back to the original owner.

  (v) The high price of items for sale in the form of credit amounts to interest which is hidden.

Views of Scholars

Twelfth Century – Sixteenth Century

Rapid development in the field of business and trade in the early 12th century assigned a prominent role in the economy to money and credit. Traders needed more money to finance their trade; consequently, credit became one of the important sources of financing at that time. When the amount of commercial loans increased, the issue of taking interest on loans became a topic of discussion. Two important elements were found in the nature of lending during the 12th century. First, there were commercial loans as well as consumption loans. Secondly, there was an inclination towards the development of a money and capital market or the establishment of the market interest rate (Divine, 1959). The fact that commercial loans were different from consumption loans gave rise to demands for the extension of the concept of interest. Discussions were not merely from the moral perspective as deliberated by early Christian teachings, but also involved the concept of debtor-creditor relationship.

Prior to this, discussions on interest only revolved around aspects of Christianity. The early priests mostly used verses found in their holy books. They regarded the practice of taking interest as inhumane, immoral, an exploitation of the poor and in conflict with the teachings of Christianity. Very rarely did the discussions revolve around economic or legal aspects. These priests were the only ones to have gone to great lengths to discuss the issue of interest, although they were not comprehensive in principle (Bohn-Bewark, Vol. 1, 1959).

In their discussions on interest, the scholars, in addition to moral issues extended their consideration to other aspects, such as issues of types and forms of laws, individual rights on holding property, characteristics and meaning of justice, forms of profit, intentions of human actions and the difference between individual and public sins with respect to interest (Noonan, 1957). This group of scholars were seen as the pioneers who paved the way for the new interpretation of the word "interest". They eventually assigned different meanings to the words "interest" and "usury". "Interest" was regarded as interest rate which was valid or legal, while "usury" was seen as excessive interest rate. In addition, this group was also the most significant contributor in the re-elaboration of the meaning of the word "interest". Robert of Courcon (1158–1218) and

Willian of Auxxerre (1160–1220) were pioneer theologians in the discussion of the concept of interest. Other priests who made major contributions to the development of the concepts of interest and usury were St. Raymond of Pennaforte (1180–1278), Alexander of Hales (1168–1245), St. Albert the Great (1206–1280), St. Bonaventure (1221–1274) and St. Thomas Aquinas (1225–1274). However, it is the analysis on interest made by St. Thomas Aquinas which was said to have a significant influence on subsequent scholastic theory on interest.

The following are among the major issues concerning interest which were resolved by the scholars: first, the intention or action to acquire profit through lending was regarded as a sin and injustice. Secondly, the taking of interest from a loan was permitted. However, whether or not it was illegal depended on the intention of the creditor. Interest was considered legal if the interest was paid to the lender as compensation for granting a loan for benevolent purposes. The scholars declared the rights of the creditor to seek compensation in advance, but bad debt risks could not be used as grounds for permitting the creditor to receive interest.

Views of Reformists

Sixteenth Century – 1836

The era of the reformists began in the middle of the 16th century. This group made changes and formed new perspectives on interest and their views were somewhat different from those of the scholars. The champion of this group was a Protestant leader named John Calvin (1509–1564). His views were shared by two other famous reformists, namely Charles Du Moulin (1500–1566), a French Catholic lawyer and jurist, and Clude Saumaise (1588–1653). Among other reformists involved were Martin Luther (1483–1546), Melanchthon (1497–1560) from Germany and Zwingli (1484–1531) from Switzerland.

Calvin in his analysis on interest used what he called the Golden Rule in which interest was redefined (Noonan, 1957). According to him, interest was regarded a sin only when it harmed someone. Calvin also rejected Aristotle's view that money was sterile. Calvin argued that money was something that multiplied. A person who borrowed money would not leave it idle, but would instead use it to add to his commodities and income. Although Calvin did not agree to the prohibition of taking interest, neither did he agree with the universal permissible interest. However, Calvin preferred interest to be abolished completely. He felt that moderate interest might be necessary for business, but the practice of taking interest must not be made an occupation. Anyone making an income from lending with interest should be expelled from the Church. Interest must not be taken from the poor and must not exceed the maximum legal rate. Lenders should adhere to the words of God and not custom. Taking interest was not considered a normal practice, and the lender should not receive greater profit from the loans than the borrower. The general concept of interest introduced by Calvin is that interest is not a sin as long as it does not burden or hurt the debtor, and interest is lawful on loans to the wealthy who borrow for the sheer purpose of increasing their profits.

Charles Du Moulin (Molinaeus), a renowned French lawyer, was the first Catholic writer to urge for the legitimateness of moderate interest. According to Molinaeus, both the *Old Testament* and the *New Testament* prohibited the taking of interest by condemning it as a sin against charity. He argued that the prohibition was only directed towards the taking of interest from the poor, and nowhere was it stated in the divine or natural law that lending money at interest was prohibited. In the case of business loans, Molinaeus stand was that it was unjust for the creditor to have a share in the profit acquired by the debtor merely on grounds that he provided the loan. Instead, Molinaeus stated that interest charged by the creditor was charges for the function of money which had a value.

Hence, it was considered appropriate if payment were to be imposed for that price.

Claude Saumaise (Salmasius), a follower of Calvin, was regarded as the most outspoken leader in the defence of interest. While Calvin was hesitant in allowing interest of any type, and Molinaeus was against taking interest from the poor, Salmasius on the other hand defended all moneylenders including those who made profits from the poor. According to Salmasius, money could be sold just like any other items in business. If it was legal for other businesses to buy and sell goods with money, there should be no reason why making money from money should be illegal. Given that every person made his living from someone else, this rule was also applicable in matters involving interest. Salmasius argued that the moneylenders were actually providing a very useful service, that is fulfilling the needs of society. Since the moneylenders were granted licence by the government, this implied that they had been endorsed by the government and thus were considered as government officials such as tax collectors. In this case, if moneylenders were guilty of sin, then the government was also guilty. Salmasius disregarded all divine prohibition of interest. His inclination was towards secular laws in managing interest and profit. In conclusion, the reformists supported the full legitimization of interest on the basis that it did not hurt or burden debtors. Instead, they believed interest help businessmen by stimulating economic growth. Therefore, issues of morality and impious were no longer of concern.

THE CONCEPT OF *RIBA* FROM THE ISLAMIC PERSPECTIVE

In the past, there have been disputes among Muslim scholars as to whether *riba* as spoken by the Muslims refers to the English term "interest" or "usury". If we re-examine the meaning of the terms "interest" and "usury" as held today, interest is money which is paid at a fixed rate (usually in percentage form) against a particular loan. Usury is the act of lending money at an exceedingly high interest rate, and this rate is normally regarded as illegal by law. Based on these definitions, there is clearly a major difference in meaning between interest and usury. This has led some scholars to believe that what Islam forbids is usury and not interest. They claimed that interest paid on loans for investment in productive activities does not contravene the Quran for the Quran refers only to usury on non-productive loans which prevailed in pre-Islamic times when people were not familiar with productive loans and their effects on economic development (Mannan, 1986).

There is a general consensus among Muslims scholars and *ulama* that the word *riba* encompasses both interest and usury (Khan and Mirakhor, 1987). This simply means that in Islam there is no such thing as acceptable *riba* and extreme *riba* does not exist from the legal perspective. *Riba* is considered *riba* regardless of the amount involved. The Islamic Research College, University of al-Azhar, Egypt at its second annual conference in 1965 had discussed matters related to *riba* and banking operations. A resolution was reached whereby it was determined that interest imposed by banks on all types of loans constitutes *riba*, regardless of whether the loan is for consumption or production or whether the amount involved is big or small. All types of interest without exception is regarded *haram* or unlawful (Homoud, 1985).

Prohibition Against *Riba*

Muslims are prohibited from dealing with *riba*. Ahmad (1992), an Islamic scholar, asserted that there should not be two different opinions on the categorical prohibition of *riba* in Islam. Differences, however, lie in the interpretation of its scope and coverage.

The prohibition of *riba* is not only revealed in various verses of the Quran, but also in several *Hadith*. The Prophet Muhammad (p.b.u.h.) clearly condemned the accepter and provider of *riba*.

Prohibition Against *Riba* by the Quran

The prohibition of *riba* in the Quran developed gradually and appeared in four revelations. The first revelation is in *Surah ar-Ruum*, verse 39, the second in *Surah an-Nisaa*, verse 61, the third in *Surah Ali Imran*, verses 130 to 132, and the fourth in *Surah al-Baqarah*, verses 275 to 281.

In *Surah ar-Ruum*, verse 39, Allah (s.w.t.) says:

> *That which ye lay out for increase through the property of (other) people, will have no increase with Allah: but that which ye lay out for charity, seeking the Countenance of Allah, (will increase): it is these who will get a recompense multiplied.* (Q30: 39)

The first revelation occurred in Mecca at the time when the city was prosperous with business and trade. Traders were not only actively involved in imports and exports and facilitated the transit of goods, but they also participated in loans for interest, speculations and aleatory transactions. These activities were performed because of the traders' unwillingness to see their capital lying idle while waiting for the arrival or departure of laden caravans. This situation whereby traders involved themselves in *riba* was said to be the reason for the verse concerned to be revealed to the Prophet (p.b.u.h.) by Allah (s.w.t.) (Saleh, 1986).

The above verse strongly prohibits Muslims from taking *riba*. The principle is that any profit Muslims seek to gain should be through their own exertion and not through exploitation of other people. Muslims must show their love for their neighbours by spending their own resources or by the utilization of their own talents and opportunities in the service of those who need them.

The reward will not be merely what they deserve but it will be multiplied many times (Ali, 1989).

Further, Allah (s.w.t.) says:

That they took interest, though they were forbidden; and that they devoured men's substance wrongfully – We have prepared for those among them who reject Faith a grievous punishment.   (Q4: 161)

The second verse on *riba* which was sent down by Allah (s.w.t.) in Medina has created some misunderstanding among intellectuals as to whether the prohibition is directed at Muslims or at the Jews. Hitti (1970), a renowned historian of Islam was of the view that the prohibition is meant for the Jews in Medina. His view was based on Allah's (s.w.t.) words in verse 160:

For the iniquity of the Jews We made unlawful for them certain (foods) good and wholesome which had been lawful for them – in that they hindered many from Allah's Way.   (Q4: 160)

However, Saleh (1986) disagreed with Hitti's opinion. He refuted it on two grounds. First, the practice of *riba* occurred while the Prophet (p.b.u.h.) was still in Mecca, where there were few Jews at that time. Secondly, the Jews in Medina in those times were mostly involved in the agricultural sector and not in the commercial sector. According to Saleh, those involved in *riba* comprised the Muhajirun (Meccans who accompanied the Prophet (p.b.u.h.) in his migration to Medina) and the Ansar (Medinan Muslims) who dealt with usury in Medina. To support his view, Saleh used the following two statements issued by Abu Hurairah (19 SH/600–59 H/678) and Abdullah Ibn Salam (d. 43 H/663–4), Companions of the Prophet (p.b.u.h.).

In Sahih Bukhari's collection of *Hadith*, Abu Hurairah said:

You people say that Abu Hurairah tells many narrations from Allah's Apostle and you also wonder why the emigrants and Ansar do not narrate from Allah's Apostle as Abu Hurairah does. My emigrant

brothers were busy in the market while I used to stick to Allah's Apostle
content with what fills my stomach; so I used to be present when they
were absent and I used to remember when they used to forget, and my
Ansar brothers used to be busy with their properties and I was one of
the poor men of Suffa. I used to remember the narrations when they
used to forget.   (*Khan*, 1986, p. 149)

Abdullah Ibn Salam was reported to have said that the practice
of *riba* was widespread in Medina, which was considered to have
occurred after the death of the Prophet (p.b.u.h.) and after the Jews
were banished from Medina (Saleh, 1986).

Surah Ali Imran, verses 130–132, state:

O ye who believe! Devour not interest, doubled and multiplied; but
fear Allah; that ye may (really) prosper.

Fear the Fire, which is prepared for those who reject Faith:

And obey Allah and the Messenger; That ye may obtain mercy.
                                                       (Q3: 130–132)

The above prohibition was sent down by Allah (s.w.t.) in the
wake of the Battle of Uhud, in the third Hijrah year. Al-Fahkr
ar-Razi (543 H/1149–606 H/1209) believed there were two possible
reasons for the revelation of this verse. First, this verse may have
an association with the preceeding verse, where it is stated that
the Musyrikin had spent money on the troops who participated
in the battle, for which the money had been raised through *riba*.
Another possibility for the practice of *riba* by Muslims at that time
was to raise money to finance the battle against the Musyrikin
(Homoud, 1985).

The above verse shows that the prohibition is for all kinds of
riba. The words "doubled" and "multiplied" in the verse, however,
have created some anomalies among Muslim jurists and scholars.
Some interpreted it to mean that it only refers to *riba* which is
doubled and multiplied. Nevertheless, the majority of renowned

scholars have made the resolution that the amount of *riba* has no role in determining whether or not it is *haram* (unlawful by religion, and sinful).

Qutub (1979) in his book, *In the Shades of the Quran*, expressed the view that the terms used are no more than a state of affairs and not a condition relevant to the imposition. Meanwhile, Syeikh Muhammad Abduh (1849–1905), a famous *ulama* in Egypt was reported to have said that it is not a condition of usury that the capital sum must multiply so as to render the 100 to become 200, but usury (which originally means "increase") multiplies by repetition. Shaltut (1974) also commented on the view that only excessive *riba* is forbidden by the Quran. To him, the term "multiple of multiples" was used by Allah (s.w.t.) to emphasize and condemn the wrongdoings. Homoud (1985) explained that the *riba* which existed in the pre-Islamic era was not about the 100 becoming 200, but rather the multiplicity of ages of the camels lent.

In *Surah al-Baqarah*, verses 275–281, Allah (s.w.t.) says:

> *Those who devour interest will not stand except as stands one whom the Evil One by his touch hath driven to madness. That is because they say: "Trade is like usury", but Allah hath permitted trade and forbidden usury. Those who, after receiving direction from their Lord, desist, shall be pardoned for the past; their case is for Allah (to judge); but those who repeat (the offence) are Companions of the Fire: they will abide therein (forever).*

> *Allah will deprive usury of all growth, but will give increase for deeds of charity: for He loveth not creatures ungrateful and wicked.*

> *Those who believe, and do deeds of righteousness, and establish regular prayers and regular charity, will have their reward with their Lord: on them shall be no fear, nor shall they grieve.*

> *O ye who believe! Fear Allah, and give up what remains of your demand for usury, if ye are indeed believers.*

If ye do it not, take notice of war from Allah and His Messenger: but if ye turn back, ye shall have your capital sums: deal not unjustly, and ye shall not be dealt with unjustly.

If the debtor is in a difficulty, grant him time till it is easy for him to repay. But if ye remit it by way of charity, that is best for you if ye only knew.

And fear the Day when ye shall be brought back to Allah. Then shall every soul be paid what it earned, and none shall be dealt with unjustly.   (Q2: 275–281)

The above verses were sent down in Thaif at the time when the mission of the Prophet (p.b.u.h.) was almost complete. The verses very strongly condemn the practice of *riba*. In verse 275, Allah (s.w.t.) clearly mentioned that there is a difference between trade and *riba*. While trade is permissible, *riba* is forbidden. The word "stand" in this verse has two meanings. Some Islamic scholars interpreted it to mean the conditions of those who take *riba* on the Day of Judgement. Others were of the opinion that it describes the conditions of those who associated themselves with *riba*; this attitude would cause disruption in life.

Surah al-Baqarah, verses 276 and 277 elaborate upon the idea that Allah (s.w.t.) will not bless those who take *riba* and will destroy property which has the element of *riba*. In this case, the destruction of property may be in this world or in the Hereafter. Similarly, those who take *riba* will be punished in both worlds. In the subsequent verses, there is a reminder that Muslims must fear Allah (s.w.t.) and abandon the remnants of *riba* that occurred during the pre-Islamic days. The inability to comply with this instruction will bring war from Allah (s.w.t.) and the Prophet (p.b.u.h.).

This statement serves as a serious warning to Muslims that they should not associate themselves with *riba*. They are allowed to demand only the principal amount from the borrowers and they are urged to deal justly and fairly with debtors. In the event that the debtor is unable to pay his debt, the lender has two alternatives. The lender can either extend the repayment or to convert the loan to charity. Of the two choices, verse 280 suggests that the second is better for Muslims. The main point is that whoever transgresses Allah's (s.w.t.) commands will be punished in this world through disruption and failure in this life and also in the Hereafter. This fact is found in verse 72 of *Surah al-Isra'*, which states:

> *But those who were blind in this world, will be blind in the Hereafter, and most astray from the Path.* (Q17: 72)

Prohibition Against *Riba* by the *Hadith*

In line with its function as the original and eternal source of *Syariah* law, the Quran neither defines *riba* nor provides any detailed explanation of *riba* (Ahmad, 1992). The prohibition of *riba* is revealed in four chapters of the Quran which serves as a universal and fundamental guideline for Muslims. *Hadith,* on the other hand, is a source of reference which enables Muslims to confirm or to acquire further explanation on the rules stipulated in the Quran. The *Hadith* reports prohibition of *riba* in numerous accounts. Sometimes there are slight differences among the narrators. *Hadith* related to *riba* can be classified into three areas, namely directive *Hadith*, explanatory *Hadith* and reminder *Hadith*. Directive *Hadith* is *Hadith* that prevents Muslims from dealing in any kind of *riba*. Explanatory *Hadith* is *Hadith* that explains the types of *riba* and the circumstances of trade that generate *riba*. Reminder *Hadith* is a *Hadith* that visualizes the consequences for those who associate themselves with *riba*. This classification is however not absolute. There is a possibility that some *Hadith* belong to more than one classification. For instance, the *Hadith* which says, "Gold for gold, silver for silver…" is suitable for both the directive and explanatory categories. Some of the *Hadith* related to *riba* are given on the next page.

Directive Hadith

(i) *"If they accept, well and good and, failing which, warn them of war."*

This *Hadith* was taken from the the Prophet's (p.b.u.h.) letter to Itab bin Osaid, the governor of Mecca, when the Thaqeef claimed their debts from Bani Mogheera (Homoud, 1985, p. 80).

(ii) *O People, just as you regard this month, this day and this city as Sacred, so regard the life and property of every Muslim as a sacred trust. Return the goods as entrusted to you to their rightful owner. Hurt no one so that no one may hurt you. Remember that you will indeed meet your Lord, and that He will indeed reckon your deeds. Allah has forbidden you to take riba, therefore all riba obligations shall henceworth be waived. Your capital, however, is yours to keep. You will neither inflict nor suffer inequality. Allah has judged that there shall be no riba and that all riba due to Abbas ibn' Abd'al Muttalib shall henceforth be waived.*

This *Hadith* is the last sermon delivered by the Prophet (p.b.u.h.) on the Ninth Day of Dzul Hijjah 10 AH (after *Hijrah*) (Chapra, 1992, p. 380).

(iii) Narrated by 'Aun bin Abu Juhaifa:

> *My father bought a slave who practised the profession of cupping. My father broke the slave's instruments of cupping. I asked my father why he had done so. He replied, "The Prophet (p.b.u.h.) forbade the acceptance of the price of a dog or blood, and also forbade the profession of tattooing, getting tattooed and receiving or giving riba (usury), and cursed the picture-makers."*
>
> (*Khan*, 1989, p. 169)

(iv) Narrated by Abu Said Al-Khudri and Abu Hurairah:

> *Allah's Apostle (p.b.u.h.) appointed somebody as a governor of Khaibar. That governor brought to him an excellent kind of dates*

(from Khaibar). The Prophet (p.b.u.h.) asked, "Are all the dates of Khaibar like this?" He replied, "By Allah, no, O Allah's Apostle! But we barter one Sa of this (type of dates) for two Sas of dates of ours and two Sas of it for three of ours." Allah's Apostle (p.b.u.h.) said, "Do not do so (as that is a kind of usury) but sell the mixed dates (of inferior quality) for money, and then buy good dates with that money."   (Khan, 1989, p. 222)

Explanatory Hadith

(i) Narrated by Ibn Shihab:

Malik bin Aus said, "I was in need of change for one hundred Dinars. Talha bin 'Ubaid-Ullah called me and we discussed the matter, and he agreed to change (my Dinars). He took the gold pieces in his hands and fidgeted with them, and then said, 'Wait till my storekeeper comes from the forest.' Umar was listening to that and said, 'By Allah! You should not separate from Talha till you get the money from him, for Allah's Apostle (p.b.u.h.) said, 'The selling of gold for gold is Riba (usury) except if the exchange is from hand to hand and equal in amount, and similarly, the selling of wheat for wheat is Riba (usury) unless it is from hand to hand and equal in amount, and the selling of barley for barley is usury unless it is from hand to hand and equal in amount, and dates for dates is usury unless it is from hand to hand and equal in amount'.' "

(Sidiqi, undated, p. 833)

(ii) Narrated by Ibn 'Umar:

The Prophet (p.b.u.h.) said, "The selling of wheat for wheat is Riba (usury) except if it is handed from hand to hand and equal in amount. Similarly the selling of barley for barley is Riba except if it is from hand to hand and equal in amount, and dates for dates is usury except if it is from hand to hand and equal in amount."

(*Khan*, 1986, p. 210)

(iii) Narrated by Abu Said Al-Khudri:

Allah's Apostle (p.b.u.h.) said, "Do not sell gold for gold unless equivalent in weight, and do not sell less amount for greater amount or vice versa; and do not sell silver for silver unless equivalent in weight, and do not sell less amount for greater amount or vice versa and do not sell gold or silver that is not present at the moment of exchange for gold or silver that is present."

(*Khan*, 1986, pp. 212–213)

(iv) Narrated by Abu Salih Az-Zaiyat:

I heard Abu Said Al-Khudri saying: "The selling of a Dinar for a Dinar, and a Dirham for a Dirham (is permissible)." I said to him, "Ibn 'Abbas does not say the same." Abu Said replied, "I asked Ibn 'Abbas whether he had heard it from the Prophet (p.b.u.h.) or seen it in the Holy Book. Ibn 'Abbas replied, 'I do not claim that, and you know Allah's Apostle (p.b.u.h.) better than I, but Usama informed me that the Prophet (p.b.u.h.) had said, 'There is no riba (in money exchange) except when it is not done from hand to hand (i.e. when there is delay in payment)'.'"   (*Khan*, 1986, p. 213)

(v) Narrated by Abu Said al-Khudri:

Once Bilal brought Barni (i.e. a kind of dates) to the Prophet (p.b.u.h.) and the Prophet (p.b.u.h.) asked him, "From where have you brought these?" Bilal replied, "I had some inferior dates and exchanged two Sas of it for one Sa of Barni dates in order to give it to the Prophet (p.b.u.h.) to eat." Thereupon the Prophet (p.b.u.h.) said, "Beware! Beware! This is definitely riba! This is definitely riba! Don't do so, but if you want to buy (a superior kind of dates) sell the inferior dates for money and then buy the superior kind of dates with that money."   (*Khan*, 1986, p. 291)

(vi) Narrated by Abu Bakra:

> *Allah's Apostle (p.b.u.h.) said, "Don't sell gold for gold unless equal in weight, nor silver for silver unless equal in weight, but you could sell gold for silver or silver for gold as you like."*

(Khan, 1986, p. 214)

(vii) 'Ubada ibn al-Samit reported:

> *Allah's Messenger (p.b.u.h.) as saying, Gold is to be paid for by gold, silver by silver, wheat by wheat, barley by barley, dates by dates, and salt by salt, like for like and equal for equal, payment being made hand to hand. If these classes differ, then sell as you wish if payment is made hand to hand.*

(Sidiqi, undated, p. 834)

(viii)Abu Sa'id al-Khudri reported:

> *Allah's Messenger (p.b.u.h.) as saying, "Gold is to be paid for by gold, silver by silver, wheat by wheat, barley by barley, dates by dates, salt by salt, like by like, payment being made hand to hand. He who made an addition to it, or asked for an addition, in fact dealt in usury. The receiver and the giver are equally guilty."*

(Sidiqi, undated, p. 834)

(ix) Abu Hurairah reported:

> *Allah's Messenger (p.b.u.h.) as saying, "Gold is to be paid for by gold with equal weight, like for like, and silver is to be paid for by silver with equal weight, like for like. He who made an addition to it or demanded an addition dealt in usury."*

(Sidiqi, undated, p. 834)

(x)   Abu Minhal reported:

> *"My partner sold silver to be paid in the (Hajj) season or (in the days of) Hajj. He (my partner) came to me and informed me, and I said to him: 'Such transaction is not desirable'. He said:*

'I sold it in the market (on loan) but nobody objected to this'. I went to al-Bara' b. 'Azib and asked him, and he said: 'Allah's Apostle (p.b.u.h.) came to Medina and we made such transaction, whereupon he said: 'In case the payment is made on the spot, there is no harm in it, and in case (it is sold) on loan, it is usury'. You'd better go to Zaid b. Arqam, for he is a greater trader than I'; so I went to him and asked him, and he said the same."

(*Sidiqi*, undated, p. 835)

Reminder Hadith

(i) Narrated by Samura bin Jundab:

> *The Prophet (p.b.u.h.) said, "This night I dreamt that two men came and took me to a Holy land whence we proceeded on till we reached a river of blood, where a man was standing, and on its bank was standing another man with stones in his hands. The man in the middle of the river tried to come out, but the other threw a stone in his mouth and forced him to go back to his original place. So, whenever he tried to come out, the other man would throw a stone in his mouth and force him to go back to his former place. I asked, 'Who is this?' I was told, 'The person in the river was a riba-eater.'"*

(*Khan*, 1986, pp. 168–169)

(ii) *'Abdullah b. Mas'ud said that Allah's Messenger (p.b.u.h.) cursed the one who accepted interest and the one who paid it. I asked about the one who recorded it, and two witnesses to it. He (the narrator) said: "We narrate what we have heard."*

(*Sidiqi*, undated, p. 839)

(iii) *Jabir said that Allah's Messenger (p.b.u.h.) cursed the accepter of interest and its payer, and the one who records it, and the two witnesses, and he said: "They are all equal."*

(*Sidiqi*, undated, p. 839)

(iv) Narrated by Abu Hurairah:

> *Allah's Messenger (p.b.u.h.) said, "On the night of Ascension I came upon people whose stomachs were like houses with snakes visible from the outside. I asked Gabriel who they were. He replied that they were people who had received interest."*
>
> (Chapra, 1992, p. 381)

(v) Narrated by Abdullah ibn Hanzalah:

> *Allah's Messenger (p.b.u.h.) said, "A Dirham of riba which a man receives knowingly is worse than committing adultery thirty six times."*   (Chapra, 1992, p. 381)

(vi) Narrated by Abu Hurairah:

> *Allah's Messenger (p.b.u.h.) said, "Allah would be justified in not allowing four persons to enter heaven or to taste its blessings: he who drinks habitually, he who takes riba, he who usurps orphan's property without right, and he who is undutiful to his parents."*
>
> (Chapra, 1992, p. 383)

(vii) Narrated by Abu Hurairah:

> *Allah's Messenger (p.b.u.h.) said, "Riba has seventy segments the least serious being equivalent to a man committing adultery with his own mother."*   (Chapra, 1992, p. 381)

(viii) Narrated by Abu Hurairah:

> *The Prophet (p.b.u.h.) said, "There will certainly come a time for mankind when everyone will take riba and if he does not do so, its dust will reach him."*   (Chapra, 1992, p. 381)

Classification of *Riba*

There is no standardization among the earlier and contemporary Muslim scholars in classifying *riba*. The method of classification can be divided based on time, origin or source of prohibitions and the nature of transactions that generate *riba*.

The first classification of riba is termed pre-Islamic *riba*. This terminology is often used by the majority of past and present Muslim scholars and jurists in explaining the *riba* which was in existence prior to the introduction of Islam to Arabs. Pre-Islamic *riba* is also known as *Riba al-Jahiliyyah* among certain Muslim writers. *Riba al-Jahiliyyah* refers to the practice of increasing the amount of debt as a result of extension of the term of maturity, either from the date of maturity or from the actual date of debt. According to Homoud (1985), al-Tabiri in his interpretation of *riba* which is forbidden by Allah (s.w.t.) stated that, "In the pre-Islamic times when a man is indebted to another he used to say: 'I give you so much if you extend the date for payment.'" With that, the creditor would extend the date of payment. Al-Fahkr ar-Razi, in his deliberation about the business practices of pre-Islamic Arabs believed that Arabs with debt used to pay money monthly and left the principal intact. On maturity, the debtor had to pay the principal amount. In the case of inability or failure to repay, there was the possibility that the creditor would increase the amount of principal and extend the repayment term. This additional amount, according to ar-Razi, is called *Riba al-Jahiliyyah* (Homoud, 1985).

Besides the above classification, another type of *riba* is classified based on the prohibitions of the Prophet (p.b.u.h.). Abu Zahra (1955) in his book, *Khatem An-Nabiyayn* classified *riba* into two groups. The first is called debt *riba*. In this situation, when money is loaned as debt, the principal would increase each time the repayment date is extended. The surplus or additional payment is regarded as payment in return for the extended repayment date; this additional payment is termed *riba*. In the second classification, the *riba* is called sales *riba*, which according to Abu Zahra, is known as such because the Prophet (p.b.u.h.) called it *riba* (Homoud, 1985). Similarly with al-Jassas (1927) in *The Rules of al-Quran,* who described the sales *riba* which was unknown in the pre-Islamic period. Sales *riba* is divided into two categories, increased *riba* and delayed payment *riba*. Increased *riba* occurs when an item which is subject to *riba* is sold with an addition of one consideration over the other. The delayed payment *riba,* on the other hand, may occur in case of the sale of an item subjected to *riba* for an item of its kind. *Riba* is committed if the payment of either consideration is delayed (Homoud, 1985). Pre-Islamic *riba* is also called *Riba* al-Quran, while sales *riba* is called *Riba al-Sunnah.*

Ismail (1992) referred to the works of al-Arabi, al-Qurtubi and al-Jassas in his discussion on deferred contract of exchange mentioned in the Quran. He concluded that the word *riba* as unanimously agreed by all three exegetists is known as *Riba al-Duyun.* This *riba* can be further divided into two components, *Riba al-Jahiliyyah* and *Riba al-Qardah.* According to Ismail, *Riba al-Jahiliyyah* arises when the creditor in any deferred contract of exchange, either in *al-bai bithaman ajil* (deferred sale), *bai al-istisna* (sale on order) or *al-Ijarah* (leasing), demands from the debtor an amount over and above which was initially agreed to in the original contract. *Riba al-Qardah* is a similar additional consideration of time, except that it is not an inducement for extending the period of liability arising from a contract of exchange, but rather the period of liability of a straight loan.

Al-Tabiri also believed that the prohibition against *riba* in the Quran in verse 130 of *Surah Ali Imran* refers to the *riba* which occurred during pre-Islamic period. This *riba* covered the practice of deferring debt with additional condition of an increase in the amount of repayment. Ahmad (1992) when commenting on al-Tabiri's view believed that the practice of increasing the amount of debt due to an extension in maturity is also known as *dayn mu'ajjal.* He further argued that al-Tabiri's view created an ambiguity in two areas. First, it is unclear whether *dayn mu'ajjal* emerged from sale transactions or from loan dealings. Secondly, whether the stipulation of *riba* occurred in the first term or during subsequent terms. Ahmad (1992) concluded that *dayn mu'ajjal* mostly originated from the practice of *bay' bi'l-nasiah*, which is credit sale with a fixed term (trade credit) to the agreed price. This usually results in *riba* dealings which cause the multiplication of the debt. Ibn al-Qayim (1292–1350) also classed *riba* into two groups, namely overt *riba* and covert *riba*. Overt *riba* is, according to Ibn al-Qayim, deferred payment *riba* which was practised during the pre-Islamic period while covert *riba* is the increased *riba*, forbidden by the Prophet (p.b.u.h.) (Homoud, 1985). However, these classifications are seldom used by other Muslim scholars.

Modern Muslim scholars and jurists prefer to use Arabic terminologies in elaborating *riba*. The terms frequently used are *Riba al-Nasiah* and *Riba al-Fadl*. The word *nasiah* comes from the root *nasa'a* which means "to postpone, defer or wait". It refers to the time that is allowed for the debtor to repay the loan after its due date. In return, the debtor must pay an additional amount or premium on the extended paying period. This additional amount is considered *riba* in Islam. Thus, *Riba al-Nasiah* is *riba* which had existed since the pre-Islamic period and which is forbidden by the Quran. In other words, this *riba* is the same as *Riba al-Jahiliyyah*. Since its prohibition is mentioned in the Quran, some writers refer to it as *Riba al-Quran*. This is also the *riba* which was mentioned by the Prophet (p.b.u.h.) in the *Hadith* narrated by Usama Ibn Zaid which means: "There is no *riba* except in *nasiah*" (Chapra, 1992, p. 35). *Riba al-Nasiah* is also sometimes referred to as *Riba al-Duyun, Riba al-Mubashir* and *Riba al-Jali*.

Riba al-Fadl is *riba* which occurs as a result of trade or sale transactions. It covers all on-the-spot transactions involving cash payment and immediate delivery of goods. The prohibition of this kind of *riba* is based on the *Hadith* that says: "Gold for gold, silver for silver...." Thus, this *riba* is what Muslim scholars have termed as sales *riba* and *Riba al-Sunnah*. It is also sometimes known as *Riba al-Buyu, Riba Ghyr al-Mubashir* and *Riba al-Khafi* (Chapra, 1992). Homoud (1985) subsequently divided this sales *riba* into two types, increased *riba* and delayed payment *riba*.

This classification of *riba* may be seen from various perspectives. First, it may be seen in terms of time occurrence; secondly, from the source of the prohibition, whether the Quran or *Hadith*; and thirdly, the nature of transaction that can generate *riba*, that is, whether loan or sale, or whether spot or deferred. Table 4–1 shows the classification of *riba* based on time, that is pre-Islamic *riba* and post-Islamic *riba*.

TABLE 4–1   Classification of *Riba*

	Pre-Islamic Riba	*Post-Islamic Riba*
Time of Occurrence	Before the establishment of Islam	After Islam became established
Source of Prohibition	al-Quran	*Hadith*
Area of Emergence	Extension of debt	Point of sales: – increment – deferred
Common Terminology	Debt *riba* *Riba al-Quran* *Riba al-Jahiliyyah* *Riba al-Nasiah* *Riba al-Duyun* *Riba al-Mubashir* *Riba al-Jali*	Sales *riba* *Riba al-Hadith* *Riba al-Sunnah* *Riba al-Fadl* *Riba al-Buyu* *Riba Ghyr al-Mubashir* *Riba al-Khafi*

Based on the classification in Table 4–1, it may be concluded that pre-Islamic *riba* is *riba* resulting from the extension of debt. The debt could either be from business transactions or a straight loan. Post-Islamic *riba,* on the other hand, is *riba* originated from sales, and may be further classed into increased *riba* or *riba* which occurs due to unequal exchange value, and delayed payment *riba* or *riba* which emerges due to increase in price or exchange value as a result of extension of the payment period.

An important criteria which differentiates pre-Islamic *riba* and post-Islamic *riba* is the additional prohibition imposed associated with the sale of business goods. Debt *riba* which was known to the pre-Islamic Arabs has not necessarily ceased to exist in the post-Islamic period. For instance, *riba* of a direct loan is considered pre-Islamic *riba* even though the time of occurrence is the post-Islamic period. Nevertheless, the majority of writers nowadays prefer to use the terms *Riba al-Nasiah* (debt *riba*) and *Riba al-Fadl* (increased *riba)* in their writings. In Islamic banking system, the *riba* normally being discussed is debt *riba* or *Riba al-Nasiah*. Hence, the interest imposed by conventional banks is grouped as *Riba al-Nasiah*.

Apart from the various types of *riba* mentioned, there is one more type of *riba* discussed by the *ulama* of Shafiis called *Riba al-Yad*. This type of *riba* comes into effect when different goods of the same group (such as wheat with barley) are traded with deferment on the exchange period or without mentioning the term of deferment. The Hanafiis, nevertheless, categorize this type of *riba* as *Riba al-Nasiah* (Al-Zuhayli, 2003).

Riba Among Muslims

Unlike the Christians who were engaged in a long debate on the legality of taking interest, Muslims were not involved in such a debate. There are several possible reasons for this. First, the Quran has given clear guidelines on the prohibition of *riba*. Secondly, the Muslims during the early days, had the opportunity to obtain clarification and guidance on this matter from the Prophet (p.b.u.h.). This was made even easier by the fact that the Prophet (p.b.u.h.) was Himself someone who possessed understanding and skills of the methods of business. The explanation and guidance are found in the *Hadith* related to *riba*. In addition, the caliphs (successors of the Prophet (p.b.u.h.)) also commented on the matter of *riba*. For example, Umar did not accept a gift of dates from a debtor, and he explained that such practice was considered *riba* (Homoud, 1985).

In view of such instance, there is little controversy with regard to the concept and doctrines of *riba* among Muslims. However, there was some confusion among the early Muslims regarding sales *riba* on one occasion. The account was written by As-Sarkhassi in his book *Al Mabsut*. He reported Ibn Abbas and Abu Said al-Khudri had some misunderstanding about sales *riba*. Abu Said warned Ibn Abbas by saying:

> *"Oh ye Ibn Abbas, until when would you let people eat usury; did you accompany God's Messenger, God's prayer and peace be upon him, as no one else did; did you hear from him what was not heard by any one else?" Ibn Abbas retorted, "No, but Ussama ben ZAYD related to me that the Prophet, God's prayer and peace be upon him, said, 'There is no usury except in delayed payment';" then Abu Sa'id said: "By God I will not stay with you under the same roof so long as you persist in this say."* (Homoud, 1985, p. 82).

Although the discussion on *riba* among Muslims has yet to reach a final conclusion, this does not mean that *riba* is a less significant matter among Muslims. On the contrary, jurists of all four Muslim *mazaahib* of *Hanafi*, *Maliki*, *Shafii* and *Hanbali*, have discussed and issued specific guidelines on *riba* to be followed by Muslims. There are some differences of opinion among the *mazhab* with regard to the scope of the ban on *riba*, the transactions that constitute *riba* and the types of properties subjected to *riba*. Modern Muslim scholars are not left behind in the discussion of this issue. Sometimes the discussions appear to be going along the route that had been taken by the Christian scholars and reformists during the process of legalizing *riba*.

Views of the Mazhab on Riba

There are slight differences of opinion among the four *mazaahib* on the prohibition and the form of *riba* involving debts or loans. With regard to debt *riba*, they are all in agreement that every loan that produces an advantage is *riba*. However, Ibn Hazm (384 H/994–456 H/1064) in his book, *Al-Muhalia* was of the view that *riba* is not allowed in a sale or delayed payment except in six items, namely gold, silver, wheat, barley, dates and salt; but for loans, *riba* covers everything (Homoud, *1985*). *Riba*, however, is not committed in the case of an additional amount paid by the debtor over the principal if there is no expressed agreement which requires the debtor to do so. This is in line with the *Hadith* narrated by Abu Hurairah who reported that the Prophet (p.b.u.h.) had said, "The best of you is he who repays best." (Homoud, 1985, p. 87). There are some differences of opinion among the *mazhab* related to the *Hadith*, "Gold for gold, silver for silver..." Based on this *Hadith*, the meaning of *riba* in the *Syariah* context is the unlawful gain derived from the exchange of two or more items in the same *jins* (group) that are governed by the same *illa* (process of formation).

The various views of the *mazaahib* on *Riba al-Fadl* and *Riba al-Nasiah* may be summarized below (Saleh, 1986, pp. 20–26). The description only covers the four principal *mazaahib*. The opinions of other *mazaahib* will not be discussed. (Al-Zuhayli (2003) has also written in detail on this matter.)

Hanafis

(i) The exchanged countervalues are all measurable or all weighable and belong to the same genus. For example, the sale of wheat for wheat.

No gain permitted in a hand-to-hand transaction and no deferred transaction, even without gain.

(ii) The exchanged countervalues are all measurable or all weighable but belong to different genera. For example, the sale of gold for silver.

No deferred transaction permitted, even without gain. Increase permissible in a hand-to-hand transaction.

(iii) The exchanged countervalues are not measurable or weighable but belong to the same genus, such as the sale of an animal for an animal.

No deferred transaction permitted even without gain. Gain permissible in a hand-to hand transaction.

(iv) One of the exchanged countervalues is measurable while the other is not (whether weighable or not). For example, sale of wheat for silver or pomegranate.

Gain permissible whether in a hand-to-hand transaction or in a deferred one.

(v) One of the exchanged countervalues is weighable while the other is not (whether measurable or not). For example, the sale of gold for wheat or quinces.

Gain permissible whether in a hand-to-hand transaction or in a deferred one.

(vi) The exchanged countervalues are not measurable or weighable, and furthermore belong to different genera. For example, the sale of pomegranates for apples.

Gain permissible whether in a hand-to-hand transaction or in a deferred one.

Shafiis

(i) The exchanged countervalues are all currencies or all foodstuffs and belong to the same genus. For example, the sale of gold for gold or dates for dates.

No gain permitted in a hand-to-hand transaction and no deferred transaction permitted, even without gain.

(ii) The exchanged countervalues are all currencies or all foodstuffs but belong to different genera. For example, the sale of gold for silver or dates for wheat.

No deferred transaction permitted even without gain. Gain permissible in a hand-to-hand transaction.

(iii) One of the exchanged countervalues is foodstuffs, the other is not. For example, the sale of wheat for iron.

No deferred transaction permitted even without gain. Gain permissible in a hand-to-hand transaction.

(iv) The exchanged countervalues are neither foodstuffs nor currencies, whether or not they belong to the same genus. For example, the sale of chalk lime for lime or lime for lead.

Gain permissible whether in a hand-to-hand transaction or in a deferred one.

(v) One of the exchanged countervalues is currency, the other is not, whether or not foodstuffs. For example, the sale of rice for silver and iron for gold.

Gain permissible whether in a hand-to-hand transaction or in a deferred one.

Hanbalis

(i) The exchanged countervalues are all measurable or all weighable and furthermore are foodstuffs. For example, the sale of rice for rice or grain for grain.

No gain permitted in a hand-to-hand transaction and no deferred transaction permitted, even without gain.

(ii) The exchanged countervalues are of the same genus (*jins*) and all foodstuffs, but neither measurable nor weighable. For example, the exchange of watermelons for apples, or all measurable or all weighable but not foodstuffs, such as the exchange of gold for silver.

Gain permissible in a hand-to-hand transaction but no deferred transaction permitted, even with no gain.

(iii) The exchanged countervalues belong to different genera and are properties governed by one *illa*, that is, they are all measurable or weighable or all foodstuffs. For example, the sale of wheat for barley.

Gain permissible in a hand-to-hand transaction but no deferred transaction permitted, even with no gain.

(iv) One of the exchanged countervalues is currency and the other one an article susceptible to *riba*, that is, measurable, weighable or foodstuffs.

Gain permissible whether in a hand-to-hand transaction or in a deferred one.

(v) The exchanged countervalues belong to different genera and are governed by different *illa*. For example, one is measurable (wheat) and the other is weighable (meat).

Gain permissible in a hand-to-hand transaction but conflicting opinion regarding deferment, with trend towards permission.

(vi) The exchanged countervalues are all neither measurable nor weighable nor foodstuffs. For example, the sale of riding animals.

Gain permissible whether in a hand-to-hand transaction or in a deferred one.

Malikis

(i) The exchanged countervalues are all currencies or all storable nourishment for mankind and belong to the same genus. For example, the exchange of dinars for dinars or wheat for wheat.

> *No gain permissible in a hand-to-hand transaction and no deferred transaction even with no gain.*

(ii) The exchanged countervalues are all currencies or all storable nourishment for mankind but belong to different genera. For example, the exchange of dirhams for dinars or wheat for broad beans.

> *No deferred transaction permitted even with no gain. Gain permissible in a hand-to-hand transaction.*

(iii) The exchanged countervalues are all foodstuffs which are not governed by the Maliki's *illa* whether or not they belong to the same genus. For example, the sale of bananas for lettuce.

> *No deferred transaction permitted even with no gain. Gain permissible in a hand-to-hand transaction.*

(iv) The exchanged countervalues are neither edible nor drinkable but are all either weighable or measurable, belong to the same genus and furthermore serve the same purpose. For example, the sale of material for material.

> *No deferred transaction permitted even with no gain. Gain permissible in a hand-to-hand transaction.*

Apart from the opinions expressed by the four *mazhab* on the existence of the elements of *riba* in various situations and types of transactions, these *mazhab* also have differing opinions on whether Muslims are allowed to deal with *riba* with non-Muslims. According to Muslim jurists, transactions carried out by Muslims may be done in three different regions. The first region is known as *dar al-Islam*, and comprises countries where Islamic laws are applied and are under the rule of Muslims leaders. The second region is called *dar al-Harb*. Countries in this category have the potential to be at war with Muslims. The third region is called *dar al-Sulh*, and comprises countries which have an agreement with Islamic countries and are neither under the rule of a Muslim sovereign nor potentially at war with the Muslims (Saleh, 1986).

Imam Abu Hanifa (80 H/699–150 H/767), the founder of the Hanafi School of Law, allowed Muslims to enter non-Muslim territories and trade on the basis of *riba*. Abu Hanifa also allowed Muslims to trade on a similar basis with converted Muslims from non-Muslim countries. The Imamate of Syiah is also of the opinion, with regard to transaction with non-Muslims, that it is unlawful for Muslims to accept *riba* but not to give *riba* (Homoud, 1985). The Shafiis, Malikis and Hanbalis do not share the opinion of the Hanafis. They believe that there should be no segregation in the prohibition of *riba*. Since *riba* is prohibited in Muslim territories, the same rule should be applied in non-Muslim territories. Similarly, if it is unlawful for Muslims to accept or give *riba* to fellow Muslims, the same should be applied to transactions with non-Muslims (Homoud, 1985).

Views of Modern Scholars

One of the controversial views pertaining to *riba* was given by Syeikh Muhammad Abduh (1849–1905), the *Mufti* of Egypt. Abduh was known as a person with sharp intellect and an open mind. Many alleged that Abduh had issued a *fatwa* that the interest paid by the Post Office Savings Fund was not *riba*. However, Muhammad Rasyid Redha (a student of Abduh) denied that the *Mufti* had issued such a *fatwa*, but confirmed that certain government officials including the Director of Posts had a private discussion with the

Mufti on this matter. The magazine, *al-Manar*, in its December 1903 issue, published a statement from Abduh which read: *"The stipulated usury is not permissible in any case, whereas the Post Office invests the monies taken from the people, which are not taken as loans based on need, it would be possible to apply the investment of such monies on the rules of partnership in commendam."* (Homoud, 1985, p. 122). This statement created much controversy regarding its validity and authenticity.

Another somewhat different view on *riba* was expressed by Jawish (1908). He believed that *riba* as referred to in the Quran is the multiple delayed payment *riba*, and not interest on loans. With regard to *riba* on loans, Jawish believed that it was taken not from the Quran but from precedural rules. Redha (1929) also expressed his opinion on matters relating to *riba*. One of the most controversial statements he issued is that it is permissible for a person to borrow $100 and sign a note for $120, and this practice is not absolute *riba*. According to Redha, delayed payment *riba* takes place upon the extension of debt upon maturity.

Statements made by Jawish and Redha did not openly encourage Muslims to be involved in *riba*. Maruf Dawalibi, a modern Muslim scholar believed that a reasonable interest rate should be allowed for loans of production. This view was supported by another scholar, Syeikh Abdul Jalil Isa. During the Scientific Conference of Islamic Jurisprudence held in Paris in the year 1951, Dawalibi said:

The banned usury takes place in loans meant for consumption and not for production, wherein the former sector the usurers take advantage of the need of the poor and destitute to exhaust them with exorbitant usury they impose on them. Nowadays, as the economic systems have been developed and many companies have been established, where most of the loans are being granted for production not for consumption, it is necessary to consider what development must be introduced to the stipulations in consequence of this development of civilization.

(Homoud, 1985, p. 120)

Abdullah Yusuf Ali (1872–1948), one of the leading contemporary Muslim scholars, was reported as saying:

> *Our ulama (Muslim learned scholars) both ancient and modern, have worked out a great body of literature on riba, based mainly on economic conditions as they existed at the rise of Islam. I agree with them on the main principles, but respectfully differ from them on the definition of riba. The definition I would accept would be: undue profit made, not in the way of legitimate trade, out of loans of gold and silver, and necessary articles of food, such as wheat, barley, dates and salt (according to the list mentioned by the Holy Apostle himself). My definition would include profiteering of all kinds, but exclude economic credit, the creature of modern banking and finance.*
>
> (Zakaria, 1989, p. 41)

During the 1965 conference organized by Islamic Research College, University of al-Azhar, Egypt, the decision on the legality of *riba* was made whereby a resolution was passed which reaffirmed that interest on all types of loans, regardless of the size is considered *riba* and *haram* (illegitimate). The decision made was regarded as the conclusion to the discussion on the status of the legality of *riba* as offered by modern conventional banks. On *Riba al-Fadl*, a controversial view was offered by Mahmud Abu al-Saud (1992). He believed that this type of *riba* is lawful and defined it as any arrangement whereby an immediate exchange of goods of the same kind takes place when one person receives from the other something more in quantity than what he has given. Since the transaction involved is merely an exchange or barter, it cannot be regarded as such except when there is a difference between the things exchanged. Al-Saud subsequently gave the example of a person who wished to exchange low quality dates with dates of a superior quality. It was reasonable to expect that the number of the inferior dates exchanged would be more than that of the superior quality dates. Therefore, in this case the exchange process was lawful and permissible. This view, according to him, is in line with the opinion given by one of the early Muslim scholars, Ibn Hazm (384 H/994–456 H/1064), but contrary to the opinion of Ibn Qayyim (1292–1350) (al-Saud, 1992). In contrast to the view expressed by al-Saud, Syeikh Tantawi, the Grand *Mufti* of Egypt and the Chairman of the al-Azhar Research Academy, stated that interest-paying government bonds were in conformity with Islam. This caused an outrage from many Muslim scholars (Mallat, 1996). Apart from this, on 12 July 1989, Syeikh Tantawi also issued a *fatwa* in the *Al-Ahram* newspaper that the interest from certificates of investment issued by Bank Al-Ahli in Egypt was not *haram*. A further two *fatwa* were released by Syeikh Tantawi, in November 1989 and 1991, where he declared that bank interest was permissible in Islam (Al-Zuhayli, 2003). However, Syeikh Tantawi had earlier issued a contradicting *fatwa*, where he declared that interest given by banks was *haram*.

Countries in South East Asia, with the exception of Indonesia, have not discussed the permissibility or prohibition (*halal* or *haram*) of *riba* in detail or depth. In Malaysia, for instance, a complete collection of *fatwa* on *riba*, whether those issued by individuals or organizations, has yet to be published. To date, no scholars and *ulama* have openly declared that bank interest is not *haram*. This does not, however, mean that scholars in Islamic studies, *ulama* (*mufti*), and Religious Councils have never issued any *fatwa* on *riba*. For example, the late Syeikh Alwi bin Tahir al-Haddad, the former *Mufti* of Johore, frequently issued *fatwa* on this matter which were used as a source of reference by the *Mufti* of Brunei. A collection of *fatwa* by Syeikh Alwi was published in *Kumpulan Fatwa-Fatwa Mufti Kerajaan Johor Penggal 1 dan 2*. The staff of the *Mufti* Department of the Government of Brunei Darussalam were among those who had published collections of *fatwa* on matters associated with *muamalat* with a special chapter on the issues of *riba* (Jabatan *Mufti* Kerajaan Brunei, 2000). *Fatwa* on *riba* have been issued by the *Mufti* of Brunei since 1964. Based on the compilations issued from 1962 to 1999, there was no *fatwa* found to be against the views of the mainstream.

The discussions on *riba* by Muslim scholars in Indonesia were conducted on a larger scale compared to Malaysia. Apart from the *fatwa* issued by the scholars, Islamic groups or associations also issued their own *fatwa* on *riba*. Discussions on *riba* in Indonesia were ˙conducted in 1927 by the group, Nadhatul Ulama in Surabaya, and subsequently in Magelang in 1939 and Cilacap in 1981. However, their views on the legality of *riba* were inconsistent. Some contended that *riba* was *haram*, others argued that it was *halal*, while there were also those who declared it to be something of doubt or *syubhah*. Detailed study conducted by Antonio (2004) on the views of the Indonesian society on *riba* had shown inconsistencies in the views among the scholars and *ulama*. These contradictory views continue to this day. In his study, Antonio investigated the opinions of 45 renowned Indonesian scholars and *ulama*, including *ulama* from Muhammadiah, Nadhatul Ulama, Persatuan Islam and Majlis Ulama Indonesia. There was a surprising finding from his study: 24 participants believed that interest paid or imposed by banks was not *haram*. Many were of the view that *riba* was only *haram* if it harmed or hurt the recipient, and that only exorbitant interest was regarded as *riba*. Among the renowned *ulama* and scholars who regarded *riba* as *halal* were Ibrahim Hosen, Abdurrahman Wahid (a former President of Indonesia) and Hasan Basri.

SUMMARY

Islam forbids its followers to accept and give *riba*. This prohibition is clearly stated in the Quran and *Hadith*. Nevertheless, the involvement of humans in interest loans had existed since the Sumerian period. The practice of applying interest on the lending system was then continued by other civilizations such as Babylonian, Assyrian, Neo-Babylonian, Persian, Greek and Roman civilizations. Nonetheless, religions at that time held differing views on this practice of accepting and giving interest. In addition, various views and conceptions were also presented by religious scholars and philosophers of earlier civilizations which at times differed from those of scholars in other civilizations. For example, the original concept of interest was that of compensation on the loss on the part of the creditor resulting from the debtor's failure to repay his debt upon maturity. Today, interest is defined as the additional amount required to be paid by the borrower on repayment of his loan. As for usury, it originally meant "interest". However, when the Christians legalized interest in 1836, usury was regarded as illegal interest or a rate exceeding the legal rate set by the authorities. From the Islamic perspective, *riba* refers to the amount of extra payment made on the principal loan, regardless of the size of the amount borrowed.

Although the Jews were not prohibited from taking interest from foreigners outside the Jews community, they were forbidden from taking interest from their own kind. The Christians, on the other hand, were originally prohibited from charging interest on loans. From the early Christian period until the 12th century, various condemnations were thrown by Fathers of the Church towards those who dealt with interest. In fact, some went to the extent of declaring that those involved in interest were to be ostrasized from the religion. However, the rapid development of trade and commerce in the 12th century changed the conceptions about interest to the extent that some Christian scholars began to view it as legal. Eventually, the discussion on the concept of interest took on various angles including legislative, economic, social and religious perspectives. In time, interest was made permissible in Christianity.

In contrast with other religions, Islam offers a definite guidance which forbids Muslims from dealing with *riba*. The prohibition of *riba* is revealed in four chapters in the Quran. *Hadith* related to *riba* can be classified directive *Hadith*, explanatory *Hadith* and reminder *Hadith*. Guidance given by both sources had prevented any serious conflicting views on *riba* among Muslim scholars. All scholars concurred that *riba* is illegitimate or *haram* regardless of the size of the loan. Furthermore, all types of *riba* are considered illegal regardless of whether they originate from productive loans or consumption loans. Presently, a group of scholars and *ulama*, particularly in Indonesia, proclaimed that interest as practised by conventional banks is not *haram*. The most distinct group voicing this stand are the *ulama* and religious figures in Indonesia. They based their arguments on the grounds that interest is only regarded as *haram* if the amount is exorbitant and it oppresses the debtor. In addition to this point, other reasons for legalizing *riba* were inflation and that lending money creates economic benefits. This is actually perturbing, for these reasons put forward by the Muslim scholars were the very ones given by Christian scholars 500 years ago when they legalized *riba*. If these arguments continue to gain ground, it will hardly come as a surprise if one day all *ulama* were to contend that *riba* is *halal*. If this happens, there will no longer be any difference between Islamic and conventional banks.

REFERENCES AND FURTHER READING

Abu Zahra, Muhammad. *Tahrim ar-riba Tanzim Iqtisadi*. Kuwait: Maktaba Al-Manar, 1955.

Ahmad, Ziauddin. "The Theory of Riba." *Islamic Studies*, Winter (1978): 171–185.

Ahmad, Ziauddin. "The Theory of Riba." In *An Introduction to Islamic Finance*, edited by Syeikh Ghazali Syeikh Abod. Syed Omar and Aidit Ghazali, 56–69. Kuala Lumpur: Quill Publishers, 1992.

Ali, Abdullah Yusuf. *The Holy Qur'an: Text, Translation and Commentary*. Maryland (USA): Amana Corporation, 1989.

Al-Jassas, Al-Hanafi. *The Rules of the al-Quran.* Egypt: al Matba'at al Bahiyyah, 1927.

ALKITAB, Lembaga Alkitab Indonesia. Jakarta, 1988.

Al-Saud, Mahmud Abu. "Islamic View of Riba (Usury and Interest)." In *An Introduction to Islamic Finance,* edited by Syeikh Ghazali Syeikh Abod, Syed Omar and Aidit Ghazali, 70–93. Kuala Lumpur: Quill Publishers, 1992.

Al-Zuhayli, Wahbah. *Financial Transactions in Islamic Jurisprudence.* Vol. 1, translated by Mahmoud A. El-Gamal. Beirut (Lebanon): Dar al-Fikr al-Mouaser, 2003.

Antonio, Muhammad Syafii. *Islamic Banking in Indonesia: A Study of Riba and the Development of the Islamic Banking Industry and Its Role in the Advancement of Small and Micro Financing.* Unpublished PhD dissertation, University of Melbourne, 2004.

Barnhart, Robert K. *The Barnhart Dictionary of Etymology.* USA: The H.W. Wilson Company, 1988.

Boardman, John, Jasper Griffin and Oswyn Murry (eds). *The Oxford History of the Classical World.* Oxford and New York: Oxford University Press, 1986.

Bohm-Bawerk, Eugen Von. *Capital and Interest: Vol. I, History and Critique of Interest Theories,* translated by George D. Huncke and Hans F. Sennholz. Illinois (USA): Libertarian Press South Holland, 1959.

Bohm-Bawerk, Eugen Von. *Capital and Interest: Vol. II, Positive Theory of Capital,* translated by George D. Huncke and Hans F. Sennholz. Illinois (USA): Libertarian Press South Holland, 1959.

Catholic Encyclopedia, The. Vol. 15. New York (USA): Robert Appleton Company, 1912.

Chapra, Muhammad Umar. "The Nature of *Riba* and Its Treatment in the Quran, Hadith and Fiqh." In *An Introduction to Islamic Finance*, edited by Syeikh Ghazali Syeikh Abod, Syed Omar and Aidit Ghazali, 33–55 and 379–391. Kuala Lumpur: Quill Publishers, 1992.

Dempsey, Bernard W. *Interest and Usury*. London (UK): Dennis Dobson Ltd, 1948.

Departemen Agama Republik Indonesia. *Al-Quran dan Terjemahannya*. Jakarta, 1974.

Divine, Thomas F. *Interest: An Historical and Analytical Study in Economics and Modern Ethics*. Milwaukee (USA): The Marquette University Press, 1959.

Encyclopaedia Judaica. Vol. 16. Jerusalem (Israel): Keter Publishing House Jerusalem Ltd., 1972.

Fisher, Irving. *The Theory of Interest*. New York (USA): Kelley & Millman, Inc., 1954.

Gottwald, Norman K. *The Ibrani Bible, A Socio-Literary Introduction*. Philadelphia (USA): Fortress Press, 1985.

Hasting, James. *Encyclopaedia of Religion and Ethics*. Edinburgh (UK): T&T Clark, 1921.

Hitti, Philip K. Islam. A Way of Life. Minneapolis (USA): University of Minnesota Press, 1970.

Holy Bible: New International Version. Michigan (USA): Zondervan Publishing House, 1986.

Homer, Sydney. *A History of Interest Rates*. 2nd ed. New Brunswick (New Jersey, USA): Rutgers University Press, 1977.

Homoud, Sami Hassan. *Islamic Banking: The Adaptation of Banking Practice to Conform with Islamic Law*. London: Arabian Information Ltd., 1985.

Ismail, Abdul Halim. "The Deferred Contracts of Exchange in Al-Quran." In *An Introduction to Islamic Finance*, edited by Syeikh Ghazali Syeikh Abod, Syed Omar and Aidit Ghazali, 284–313. Kuala Lumpur: Quill Publishers, 1992.

Jabatan *Mufti* Kerajaan Brunei. *Fatwa Mufti Kerajaan: Isu-Isu Kewangan*. Brunei Darussalam, 2000.

Jain, L.C. *Indigenous Banking in India*. London: Macmillan & Co., 1929.

Jawish, Abdul Aziz. *al-Islam Din al-Fitrat wa al-Hurriyah*. Cairo (Egypt): Dar al Maaraf, 1908.

Kamus Dwibahasa: Bahasa Inggeris-Bahasa Malaysia. Kuala Lumpur: Dewan Bahasa dan Pustaka, 1985.

Keynes, John Maynard. *The General Theory of Employment, Interest and Money*. London: Macmillan & Co., 1939.

Khan, Mohsin S. and Abbas Mirakhor (eds). "The Framework and Practice of Islamic Banking." In *Theoretical Studies in Islamic Banking and Finance*, 3–13. Houston (USA): Institute for Research and Islamic Studies, 1987.

Khan, Muhammad Muhsin, trans. the Translation of the Meanings of Sahih al-Bukhari, Vol. III. Lahore (Pakistan): Kazi Publication, 1986.

Mallat, Chibli. "Tantawi on Banking Operations in Egypt." In *Islamic Legal Interpretation of Mufti and Their Fatwa*, edited by Muhammad Khalid Masum, Brikley Messick and David S. Powers. Cambridge: Harvard University Press, 1996.

Mannan, Muhammad Abdul. *Islamic Economics: Theory and Practice*. London (UK): Hodder and Stoughton, 1986.

Nelson, Benjamin N. *The Idea of Usury*. Princeton (USA): Princeton University Press, 1949.

Noonan, John T. Jr. *The Scholastic Analysis of Usury*. Cambridge (USA): Harvard University Press, 1957.

Oxford English Dictionary. 2nd ed. Volume VII and Volume XIX. Oxford (UK): Clarendon Press, 1989.

Qutub, Sayid. *In the Shades of the Quran*. London (UK): MWH Publishers, 1979.

Saleh, Nabil A. *Unlawful Gain and Legitimate Profit in Islamic Law: Riba, Gharar and Islamic Banking*. Cambridge (UK): Cambridge University Press, 1986.

Shaltut, Mahmud. *Al-Islam, Aqidah wa Shariah*. Cairo (Egypt): Dar al Shuruq, 1974.

Siddiqi, Hamid, trans. *Sahih Muslim*. Vol. 3 Beirut (Lebanon): Dar al Arabia Publishing, Printing & Distribution, undaled.

Tanner, Norman P. *Decrees of the Ecumenical Councils*. Vol. I and Vol. II. London and Washington: Sheed & Ward and Georgetown University Press, 1990.

Thomas, J.A.C. *Textbook of Roman Law*. Amsterdam (Holland): North-Holland Publishing Company, 1976.

Zakaria, Rafiq. *The Struggle Within Islam: The Conflict Between Religion and Politics*. London (UK): Penguin Books, 1989.

www.americanfinance.com/financing/HistoricalCritiqueUsury.shtm

CHAPTER 5

LAWS AND REGULATIONS OF ISLAMIC BANKING

This chapter discusses the laws and regulations to be complied with and adhered to by an Islamic bank. As institutions based on Islamic doctrines, Islamic banks must operate within the ambit of Islamic principles and laws. In addition, the banks must conform to man-made laws or positive laws.

INTRODUCTION

Islamic banks all over the world are required to comply with two kinds of laws, namely Islamic laws and positive laws. Just as every Muslim individual is required to do what is commanded of him and to avoid what is forbidden in Islam, such is also the case with Islamic banks. The failure to do as recommended by Islamic teachings would mean that the Islamic banks have not yet fully internalized and implemented what is required of them. Hence, using Islamic terminologies or labelling themselves as Islamic banks would be questionable. The Islamic laws which need to be complied with by Islamic banks are known as *Syariah* law. Positive laws, on the other hand, are rules and regulations imposed by the government of the country where the banks operate.

Although Islamic banks are subject to *Syariah* law, this does not mean that there exist specific *Syariah* laws for the control or administration of Islamic banking operations. Today, there does not yet exist an Islamic organization in the world which issues *Syariah* laws containing provisions to cover the total running and operations of an Islamic bank. Nevertheless, all regulations and general guidelines related to the running of Islamic banks are found in the sources of *Syariah* law. *Syariah* law comes from four sources, namely the Quran, *Hadith*, *ijma* and *qiyas*.

Mannan (1986) in his book, *Islamic Economics: Theory and Practice*, stated that the uniqueness of Islam lies in its comprehensive principles which can be certified at all times, for all mankind. Islamic laws as a whole are founded on eternal miracle (*mukjizat*). The meaning of "miracle" here is that the laws are comparable not only with fluctuating laws but also with simple and concise laws. In addition, Islamic laws constantly discover new truths and guidance for every period and level. Guidance is provided to mankind by Allah (s.w.t.) to the Prophet (p.b.u.h.) through divine inspiration (*wahyu*) which is fundamental and eternal. Islamic law is an all-embracing body of religious duties, the totality of Allah's (s.w.t.) commands that regulate the life of every Muslim in all its aspects, including religious practices, politics and legislation (Schacht, 1964). Schacht, an authority on Islamic civilization, opined that Islamic law was created not by an irrational process of continuous revelation but by a rational method of interpretation, which took into consideration both religious standard and moral values.

Maududi (1983) in his book, *Islamic Law and Constitution*, presented the view that the principal objectives of *Syariah* are to construct human life on the basis of *marufat* or virtues and to cleanse it of the *munkarat* or vices. The concept of *marufat* symbolizes all the virtues and good qualities that have been accepted as good by the human conscience. On the other hand, *munkarat* denotes all the sins that have been condemned by human nature as evil. The *Syariah* gives a clear view of these *marufat* and stresses that they are the norms to which individuals and social behaviour must conform.

Positive laws or the laws that are given by a person of authority are distinct from moral and sacred laws given by God or with God's guidance. Positive laws at times refer to Western laws and also secular statutes borrowed by Islamic countries (Saleh, 1986). The use of these Western laws is the result of historical factors; most Islamic countries had at one time or another been colonized by Western powers. Hence, among the legacies of the colonizers are the laws which have been formulated on the basis of laws used in the colonizers' countries. Malaysia, for instance, applies laws which are mostly guided by English laws. Hence, Islamic banks are required to comply with not only *Syariah* law but also these positive laws. In general, most laws that are formulated and imposed on Islamic banks are under the control and supervision of the central bank of the particular country. For example, the establishment of Islamic banks in Malaysia is governed by the *Companies Act 1965* and its operations are subject to the *Islamic Banking Act 1983*. Hence, Islamic banks must conform to all requirements as stipulated in both the acts. Similarly, other governments have passed special laws that govern the operations of Islamic banks in their countries. For example, Islamic banks in Pakistan and Iran are required to comply with not only ordinary laws but also specific laws issued to monitor and regulate Islamic banks.

THE CONCEPT AND MEANING OF *SYARIAH*

The word *Syariah* originates from *syar*, which means "the path or the road leading to the water", and the verb *syara'a* literally means "to chalk out or mark out a clear road to the water". In the religious sense, it means the path to a perfect life or "the highway of good life". In other words, *Syariah* is the way which directs man's life to the right path (Rahman, 1979). From the words "to the right path", came the meaning of "law" (Denny, 1985). The word *Syariah* also has its correlation with the word *din* which means submission or following. *Syariah* is the stipulation of methods or ways and the principal subject is Allah (s.w.t.), while *din* is in compliance with the methods stipulated and the principal subject is man. Hence, one can use the words *Syariah* and *din* interchangeably because both use the stipulations or commands given by way of the Quran (Rahman, 1979).

The concept of *Syariah* encompasses not only the conduct of man in his life towards realizing the Divine Will, but also covers all behaviour – spiritual, mental and physical. This means that the concept of *Syariah* is greater than law, covering all aspects of living including faith and practices, personal behaviour, legal and social matters. In other words, *Syariah* is an all-encompassing, comprehensive principle of a total way of life. Denny (1985) stated that *Syariah* contains all aspects which may positively be termed laws and is the centre of the Islamic legislation system. *Syariah* is something that is perfect and real. *Syariah* also unites and guides Muslims at all times and in all situations. It is brought down from generation to generation and disseminated to all Islamic areas. Further, according to Denny, *Syariah* lifts the spirit and renders a feeling of stability and calm among Muslims.

Ismail (1992) in his elaboration on the origins of Islamic finance and banking, perceived Islam as comprising three basic elements, namely *Aqidah*, *Syariah* and *Akhlaq*. *Aqidah* covers all aspects of belief and faith of Muslims towards Allah (s.w.t.) and His commands. *Syariah* covers all forms of actions or practices of Muslims to demonstrate their belief and faith. *Akhlaq* encompasses aspects of action, behaviour and work ethics of Muslims when performing an action. The *Syariah* aspect may be further divided into two parts, namely *Ibadat* and *Muamalat*. *Ibadat* is concerned with the practicalities of a Muslim's worship of Allah (s.w.t.), while *Muamalat* is about man-to-man relationship. Hence, aspects such as political, economic and social activities, are all under the ambit of *Muamalat*. Since finance and banking activities are part of the economic activities, these activities are therefore linked to *Syariah* principles through *Muamalat*. The relationship between *Syariah* and the Islamic banking system is shown in Figure 5–1.

FIGURE 5–1 Relationship Between Islamic Banking System and Syariah

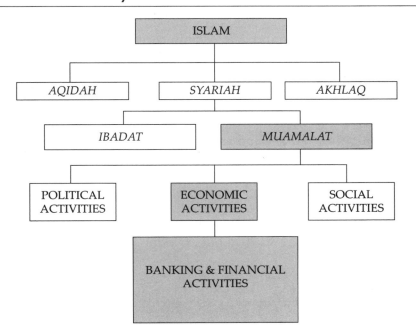

Source: Ismail, 1992, p. 250.

Doi (1984) was of the view that *Syariah* is different from all other laws because the Quran and *Sunnah* are gifts from Allah (s.w.t.) whose value to the *ummah* is beyond any form of comparison. Since the various communities in the *ummah* are collectively responsible for administering justice, Muslims or others living in peace and harmony in Islamic countries have the right not to be violated by any ruler or legislative council. Ali (1950) saw Islam as two parts, theoretical and practical. The theoretical aspects include matters related to faith and its doctrines, and these aspects are called *usul* or the origins of a principle. These theoretical aspects are also commonly termed as *aqa'id* (singular: *aqidah*) which means beliefs. Practical aspects include all that a Muslim is required to do. These practical aspects are known as *furu* (singular: *far*) which means branch; it is also called *ahkam* (singular: *hukm*) which means ordinances or regulations of Islam. Consequently, the existence of Islamic banking system is governed by the practical aspects of Islam and must therefore conform to the *ahkam* of Islam. These aspects may be listed or are found in all Islamic *ahkam*.

There are five types or categories of *ahkam* in *Syariah* law as listed below.

(i) *Fard* or *wajib*

Compulsory duties and acts to be performed by all Muslims. Performance is rewarded and omission is punished.

(ii) *Sunna, masnun, mandub* or *mustahabb*

Duties and acts that are recommended but not required. Performance is rewarded, but omission is not punished.

(iii) *Ja'iz* or *mubah*

Indifferent actions whose performance or omission is neither rewarded nor punishable.

(iv) *Makruh*

Actions that are disapproved but not punished or forbidden.

(v) *Haram*

Actions that are both forbidden and punishable.

SOURCES OF *SYARIAH*

There are four fundamental sources of *Syariah* law. The first source is the Quran, the holy book of the Muslims. The Quran is the authentic and eternal source of *Syariah* law. It constitutes messages that Allah (s.w.t.) presented to the Prophet (p.b.u.h.) for the guidance of mankind. These messages are universal, eternal and fundamental.

The second source of *Syariah* law is the *Hadith*, which is next in importance to the Quran. *Hadith* refers to information, accounts, narratives, stories and records of the *Sunnah* of the Prophet (p.b.u.h.) which have been handed down from generation to generation to become the rule of faith and practice of Muslims. *Sunnah* (plural: *sunan*) describes the customs, habits and usages of the Prophet (p.b.u.h.). It also describes the Prophet's (p.b.u.h.) behaviour, actions, his sayings and declarations under a variety of circumstances in life.

The third source is called *ijma*. *Ijma* means a consensus of opinion of the *mujtahid* or an agreement of Muslim jurists of a particular age on a question of law. *Mujtahid* are learned scholars of Islam or those authorized to exercise independent legal reasoning. The process whereby these experts discuss in full seriousness the solution to a particular religious issue is called *ijtihad*.

The fourth and final source is *qiyas* which literally means "measuring by" or "comparing with" (Ali, 1950). In *Syariah* terms, *qiyas* is the process of reasoning by analogy of the *mujtahid* with regard to difficult and doubtful questions of doctrine or practice, by comparing them with similar cases already settled by the authority of the Quran and *Hadith* and thus arriving at solutions of undecided questions.

Both the Quran and *Hadith* are also known as *al-adillat-al-qatiyyah* meaning absolutely certain arguments of infallible proof. This is because these two sources contain absolute truth and undoubted fundamental doctrines of Islam. These sources are also sometimes referred to as *usul* or the principal root of *Syariah*. *Ijma* and *qiyas* are known as *al-adillat-al-ijtihadiyyah* or arguments obtained by exertion. These two sources are also called *furu* or a branch of *Syariah* law. Within these four frameworks, the *Syariah* law is able to deal with the complexity of today's dynamic world and is capable of handling various conflicting problems of modern life.

The First Source: The Quran

The Quran is the foundation of Islam and is the principal Book on the religion and moral principles. The Quran was revealed by Allah (s.w.t.) to the Prophet (p.b.u.h.) through a process called *wahy matluww* or revelation that is recited. In this case, Gabriel or the Holy Spirit who acted as an intermediary gave directly to the Prophet (p.b.u.h.) divine messages from Allah (s.w.t.). This holy Book consists of 114 chapters of different lengths, called *surah*, each one with its own title. The actual meaning of *surah* is eminence or high degree. The *surah* contain verses which are meant as guidance or communication from Allah (s.w.t.). Without counting *"Bismillah..."* as a verse, there are 6,240 verses in the Quran. However, there exist minor disagreements in opinion in terms of the total number of verses as a result of the different methods used to compute them by centres of Quranic learning (Ali, 1950). According to Doi (1984), the total number of verses in the Quran is 6,666.

In general, the longer *surah* are placed in the earlier part of the Quran. Some of the verses in the *surah* are arranged according to the occurrence of events, while some are grouped according to the matter being discussed. Basically, chapters in the Quran are divided according to the place of revelation. The *surah* revealed in Mecca are called Mecca *Surah* and those revealed in Medina are called Medina *Surah*. According to Ali (1950), 92 *surah* were revealed in Mecca and the rest in Medina.

There are three broad features which distinguish the two revelations. First, Mecca revelation deals chiefly with faith in God and is particularly devoted to grounding Muslims in the faith, while Medina revelation is chiefly intended to translate that faith into action. Secondly, Mecca chapters are generally prophetical, while those from Medina deal with the fulfilment of prophecy. Thirdly, while the Mecca revelation describes how true happiness of mind may be sought in communication with God, the Medina verses point out how man's dealing with man may also be a source of bliss and comfort to him.

The word *Quran* itself is frequently mentioned in the Quran (Q2: 185; Q10: 37 and 61; Q17: 106). Imam Allama Abu-l-Fadzl Jamal al-Din Muhammad ibn Mukarram in his writing, *Lisan al-Arab*, said that the root of the word *Quran* is the word *Qara'a* which means "to put together items". Imam Abu-l-Qasim al-Husain ibn Abu-l-Fadzl al-Raghib in his book, *Al-Mufridat fi Gharibi-l-Quran* stated that the word *Quran* means "to read" or "to verbalize". This is because in reading or verbalizing, letters and words are joined according to certain rules (Ali, 1950). Due to the fact that this Book contains *wahyu* from Allah (s.w.t.) which was revealed to the Prophet (p.b.u.h.) from time to time, it is also known as *Kalam-Allah* or words from Allah (s.w.t.).

The Quran is also known by various other names, and these names are mentioned in a number of verses in the Quran itself. Among them are *al-kitab* (Q2: 2) which means complete writings; *al-Khair* (Q3: 103) which means good; *al-Bayan* (Q3: 137) which means explanation; *al-Burhan* (Q4: 175) which means view; *al-Muhaimin* (Q5: 48) which means guardian; *al-Nur* (Q7: 157) which means light; *al-Mau'izah* (Q10: 57) which means advisor; *al-Shifa* (Q10: 57) which means healer; *al-Hukm* (Q13: 37) which means judge or implementor of rules; *al-Dikra* and *al-Tadhkirah* (Q15: 9) which mean provider of reminders or source of nobility and victory for man; *al-Hikmah* (Q17: 39) which means wisdom; *al-Haqq* (Q17: 81) which means truth; *al-Rahmah* (Q17: 82) which means forgiver; *al-Qayyim* (Q18: 2) which means care-giver; *al-Furqan* (Q25: 1) which means the one that differentiates between truth and falsity and between pure and fake; *al-Tanzil* (Q26: 192) which means statements from up high; *Ahsan-al-Hadith* (Q39: 23) which means the best sayings; *al-Ruh* (Q42: 52) which means the soul of life; and *al-Naimah* (Q93: 11) which means blessings.

Apart from the abovementioned names, there are many more names which can be used to describe the Quran. Among the important issues that Islamic scholars frequently argue about is the interpretation and commentary of the real meaning of the verses of the Quran. The rule for the interpretation of the Quran is given in verse 7, *Surah Ali Imran*.

> *It is He who has sent down to thee the Book: in it are verses basic or fundamental (of established meaning); they are the foundation of the Book: others are allegorical. But those in whose hearts are perversity follow the part thereof that is allegorical, seeking discord, and searching for its hidden meanings, but no one knows its hidden meanings except Allah. And those who are firmly grounded in knowledge say: "We believe in the Book; the whole of it is from our Lord": and none will grasp the Message except men of understanding.* (Q3: 7)

Fundamental (*muhkamaat*) verses are those whose meanings are clear and can be easily understood. Allegorical (*mutasyaabihaat*) verses carry various meanings and the intended meaning cannot be determined unless by in-depth study, and even then the full actual meaning is only known to Allah (s.w.t.). The verse above also provides a clear guideline to those intending to interpret the Quran. Abdullah Yusuf Ali (1872–1948), a renowned interpreter of modern times, believed that the verses can be divided into two parts which are closely interconnected. The first part is the essence or foundation of the holy Book or better known as "the mother of the Book", and the second is the part where the meaning is not so clear. Abdullah Yusuf Ali further said that it is fascinating to seek the meaning of something unclear, using ingenuity to discover the hidden meaning. Nevertheless, such effort requires spiritual elements and its depth is beyond the human language. Those of wisdom may obtain a certain amount of light from it, but nobody should be dogmatic, claiming his interpretation alone to be correct and irrefutable, as only Allah (s.w.t.) alone knows the true meaning of the verses. According to Ali (1950), the most important principle and one which must be borne in mind in interpreting the Quran is that the meaning must be sought within the Quran itself. The interpretation made must not be in conflict with other verses, in particular with the verses whose meanings are clear.

Doi (1984) classified those who produce wrong interpretations into four groups, namely *fasidun*, that is those who cause destruction or disasters; *fasiqun*, those who rebel; *zalimun*, those who do wrong; and *kafirun*, the non-believers. According to Doi, the following characteristics are required of those who wish to interpret the Quran:

- Possess in-depth and detailed knowledge of the Arabic language.

- Possess wide knowledge of *Ilm al-Ma'ani* or rhetorics (the art of using words effectively).

- Possess great, profound and complete knowledge of *Hadith*.

- Able to use knowledge of *Hadith* to identify verses which are unclear in meaning (*mubham*) and to provide an explanation for them in a concise (*mujmal*) manner.

- Highly knowledgeable in *asbab al-Nuzul*, that is, knowledge about the reasons why particular verses were sent down by Allah (s.w.t.).

- Highly knowledgeable in *nasikh* and *mansukh*, that is, knowledge about the abolition of a verse and its replacement by another.

- Highly knowledgeable in *usul al-Fiqh*, that is, knowledge about the origins of Islamic legislation.

- Knowledgeable in *ilm al-Tajwid*, that is, knowledge about the reading of the Quran.

- God-fearing (*taqwa*).

The Second Source: *Hadith*

The word *Hadith* means a story, a narration or a report. The original meaning of the word is "being new" and "occurring, taking place, coming to pass", and extends to talking about or reporting what has happened. Hence, *Hadith* is a narration or report of something which has occurred. These reports or sayings are conveyed to another party through hearing or through revelation. The Quran mentions the word *Hadith* in *Surah* 18, verse 6 and *Surah* 39, verse 23. *Hadith* is also known as tradition since it was passed down from person to person and from generation to generation. In the context of *Syariah*, *Hadith* refers to the *Sunnah* of the Prophet (p.b.u.h.). As a source of *Syariah* law, *Hadith* is used to confirm, verify, extend, elaborate, explain and complement the verses of the Quran.

Sunnah literally means a way or rule or manner of acting or mode of life (Ali, 1950). The Quran also mentions *Sunnah* in general to mean "ways" or "rules". The term *sunnat al-awwalin* is used in several Quranic verses (Q8: 38; Q15: 13; Q18: 55; and Q35: 43) where the term means "the ways or examples from people in the past", and it describes the way Allah (s.w.t.) deals with mankind. Rahman (1979) described the word *Sunnah* as "a trodden path" and each part of the path is considered a *Sunnah*, regardless of its position, whether near to the starting point or remote from it. There are three types of *Sunnah*. The first is *qaul* or the words spoken by the Prophet (p.b.u.h.) which are related to religious issues. The second is *fi'il*, which describes the actions or practices of the Prophet (p.b.u.h.). The third is *taqrir*, which means the Prophet's (p.b.u.h.) silent approval of the actions or practice of another. If He does not forbid someone from performing a certain action, it is taken as the Prophet (p.b.u.h.) agreeing to the action.

The use of *Hadith* as the second most important source in *Syariah* is in agreement with a number of verses in the Quran. In those verses, Allah (s.w.t.) commands the believers to obey Allah (s.w.t.) and His Apostle. The following are examples of such verses.

Allah (s.w.t.) says in Surah Ali Imran, verses 31–32:

> Say: "If ye do love Allah, follow me: Allah s.w.t. will love you and forgive you your sins: for Allah s.w.t. is Oft-Forgiving, Most Merciful."

> Say: "Obey Allah s.w.t. and His Messenger": But if they turn back, Allah s.w.t. loveth not those who reject Faith.   (Q3: 31–32)

In *Surah an-Nisaa*, verse 59, Allah (s.w.t.) says:

> O ye who believe! Obey Allah, and obey the Messenger, And those charged with authority among you. If ye differ in anything among yourselves, refer it to Allah s.w.t. and His Messenger, if ye do believe in Allah s.w.t. and the Last Day: that is best, and most suitable for final determination.   (Q4: 59)

Further, Allah (s.w.t.) says in *Surah al-Hasyr*, verse 7:

> ... So take what the Messenger assigns to you, and deny yourselves that which he withholds from you. And fear Allah; for Allah s.w.t. is strict in Punishment.   (Q59: 7)

After the death of the Prophet (p.b.u.h.), the need to understand the sayings and deeds of the Prophet (p.b.u.h.) gave rise to the widespread usage of the *Hadith* among the Muslim *ummah*. The period in which the *Hadith* was extensively used may be divided into four. The first was the period of the Companions (*Sahabat*); the second period was the time after the Companions or the period of the followers of the Companions; the third was the period after the followers of the Companions. It was in this third period that studies began towards arranging the *Hadith* according to particular groupings. Among the Companions who contributed towards the development of the *Hadith* are as follows (Doi, 1984):

- Companions who narrated more than 1,000 *Hadith*:

  Abu Hurairah 'Abdur Rahman (m. 59 H)   – 5,374 *Hadith*
  AbdAllah s.w.t. bin 'Abbas (d. 68 H)   – 2,660 *Hadith*
  Ummal-Muminin (d. 58 H)   – 2,210 *Hadith*
  'Abdallah s.w.t. bin 'Umar (d. 78 H)   – 1,560 *Hadith*
  Anas bin Malik (d. 93 H)   – 1,286 *Hadith*
  Abu Said Khudri (d. 74 H)   – 1,170 *Hadith*

- Companions who narrated between 500 and 1,000 *Hadith*:

  'Abdallah s.w.t. bin 'Umru bin al-'As (d. 63 H)
  Saydina 'Umar (d. 23 H)
  Saydina 'Ali (d. 40 H)

- Companions who narrated between 100 and 500 *Hadith*:

  Saydina Abu Bakr (d. 13 H)
  Saydina Uthman (d. 36 H)
  Umm Salmah (d. 59 H)
  Abu Musa Ash'ari (d. 52 H)
  Abu Dhar Ghaffari (d. 32 H)
  Abu Ayyub Ansari (d. 51 H)
  Ubayy bin Ka'ab (d. 19 H)
  Mu'adh bin Jabal (d. 18 H)

The second period of the development of the *Hadith* was the period after the Companions, around the middle of the second century of *Hijrah*. Among the followers of the Companions, or the *Tabi'in*, who contributed a great deal to the development of *Hadith* were Said bin Musayyib (d. 105 H), Urwah bin Zubair (d. 94 H), Salim bin 'Abdallah s.w.t. bin 'Umar (d. 106 H), Nafi Maula 'Abdallah s.w.t. bin 'Umar (d. 117 H) and other followers of the Companions such as Muhammad bin Shitab Zuhari (d. 124 H), 'Abdal-Malik bin Jarih (d. 150 H), Imam Auzai (d. 157 H), Ma'mar bin Rashid (d. 153 H), Sufyan al-Thawri (d. 161 H), Hammad bin Salmah (d. 167 H), Abdallah s.w.t. bin Mubarak (d. 181 H) and Imam Malik bin Anas (d. 179 H).

The second period started at the end of the second century of *Hijrah*. During this period, attempts were made to compare the *Hadith* of the Prophet (p.b.u.h.) as reported by the Companions against what was reported by the followers of the Companions. At that time, there were two types of *Hadith*, *Musnad* and *Jami'* or *Musannaf*. *Musnad* comes from the word *sanad* which means authority. The presentation order of *Hadith* based on *musnad* is made according to the names of the first Companions who had narrated the *Hadith*, rather than based on topics. Hence, a *Hadith* has two important elements, that is, *isnad*, which means the link or chain of authority right up to the root source of a *Hadith*, and *matn*, which is the meaning of the content of the *Hadith*. The most important compilation of *Hadith* that followed this method of presentation order is Imam Ahmad ibn Hanbal's (164 H/778–241 H/855) *Musnad*.

Presentation based on *jami'* (something collected together) or *musannaf* (implemented or obeyed together) was carried out later than the *musnad* method. In this method, compilations and presentations were done based on the subject covered in a particular *Hadith*. Some of the most important *Hadith* in this group are those by Imam Muhammad bin Ismail al-Bukhari (d. 256 H/870), Imam Muslim bin Hajjaj al-Qushayri (d. 261 H/875), Imam Abu Daud

Ashath al-Sijistani (d. 275 H/889), Imam Abu Ismail al-Tirmidhi (d. 279 H/893), Imam Muhammad bin Yazid Ibn Majah al-Qazwini (d. 273 H/886) and Imam Ahmad bin Shu'aib al-Nasai (d. 303 H/916).

The third period of the development of the *Hadith* began in the early fifth century of *Hijrah* and continues until today. However, most of the works in this period are in the form of commentaries of earlier works. Among the well-known works are *Miskat al-Masabih* by Wali al-Din al-Khatib, *Riyad al-Salihin* by Abu Zakariya Yahya bin Sharf al-Nawawi (d. 676 H), *Muntaqi al-Akhbar* by Abul Barakat Abdus Salam Ibn al-Taimiyyah (d. 652 H), *Bulugh al-Maram* by Hafiz Ibn Hajar (d. 752 H) and *Subul al-Salam* by Muhammad bin Isma'il (d. 1182 H).

A variety of methods are used by learned scholars in classifying *Hadith* into categories or organizing them into particular groupings. A *Hadith* may be classified according to: the number of narrators who narrated it; the features of the *isnad*, that is the features that link the narrator and the source of the *Hadith*; whether a particular *Hadith* is adopted or rejected; and finally, specific characteristics found in the *isnad* and *matn* of a particular *Hadith*.

The first method of classification that is based on the number of narrators, may be further broken down into the following types:

- *Mutawatir hadith*

  Hadith of this type were narrated by many narrators with no conflict among them.

- *Mashur hadith*

  Hadith of this type were narrated by more than two narrators. Not all *Hadith* of this type can be regarded as *sahih*, that is, not all can be regarded as adoptable or unquestionable in their truth.

- *Aziz hadith*

  This type of *Hadith* came from only one narrator, but this individual was someone who was fully trusted and accepted as a narrator of *Hadith*. The *Hadith* recited by this individual was later taken and narrated by two or three other narrators.

• *Ghaib hadith*

This *Hadith* came from one source, whether from among the Companions or an individual who came later.

• *Fard hadith*

This *Hadith* was narrated by only one narrator at each phase or was only narrated by narrators in the same region.

• *Shadhdh hadith*

This *Hadith* came from only one narrator, but this individual was someone who was fully trusted, and the content of the *Hadith* differed from what was narrated by other narrators.

• *Ahad hadith*

This is a lone *Hadith* and it was narrated by only one narrator.

Under the second method of classification, the *isnad* system, *musnad* is used to group *Hadith* where the *isnad* or link reaches the Prophet (p.b.u.h.) directly. This type of *Hadith* is also called *marfu hadith*, regardless of whether or not the link is broken. *Mawkuf hadith* has at the beginning of its *isnad* the Companions of the Prophet (p.b.u.h.), while *maktu hadith* begins with those after the Companions. The *Hadith* whose *isnad* is not broken is termed *muttasil marfu* if the link reaches up to the Prophet (p.b.u.h.), and *muttasil mawkuf* if it ends with the Companions. *Munfasil,* which means broken or separated, is a *Hadith* with breaks in the link. Imam Shafii and al-Tabrani used the term *munkati* for this type of *Hadith*. If the names of one or two narrators or all the names of the narrators are not mentioned in the *isnad*, then the *Hadith* is termed *mu'Allah s.w.t. hadith*, which means "hanging". *Mursal hadith* is where the narrator after the period of the Companions directly extracted the sayings of the

Prophet (p.b.u.h.) without mentioning the name of the Companion concerned. *Mu'allal* or *ma'lul hadith* is a *Hadith* which is weak or defective in terms of its *isnad* or *matn*.

The third method, based on whether the *Hadith* can be adopted or rejected, is frequently used. A *Hadith* can be accepted if it falls into one of the categories of *makbul, maruf* or *mahfuz*. *Makbul hadith* is one that fulfils all conditions for adoption, and is generally known as *sahih* and *hasan*. *Maruf hadith* (can be accepted) is a *Hadith* that is somewhat weak but is verified by other *Hadith* of the same standing. *Mahfuz hadith* (fixed in the mind) is of higher standing than *shadhdh hadith*.

Hadith which are rejected are those from the group of *mardud, munkar, matruk, matruh* and *mawdu*. *Mardud hadith* is a *Hadith* which is a contrast to *makbul*; its narrators were weak or unknown and its narration differs from what was narrated by those who were trusted. *Munkar hadith* (ignored) is a *Hadith* narrated by only one narrator and differs from what had been narrated by those who were trusted. *Matruk hadith* (disregarded) came from a narrator known to be a liar or someone who openly behaved immorally and told lies. *Matruh hadith* (discarded) is of the same standing as *matruk*. *Mawdu hadith* (imaginary) is a *Hadith* which had been purposely made up, and of all the rejected *Hadith*, this is of the lowest type and as such is regarded as dangerous.

The fourth method which groups *Hadith* based on specific characteristics found in the *isnad* and *matn* is seldom used. Narrators of this type of *Hadith* had the tendency to add their own words; or to speak on the basis of oath or word of honour, etc. In terms of *Syariah*, not all *Hadith* can be used as a source for formulating laws. *Hadith* in the category of *sahih* (sound) are the primary source of *Syariah* law. *Sahih hadith* are normally broken down into seven main classes as follows:

(i) *Hadith* compiled by both Imam Bukhari and Imam Muslim.

(ii) *Hadith* compiled by Imam Bukhari only.

(iii) *Hadith* compiled by Imam Muslim only.

(iv) *Hadith* not compiled by Imam Bukhari or Imam Muslim but possess the *shurut* (conditions) of both.

 (v) *Hadith* which satisfy the *shurut* of Imam Bukhari.

(vi) *Hadith* which possess the *shurut* of Imam Muslim.

(vii) *Hadith* which are reliable and are compiled by other groups which can be trusted.

The second group of *Hadith* which can be used as a source in formulating law is *hasan* (fair). This kind of *Hadith* is not considered very strong, yet it is necessary for establishing a point of law. Most of the *Hadith* concerning legal matters are of this type. The final category of *Hadith* is *daif* (weak) or *sakim* (infirm). A *Hadith* of this type is not acceptable for making rulings although it may be used to strengthen a *hasan hadith* if it has similar narration. However, the usage is considered appropriate only if it deals with exhortations, stories and good behaviour.

Apart from the *Hadith* described above, there is one other type of *Hadith* which is called *kudsi hadith* or sometimes known as *ilahi hadith* or *rabbani hadith*. This type of *Hadith* is different from the *nabawi hadith* which is taken from the *Sunnah* of the Prophet (p.b.u.h.). This *Hadith* contains Allah's (s.w.t.) *wahyu* (divine revelation). Not all *wahyu* from Allah (s.w.t.) was sent to the Prophet (p.b.u.h.) through the angel Gabriel. There were some *wahyu* acquired by the Prophet (p.b.u.h.) through inspiration and dreams. The biggest compilation of *kudsi hadith* was produced by Muhammad al-Madani (d. 881 H/1476) in his book *al-Ithafat al-saniyya fi 'l-ahadith al-kudsiyya*.

The Third Source: *Ijma*

Ijma (consensus) was originally the agreement of qualified legal scholars in a particular generation, and such a consensus of opinion is deemed infallible. The emergence of the concept of *ijma* as a source of law is in line with one *Hadith* which states:

"My umat will never agree upon an error."

Imam Shafii was the first person to introduce this concept as a source of law after the Quran and *Hadith*. He refuted that the agreement reached by Islamic scholars in a certain district cannot be used for the whole Muslim *ummah*. Instead, Imam Shafii was of the view that there exists only one agreement, which is the agreement reached by the whole Muslim *ummah*. *Ijma* of this kind must be adhered to and is called *ijma* of the society. Rahman (1979) regarded *ijma* as absolutely authoritative not only for discerning the right at present and in the future but also in the past. *Ijma* also establishes what the *sunnah* of the Prophet (p.b.u.h.) had been and indeed what the right interpretation of the Quran is. *Ijma* among the Muslims is not an agreement that can be achieved easily; it must be arrived at by *ijtihad* or exertion. *Ijtihad* is a conscientious examination and meditation on the subject under consideration. The desired consensus is normally achieved in three ways. First, it could be reached by agreement of words or declaration of opinion in words; secondly, by agreement of act, practice or expressed in unanimity of action or practice; and thirdly, agreement of silence or tacit assent by silence or by non-interference. In addition, there is overall consensus where all parties agree to the decision made.

Mujtahid (learned scholars) who are involved in the process must be men of honesty and of integrity. Their minds must not be iniquitous (*fasiq*) or blinded by passion (*hawa*). In general, there are three classes of *mujtahid* who are given this responsibility. The first is the absolute *mujtahid* who has absolute authority and whose sphere of exertion embraces the whole law. The second is the *mujtahid* from a particular *mazhab* or special school of theology who is an authority within the sphere of one of the special theological systems. The last is the *mujtahid* of special questions and cases which have not been decided or resolved by any of the *mazhab* in the past.

The Fourth Source: *Qiyas*

The final source of *Syariah* law is *qiyas*. The actual meaning of *qiyas* is "measuring by" or 'comparing with". In short, *qiyas* is an approach to solve difficult and confusing problems associated with issues of doctrines or religious practices. The approach uses wisdom of thought, by seeking realistic reasons and rationale and comparing the problem at hand with similar problems which have in the past already been resolved by the Quran and *Hadith*.

This approach of using reasoning or the exercise of judgement, in theological as well as in legal matters, plays a vital part in Islam and the Quran clearly recognizes this process as stressed by Allah (s.w.t.) in *Surah An-Nisaa*, verse 83 (Q4: 83) as follows:

> *When there comes to them some matter touching (public) safety or fear, they divulge it. If they had only referred it to the Messenger, or to those charged with authority among them, the proper investigators would have tested it from them (direct). Were it not for the Grace and Mercy of Allah unto you, all but a few of you would have followed Satan.*   (Q4: 83)

Abu-l-Faidz Sayyid Muhammad Murtadza al-Husaini in his book *Taj al-Arus*, stated that the authentic word for "seeking knowledge" is *yastanbitun*. This word originates from the word *istanbat* which is taken from the word *nabat al-bi'ra* which means "he digs a well to bring out water". Hence, the word *istanbat* used among the *mujtahid* is taken to mean "to seek and acquire meanings or hidden meanings through the process of *ijtihad*" and this applies also to the solution acquired through *qiyas* or comparisons (Ali, 1950). Those who do not use their reasoning faculty are compared to animals and are regarded as deaf, dumb and blind. Allah (s.w.t.) clearly states this in *Surah al-Baqarah*, verse 171 (Q2: 171):

> *The parable of those who reject Faith is as if one were to shout like a goat-herd, to things that listen to nothing but calls and cries: deaf, dumb and blind, they are void of wisdom.*   (Q2: 171)

Similarly, it is stated in *Surah al-A'raaf*, verse 179 (Q7: 179):

> *Many are the Jinns and men We have made for Hell: they have hearts*
> *wherewith they understand not, eyes wherewith they see not, and ears*
> *wherewith they hear not. They are like cattle – nay more misguided:*
> *for they are heedless (of warning).*   (Q7: 179)

Verse 22 of *Surah al-Anfaal* (8: 22) also explains:

> *For the worst of beasts in the sight of Allah s.w.t. are the deaf and the*
> *dumb – those who understand not.*   (Q8: 22)

The deaf and the dumb in the verse above are those people who
refuse to listen, utter or express, and understand the truths regarding
Allah (s.w.t.). Further, in *Surah al-Furqan*, verse 44 (Q25: 44), Allah
(s.w.t.) says:

> *Or thinkest thou that most of them listen or understand? They are*
> *only like cattle – nay, they are worse astray in Path.*   (Q25: 44)

While condemning those who do not exercise their reason or
judgement, Allah (s.w.t.) praises those who perform *ijtihad* and use
their wisdom. This is evident in *Surah Ali Imran*, verses 190 and 191
(Q3: 190 and 191) which say:

> *Behold! In the creation of the heavens and the earth, and the alternation*
> *of Night and Day – there are indeed signs for men of understanding*
> *– Men who celebrate the Praises of Allah, standing, sitting, and lying*
> *down on their sides, and contemplate the (wonders of) creation in the*
> *heavens and the earth, (with the thought): "Our Lord! Not for naught*
> *hast Thou created (all) this! Glory to Thee! Give us salvation from the*
> *Penalty of the Fire."*   (Q3: 190 and 191)

It is also reported that the Prophet (p.b.u.h.) himself sanctioned
and encouraged reasoning and the exerting of the faculties of

one's mind in order to find the proper solutions for difficult and doubtful   cases of law. The Prophet (p.b.u.h.) is reported by Abu Daud in his *sunan* to have approved Mu'adh's answer that he would use his own considerations in the event that a solution cannot be found in the Quran and *Hadith*. In another *Hadith*, it was reported that the Prophet (p.b.u.h.) had said:

> *When a judge gives a decision, having tried his best to decide correctly and is right, there are two rewards for him; and if he gave a judgement after having tried his best (to arrive at a correct decision) but erred, there is one reward for him.*   (Siddiqi, Vol. 3, p. 930)

The above *Hadith* proves that Muslims need not worry or be afraid to perform *ijtihad*. This is because Islam acknowledges and accepts the possibility of Muslims erring in making decisions. Following this, there will probably exist differences of opinion between one generation and another. Normally, there are four aspects that need to be considered in *qiyas*. First, the matter at hand; secondly, the matter to be used for comparison; thirdly, the similarities that exist between the two matters; and fourthly, the decision made through the process of comparison. Use of the *qiyas* method needs to comply with certain conditions, which are:

(i) The definition or practice which will be created is general in nature and its use is not for something specific.

(ii) The reasons for a particular prohibition or command must be known and understood.

(iii) The decision made must be based on the Quran or *Hadith*.

(iv) The decision reached must not be in conflict with verses in the Quran and *Hadith*.

GENERAL LAWS OF *SYARIAH* IN ISLAMIC BANKING SYSTEM

The fundamental goal of *Syariah* is to construct life on the basis of virtues and to cleanse it of vices. Consequently, *Syariah* is expected to provide not only the right path, but also to govern all activities of Muslims towards the betterment of the whole *ummah*, including attaining rewards in the Hereafter. In reality, instead of being governed by the *Syariah*, Muslims are constantly bound by customary and positive laws. This situation which prevails in modern times commenced during the mediaeval age of Islam when the *Syariah* was frequently set aside by orders of the Caliphs and governors, particularly in matters related to commerce.

The absence of *Syariah* to govern the activities of Muslims has given rise to a new dimension in the status of the relationship between Muslims and *Syariah*. The status of this relationship has become mere moral ties rather than legislative bonds. This state of affairs occurs even in the Islamic banking system. The moral relationship is usually based on the principles given by the Quran and *Hadith*. The Quran is primarily a book of religious and moral principles and exhortations. Although the Quran is not a legal document, nevertheless, it embodies important legal enunciations. Mannan (1986) opined that if in the modern context laws are regarded as what man formulates, the Quran does not carry that meaning and neither is it the essence of ethics. Instead, the Quran contains basic principles and focuses on noble qualities, and on the journey and state of man for attaining mercy and bounty when they are knowledgeable of the principles. Abd al-Wahhab ibn Khallaf, a scholar from Egypt, according to Zakaria (1989), had produced classification of legal provisions found in the Quran. The essence of the verses relates to the key aspect of a particular matter, although there is no clear elaboration. This relevance to laws covers aspects such as sources of laws, constitutional provision, international law, etc. The breakdown is as follows:

- Source of laws   : 50 verses

- Constitutional provisions   : 10 verses

- International law   : 25 verses

- Jurisdiction and procedures   : 13 verses

- Penal law   : 30 verses

- Civil law   : 70 verses

- Family and personal law   : 70 verses

- Financial and economic directives : 20 verses

In relation to Islamic banking system, the Quran has given clear and explicit guidelines that such operations must be free from all elements of *riba*. As an ordinary business entity, Islamic bank is expected to conform to the rules and guidelines given by the Quran on conducting its business. For example, Islamic banks are required to fulfil their obligations to their shareholders, depositors, business partners, borrowers and other customers. This instruction is clarified by Allah (s.w.t.) in *Surah al-Baqarah*, verse 177 (Q2: 177), *Surah al-Ma'idah*, verse 1 (Q5: 1), *Surah an-Nahl*, verse 91 (Q16: 91) and *Surah al-Israa'*, verse 34 (Q17: 34). Islamic banks are also expected to uphold trust, justice and fairness in their dealings as urged in the Quran by verses 58 and 135 of *Surah an-Nisaa'* (Q4: 58 and 135), verses 8 and 87 of *Surah al-Ma'idah* (Q5: 8 and 87), verse 152 of *Surah al-An'am* (Q6: 152), verse 90 of *Surah an-Nahl* (Q16: 90), verse 35 of *Surah al-Isra'* (Q17: 35), verse 8 of *Surah al-Mu'minun* (Q23:8), verses 8 and 9 of *Surah al-Rahman* (Q55: 8 and 9) and verses 32 and 33 of *Surah al-Ma'arij* (Q70: 32 and 33).

The Quran also provides guidance to Islamic banks for dealing with those who borrow from them. This is found in *Surah al-Baqarah*, verse 280 (Q2: 280) and *Surah Ali Imran*, verse 75 (Q3: 75). In terms of business procedures, the Quran prescribes details regarding the prosecution of contracts and other covenants involved in contracts.

This is stated in *Surah al-Baqarah*, verses 282 and 283 (Q2: 282 and 283). Islamic banks are forbidden from venturing into businesses which are unproductive or non-beneficial, as stated in *Surah al-Baqarah*, verse 188 (Q2: 188). In addition, Islamic banks are prohibited from having dealings with businesses which promote obscenity or which involve the manufacturing, selling and transporting of liquor, the making and selling of idols and services rendered in or to pagan places of worship, fortune telling and gambling, prostitution, and businesses involving usury and bribery. These prohibitions are proclaimed through verse 188 and verses 275 to 280 of *Surah al-Baqarah* (Q2: 188, 275–280), verse 130 of *Surah Ali Imran* (Q3: 130), verses 42 and 90 of *Surah al-Ma'idah* (Q5: 42 and 90) and verse 19 of *Surah al-Nur* (Q24: 19).

There are also many *Hadith* especially in the *sahih* category which are very relevant and serve as guidelines to Islamic banking system. Among the most important *Hadith* are the ones that forbid the taking of *riba*. Apart from that, there are also many other *Hadith* in the areas of sales, *salam* (sale in which a price is paid for goods to be delivered later); renting, *hiwalah* (transfer of a debt from one person to another); representation; lending; payment of loans; freezing of property; bankruptcy; partnership; mortgaging; witnesses and conditions of transactions. These *Hadith* are an important source of reference for Islamic banks in their daily operations.

The concepts of *ijma* and *qiyas* are becoming increasingly important in formulating new *Syariah* laws in today's modern business world, especially in finance and banking. These concepts should be taken seriously by Islamic scholars and jurists due to four main reasons. The first reason is based on the concept of *Syariah* itself which contains issues of legislation and religion. Matters related to religion are based on spiritual experience. Belief in Allah (s.w.t.) and the Prophet (p.b.u.h.) and other aspects involving belief and faith (*iman*) are not exchangeable. However, matters involving legislation are based on needs and desires of society as stated through laws passed by the government or other law-making authorities. Laws differ between countries and periods. According to Fyzee (1982), laws can never be permanently static because only non-living things are static. The changes that take place are the results of man's control over situations, their views and perceptions about life, and their desire to improve their living status. Many believe that what have been established should be adhered to and not be amended. However, this statement is something which should be re-evaluated and its truth re-examined. This echoes Allah's (s.w.t.) words in *Surah Ali-Imran*, verse 7 (Q3: 7). This verse can be interpreted to mean that laws can be changed, while matters related to religion are eternal and are not amendable.

Secondly, Islam has already set a very high ethical goal which requires each of its followers to achieve the standard it has set. Every regulation and legislation formulated is something that approaches the level of perfection. Islam also encourages its followers to determine the essentials that they need to have in life in order to reach that level of perfection. Once the essentials have been determined then the method to achieve them must be provided based on current situations. All this proves that Islam is unambiguous and easy to understand; and has the capacity to be constantly renewed and revived, fitting to the time and situation.

The third reason lies on the basis of what had occurred during the time of the Prophet (p.b.u.h.). During this period, the laws available, through the Quran or the Prophet's (p.b.u.h.) *Sunnah* were only civil laws which were much needed by the society then. The regulations and legislation were minimal and what were given illustrate that Islam outlines the necessary guidelines fitting to the situations. This clearly implies that Islam prefers or encourages its followers to seek methods for resolving issues that are apt to the time and situation at hand. In doing so, the Muslim *ummah* will continuously increase and expand their knowledge, and use their expertise and intelligence. All these actions and practices would eventually benefit the whole of the Muslim *ummah*.

The fourth reason which makes it possible for the concepts of *ijma* and *qiyas* to become increasingly important in shaping *Syariah* legislation is seen through the lessons learnt from the teachings of the Prophet (p.b.u.h.). Mahmasni (1982) believed that the teachings of the Prophet (p.b.u.h.) do not restrain the Muslim *ummah* except in matters related to religion, moral and other matters associated with them. He further argued that Muslims are not obligated to follow the *Hadith* on the opinions of the Prophet (p.b.u.h.) related to everyday living. To back his view, Mahmasni extracted a *Hadith* which reported the Prophet (p.b.u.h.) to have passed an orchard, where several people were conducting pollination on date palms, and the Prophet (p.b.u.h.) asked: *"What are the people doing?"* Upon being told what the farmers were doing, the Prophet (p.b.u.h.) said: *"If they don't do it, the plants will flourish."* On hearing this, the farmers left their task and as a result the dates did not ripen. When the Prophet (p.b.u.h.) was told of this outcome, he said:

> *I am but an ordinary man; if I instruct you to perform anything related to religion, you are obligated to conform to it. However, if I ask you to do something based on my opinion, I am but human. You have better knowledge in matters related to your living.*
>
> (Mahmasani, 1982, p. 186)

Based on the above *Hadith*, some are of the views that there is no connection between Islam and everyday living except in matters of religion. Issues of religion cover matters of belief and faith, practices to enhance belief and faith, as well as moral principles and regulations, and legislative basis for certain actions.

In conclusion, the role played by *ijma* and *qiyas* is to specify, whether in terms of theory or practice, legislative issues related to the actions of Muslims and at the same time make known the commands stipulated by the Quran and *Hadith*. In other words, both these sources have the role of *dalil sharia* or evidence of *Syariah* in matters of *mualamat*, without touching issues of *ibadat* or *i'tikadat*. Nuwayhi (1982) stated that there are groups who are highly fanatic with their views that the Quran, *Hadith* and all the four *mazaahib* have already projected and provided answers to every issue that exists in modern legislation and regulations. This view in actuality demonstrates two facets of ignorance. First, it shows their ignorance in modern legislation which is filled with a range of aspects, of very wide coverage and of varied interpretations. Secondly, they are ignorant of the fact that Islamic legislative system itself took a long time to develop and that it passed through various processes based on needs and situations.

Nevertheless, *Syariah* law must comply with certain fundamental principles. Doi (1984) stated that the basis of *Syariah* principles may be summarized as follows:

(i) Interest of society is of higher priority compared to individual interest.

(ii) Although both overcoming suffering and encouraging profit or benefit are the foremost objectives of *Syariah*, overcoming suffering is given more importance.

(iii) A big loss cannot be tolerated with the intention to avoid a small loss, or a big profit cannot be sacrificed for the sake of obtaining a small profit. Similarly, a small loss may be accepted in order to avoid a bigger loss, or a small profit may be sacrificed for the sake of obtaining a bigger profit.

SPECIFIC *SYARIAH* LAWS RELATED TO ISLAMIC BANKING SYSTEM

In reality, no Muslim country has yet to formulate a law founded on *Syariah* for its banking system. This is due to the fact that the ones formulating laws are people, and these people would look at it from the perspective of current situations. So eventually the law formulated becomes positive law or man-made law. Although formulating a complete set of *Syariah* laws for Islamic banking has a long way to go, it is something that must be done continuously. Among the earliest systematic *Syariah* law related to *muamalat* or business is *MajAllah s.w.t. el-Ahkam-I-Adliya* or more commonly known as *The Mejelle*. These laws were developed during the period between 1869 and 1876 upon the wish of the Uthmaniyyah Sultan of Turkey who had wanted to implement a process of renewal called *Tanzimat* or restructuring. This legislation was to replace the *Penal Code of 1850* and *Commercial Code of 1861* which were created based on European laws. The formulation efforts were carried out by the Legislative Commission headed by Ahmad Djevdet Pasha who was the Minister of Justice at that time. On completion, *The Mejelle* contained 16 books (or parts) and 1,851 articles. Only the first 12 books had relevance to business, while the last four books (books 13 to 16) were related to matters of procedure and evidencing in court. The introduction or *mukkaddime* had 100 articles which functioned as a guide to judges and lawyers in making decisions or providing views on a matter being discussed. The books in *The Mejelle* which had relevance to business are as follows:

- Book 1 (7 chapters): Sale and purchase (*'bai*)

- Book 2 (8 chapters): Rent/hire (*ijarah*)

- Book 3 (3 chapters): Security/guarantee (*kafalah*)

- Book 4 (2 chapters): Transfer of debt (*hiwalah*)

- Book 5 (4 chapters): Pawn/lease (*rahn*)

- Book 6 (3 chapters): Trusteeship of property (*emanet*)

- Book 7 (2 chapters): Gift (*hibah*)

- Book 8 (2 chapters): Breach of trust and destruction

- Book 9 (3 chapters): Restriction, compulsion and advancement

- Book 10 (8 chapters): Corporatization and partnership

- Book 11 (3 chapters): Representative or agency (*wakalah*)

- Book 12 (4 chapters): Solution and release

Even though *The Mejelle* was certified by the Uthmaniyyah Sultanate, the laws were not regarded as binding. This was because the judges were free to make their own decisions. Eventually, on 17 February 1926, the Turkish government decided to use new laws based on the *Swiss Code* and with that *The Mejelle* was no longer applied. When Islamic banks were established, efforts began in the search for *Syariah* which had relevance to the Islamic banking system. Up until today, there is still no law formulated specifically for this purpose, even if, at the very least, to match *The Mejelle*. In fact, there is yet no publication that covers the scope of what *Syariah* upholds, that is, development of laws with considerations from the angles of the Quran, *Hadith*, *ijma* and *qiyas*. Although there are several publications and writings of intellectuals which touch on the issues of *Syariah* and Islamic banking, these writings only touch the surface. One example is the writings of Syafii Antonio, who tried to promote the basis of rules which are related to the *Syariah* principles used. It is cited that, for instance, the *musyarakah* principle has as its basis *Surah an-Nisa*, verse 12 and *Surah Shad*, verse 24. Meanwhile, the *Hadith* which has relevance to the *musyarakah* principle is the *Hadith* narrated by Abu Daud and compiled by Hakeem in the book *al-Buyu*; and from the angle of *ijma* it is the one from Ibnu Qudamah in the book *al Mughni*.

Apart from this, there are other literature which may be regarded as initial efforts to promote *Syariah* in Islamic banking in Malaysia. For example, Abdul Halim El-Muhammady in 2001 wrote a general reading material titled *Muamalat Laws & Their Application to Islamic Banking Products*. Although it is not considered a law book, the effort may pave the way for more substantial literature with various comparative sources. In addition to writings, there are also publications of *fatwa* related to Islamic banking. These include *fatwa* by Fiqh Academy OIC, *fatwa* by the Syariah Advisory of the Securities Commission of Malaysia and *fatwa* by the Fatwa Council of Bank Muamalat Indonesia. These *fatwa* could be used as the basis for *ijma*. Nevertheless, creating a comprehensive *Syariah* law is not an easy task. The endeavour requires sacrifice from all parties, especially the government. The aspects of Islamic banking legislation required to be developed encompass the following:

- The relationship between the bank and its customers (interpretation of a bank and customer, responsibility to be fulfilled, contracts involved, customer as business partner, bank as trustee, representative and chargee, etc.).

- The aspects of legislation underlying the products and services offered by the bank to its customers (the tasks of receiving money, cheque collection and payment, money order remittance services within and out of the country, tasks related to travellers cheques and foreign exchange).

- The aspects of legislation related to customers and the types of customers (types of customers, accounts which could be opened by customers, closure and methods of account management).

- Duties and responsibilities of the bank as issuer and collector of customers' funds (the processes of cheque cashing, cheque collection, responsibility to pay or return the cheque which has been cashed, negotiation and assigning a value to a cheque).

- Legal action on customers (the right to take action, when the action can be taken and method of action, process of securities sale and dissolution).

- Aspects of financing (business that could be financed, form of financing and amount, properties that could be accepted as securities and the process of approving the securities).

- Aspects of guarantee and representatives (the rights of guarantors and representatives, responsibilities that must be fulfilled, release of responsibility and compensation claims, if any).

POSITIVE LAWS AND REGULATIONS

Basically, there is no uniform law to be followed by Islamic banks throughout the world. In most Islamic countries, special laws are formulated and passed prior to the establishment of the Islamic bank. These laws would normally specify the rules and regulations to be followed by institutions wishing to engage in banking business based on Islamic principles. The laws created are at times general in form, meant for the monitoring of all the Islamic banks in a country, and then there are also laws which are specific. The specific laws are usually created to meet the needs of a particular bank only, and its jurisdiction does not cover all other Islamic banks.

In Malaysia, however, the *Islamic Banking Act 1983* was passed by Parliament prior to the establishment of Bank Islam Malaysia Berhad and this Law applies to any Islamic banking institution wishing to operate in Malaysia. The Law consists of eight parts as follows:

  (i) Short title, commencement, application and interpretation.

 (ii) Provisions related to licensing.

(iii) Financial requirements and duties.

(iv) Matters related to ownership, control and management.

 (v) Restrictions on business.

(vi) Powers of supervision and control.

(vii) Miscellaneous matters such as indemnity, priority of sight and savings account liabilities and penalties on directors and managers.

(viii) Provision for consequential amendments that need to be made to other related Acts to enable Islamic banks to carry out their operations.

In Turkey, the decision to allow Islamic banks to operate is contained in the *Decree 83/7506* issued in December 1983 and published in the *Official Gazette No. 18256* dated 19 December 1983. The decree contains 17 articles and deals with the method and procedures of the establishment of "Special Finance Houses", their activities and liquidation, under the Protection of the Exchange Value of the Turkish *Currency Law No. 1567* and *Decree No. 70* regarding banks. More comprehensive rules and regulations for Islamic banks were formulated by the Undersecretariat of the Treasury and Foreign Trade and published in the *Official Gazette No. 18232* on 25 February 1984. In it are 35 articles covering the founding structure, operation and liquidation of the Special Finance Houses. The decree also covers matters such as the minimum amount of capital required to set up a finance house and the types of accounts that the finance house may offer to the public (Baldwin, 1990). Special Finance Houses gained the "bank" status when the *Banking Law No. 5411* was enacted in November 2005. Pursuant to this Law, Special Finance Houses were renamed "Participation Banks". In Egypt, a special act was passed for the purpose of establishing a particular bank. Faisal Islamic Bank of Egypt for instance, was established under the *Special Act (No. 48) 1977*. This Act outlines various privileges for this bank and confers on it full authority beyond any influence from government agencies, with the exception of the central bank. Again, when the Islamic International Bank for Investment and Development wanted to be incorporated in 1980, a special ministerial decree was issued in accordance with the *Investment Law of Arab and Foreign Funds* and *Free Zones Law (No. 43)*

1974 (El-Ashker, 1990). In 2006, the Islamic International Bank for Investment and Development was merged with the United Bank of Egypt and Nile Bank to form a new entity called the United Bank.

In Jordan, the establishment of Jordan Islamic Bank was within the ambit of the *Temporary Special Law (No. 13) 1978*. The enactment of the *Banking Law No. 28* of 2000 which was published in the *Official Gazette No. 4448* dated 1 August 2000 as amended by *Temporary Law No. 46* of 2003 and published in the *Official Gazette No. 4600* dated 1 June 2003, outlines the definition of an Islamic bank, its objectives, activities the bank may carry out and other conditions and restrictions as imposed by the central bank. The *Banking Law*, among others, states that the Islamic banks in Jordan may carry out activities such as the following (www.cbj.gov.jo):

- Accept monetary deposits in various types of accounts including credit accounts, mutual fund accounts or private investment accounts.

- Issue Islamic bonds or *sukuk*.

- Carry out finance and investment activities that are in accordance with *Syariah* principles.

- Carry out all traditional interest-free banking acitivities in accordance with the law and regulations as set out and permitted by the Central Bank of Jordan.

In Kuwait, a special government decree which recognized the Islamic nature of banking was passed by the government before the establishment of Kuwait Finance House on 23 March 1977 (Wilson, 1990). With the amendment of the *Central Bank of Kuwait Law (Act No. 32/1968)* in 2003, Islamic banks in Kuwait are now regulated by the Central Bank of Kuwait. The Law provides the regulatory and supervisory framework for Islamic banking as well as the framework for *Syariah* governance. Under *Article 93* of the Law, Islamic banks in Kuwait are required to establish an independent Syariah Supervisory Board when applying for registration.

However, the Board reports directly to the Ministry of Awqaf and Islamic Affairs, and not the Central Bank.

Although both Iran and Pakistan have converted their entire banking system to the Islamic banking system, there are no similarities in the banking laws in these two countries. In Iran, as a result of the revolution in 1979, the banking system was nationalized and the *Law for Usury-Free Banking* was passed in parliament in August 1983. This Law is broadly divided into four chapters: (i) Aims and duties of the banking system; (ii) The mobilization of monetary resources; (iii) The granting of facilities; and (iv) The Central Bank of the Islamic Republic of Iran and the monetary policies (Herdayati, 1993). Although Iran has introduced a specific law for the Islamic banking system, it does not mean that all previous laws which regulated the banking system are no longer operative. Instead, all provisions in the *Money and Banking Law 1972* which do not violate the principles set forth in the new law remain effective (Shojaeddini, 1993).

Unlike Iran, Pakistan does not have a comprehensive single law which deals with Islamic banks. The process of Islamization of the whole banking system was done gradually and the rules and regulations on this matter are given on a continuing basis. The rules and regulations are usually issued in the form of declarations made by the Finance Minister and circulars issued by the State Bank of Pakistan. For example, *BCD Circular No: 13* issued by the State Bank of Pakistan in 1984 calls for the elimination of *riba* from the banking system. A similar instruction was given to the deposit facilities. The permissible modes of financing together with the possible modes of financing for various transactions were also given in this circular (Siddique, 1985). The Finance Minister also made an announcement about *Mudharabah Companies and Mudharabah (Floating and Control) Ordinance* on 26 June 1980. In January 1981 another announcement was made on *Mudharabah Companies and Mudharabah Rules 1981* (Gieraths, 1990). However, the procedure adopted by banks in Pakistan since the country pursued its Islamization process in 1985 was declared un-Islamic by the Federal Shariat Court in November 1991. Subsequently, laws involving interest which were introduced since 1985 were declared invalid and ceased to have effect as from 1 July 1992. This decision was upheld by the Supreme Court of Pakistan in December 1999. In response to this development, the State Bank of Pakistan issued detailed criteria for setting up Islamic banks in December 2001. In September 2002, *Section 23* of the *Banking Companies Act 1962* was amended in order to allow Islamic banks to establish Islamic banking subsidiaries. In January 2003, the State Bank of Pakistan issued *BPD Circular No. 01* which outlines detailed policies for the promotion of Islamic banking in the country. Among others, the Circular contained guidelines for the establishment of subsidiaries and stand-alone branches for Islamic banking by existing commercial banks. In September of the same year, the State Bank of Pakistan established an Islamic Banking Department with the task of promoting and developing Islamic banking in the country. Presently, Islamic banks in Pakistan operate under the existing laws and regulations of conventional banks.

Initially, Indonesia did not have a specific law governing the operations of its *Syariah* banks. When Bank Muamalat Indonesia, the first Islamic bank in Indonesia, was established on 1 November 1991 and began operations on 1 May 1992, there was no specific law that governed its operations. Instead, the establishment and operations of this bank were within the ambit of *Undang-Undang No. 7*, 1992, which regulates the banking system in Indonesia. This Law provides no special provision that details the rules and aspects related to *Syariah* banking operations, except for *Fasal 13C (Clause 13C)*. However, this Clause only mentions them in the form of a general statement in connection with People's Credit Banks which could provide financing services based on the principle of *bagi hasil* (division of income) or the concept of profit and loss sharing, according to what had been determined by the authorities (Antonio, 1999*)*. In line with the efforts of the Indonesian government to expand Islamic banking system in Indonesia, *Undang-Undang*

No. 7, 1992 was amended to become *Undang-Undang No. 10*, 1998 which contains many provisions that are relevant to *Syariah* banking system. These provisions include permission for commercial banks and People's Credit Banks to offer Islamic banking products. The Law also details the *Syariah* principles to be used for banking facilities and financing. However, since the year 2000, the Indonesian government, through its central bank, Bank Indonesia, has taken steps to develop a specific law for its Islamic banking system. In June 2008, the Indonesian Parliament passed the Islamic banking bill into law. The *Indonesia Law No. 21* of 2008 on Islamic Banking includes a provision for the establishment of new *Syariah* banks jointly by foreigners and Indonesian citizens or local entities. It also gives commercial banks the option to convert their operations into *Syariah*-compliant banks. Aside from this Law, Islamic banking industry in the country is also based on the rulings of the Central Bank of Indonesia.

Not all Islamic banks have gained their footing through supportive state intervention. Some Islamic banks encountered various obstacles either at the initial stage of their establishment or after they began operations. For instance, banks in Sudan are laden with problems related to regulations. In the beginning, these banks were exempted from a number of banking regulations, but these privileges were withdrawn after the government which wanted to Islamized the banking system was overthrown in the year 1985 (Ahmed, 1990). Islamic banks in the United Kingdom are also faced with various difficult issues which hinder their development. The Bank of England does not regard Islamic banks as deposit-taking institutions and therefore hinders their development (Temple, 1992). Unlike other countries, the United Kingdom does not have any specific law to govern the operations of Islamic banks in the country. Islamic banks there are governed by the Financial Services Authority (FSA).

Although most Islamic countries have enacted special laws governing the operations of Islamic banks, this does not mean that

Islamic banks are subject to that particular law. As an ordinary business entity, every Islamic bank is expected to follow the laws and regulations relevant to other business entities or laws related to activities which Islamic banks intend to perform. For example, Islamic banks in Iran are required to comply with the *Law for Usury-Free Banking 1983* and are also subject to the provisions found in *Money and Banking Law 1972*.

A similar situation is found in Malaysia. Islamic banks in Malaysia need to comply with provisions under the *Islamic Banking Act 1983*. In addition, since these banks are incorporated as public limited companies, they are within the ambit of the *Companies Act 1965*. The requirements which Islamic banks must adhere to cover issues such as the appointment of director, appointment of auditor, notice of meeting and other provisions. The requirement to comply with these regulations is clearly provided for in *Section 55* of the *Islamic Banking Act 1983*. This section states that Islamic banks established under the *Companies Act 1965* are required to comply with this Act apart from complying with the *Islamic Banking Act 1983*. In the event that conflict exists between these two Acts, then the *Islamic Banking Act 1983* would take precedence over the *Companies Act 1965*.

Apart from this, one of the important elements related to Islamic banking system in Malaysia is jurisdiction of legislation. Even though Islamic bank is an organization founded on Islam, all its business transactions are under the jurisdiction of the civil court. Hence, any legal proceedings between Islamic bank and its customers are to be handled by the civil court and not the *Syariah* court. Nevertheless, efforts have been made by various parties, including the Central Bank of Malaysia and the office of the Attorney General to study how the *Syariah* banking legislation could be developed in the interest of the Islamic religion. As a start, a high court judge has been appointed as a member of the National Syariah Supervising Board.

The legislative scope and authorities which govern Bank Islam Malaysia Berhad (BIMB) are shown in Table 5–1.

TABLE 5–1 Legislative Scope and Authorities of BIMB

Activity	Authority	Act/Regulation
1. Establishment	Company registrar	*Companies Act 1965*
2. Management	Shareholders Board of Directors Management committee	memorandum & articles of association *Islamic Banking Act 1983*
3. Licensing and supervision	Finance Ministry Bank Negara Malaysia	*Islamic Banking Act 1983*
4. Operation	Relevant authorities	*Syariah* regulations Other laws
5. *Syariah* supervision	Religious Supervision Council	*Syariah* regulations

Involvement of the Central Bank

Some of the traditional objectives of the central bank in the conventional banking system are to issue currency and to control reserves in order to maintain the value of the currency issued, to establish sound financial policies, to form stable policies of credit and banking, and to be financial advisor and banker to the government. These objectives may, however, vary from country to country, and are dependent upon and influenced by several factors. Among the factors that play a big role in determining these objectives are the political, economic and social condition of the countiry. Other countries have included objectives in accordance with their current and future needs. The Central Bank of Malaysia, for example, apart from having traditional objectives, was instrumental in assisting the government to produce a financial policy that is auxiliary for the country to achieve the objectives set out in the New Economic Policy and Vision 2020.

In line with the aforementioned objectives, a country's central bank is given the authority and responsibility through the law to regulate and supervise the country's financial system. Hence, Islamic banks being part of the financial system are also subject to the regulation and supervision of the central bank. In fact, the central bank has a function to play in the Islamic banking system just as it does in the conventional banking system. This function is also in line with the *Syariah* law, whereby Islamic banks are accountable to those who are responsible for the financial affairs of the country. To ensure the efficiency and effectiveness of the Islamic banking system, especially in countries that practise both Islamic and conventional systems, the central bank needs to play its role in the following areas (Presley, 1988):

(i) Islamic banks in most countries face difficulty in competing with conventional banks because they lack opportunity to participate as an active player in the financial market. Further, Islamic banks are also at a disadvantage compared to their counterparts when it comes to getting funds. Conventional banks are able to obtain financial aid from other banks or directly from the central bank when faced with liquidity problems. Since the mechanism of the financial market uses instruments based on interest, this assistance is inaccessible to Islamic banks. Hence, the central bank should grant financial aid to Islamic banks with liquidity problems by providing *Syariah*-compliant instruments.

(ii) The central bank should expedite the process of establishing financial instruments which are free from interest in order to enable Islamic banks to fulfil their liquidity and statutory reserve requirements. Islamic banks also need short-term investment opportunities when faced with surplus liquidity.

An efficient and effective financial market for such financial instruments could help to expedite the development and increase the profit of the Islamic bank.

(iii) The existing laws in most Islamic countries are unsuitable for Islamic banks to function fully. Hence, each Islamic country should consider establishing banking laws that encompass Islamic banking operations and are in accordance with *Syariah* principles.

(iv) The central bank should set up a special department whose responsibility is to oversee and supervise matters related to the operations of Islamic banks, especially with regard to newly-established Islamic banks or issuance of new products.

(v) A suitable method must be presented to govern the relationship between the Islamic banks and the central bank and other financial authorities. Among the aspects required in this relationship are:

- To explore suitable methods that would enable Islamic banks to provide interest-free financing and refinancing facilities.

- To seek out suitable methods for short-term investment that would enable Islamic banks to invest their surplus liquidity.

- Any facility or incentive given to customers of the conventional bank must also be given to customers of the Islamic bank.

There are many similarities in terms of powers vested in the central banks of Muslim countries in regulating and supervising Islamic banks. In Turkey for example, besides the special decree passed by the Council of Ministers, the central bank has issued rules governing the Islamic banks in the *Official Gazette No. 18348* dated 21 March 1984. This regulation contains 18 provisions that stipulate the requirements for the application and issue of licences to establish Islamic banks. The general outlines of some activities of Islamic banks are also listed in this *Gazette*. An application to operate an Islamic bank in Turkey will be scrutinized by the central bank and the licence will be issued by the Council of Ministers based on recommendations made by the central bank. The Central Bank of Turkey is also responsible for determining the reserve and liquidity ratios, and for conducting an audit on all the accounts and operations of Islamic banks in Turkey (Baldwin, 1990).

In Malaysia, the *Islamic Banking Act 1983* prescribes the powers of the Central Bank of Malaysia over Islamic banks. Applications to establish an Islamic bank in Malaysia must be forwarded to the central bank and it will scrutinize the application and make recommendations for approval and rejection. The existing licence of any Islamic bank may also be revoked on the recommendation of the central bank. Islamic banks in Malaysia must first seek approval or report to the central bank regarding the following practices and proposals:

(i) To open a new branch, agency or office within or outside Malaysia.

(ii) To establish a corresponding banking relationship with any bank outside Malaysia.

(iii) Proposed change in the control of the bank.

(iv) Whenever a loan or advance is made and secured in the aggregate by 20% or more of the paid-up capital shares of any other Islamic bank or of any licensed bank under the *Banking Act 1973* incorporated in Malaysia or of any finance company licensed under the *Finance Companies Act 1969*.

(v) To grant advances, loan and credit facilities to its directors, officers and employees.

(vi) In the case of the inability to meet its obligations or if the bank is about to suspend payment.

(vii) Proposed amendment or alteration in the memorandum and articles of association.

The Central Bank of Malaysia also has the power to conduct the following tasks:

(i) Ensure the maintenance of paid-up capital and reserve funds by the Islamic banks.

(ii) Establish the minimum amount of liquid assets to be held by the Islamic banks at all times.

(iii) Specify the types and contents of reports to be submitted to the central bank.

(iv) Prescribe the format of presentation and contents of the financial statements prepared by the Islamic banks.

(v) Impose restrictions in relation to granting of advances, loans and credit facilities.

(vi) Investigate and examine books, accounts and transactions of the Islamic banks.

Although the central bank will continue to regulate and supervise Islamic banks with various regulations and guidelines as with conventional banks, a number of adjustments need to be made. These adjustments are necessary particularly with respect to the instruments or methods used in the monetary policies. Normally, the central bank would use methods that could determine the bank's liquidity amount which would in turn determine the bank's capacity to issue credit. Some of the methods used are open market operations, discounting concept and adjustments in reserve ratio and liquidity requirement. Other methods include interest rate policy, credit policy, credit limits and loan trend. The suitability of the methods used depends largely on the political, economic and social situation of a country.

Most of the policies used for conventional banks are not suitable for Islamic banks. Determination of interest rates and open market operations are inappropriate because of the elements of interest found in government securities and treasury bills. Hence, other methods and instruments have to be developed to regulate the role of Islamic banks in the determination of the national monetary policy. Given that the role of Islamic banks in determining the national credit trend is increasing, it is imperative for such a policy to be developed. The Council of Islamic Ideology of Pakistan, in its report on the elimination of interest from the economy, expressed the view that most monetary policy instruments available to the Central Bank of Pakistan under the various banking laws of the country would also remain largely unaffected in an interest-free system. Among the regulatory instruments that would remain largely unaffected are as follows (Council of Islamic Ideology, Pakistan, 1983):

 (i) Minimum cash reserve requirement.

 (ii) Liquidity ratio requirement.

(iii) Overall ceilings on the lending and investment operations of banks.

(iv) Mandatory target for providing finance to priority sectors.

 (v) Selective credit controls.

(vi) Issue of directions to banks on various aspects of banking operations not covered by specific policy instruments.

(vii) Moral suasion.

Apart from the above methods, some Muslim countries have included additional controls in their monetary policies involving Islamic banks. Iran, for instance, as stated in *Article 20* of the

Law for Usury-Free Banking, empowered the Central Bank of Iran to supervise money and banking affairs through the application of the following instruments:

(i) Fixing a minimum and/or maximum share of profit for banks in their joint-venture and *mudharabah* activities. This ratio may vary for different fields of activities.

(ii) Designation of various fields for investments and partnerships within the framework of the approved economic policies and the fixing of a minimum expected rate of profits for various investment and partnership projects. The minimum expected rate of profit may vary with respect to different branches of activities.

(iii) Fixing the minimum and maximum profit margins banks could charge for instalment and hire purchase contracts.

(iv) Determining the types of services that the banks could provide, and the fixing of minimum and maximum commissions banks could charge for these services, and the legal fees for managing the investment deposits.

(v) Determination of the type and amount of minimum and maximum bonuses under *Article 6,* and the fixing of criteria for advertisements by banks in this respect.

(vi) Determining the minimum and maximum ratios of equity participation, *mozarebeh,* investment, hire purchase, instalment transactions, buying and selling on credit, forward sales, *mozaraah, masaqat, jo'alah* and *gharz-al-hasaneh* for banks and in each one of the various cases and fields; and fixing the maximum number of facilities that can be granted to any single customer.

In Jordan, the central bank is empowered to regulate and supervise Islamic banks as stated in *Section 15, Chapter 5* of its *Establishment Laws,* as follows:

(i) The bank may conduct any activity in various fields in accordance with normal practices and regulations adopted by commercial banks, except for activities which are in conflict with the responsibility of the bank to avoid *riba*.

(ii) In conducting its banking activities, the bank is bound by all restrictions imposed on commercial banks, including the maintenance of cash reserve requirement, and specific liquidity percentage to maintain a stable position and to protect the interest of the depositors, investors and shareholders. The bank will be subject to directives issued to it with respect to the amount and types of credit, and the usage of credit, which must be based on the country's development agenda

In Indonesia, apart from having the authority to control the banking structure akin to most other central banks, Bank Indonesia, the Central Bank of Indonesia, is also empowered under *Undang-Undang No. 10*, 1998 to regulate general banks and rural banks (People's Credit Banks) which operates *Syariah* banking. Some of the terms are as follows:

(i) *Clause 8 (2)*

The commercial bank is obligated to acquire and assimilate financing and credit guidelines based on *Syariah* principles, appropriate to the stipulations set by Bank Indonesia.

(ii) *Clause 11 (1)*

Bank Indonesia has to set the requirement on the maximum credit limit or financing based on *Syariah* principles, provision of guarantee, investment placement of letters of price, or other similar matters, which can be employed by the bank to the debtor or a group of related debtors, including to enterprises in the same group as the bank in question.

(iii) *Clause 11 (3)*

Bank Indonesia has to set the requirement on the maximum credit limit or financing based on *Syariah* principles, provision of guarantee, investment placement of letters of price, or other similar matters, which can be employed by the bank to:

- Shareholders who own 10% or more of capital in the banking sector;

- Board of Commissioners;

- Board of Directors;

- Family members to parties as meant in a, b and c above;

- Offices of other banks; and

- Enterprises in which all the above parties have interest.

(iv) *Clause 11 (4A)*

In granting credit or financing based on *Syariah* principles, the bank is prohibited from transgressing the maximum limit of credit or financing based on *Syariah* principles as stated in section (i), section (ii), section (iii) and section (iv).

Khan and Mirakhor (1987) suggested that the central bank continues its functions in determining the ratio for various types of liabilities and the maximum amount of assets that can be distributed by the Islamic bank in its partnership activities. Besides continuing to regulate and supervise as in the conventional system, the central bank may tighten its regulation over the Islamic banking system by becoming a shareholder of Islamic banks as well as other financial institutions. New opportunities would emerge if the central bank participates with other banks in profit-sharing investments and other joint ventures. However, this suggestion needs careful consideration as such action may give rise to conflict of interest and may cause central banks to deviate from their original objectives.

In contrast to its early phase of establishment, Islamic banking system is now regarded by most central banks to be an important system in determining the direction of a country's financial system. Consequently, a number of central banks have established special departments that oversee and regulate the operations of Islamic banks.

Syariah Supervisory Committee

Islamic banks are founded on religious factor. Hence, there need to be a special body which ensures that the operations of the Islamic banks do not violate any *Syariah* principles. In response to this, the majority of Islamic banks have set up special bodies known as Syariah Supervisory Committee or Syariah Supervisory Board or Syariah Monitoring Committee or Syariah Monitoring Board. This body issues its report along with the annual report of the Islamic bank.

The Accounting and Auditing Organization for Islamic Financial Institutions (AAOIFI) based in Bahrain defines the Syariah Supervisory Board as follows (AAOIFI, 2000):

> The Syariah Supervisory Board is an independent body of specialized jurists in *fiqh almua'malat* (Islamic commercial jurisprudence). However, the Syariah Supervisory Board may include a member other than those specialized in *fiqh almua'malat*, but who should be an expert in the field of Islamic financial institutions and with knowledge of *fiqh almua'malat*. This Board is entrusted with the duty of directing, reviewing and supervising the activities of the Islamic financial institutions in order to ensure that they are in compliance with *Syariah* rules and principles. The *fatwa* and rulings of the Syariah Supervisory Board shall be binding on the Islamic financial institutions.

The name of the committee and total membership of the Syariah Supervisory Board differ from one Islamic bank to another. These are shown in Table 5–2.

TABLE 5–2 Syariah Supervisory Board Information

Name of bank	Name of committee	Total membership
Abu Dhabi Islamic Bank (1999)	Syariah Supervisory and Fatwa Board	5
Albaraka Islamic Bank, Bahrain (1998)	Syariah Supervisory Board	5
Bahrain Islamic Bank (1999)	Religious Control Committee	6
Bank Islam Malaysia (1999)	Syariah Supervisory Council	5
Bank Muamalat Indonesia (1999)	Dewan Pengawas Syariah (Syariah Monitoring Council)	5
Dubai Islamic Bank (1999)	Syariah and Fatwa Supervisory Panel	4
Faysal Islamic Bank of Bahrain (1999)	Syariah Supervisory Board	6
Faisal Islamic Bank of Egypt (1998)	Syariah Supervisory Board	4
Islami Bank Bangladesh	Syariah Council	10
Jordan Islamic Bank	Syariah Consultancy Board	3
Kuwait Finance House (1999)	Syariah and Fatwa Supervisory Board	4
Qatar Islamic Bank (1998)	Syariah Control Board	4

Sources: Annual reports of related banks for the years shown in table.

Although the Accounting, Auditing and Governance Standards for Islamic Financial Institutions issued by AAOIFI in June 2000 require all Islamic financial institutions to have their own Syariah Supervisory Boards, it is possible that some Islamic banks may not have one. For example, Albaraka Bank in South Africa may not have established this supervisory committee, since the bank's annual statement does not contain any report from the committee. Similarly with Tadamon Islamic Bank in Sudan. The establishment article of this bank only requires a report issued by the Fatwa and Research Administration of the bank itself, and does not necessitate the need for a Syariah Supervisory Committee (*Annual Report*, Tadamon Islamic Bank, 2002). When performing its functions, this committee has the responsibility to ensure that first, the banking facilities and services offered to customers are in keeping with *Syariah* laws; secondly, the investments or projects in which the bank has interest are permissible by *Syariah*; and finally, the Islamic bank is managed according to *Syariah* principles. The duties and responsibilities of this body become more challenging if the bank concerned operates in a dual banking system, Islamic and conventional. Hence, committee members must not only possess in-depth knowledge in the field of *Syariah* but must also be knowledgeable in the modern banking system. It is also essential that members of this committee are unbiased, not easily influenced by any authority and unafraid to stand up for the truth.

The setting up of this committee may vary from country to country. In certain countries, there are provisions in the law that require Islamic banks to establish *Syariah* committees. In Malaysia, for instance, as stipulated in *Section 5* of the *Islamic Banking Act 1983*, the central bank will not recommend the granting of a licence to an Islamic bank unless it is satisfied that there is, in the articles of association of the bank concerned, provision for the establishment of a *Syariah* advisory board or committee. This committee in turn has the responsibility to advise the bank on the operations of its banking business in order to ensure that they do not involve any element that is not approved by the religion of Islam. In Jordan, the establishment of this *Syariah* committee is stated in the *Jordan Islamic Bank for Finance and Investment Law*. The provision and its contents are stated below.

Section 27:

(i) The Board of Directors shall appoint, in a period of 15 days from the date of its selection, an Islamic legislation consultant who is an acknowledged expert on Islamic principles, laws and traditions.

(ii) The consultant appointed to this post cannot be dismissed except on the basis of a board resolution adopted by a two-third majority of the members at least, and the Board giving grounds for such dismissal.

Section 28:

The Board of Directors shall determine the functions of the aforesaid Islamic legal consultant on the basis that the Board shall be under a duty to request the opinion of the Islamic legal consultant regarding the following matters:

(i) Studying the practical regulations and rules applied by the bank in its dealing with others, with a view to ensuring that they do not contain any form of usurious dealings which the bank is obligated to avoid.

(ii) Studying the causes which require the bank to bear any investment loss, with a view to finding the legal doctrinal (*fiqhi*) basis to support the resolution of the Board in this regard.

The provision on the appointment of the consultative body is also stated in the articles and memorandum of association of Kuwait Finance House, Kuwait. In contrast to the provisions in the law of Jordan Islamic Bank, provisions in Kuwait do not touch in detail on the appointment of the Syariah Supervisory Board. Instead, the law provides for the appointment of what is termed a consultative body; provisions which are of relevance to this issue are shown below.

Article 62:

The company shall retain consultative bodies specialized in economics, financial and legal studies. Such specialized body – or bodies – may be composed of a number of experts of international repute. For certain specialities, the company may retain only one expert or counsellor, but appointment of all such experts and counsellors shall be effected by the decision of the Board of Directors. The relationship between such appointees and the company shall be limited to such studies as may be assigned to them, and their researches and recommendations shall be submitted either to the Chairman of the Board of Directors or to such board members as may be delegated by the Board for the purpose.

Article 63:

Consultative bodies, experts and individual consultants shall basically execute their assignments in Kuwait. However, consultation sessions may in special cases be held outside Kuwait, under a decision to be issued by the Board of Directors covering each and every case per se on the recommendation of the Chairman or the Managing Director. In this respect, the Board's decision shall specify the person who should represent the Board of Directors at such session or sessions outside Kuwait.

Article 64:

The Board of Directors shall, upon recommendation of the Chairman or the Managing Director, determine the terms of reference for the consultative bodies, experts and individual consultants, whether their relationship with the company is permanent or occasional. Moreover, the Board of Directors shall lay down rules within the company's by-laws concerning such activities and assignments.

In Egypt, *Law No. 48 (1977)* which allowed for the establishment of Faisal Islamic Bank of Egypt also has provisions for matters pertaining to the establishment of a monitoring body called the Religious Supervisory Board.

Article 40:

The Supervisory Board shall be composed of no more than five members selected from among Islamic scholars and jurists of *Comparative Law* believing in the idea of the Islamic bank. The general meeting shall appoint them every three years and shall fix their remunerations upon the proposal of the Board of Directors.

The task of the Supervisory Board shall be to offer advice and undertake reviews as concern the application of the provisions of the Islamic *Syariah*.

In this respect, it shall have the means and the competencies available for the auditor.

The Board of Directors may invite a representative of the Supervisory Board to attend any of its meetings but he shall have no counted vote.

The Supervisory Board may request the holding of a special meeting for the Board of Directors to explain its views on matters of *Syariah* if it so deems necessary.

As an exception to the foregoing, the period of the first Supervisory Board shall be four years.

The founders shall also select the members of the first Supervisory Board immediately upon the promulgation and publication of the *Law* and the *Statutes*.

Article 41:

The Supervisory Board shall follow in its business and relations with the management of the bank and its various components the same means and shall exercise the same competencies according to the auditor under these *Statutes*.

Based on the standards issued by AAOIFI, matters related to appointment, fixing of remuneration, composition, selection and dismissal of this Board are as follows:

Appointment and Fixing of Remuneration

• Every Islamic financial institution is required to have a Syariah Supervisory Board appointed by shareholders in their annual meeting upon the recommendation of the Board of Directors by taking into consideration local legislation and regulations. Shareholders may empower the Board of Directors to determine the allowance for the members of the Syariah Supervisory Board.

• The Syariah Supervisory Board and the Islamic financial institution should agree on the terms of engagement. The terms agreed upon must be recorded in the letter of appointment.

• The Syariah Supervisory Board is required to ensure that the Islamic financial institution documents and confirms the Syariah Supervisory Board's acceptance of appointment. The letter of appointment of the Syariah Supervisory Board should in general include reference to the compliance of the Islamic financial institution with *Syariah* rules and principles.

• The Syariah Supervisory Board may appoint those among its members or other parties a supervisor(s) to help it in performing its duties.

Composition, Selection and Dismissal

- The Syariah Supervisory Board shall comprise at least three members. The Board may request the service of consultants who have expertise in business, economics, law, accounting and/or others. The Syariah Supervisory Board shall not have the director or significant shareholders of Islamic financial institutions as members.

- The dismissal of a member of the Syariah Supervisory Board requires recommendation by the Board of Directors and is subject to the approval of the shareholders in the annual general meeting.

The findings of the Syariah Supervisory Board on whether or not the activities of the Islamic bank under its supervision are *Syariah*-compliant are presented in the annual report of the particular bank. How much is presented varies from bank to bank. The reports provided by the Syariah Supervisory Boards of Bank Islam Malaysia Berhad and Kuwait Finance House are rather brief. They merely state that the operations implemented by the banks conformed to Syariah rules. There are, however, some Syariah Supervisory Boards, for instance those in Jordan, Bangladesh, Dubai and Bahrain, which give detailed views on their activities as well as the way they conduct their duties. In countries like Pakistan and Iran, the establishment of such a body is unnecessary because the government has a central body that gives a *fatwa* on banking operations. Hence, unlike the annual reports of Islamic banks in other countries, the annual reports of these banks do not contain the Syariah Supervisory Board report.

AAOIFI recommends that each report of this committee has the following basic elements:

- Title.

- Addressee.

- Opening or introductory paragraph.

- Scope paragraph explaining the nature of the work performed.

- Opinion paragraph containing an expression of opinion on the compliance of the Islamic financial institution with *Syariah* rules and principles.

- Date of report.

- Signature of the members of the Syariah Supervisory Board.

The designated name of the committee suggests that only those who are knowledgeable in *Syariah* law are competent to become board members. Hence, the question arises as to whether those from other fields and have expertise in Islamic banking may also qualify to be appointed to the committee. Other issues pertain to some Islamic scholars becoming a *Syariah* committee member of several Islamic banks and financial institutions. Currently, the trend is for there to be only one *Syariah* committee to supervise the operations of all the Islamic banks in the particular country.

SUMMARY

As a business organization founded on religion and profit, an Islamic bank is required to comply with two types of laws, that is, *Syariah* laws and positive laws. *Syariah* law is an Islamic law which covers the total way of life of Islamic organizations and society that includes both faith and practices, personal behaviour, and legal and social transactions. The aspects related to belief and faith may be regarded as the theoretical aspects of Islam while the practical aspects include all that a Muslim is required to do, that is the practical course which he must follow.

There are five categories of principles in *Syariah* law that control the behaviour of Muslims. The first is *fard* or compulsory behaviour, where the actions involved are compulsory and must be performed by all Muslims. Performance is rewarded and omission is punishable and considered sinful. The second category is *sunat*, which involves acts that are recommended but not required. Those who perform such duties or acts are rewarded, but omission is not punished. The third category, *jaiz* or *mubah*, refers to actions that are indifferent, the performance or omission of which is neither rewarded nor punishable. The fourth is *makruh*, and actions here are those that are disapproved of but not punished or forbidden. Lastly, *haram* are actions that are forbidden and performing them amounts to sinning.

There are four fundamental sources of *Syariah* laws, namely the Quran, *Hadith*, *ijma* and *qiyas*. The Quran contains the commands and messages of Allah (s.w.t.) which were sent down to Allah's Messenger (p.b.u.h.) as a guidance to mankind. *Hadith* is the compilation of information, narration, history, accounts and records of the *Sunnah* of the Prophet (p.b.u.h.), and signifies the customs, habits and practices of the Prophet (p.b.u.h.), which were handed down through generations. *Hadith* also describes the Prophet's (p.b.u.h.) behaviour, modes of actions, sayings and declarations under a variety of circumstances during his lifetime. *Ijma* is the consensus of opinion of *mujtahid* or an agreement of Muslim jurists on the matter of determining a particular legislation, while *qiyas* is the process of reasoning or the exercise of judgement in both theological as well as legal matters by analogy of *mujtahid*. The Quran and authentic (*sahih*) *Hadith* are regarded as absolute legislation and evidence whose truths are beyond question. The Quran and *Hadith* are also known as *usul* or the roots. *Ijma* and *qiyas* are branches of the *Syariah* law. Although these sources are as a whole complete, a comprehensive *Syariah* law has yet to be formulated to regulate and supervise the overall aspects of the Islamic banking system.

Besides *Syariah* law, Islamic banks are also required to comply with man-made laws called positive laws. In reality, there is no uniform law to be followed by Islamic banks. It all depends on the political climate and government policies of the country in which the bank is operating. Some countries have introduced specific Islamic banking laws for Islamic banks, while others have passed laws that must be complied with by all banks which are going to be established in those countries. Apart from conforming to specific laws, Islamic banks are also required to comply with other laws related to the banking business.

Due to the fact that the banking sector is an important sector of a country's economy, Islamic banks are also subject to the monetary control and policy of the country. The task of regulating and supervising Islamic banks is normally the responsibility of the central bank. Generally, both conventional and Islamic banks are governed by the same regulations pertaining to supervision and monitoring. However, the instruments which are related to the practice of interest rates or *riba* cannot be used by Islamic banks.

The operations and businesses of Islamic banks are carried out in accordance with *Syariah* principles. It is the duty and responsibility of a special body known as the Syariah Supervisory Board or Syariah Monitoring Council to ensure that the running and operations of the Islamic bank do not violate any *Syariah* principles. The standards and functions of this board are issued by the Accounting and Auditing Organization for Islamic Financial Institutions centred in Manama, Bahrain. Nevertheless, variations in terms of membership composition, method of appointment and tasks conducted still exist. These differences become even more apparent when different methods and contents are presented in the annual reports issued by *Syariah* boards of Islamic banks throughout the world.

REFERENCES AND FURTHER READING

Abu Dhabi Islamic Bank. *Annual Report* (various issues).

Accounting and Auditing Organization for Islamic Financial Institutions. *Accounting, Auditing and Governance Standards for Islamic Financial Institutions.* Manama (Bahrain), 2000.

Ahmed, Osman. "Sudan: The Role of the Faisal Islamic Bank." In *Islamic Financial Markets,* edited by Rodney Wilson, 76–99. London (UK) and New York (USA): Routledge, 1990.

Albaraka Islamic Bank of Bahrain. *Annual Report* (various issues).

Ali, Abdullah Y. *The Holy Quran, Text, Translation and Commentary.* Brentwood (Maryland, USA): Amana Corporation, 1989.

Ali, Maulana M. *The Religion of Islam.* Lahore (Pakistan): The Ahmadiyyah Anjuman Ishaat Islam, 1950.

Antonio, Muhammad Syafi'i. *Bank Syariah Bagi Bankir & Praktisi Keuangan.* Jakarta: Tazkia Institut, 1999.

Antonio, Muhammad Syafi'i. *Bank Syariah: Suatu Pengenalan Umum.* Jakarta: Tazkia Institut, 1999.

Bahrain Islamic Bank. *Annual Report* (various issues).

Baldwin, David. "Turkey: Islamic Banking in a Secularist Context." In *Islamic Financial Markets,* edited by Rodney Wilson, 171–189. London (UK) and New York (USA): Routledge, 1990.

Bank Islam Malaysia Berhad. *Annual Report* (various issues).

Bank Muamalat Indonesia. *Annual Report* (various issues).

Centre Culturel Islamique. *Introduction to Islam.* Paris, 1959.

Coulson, Noel J. *History of Islamic Law.* Edinburgh (UK): Edinburgh University Press, 1964.

Council of Islamic Ideology (Pakistan). "Elimination of Interest from the Economy." In *Money and Banking in Islam*, edited by Ziauddin Ahmad, Munawar Iqbal and M. Fahim Khan. Jeddah (Saudi Arabia): International Centre for Research in Islamic Economics, King Abdul Aziz University, 1983.

Denny, Frederick M. *An Introduction to Islam*. New York (USA): Macmillan Publishing Company, 1985.

Departemen Agama Republik Indonesia. *Al-Quran dan Terjemahannya*. Jakarta, 1974.

Doi, Abdul Rahman I. *Syariah: The Islamic Law*. London (UK): Ta Ha Publisher, 1984.

Dubai Islamic Bank. *Annual Report* (various issues). United Arab Emirates.

El-Ashker, Ahmed. "Egypt: An Evaluation of the Major Islamic Banks." In *Islamic Financial Markets*, edited by Rodney Wilson, 59–75. London (UK) and New York (USA): Routledge, 1990.

Faisal Islamic Bank of Egypt. *Annual Report* (various issues).

Faysal Islamic Bank of Bahrain. *Annual Report* (various issues).

Fyzee, Asaf A.A. "The Reinterpretation of Islam." In *Islam in Transition: Muslim Perspectives*, edited by John J. Donohue and John L. Esposito, 188–192. New York (USA) and Oxford (UK): Oxford University Press, 1982.

Gieraths, Christine. "Pakistan: Main Participants and Final Financial Products of the Islamization Process." In *Islamic Financial Markets*, edited by Rodney Wilson, 171–195. London (UK) and New York (USA): Routledge, 1990.

Government of Indonesia. *Undang-Undang No. 10, 1998, Undang-Undang Perbankan*. Jakarta: Penerbit Sinar Grafika, 1998.

Guillaume, Alfred. *Islam*. 2nd ed. London (UK): Penguin Books, 1977.

Herdayati, Seyed Ali Asghar. "Islamic Banking, as Experienced in the Islamic Republic of Iran." Working paper presented at the International Conference on Islamic Banking, Sydney (Australia), 9–10 November 1993.

Islami Bank Bangladesh Limited. *Annual Report* (various issues).

Ismail, Abdul H. *Bank Islam Malaysia Berhad: Principles and Operations*. Edited by Sheikh Ghazali Sheikh Abod, Syed Omar and Aidit Ghazali. Kuala Lumpur: Quill Publications, 1992.

Jordan Islamic Bank. *Annual Report* (various issues).

Khan, Mohsin S. and Abbas Mirakhor (eds). *Theoretical Studies in Islamic Banking and Finance*. Houston (Texas, USA): Institute for Research and Islamic Studies, 1987.

Klein, F.A. *The Religion of Islam*. London (UK): Curzon Press, 1985.

Kuwait Finance House. *Annual Report* (various issues).

Lewis, Bernard, Menage V.L., Ch. Pellat and Schacht J. *The Encyclopedia of Islam* (new edition). Leiden (Netherlands): E.J. Brill, 1971.

Mahmasani, Subhi. "Adaptation of Islamic Jurisprudence to Modern Social Needs." In *Islam in Transition: Muslim Perspectives*, edited by John J. Donohue and John L. Esposito, 181–187. New York (USA) and Oxford (UK): Oxford University Press, 1982.

Mannan, Muhammad A. *Islamic Economics: Theory and Practice*. Cambridge (UK): Hodder and Stoughton, 1986.

Maududi, Abul Ala. *Islamic Law and Constitution*. Lahore (Pakistan): Islamic Publication, 1983.

Nuwayhi, Muhammad. "A Revolution in Religious Thought." In *Islam in Transition: Muslim Perspectives*, edited by John J. Donohue and John L. Esposito, 160–168. New York (USA) and Oxford (UK): Oxford University Press, 1982.

Presley, John R. (ed.). *Directory of Islamic Financial Institutions*. London (UK): Croom Helm, 1988.

Qatar Islamic Bank. *Annual Report* (various issues).

Rahman, Fazlur. *Islam*. 2nd ed. Chicago (USA): The University of Chicago Press, 1979.

Saleh, Nabil A. *Unlawful Gain and Legitimate Profit in Islamic Law*. Cambridge (UK): Cambridge University Press, 1986.

Schacht, Joseph. *An Introduction to Islamic Law*. Oxford (UK): The Clarendon Press, 1964.

Shallah, Ramadan. "Jordan: The Experience of the Jordan Islamic Bank." In *Islamic Financial Markets*, edited by Rodney Wilson, 100–128. London (UK) and New York (USA): Routledge, 1990.

Shojaeddini, Mohammad Reza. "Instruments of Monetary Policy in Islamic Banking." Working paper presented at the International Conference on Islamic Banking, Sydney, Australia, 9–10 November 1993.

Siddiqi, Hamid. trans. *Sahid Muslim*. Vol 3. Beirut (Lebanon): Dar al Arabia Publishing, Printing & Distribution, undated.

Siddiqi, Muhammad Iqbal. *Model of an Islamic Bank*. Lahore (Pakistan): Kazi Publication, 1986.

Siddique, Muhammad. *Islamic Banking System: Principles and Practices*. Islamabad (Pakistan): Research Associates, 1985.

Tadamon Islamic Bank. *Annual Report* (various issues). Sudan.

Temple, Peter. "Islamic Banking: Principle as Well as Roots." *Accountancy*. Vol. 110, Iss. 1187 (July 1992): 46–47.

The Mejelle: Being an English translation of Majallah el-Ahkam and a Complete Code on Islamic Civil Law, translated by C.R. Tyser, D.G. Demetriades and I.H. Effendi. Kuala Lumpur: The Other Press, 2001.

Wilson, Rodney. "Kuwait: Islamic Banking for a Consumer Society." In *Islamic Financial Markets*, edited by Rodney Wilson, 100–128. London (UK) and New York (USA): Routledge, 1990.

Zakaria, Rafiq. *The Struggle Within Islam: The Conflict Between Religion and Politics*. New York (USA): Penguin Books, 1989.

CHAPTER 6

OPERATIONAL ASPECTS AND PRACTICES OF ISLAMIC BANKING SYSTEM

This chapter discusses the operational aspects and practices of a number of Islamic banks. The discussion includes comparisons of the Syariah principles governing the operations and practices of Islamic banks, the services provided, investment, and social and welfare activities among Islamic banks in certain countries. The recommendations of the Accounting and Auditing Organization for Islamic Financial Institutions for the presentation of accounts, financial management and presentation of financial statements for Islamic banks are also detailed.

INTRODUCTION

Islamic banks are for Muslims who do not wish to have transactions with conventional banks because of the presence of elements of *riba* in their transactions. Hence, Islamic banks must make available services similar to those provided by conventional banks. Further, the services should be portrayed as having better features than those of conventional banks. By virtue of the fact that conventional banks have been established in the world for some time already, they have various advantages over Islamic banks. The experience and expertise that conventional banks possess enable them to not only provide services which are efficient and comprehensive, but also to realize the needs of customers and subsequently meet those needs. As a result, conventional banks have the capacity to instil loyalty in their customers, making it difficult for other financial institutions to attract them.

The case is different with Islamic banks. The majority of Islamic banks have only been in the market between 10 to 20 years. In fact, a number of Islamic banks were only established in the early 20th century. For instance, many Islamic banks in Indonesia were established after the country suffered an economic crisis at the end of the 1990s. Although these banks are still in their early stage of development, most have successfully provided banking services that are efficient and effective to their customers, and nearly all have recorded profits. In addition to the increasing trend in the level of yearly profits, other statistics also indicate an increasing amount of deposits and financing. These data prove that Islamic banks not only have managed to establish themselves as a viable alternative to conventional banks but they have also been able to improve themselves in terms of profitability and patronage. Moreover, Islamic banks not only serve the needs of Muslim customers; they have extended their operations to service non-Muslims. For example, Bank Islam Malaysia Berhad (BIMB) which began operations in 1984, as at the end of August 1993, had 350,000 customers of whom 17,000 were non-Muslims. By the end of 2007, BIMB customers totalled more than one million whereby about 10% were non-Muslims. Similarly, Bank Muamalat Malaysia Berhad which started operations as a full-fledge Islamic bank at the end of 1999 also recorded encouraging development. At the end of 2006, around 10% of its customers were non-Muslims.

These figures prove that Islamic banks are accepted by both Muslims and non-Muslims.

Apart from the successes of Islamic banks individually, the Islamic banking system has clearly demonstrated its capability to become a viable alternative to a country's economic management. For example, when Iran and Pakistan Islamized their respective financial systems, they received cynical views as to the viability of it. Nevertheless, more than ten years after the implementation of the Islamic system, there has been no indication that the economies of these countries have declined. On the contrary, based on the statistics issued by the International Monetary Fund, the amount of deposits in both countries had increased. For example, after the nationalization of its banking system, banks in Iran had total deposits of IRR980.88 billion in the current account and IRR1,776.74 billion in the fixed deposit and savings account in 1980. (The currency of Iran is the Iranian Rial or IRR.) These figures increased to IRR2,864.9 billion for the current account and IRR4,339.2 billion for the fixed deposit and savings account at the end of 1986 and continued to increase to reach IRR7,850.9 billion and IRR13,341.6 billion for the current account and fixed deposit and savings account, respectively at the end of 1991. The amount of both types of deposits soared to IRR353,093.3 billion for the current account and IRR869,654.5 billion for the fixed deposit and savings account at the end of 2007.

Similar trends were also observed in Pakistan. Although some are of the view that Pakistan has not fully Islamized its entire economic system, some of its banks did adopt the Islamic economic system. At the end of 1980, the country's banking sector recorded total deposits of Rs33,698 million and Rs30,650 million in the current account and fixed deposit, respectively. (The official currency of Pakistan is the rupee or Rs.) The amount of deposits in Pakistan has continued to record a yearly increase. For example, the amount of deposits in the current account was Rs69,103 million in 1985 and this increased to Rs138,725 million in 1990,

Rs340,332 million in 1995 and Rs458,901 million in 2000. At the end of June 2008, the total deposit in the current account had soared to Rs965.4 billion. Fixed deposit was Rs82,091 million at the end of 1985, and this figure increased to Rs161,221 million in 1990, Rs424,964 million in 1995 and Rs730,112 million in 2000. Total amount of fixed deposit at the end of June 2008 was Rs1,211.5 billion. Meanwhile, total deposit in the savings account increased from Rs339,259 million in 1996 to Rs583,492 million in 2000. As at end of June 2008, the total deposit in the savings account was Rs1,572.7 billion. Based on these data, it can be concluded that the Islamic banking system is in fact practicable. The willingness of non-Muslims to patronize Islamic banks proves that this system is suitable for people of all races and religions.

APPLICATION OF *SYARIAH* PRINCIPLES

Chapter 3 has described the range of *Syariah* principles applied by Islamic banks in providing their products and services to their customers. Basically, the applications of these principles are dependent on the following:

(i) If a country has policies for the development of an Islamic banking system, then the financial authorities such as the central bank or other bodies will determine or suggest the principles to be used by Islamic banks under their supervision.

(ii) If an Islamic bank operates in a country in which the central bank is not concerned with the development of the Islamic banking system, then the principles used will depend largely on the discretion of the bank itself. Hence, the types of principles applied will be made known either through publications made by the central bank (either as published articles or through its website) or in the bank's annual report.

Differences in practices and interpretation of the principles governing banking practices do occur among Islamic banks. A list of *Syariah* principles adopted by various Islamic banks in selected Muslim countries is given in Table 6–1.

Table 6–1 shows several obvious similarities and differences in the usage of *Syariah* principles among banks in Iran, Malaysia, Pakistan, Bangladesh, Kuwait, Jordan, Bahrain, United Arab Emirates and Turkey. As explained earlier, *Syariah* principles used by Islamic banks may be classed into five categories, namely the profit-loss sharing principles, sale-based principles, fees-based or charges-based principles, free service principles and ancillary principles. The following are some of the similarities and differences:

1. Malaysia is the only country where Arabic words are used in describing all *Syariah* principles governing Islamic banking operations. Other countries, however, retain Arabic words for certain principles only and use vernacular words for others. Some of the Arabic words which are commonly used by almost all Islamic banks are *mudharabah, musyarakah, murabahah, ijarah* and *qard hassan*.

2. Although there are slight differences in spelling and pronunciation for a number of principles, they are basically the same. For instance, the *mudharabah* principle: Iran uses *mozarebeh*, Malaysia formerly called it *al-mudharabah* but now it is known as *mudharabah*, Bangladesh calls it *al-mudaraba*, Pakistan and Bahrain use *modaraba*, Kuwait and Jordan use *mudaraba* and Sudan calls it *mudarabat*. Differences in spelling and pronunciation also occur for other principles like *musyarakah, ijarah* and *qard hassan*. Turkey does not use Arabic terminologies for its principles.

3. Within the category of profit-loss sharing, most countries practise two principles, namely *mudharabah* and *musyarakah*, while Iran has more than two principles. The *musyarakah*

TABLE 6–1 Syariah Principles Used by Islamic Banks

Category	Iran	Malaysia	Pakistan	B'desh	Kuwait	Jordan	Bahrain	Turkey	UAE	Indonesia
Profit-loss sharing	Civil partnership	*Mudharabah*	Profit-loss sharing	*Mudaraba*	*Mudaraba*	*Mudaraba*	*Modaraba*	Profit-loss sharing	*Mudaraba*	*Mudharabah*
	Legal partnership	*Musyarakah*	Equity participation	*Musharaka*		*Musharaka*	*Musharaka*		*Musharaka*	*Musyarakah*
	Direct investment		Purchase of shares							
	Mozarebeh		Participation term certificate							
	Mosaqat		*Modarraba* certificate							
			Rent sharing							
Sale & purchase	Forward delivery	*Murabahah*	Repurchase agreement	*Bai-murabaha*	*Murabaha*	*Murabaha*	*Salam*		*Murabaha*	*Murabaha*
	Instalment sales	*Bai bithaman ajil*	Increment	*Bai-salam*	*Istisna*	*Salam*	*Istisna'*		*Istisna'a*	*Istisna*
		Bai al-inah	Decrement	*Bai muazzal*			*Tawarruq*			
		Bai al-salam		Purchase & negotiation			*Murabaha*			
		Bai al-istijar								
		Sarf								

TABLE 6–1 (continued)

Category	Iran	Malaysia	Pakistan	B'desh	Kuwait	Jordan	Bahrain	Turkey	UAE	Indonesia
Fees, commission fixed payment	*Jo'alah* Debt trading Hire purchase	*Al-ijarah thumma* *Al-Bai* *Al-ijarah* *Kafalah* *Al-wakalah* *Al-hiwalah* *Al-ujr*	Lease Hire purchase Development charge Service charge Financing with service charge	Hire purchase Commission Service charge	Lease Commission Service charge	Commission *Ijara* Service charge	Commission Service charge *Ijara* *Ijara wa-iktina*	Lease Service charge	Service charge *Ijara* *Wakala*	
Free service	*Gharz-al-hassanah*	*Al-qardhul hasan*	*Qarz-e-hasna*	*Quard*	*Qard hassan*	*Al-Qird al-hassan*	*Qard hassan*		*Qard hassan*	*Qard*
Other principles	*Mozaraah*	*Bai al-dayn* *Al-wadiah yad dhamanah* *Ar-rahn* *Hibah*				*Amanah*	*Amanah*	*Amanah*	*Amanah*	*Wadiah*

Sources: Iran: *The Law For Usury-Free Banking 1983*; Malaysia: www.bnm.gov.my; Pakistan: State Bank of Pakistan, *BCD Circular No. 13*, 20 June 1984; Bangladesh: *Annual Report*, Islami Bank Bangladesh Limited, 2007; Kuwait: *Annual Report*, Kuwait Finance House, 2007; Jordan: *Annual Report*, Jordan Islamic Bank, 2007; Bahrain: *Annual Report*, Shamil Bank of Bahrain (formerly known as Faysal Islamic Bank of Bahrain), 2007; Turkey: *Annual Report*, Turkiye Finans, 2007; United Arab Emirates: *Annual Report*, Dubai Islamic Bank, 2007; Indonesia: *Annual Report*, Bank Muamalat Indonesia, 2007.

principle can be divided into two, that is, (i) permanent *musyarakah* and (ii) diminishing *musyarakah*. Permanent *musyarakah*, or commonly simply referred to as *musyarakah*, is a situation where the bank participates in the equity of a company without fixing the date of termination of its participation. The returns acquired are usually based on the capital contributed. Diminishing *musyarakah* or commonly known as *musyarakah mutanaqissah*, exists when the bank agrees to transfer gradually its share to the other shareholders, so that the bank's share declines and the other shareholders' share increases until eventually the company would be fully owned by the latter.

4. Iran has three additional principles, namely civil partnership, legal partnership and direct investment, but all these principles are based on the principle of profit-loss sharing. The principle of civil partnership operates on the contribution of cash and non-cash capital by several individuals or business to a common pool on a joint-ownership basis. The partnership will be terminated as soon as the project is completed. Legal partnership involves partnership between individuals or with other entities to form a new business entity or company, where each individual involved becomes the shareholder. Direct investment occurs when the investor directly invests or provides additional capital for productive projects.

5. Pakistan, as with Iran, also has various principles within the profit-loss sharing category. Principles such as equity participation, purchase of shares, participation term certificate, *modaraba* certificate and rent sharing are those used by banks in that country to channel money to customers in need of financial aid. The returns are determined by the profitability of the issuing company. Participation term certificates are transferable financial instrument issued by a company for a specific period and are secured by a legal mortgage on the fixed assets of the company. *Modaraba* certificate is a certificate issued by

companies which are registered under the *Mudarabah (Floating and Control) Ordinance 1980*. Banks in Pakistan are allowed to purchase the certificates and the investment is almost the same as purchasing the shares of those companies except for the fact that the owner does not have authority as a shareholder. In rent sharing, the bank provides finance for the construction of buildings, complexes, etc., and receives a share of the rental income of the property. However, no information is available on the use of the *musyarakah* principle by Islamic banks in Pakistan.

6. The principles in the sale and purchase category also differ among banks. Malaysia has the most number of *Syariah* principles in this category, that is, six principles, followed by Bangladesh and Bahrain with four principles each. Islamic banks in Turkey do not have any principles listed under this category. Among the principles used by the majority of Islamic banks in the world are *murabahah*, *salam* and *istisna*. Bahrain uses a principle which is not used by banks anywhere else, that is the *tawarruq* principle, a principle associated with the financing of sale and purchase of items involving a third party. Malaysia also practises several of its own principles, namely *bai al-inah*, *bai al-istijar* and *sarf*. *Bai al-istijar* and *sarf* are also used elsewhere. *Bai al-istijar* is a sale and purchase principle used in Pakistan involving repeated deliveries. *Sarf* is a currency sale and purchase contract.

7. The number and types of *Syariah* principles used in the category of fees, commission and fixed charges also vary among Islamic banks. Islamic banks in Indonesia do not state any principles used in this category; however, in the 2003 annual reports of Bank Muamalat Indonesia and Bank Syariah Mandiri, it was mentioned that services based on fees and commission were provided. Islamic banks in Jordan and Dubai list three principles under this category; Jordan only uses *murabahah*, commission and service charge, while the United Arab Emirates uses *murabahah*, *istisna* and service charge. Islamic banks in Turkey,

Bahrain and Kuwait list five principles, namely *murabahah*, commission, service charge, *ijarah* (lease for Kuwait) and *ijara wa-iqtina* (*istisna* for Kuwait). Malaysia and Pakistan list six and five principles respectively, while Bangladesh lists seven and Iran five.

8. The number of *Syariah* principles used also differ among banks for the category of fees and commission. Malaysia uses six principles and Pakistan five. The principles used by almost all Islamic banks are *ijarah* and service charge. Among the principles which are used by a particular country are *jo'alah* in Iran and *ujr* in Malaysia, but there is actually not much difference between these two principles and the ones used by other Islamic banks. Both involve the undertaking of one party to pay a specified amount of money to another party in return for rendering a specified service in accordance with the terms of the contract. Hence, this principle is similar to the concept of service charge used by other Islamic banks.

9. The principle of *bai muazzal* used in Bangladesh is the same as the principle of *bai bithaman ajil* used in Malaysia and the principle of instalment sales used in Iran. Although these principles are not listed by Islamic banks in Bahrain, Kuwait, Jordan, Turkey and the United Arab Emirates, these banks actually do provide instalment services to their customers by applying the *murabahah* principle, known as *bay-al-mudarabah*.

10. Although Islamic banking in Pakistan and Malaysia seem to have many *Syariah* principles for their commission and fixed charges category, these principles can be brought together with the principles of service charges. In Pakistan, for instance, development charges and service charges are terms used in imposing charges on customers. In Malaysia, on the other hand, principles such as *al-wakalah, al-kafalah, al-hiwalah* and *al-ujr* are terms representing the nature of services rendered to customers and how these charges will be imposed on customers.

11. The *qard hassan* principle or free service loan is used widely by the majority of Islamic banks. Only Iran and Kuwait use this principle for deposit facilities; other banks use it for financing facilities. Islamic banks in Sudan do not adopt this principle at all.

12. There are principles that are used by Islamic banks in particular countries only. Examples are *jo'alah*, *mozaraah* and *masaqat* which are used in Iran, and *ar-rahn* and *al-wadiah yad dhamanah* which are used in Malaysia. The *rahn* principle is associated with pawning. Although other Islamic banks do not mention other ancillary principles, in practice they too require security or guarantee when offering financing and investment services.

13. Turkey is the country that registers the least number of *Syariah* principles used in its Islamic banking system. In fact, Islamic banks in Turkey such as Turkiye Finans and Bank Asya do not mention at all the *Syariah* principles that they adopt. They merely state that the facilities available are based on profit sharing. Nonetheless, these banks do provide a wide range of banking services and products.

There are many reasons for the different terminologies and principles used by Islamic banks in offering their services. First, the Islamic banks are not governed by a uniform law. In Malaysia, for example, Islamic banks are subjected to laws related to Islamic banks which have been approved by the Malaysian government, while Islamic banks in other countries are subjected to laws in their respective countries. Furthermore, every Muslim country has its own religious authority which is responsible for monitoring and supervising the activities of Islamic banks in that country. The religious authority of a particular country is independent of the religious authorities of other countries. Hence, directives of a particular law issued in a particular country are not applicable to communities beyond its jurisdiction. Secondly, currently there is no organization or party that has the authority to monitor and supervise the operations of all Islamic banks throughout the world. Although there is an association called International Association of Islamic Banks, this association does not have any legal hold on its members. In fact, membership is on a voluntary basis. As a result, each Islamic bank is free to choose the principles it wishes to adopt and apply in its banking businesses.

The absence of a comprehensive list of *Syariah* principles used by a particular Islamic bank may cause customers and financial statement users to lack a clear understanding of the *Syariah* principles underlying a particular transaction. This failure of the banks in this matter is not done consciously. It is merely because there is no legislative provision or standards which require them to do so. The standards set by the Accounting and Auditing Organization for Islamic Financial Institutions (AAOIFI) do not require Islamic banks to provide such lists. Since Islamic banks have been in operation for some time now, these banks may probably assume that the public already has a clear understanding of the *Syariah* principles adopted by them.

SERVICES PROVIDED BY ISLAMIC BANKS

As an institution which is involved in banking activities, it is only appropriate that the Islamic bank should provide services which can meet the needs of a range of users. The users may be seen as three main groups, that is, individuals, business organizations and government bodies. The individual with excess money would deposit his money in the bank for transactions, precautionary or investment purposes. Businessmen hold money for transactions and investment purposes, while government do so for investment motives. Individuals require financing from the bank for the purpose of meeting their investment and personal needs. Businessmen require financing to either start or expand their businesses. Financing required may be in the form of working capital and fixed capital financing. The government, meanwhile, needs money to finance its budget deficit.

Islamic banks also offer other facilities. In addition to catering to the needs of regular customers, the banks also provide services needed by temporary clients. Temporary clients are those who require banking services at certain times and for certain activities only. Such services include letters of credit, letters of guarantee, money order, foreign exchange, cheque and bank draft issuance, advisory services, etc. Hence, services offered by Islamic banks may be classified into three groups, namely deposit facilities, financing facilities and other facilities.

Deposit Facilities

The following are some of the similarities and differences among the deposit facilities provided by Islamic banks:

(i) Except for Turkey which offers only two types of deposit facilities, namely special current account and participation account, Islamic banks in other countries provide three types of deposit facilities, that is, current account, savings account and investment account.

(ii) There are some differences in the treatment of the savings account facility among Islamic banks. Islamic banks in Iran, Pakistan and the United Arab Emirates regard the savings account as a facility by itself. On the other hand, Bangladesh, Kuwait, Jordan and Bahrain consider it as one of the facilities within the investment account. Malaysia and Indonesia offer two types of savings account, that is, accounts using the *wadiah* and *mudharabah* principles.

(iii) In general, the investment account facility can be divided into three categories. The first category is deposits based on time, for example, tenure periods of three months, six months, nine months, etc. The second is deposits based on notice, where notice must be given by customers prior to any withdrawal. The third is deposits for specified projects or purposes. Investment deposit facilities based on notice are only available in Bangladesh, Jordan and Bahrain. Specific investment account is available in most countries except Iran, Kuwait, Pakistan and Turkey. Apart from this, there are also investment accounts with restrictions and investment accounts without restrictions. For investment accounts with restrictions, the bank cannot use the funds deposited by clients except in accordance with the specifications provided. This is not the case for investment accounts without restrictions.

(iv) Sometimes there are differences in terms of the *Syariah* principles used and in the types of deposit facilities offered among Islamic banks within the same country, as in the case of Bahrain. For example, Shamil Bank of Bahrain offers two types of deposit facilities, that is, demand deposit and investment deposit or investment account. The demand deposit is of two types, current account and savings account. Both these accounts do not give out any returns and depositors can at any time make withdrawals. Cheque books are given to the current account holders while passbooks are given to the savings account holders. Investment account is offered based on the concept of trust and is offered based on time and notice. The account holder will be given either a bank book or certificate of deposit. Here, the bank will invest the deposit made by the customers and the bank does not share in the profit acquired from the investment. Instead, the bank charges its customers a service fee. The deposit made according to this principle is not considered a liability by the bank and the amount is removed from its balance sheet.

Albaraka Islamic Bank of Bahrain also offers two types of facilities, current account and investment account. The operation of its current account is similar to those of other banks while the investment account offered is based on profit-loss sharing. In addition, this bank also manages its customers' funds, and customers can choose whether to invest in specific funds or funds based on specific *mudharabah*. Islamic Bank of Bahrain also offers two types of deposit facilities. They are current account and investment account. Its current account does not offer any returns, while its investment account is based on profit-loss sharing.

(v) Differences exist in the *Syariah* principles used by Islamic banks in their deposit facilities. For example, current accounts in Iran and Kuwait use the *qard hassan* principle, while Islamic banks in other countries use *wadiah* or trust. In the case of savings account, Iran uses the *qard hassan* principle, while Kuwait combines two principles, that is, the *mudharabah* principle for savings account with permitted investment and the *qard hassan* principle. In Malaysia, savings account is based on *al-wadiah yad dhamanah* or guaranteed deposit. Islamic banks in other countries use the profit-sharing or *mudharabah* principle for their deposit facility. For investment account, all Islamic banks use the *mudharabah* principle, except for Shamil Bank of Bahrain which uses the *wadiah* concept.

(vi) Most banks provide a guarantee to return the full amount of deposits placed by customers in deposit facilities except in the profit-loss sharing facility. Islamic banks in Iran and Malaysia provide some kind of returns to their savings account customers. These rewards are solely based on the discretion of the banks. Islamic banks in Iran do reward their current account holders but the rewards are not fixed or guaranteed. The rewards given may be in the form of cash bonus, air ticket to Mecca, carpets, cars, etc. In Malaysia, the reward for savings account holders is usually in the form of profit announced by the bank.

(vii) In addition to providing services based on the country's local currency, there are Islamic banks which accept time deposits in foreign currencies. This type of facility is offered by Islamic banks in Turkey and Jordan.

In terms of daily operations, there are some regulations and procedures that must be adhered to by Islamic banks and their customers. In most cases, the operational aspects and practices of these deposit facilities are similar to that of conventional banks. These similarities include the procedures and requirements such as the minimum deposits for opening an account, identification, method of closure and termination of operation, management of unclaimed monies, etc.

Deposit facilities provided by Islamic banks in selected Muslim countries are shown in Table 6–2.

Financing Facilities

Islamic banks also offer financing facilities to their customers. Financing for businesses include short-term and long-term financing. The former type of financing is usually for meeting working capital requirement while long-term financing covers capital expenditure or expenditure associated with long-term projects. Financing facilities offered to individual customers include financial aid in the form of housing and consumer goods loans. Since Islamic banks are prohibited from making loans other than those based on the *qard hassan* principle, all financing operations are either based on the profit-loss sharing principle or the principle of fees, commission and fixed charges.

TABLE 6-2 Deposit Facilities Provided by Islamic Banks

Iran	Malaysia	Pakistan	B'desh	Kuwait	Jordan	Bahrain	Turkey	UAE	Indonesia
Current acc.	*Mud.* fund: – Current acc. – Savings acc. – Negotiable Islamic debt certificate – Others	Current acc. Savings acc. Fixed deposit	Current acc.: – *Taka* acc. – Dollar acc. – Foreign currency acc. – Property development acc.	Non-investment deposit: – Current acc. Investment deposit: – Restricted – Non-restricted – Savings acc.	Trust acc.: – Current acc. – Demand acc. Non-restricted investment acc.: – Savings – Notice – Fixed restricted investment acc.	Current acc. Restricted investment acc. Non-restricted investment acc.	Special current acc. Participatory acc.	Current acc. Savings acc. Investment acc.	*Wadiah* acc.: – Demand – Savings Non-restricted *Mud. acc.*: – Savings – Term
Savings acc. Investment acc.	Non-*mud.* fund: – Savings acc. – Investment acc.	Term acc. Other deposits	*Mud.* deposit: – Savings – Special notice – Fund bonds Term mud.		*Muqaradah* bond				

Mud.: Mudharabah Acc.: Account

Sources: Iran: *Annual Report*, Bank Melli Iran, 2007; Malaysia: *Annual Report*, Bank Islam Malaysia Berhad, 2008; Pakistan: *Annual Report*, Muslim Commercial Bank, 2007; Bangladesh: *Annual Report*, Islami Bank Bangladesh Limited, 2007; Kuwait: *Annual Report*, Kuwait Finance House, 2007; Jordan: *Annual Report*, Jordan Islamic Bank, 2007; Bahrain: *Annual Report*, Shamil Bank of Bahrain, 2007; Turkey: *Annual Report*, Turkiye Finans, 2007; United Arab Emirates: *Annual Report*, Dubai Islamic Bank, 2007; Indonesia: *Annual Report*, Bank Muamalat, 2007.

There is no clear demarcation in terms of priority in the use of principles when meeting the financing needs of customers, be it corporate or commercial customers. However, the principles of *mudharabah* and *musyarakah* are widely used in financing working capital loans while the principles of *murabahah, bai muazzal* and *ijarah* are used to finance the purchase of fixed assets by customers. The financing principles used by Islamic banks depend a lot on the law governing their operations. In Iran, for instance, modes and scopes of financing facilities used are described in the *Law of Usury-Free Banking* as shown in Table 6–3.

TABLE 6–3 *Syariah* Principles Associated with Financing Facilities in Iran

Area	Activity	*Syariah* principle
Productive	Industrial Agricultural Mining	Instalment sale, civil partnership, legal partnership, hire purchase, forward transaction, direct investment, *qard-al-hasanah, jo'alah, mozaraah, masaqat*
Commercial	Import Export Domestic	*Modarabah*, civil partnership, legal partnership, *jo'alah*
Services		Civil partnership, legal partnership, hire purchase, instalment sale, *jo'alah*
Housing	Construction Repairs	Civil partnership, instalment sale, hire purchase, *qard-al-hasanah, jo'alah*, direct investment
Personal needs		*Qard-al-hasanah*

In Pakistan, the principles used are based on the *Circular, State Bank of Pakistan No. 13* dated 20 June 1984. It contains a list of permissible methods of financing, covering loans, trade and investment. The guidelines cover various economic activities that could be adopted by Islamic banks in Pakistan. The principle recommended for project financing is associated with the profit-loss sharing method. The minimum and maximum rates of returns that may be acquired from any principle used for trade activities and the profit rates for investment activities are pre-determined by the State Bank of Pakistan from time to time. Meanwhile, should the investment activity result in a loss, the loss is borne by all the financiers. In Malaysia, Islamic banks provide their corporate customers financing to meet working capital requirements and this project financing is based on the principles of *mudharabah, musyarakah, murabahah, bai muazzal* and *ijarah*. For the commercial customers, the banks provide personal financing for acquisition of houses, buildings, consumer goods and others. This financing is based on the principles of *bai muazzal* and *qard hassan*. Principles used by Islamic banks in Bangladesh are very similar to those adhered to by Islamic banks in Malaysia, but the banks in Bangladesh have an additional principle, namely the *bai-salam* principle. Overall, most of the *Syariah* principles used by Islamic banks are based on *mudharabah, musyarakah, murabahah, bai muazzal, ijarah* and *qard hassan*. However, Islamic banks differ in the priority of principles used and the extent to which particular principles are used depends a lot on the management of that particular Islamic bank.

The financing activities of Islamic banks in selected countries based on *Syariah* principles are shown in Table 6–4. Referring to Table 6–4, there exist several similarities and differences among Islamic banks in providing financing to clients. The following are some of the more obvious similarities and differences:

(i) Although the principles of *mudharabah* and *musyarakah* (profit-loss sharing) are recommended by Islamic scholars, there are still some Islamic banks which do not apply these principles while others channel a very small portion of their funds into these modes of financing. For instance, in their annual reports, Kuwait Finance House and Albaraka Turk, Turkey, did not show any record of financing based on the principles of *mudharabah* and *musyarakah*. Meanwhile, Bank Islam Malaysia and Islami Bank Bangladesh channelled only 1% of their total financing portfolio into the *musyarakah* principle. The highest percentage of *musyarakah* financing was recorded by Bank Muamalat Indonesia, that is 43.2%, followed by Shamil Bank of Bahrain and Dubai Islamic Bank at 8.8% and 7.8%, respectively. However, Bank Muamalat Indonesia and Dubai Islamic Bank are two banks which actively apply the *mudharabah* principle. At the end of 2007, the percentage of such financing for Bank Muamalat Indonesia was 56.8% while it was 11.3% for Dubai Islamic Bank. Shamil Bank of Bahrain had the third highest percentage of financing under this principle with 9.7% of total financing.

(ii) As for the *qard hassan* principle or goodwill loan, only Islami Bank Bangladesh and Islamic International Arab Bank gave out financing via this principle, that is only 1.3% and 0.2% of their total financing, respectively. There are two possible reasons for these low rates. First, there is a possibility that the managements of Islamic banks view this type of financing as not bringing any economic returns. Secondly, the banks may feel that they have already performed many other social activities and hence regard *qard hassan* loans as unwarranted.

(iii) All the Islamic banks focus on sale-based principles, in particular *murabahah* and *bai bithaman ajil*. Only Bank Islam Malaysia provided financing based on the *Syariah* principle of *bai bithaman ajil*, that is, 52.8% of its total financing. Dubai Islamic Bank and Shamil Bank of Bahrain channelled 91% and 75% respectively of their financing activities into *murabahah*. Bank Islam Malaysia had the lowest percentage of *murabahah* financing, that is 17.7%.

(iv) The *ijarah* principle is now gaining the attention of Islamic banks worldwide. Islamic International Arab Bank, Jordan allocates the most funds for financing under this principle. Dubai Islamic Bank channelled 18.5% while Islami Bank Bangladesh and Bank Islam Malaysia channelled 4.9% and 2.6% respectively of their funds into *ijarah* financing.

(v) The *istisna* principle was used in the financing activities of Dubai Islamic Bank, Kuwait Finance House and Bank Islam Malaysia. The *istisna* financing of these banks stood at 13.5%, 8.9% and 4.9% of their total financing, respectively.

TABLE 6–4 Percentage of Financing Based on *Syariah* Principles

Principle	A	B	C	D	E	F	G	H
Musyarakah	–	8.8	0.1	43.2	–	–	7.8	0.1
Mudharabah	0.09	9.7	*	56.8	–	–	11.3	3.8
Murabahah	17.7	75.0	50.9	–	91.0	–	45.1	68.1
Bai bithaman ajil	52.8	–	–	–	–	–	–	–
Ijarah	2.6	4.9	–	–	–	–	18.5	19.3
Qard hassan	–	–	1.3	–	–	–	–	0.2
Istisna	4.9	–	–	–	8.9	–	13.5	–
Other principles	21.9	1.6	47.7	–	–	–	3.8	8.5
Total	100	100	100	100	100	–	100	100

* Less than 0.05%. A = Malaysia, Bank Islam Malaysia (Figures as of 30/6/2008).

B = Bahrain, Shamil Bank of Bahrain (Figures as of 31/12/2007).

C = Bangladesh, Islami Bank Bangladesh (Figures as of 31/12/2007).

D = Indonesia, Bank Muamalat Indonesia (Figures as of 31/12/2007).

E = Kuwait, Kuwait Finance House (Figures as of 31/12/2007).

F = Turkey, Albaraka Turk (Figures as of 31/12/2007).

G = United Arab Emirates, Dubai Islamic Bank (Figures as of 31/12/2007).

H = Jordan, Islamic International Arab Bank (Figures as of 31/12/2007).

Islamic banks tend to finance all sectors within the economy as shown in Table 6–5.

TABLE 6–5 Distribution of Financing Based on Sector (%)

Sector	A	B	C	D	E	F	G	H
Agriculture	1.1	–	12.6	*	–	4.1	–	0.6
Manufacturing	11.2	12.2	56.0	0.3	25.6	51.3	24.5	6.8
Construction	5.6	5.65	–	3.5	14.6	16.9	–	9.3
Wholesale and retail	5.0	–	–	0.9	–	–	7.9	36.8
Communication and warehousing	0.8	–	–	–	–	–	–	–
Services and financial	1.0	57.5	–	62.3	54.0	21.4	7.6	10.2
Real estate	31.7	–	–	–	–	–	37.1	20.9
Consumerism	18.9	–	–	–	–	–	13.9	10.8
Miscellaneous	24.7	24.7	31.4	33.0	5.8	1.6	9.0	4.4
Total	**100**	**100**	**100**	**100**	**100**	**100**	**100**	**100**

* Less than 0.1%. Note: List of banks is as in Table 6–4.

From Table 6–5, it can be seen that there is no uniformity or standardization among Islamic banks in the distribution of financing. Bank Islam Malaysia, for example, concentrates more on the real estate and miscellaneous sectors, such as construction and services. The real estate sector is also the focus of Dubai Islamic Bank and Islamic International Arab Bank. It is because of this high concentration in the housing sector that at the end of the 2008 financial year, Bank Islam Malaysia recorded *bai bithaman ajil* as having the highest percentage of financing used, that is 52.8% of its total financing. As for the wholesale and retail sector, Islamic International Arab Bank has the highest concentration of financing in this sector. Bank Islam Malaysia, Dubai Islamic Bank and Islamic International Arab Bank are involved in financing the consumerism sector, that is 18.9%, 13.9% and 10.8%, respectively. Only five Islamic banks are involved in the agriculture sector with Bank Muamalat Indonesia channelling less than 0.1% to this sector. For Islami Bank Bangladesh, 12.6% of its total financing was channelled into the agriculture sector in 2007, while it was 4.1%, 1.1% and 0.6% for Albaraka Turk, Bank Islam Malaysia and Islamic International Arab Bank, respectively. Bank Muamalat Indonesia, Shamil Bank of Bahrain and Kuwait Finance House allocated a major portion of their financing, that is 62.3%, 57.5% and 54% respectively, to the services and financial sector. All eight Islamic banks listed in the table provide financing to the manufacturing sector with Islami Bank Bangladesh and Albaraka Turk channelling the most funds, that is 56% and 51.6% of their total financing, respectively into this sector.

The concentration of an Islamic bank's financing in a particular sector is dependent on several factors, which may be categorized as internal and external factors. External factors consist of aspects such as economic situation, regulations set by the central bank, competition and the perception of the local community towards the bank. If the bank is operating in a country where the industrial sector is developing rapidly, then there is a high possibility that financing will be concentrated in the manufacturing sector. Similarly, if the country is an agricultural country, then the agriculture sector will be given more attention. Apart from that, the role of the central bank is also significant in setting the direction and amount of financing. For instance, the bank must comply with the directives of the central bank on the issuance of certain financing.

Customer factor is also an important determination of the amount of financing. If the majority of customers are drawn by certain factors to patronize an Islamic bank, then they would obtain financing from an Islamic bank. In contrast, if they prefer to conduct their banking business with the conventional banks, Islamic banks may end up financing the less preferred sectors. Internal factors include the management perception, financing costs and effectiveness and efficiency in providing products and services. If the management merely wants to finance sectors that are secure and provide short-term returns, there is a high probability that sectors with high risks like agriculture would receive less financing. Instead, the banks would be more heavily involved in financing the real estate sector which is regarded as more secure. In addition, financing costs charged by Islamic banks are higher than those of conventional banks. This obviously makes conventional banks more attractive. A number of studies have shown that customers patronize Islamic banks on the basis of economic factors rather than religious factors. The final factor is the efficiency of the bank in giving out loan approvals and the applicability of the financing provided. Customers prefer banks that grant immediate financing approval and do not impose too many conditions.

Other Facilities

Apart from deposit and financing facilities, Islamic banks also provide other facilities to their customers. Such facilities depend on the capability and capacity of the particular bank. For a newly-established bank, there is a high possibility that it would be providing only basic facilities. For example, some Islamic banks do not issue letters of credit to their customers. In Indonesia, for instance, only certain banks are allowed to conduct international trade transactions. Others do not perform foreign exchange businesses. However, most Islamic banks offer facilities such as letters of credit for international and domestic trade, letters of guarantee, foreign exchange, local and overseas money order, cheque and bank draft issuance, issuance and underwriting of Islamic securities, syndicated loan, advisory service and consultancy service. Letters of credit are normally issued to customers who wish to import goods from overseas, and most letters of credit use the *mudharabah* principle. In a *mudharabah* letter of credit, the bank acts as the middleman and imports the goods required by the customer and subsequently resells the goods to the customer. The following are the basic steps involved in a letter of credit transaction.

1. The customer asks the bank to open a letter of credit for the purpose of importing a particular commodity. The customer will provide the bank with all the information about the exporter and the commodity he intends to purchase (type, price, quantity, size, etc.).

2. If approval is granted, and after receiving a guarantee either in the form of deposit or other forms, the bank will issue a letter of credit (the bank that issues the letter of credit is called the issuing bank), the contents of which are in accordance with the customer's request. This letter will be sent to the bank that is acting as his representative (known as the representative bank) where the exporter resides.

3. The customer will sign an "agreement to purchase" the imported commodity. The bank and customer will negotiate on the cost of the commodity to be sold and the terms of delivery.

4. The exporter will execute the delivery of the commodity as stipulated in the letter of credit, after which all delivery documents will be submitted to the representative bank. The representative bank in turn delivers the documents to the issuing bank.

5. When all the documents have reached the issuing bank and the issuing bank endorses its ownership rights on the commodity,

the customer will then sign a letter of sale and purchase agreement of the commodity.

Bank Islam Malaysia issues its letters of credit by using three separate methods based on *wakalah, musyarakah* and sale with profit mark-up (*murabahah*). The choice of method depends on the needs of the customer. The following are the transactions involved in the use of such services.

Wakalah Letter of Credit

When the *wakalah* principle is applied, the bank acts as the agent or representative in the transaction involving the purchase of the commodity on behalf of its client, and the bank receives a payment for the service provided. The steps involved are as follows:

1. The customer informs the bank of his letter of credit requirement and negotiates the terms.

2. The customer will place a deposit towards the purchase of the goods in the deposit account based on the *wadiah* principle.

3. The bank establishes the letter of credit.

4. Upon receipt of the documents or information via telex regarding negotiations of the letter of credit, the bank will remit the payment to the seller utilizing the customer's deposit.

5. The bank charges the customer a commission fee based on the principle of fees, commission and fixed payment, and management expenditure associated with the facility and service of letters of credit.

6. The bank submits the related documents to the customer.

Musyarakah Letter of Credit

Under this principle, the bank acts as the partner in the transaction involving purchase of the goods concerned. In addition to managing all the relevant documents for the import of the goods, the bank also issues part of the capital to finance the purchase of the goods. The steps involved are as follows:

1. The customer informs the bank on the type and features of the goods he intends to import or purchase, as well as the terms for issuance of the letter of credit.

2. The customer deposits his share of the financing with the bank under the *wadiah* principle.

3. The customer and the bank both agree to contribute their capital and expertise in the import or purchase of the goods based on the *musyarakah* principle and seal the agreement which contains terms based on *musyarakah*, such as contribution of their respective portions of capital, profit apportionment ratio and other such matters.

4. The bank issues the letter of credit.

5. Upon receipt of the documents or information via telex regarding negotiations of the letter of credit, the bank will remit the payment to the seller utilizing the customer's deposit and the bank's share of financing.

6. The bank imposes a commission fee on the customer based on the principle of service reward and management expenditure associated with the facility and service of letters of credit.

7. The bank releases the documents to the customer, and the customer takes possession of the goods in the manner set forth in the agreement.

8. The bank and customer share in the profit from the venture as provided for in their agreement.

Murabahah Letter of Credit

Under this principle, the Islamic bank acts as the businessman. The bank will first purchase the goods from a producer, and then resell it to the client at a higher price. The steps involved are as follows:

1. The customer informs the bank on the type and features of the goods he intends to import or purchase, as well as the terms for issuance of the letter of credit.

2. The customer negotiates with the bank for it to purchase the goods in advance and to subsequently sell the goods to the customer at a sale price comprising its cost and a profit margin.

3. The bank issues the letter of credit.

4. Upon receipt of the documents or information via telex regarding negotiations of the letter of credit, the bank will remit payment to the seller utilizing its own fund.

5. The bank sells the goods to the customer based on the *murabahah* principle.

6. The bank charges the customer a commission fee based on the principle of fees, commission and fixed payment, and management expenditure associated with the facility and service of letters of credit.

Kafalah Letter of Guarantee

The issuance of letters of guarantee is based on the principle of fees, commission and fixed payment. Bank Islam Malaysia issues this letter of guarantee based on the principle of *kafalah* or secured debt. The steps involved in using a letter of guarantee are as follows:

1. The customer submits an application to the bank to issue a letter of guarantee to a third party for the purpose of settlement of a loan or successful performance of a task.

2. The bank issues a letter of guarantee to the third party and agrees to assume the liability of the customer in the case of default or breaching of contract as agreed between the customer and the third party.

3. The customer may be required to place a certain amount of deposit, which the bank accepts under the principle of *wadiah*.

4. The bank charges the customer a fee for the service provided based on the principle of *ujr*.

Services such as money order, foreign exchange, sale and purchase of travellers cheque, etc., are based on fees, commission and fixed payment. For foreign exchange transactions, spot rate and not forward rate is used. For example, Islami Bank Bangladesh offers no forward transactions for foreign exchange facilities. However, the additional facilities provided by Islamic banks vary from one bank to another due to factors such as expertise, location and emphasis on facilities extended by the bank. For instance, the involvement of a bank in international trade can be seen from the amount of contingent liabilities of the bank. The contingent liabilities of selected banks are shown in Table 6–6.

TABLE 6–6 Percentage Breakdown of Contingent Liabilities

Type of Liability	A	B	C	D	E	F	G	H
Letters of credit	5.6	24.7	79.7	19.1	31.9	18.4	34.2	19.1
Letters of guarantee	6.8	–	6.1	80.9	50.3	75.1	57.7	11.0
Foreign exchange contract	31.0	–	–	–	–	–	–	–
Bills for collection	5.5	–	12.5	–	–	–	–	–
Other liabilities	51.1	75.3	1.8	–	17.8	17.8	8.1	69.9
Total	100	100	100	100	100	100	100	100
Total assets (%)	39.6	6.9	30.9	8.8	14.3	27.3	21.5	11.5

Note: List of banks is as in Table 6–4.

From Table 6–6, we can conclude that:

(i) The types of international services offered differ among Islamic banks. While letter of credit is available at all banks, facilities such as letter of guarantee, foreign exchange and bills for collection are available only at selected banks.

(ii) Bank Islam Malaysia is the only Islamic bank that provides all facilities in international trade. Foreign exchange futures contract is not provided by banks in West Asia. Likewise for bills for collection services.

(iii) There are also some differences in terms of emphasis on facilities extended by Islamic banks to their customers. Islamic bank in Bangladesh seems to concentrate on letters of credit facilities, whereas Islamic banks in Indonesia, Turkey,

Dubai and Kuwait tend to concentrate on providing letters of guarantee. Meanwhile, Islamic banks in Bahrain and Jordan are more inclined towards other liability facilities. These other facilities may be forms of financing that have already been approved but not yet used by customers.

(iv) The extent of additional facilities provided also varies between Islamic banks. Bank Islam Malaysia has the highest exposure in terms of contingent liabilities; its contingent liabilities are 39.6% of total assets. This is followed by Islami Bank Bangladesh with 30.9% and Albaraka Turk with 27.3%. The banks with the lowest exposure are Islamic International Arab Bank, 11.5%, Shamil Bank of Bahrain, 6.9% and Bank Muamalat Indonesia, 8.8%.

SOURCES OF FUNDS

Generally, there are three main sources of funds for Islamic banks, namely deposit, other liabilities and shareholders' funds. The amount of capital issued depends on the financial strength of those who wish to establish the Islamic bank concerned. The Dallah Albaraka Group has invested a huge part of its funds for the establishment of Islamic banks. Bank Negara Malaysia has set a minimum share capital requirement of RM300 million for foreigners wishing to set up Islamic banks in Malaysia. This deposit in turn is divided into several types, as already explained in the previous section (Deposit Facilities). Other contributions are funds acquired from other liabilities, which are usually in the form of short-term liability. Meanwhile, shareholders' funds consist of paid-up capital, various reserves and retained earnings. The sources of funds of Islamic banks in particular countries are shown in Table 6–7.

TABLE 6–7   Sources of Funds of Islamic Banks (%)

Source of funds	A	B	C	D	E	F	G	H
Deposit	88.4	72.3	86.9	87.0	74.4	81.2	77.6	84.8
Shareholders' funds	5.6	20.5	6.2	8.0	16.0	14.5	12.7	12.5
Others	6.0	7.2	6.9	5.0	9.6	4.3	9.7	3.1
Total	100	100	100	100	100	100	100	100

Note: List of banks is as in Table 6–4.

Based on the figures shown in Table 6–7, Bank Muamalat Indonesia is the bank with the highest amount of funds deposited by customers, about 87% of its overall assets at the end of the 2007 financial year. The percentage figures for other Islamic banks are within the range of 70% to 90%. Shamil Bank of Bahrain has the lowest percentage figure, only 72.3% in the year 2007, followed by Kuwait Finance House with 74.4%. The low percentage figure registered by Shamil Bank is due to the fact that investment accounts are not considered as liabilities, and hence are consequently removed from the financial statement, while deposit account is shown to be consisting of current account and savings account only. Shamil Bank also has the highest percentage of shareholders' fund, that is 20.5%. Banks which recorded low shareholders' funds are Bank Islam Malaysia with 5.6%, Islami Bank Bangladesh, 6.2% and Bank Muamalat Indonesia, 8%. In line with Basel II (an effort by the Basel Committee on Banking Supervision to update the original international bank capital accord), banks worldwide must hold capital reserves appropriate to the risk the bank exposes itself to through its lending and investment practices. The composition of deposits of Islamic banks is shown in Table 6–8.

TABLE 6–8 Deposit Composition of Islamic Banks (%)

Source of funds	A	B	C	D	E*	F	G	H
Current accounts	28.2	26.9	11.5	10.6	–	14.4	21.2	21.3
Savings accounts	11.7	–	37.5	38.0	–	–	13.4	4.1
Investment accounts	30.5	50.0	18.7	51.4	–	85.6	64.0	74.6
Other accounts	29.6	23.9	32.3	–	–	–	1.4	–
Total	100	100	100	100	–	100	100	100

Note: List of banks is as in Table 6–4.

*No breakdown of deposit account is shown by Kuwait Finance House.

Based on **Table 6–8**, the following are the deposit composition of Islamic banks.

(i) Except for Shamil Bank of Bahrain and Albaraka Turk, Turkey, Islamic banks in other countries offer three types of deposit facilities to their customers, namely current account, savings account and investment account. Although current account does not give out any reward, most of the deposit made by customers is of this form. Bank Islam Malaysia has the highest percentage of current accounts, that is, 28.2%, followed by Shamil Bank of Bahrain with 26.9%. Furthermore, total fund deposited in the current account facility is more than 10% on average; thus suggesting that customers do not require rewards or *hibah*. However, the investment account facility has the highest percentage of deposited funds. Albaraka Turk, Turkey has the highest percentage of investment accounts, that is, 85.6%, followed by Islamic International Arab Bank, Jordan with 74.6%. All investment deposits available at Islamic banks are governed by the profit-loss sharing or *mudharabah* principle.

(ii) Savings account is not very popular among depositors in Jordan and Malaysia, comprising only 4.1% and 11.7% of total deposits of Islamic International Arab Bank and Bank Islam Malaysia, respectively. This is in contrast with other banks such as Islami Bank Bangladesh and Bank Muamalat Indonesia which have recorded relatively higher percentage of savings accounts; 38% and 37.5%, respectively. Two factors contributing to this difference have been identified. First, other banks apply the *mudharabah* principle while Malaysia uses the *wadiah* principle. Secondly, other banks offer various forms of savings accounts, and thus are better able to attract depositors.

(iii) Bangladesh and Malaysia are two countries where "other deposits" constitute a relatively high percentage of the banks' deposit composition. During the 2007 financial year, other accounts comprised 32.3% of the total deposits in Bangladesh, while in Malaysia it was 29.6%. In Bangladesh, the bulk of this deposit is mainly from the marginal deposits required by the banks prior to the issuance of letters of credit and letters of guarantee. In the case of Malaysia, customers who deposit their money into this facility are mainly the government and government agencies.

USES OF FUNDS

How Islamic banks use their funds is represented by the types of assets held which mainly belong to five main categories, namely cash, financing, investment, fixed assets and others. Cash includes cash in hand, balance with the central bank or reserves and balances with other financial institutions. Banks normally do not hold high percentages of cash. The amount of reserves each bank keeps with the central bank depends on the ratio set by the central bank of the particular country. It also depends to a large extent on how the central bank implements its financial policies as well as on the country's inflation rate. Financing comprises all loans extended under the principles of *mudharabah, musyarakah, murabahah, bai muazzal, ijarah* and *qard hassan*. Investment includes investment in government securities, treasury bills and investment in subsidiaries and associated companies. Fixed assets include all land and buildings, vehicles, factories, furniture and fixtures. All other assets which cannot be categorized under the four mentioned categories are classified as other assets. The uses of funds by Islamic banks are shown in Table 6–9.

TABLE 6–9 Uses of Funds by Islamic Banks (%)

Uses of funds	A	B	C	D	E	F	G	H
Cash	42.2	28.2	8.9	1.6	6.3	4.0	5.9	5.9
Financing	38.5	39.4	75.7	38.7	57.5	73.0	58.4	51.1
Investment	15.6	26.9	10.6	0.4	6.7	0.1	11.3	4.3
Fixed assets	0.5	0.6	4.5	0.7	4.6	1.1	0.8	1.5
Other assets	3.2	4.9	0.3	58.6	24.6	21.8	23.6	37.2
Total	100	100	100	100	100	100	100	100

Note: List of banks is as in Table 6–4.

Table 6–9 shows that there exist similarities and differences in terms of the uses of funds by Islamic banks. Variations are reflected by the differences in terms of preferences as well as in the percentage of funds allocated for various categories of assets. The following are some prominent features in terms of the uses of funds among Islamic banks.

(i)   With the exception of Bank Islam Malaysia, Bank Muamalat Indonesia and Shamil Bank of Bahrain, Islamic banks in other countries are concentrating on financing activities. For example, Islami Bank Bangladesh and Albaraka Turk have channelled more than 70% of their funds into these activities. Other banks which concentrate on financing activities are Dubai Islamic Bank, 58.4%, Kuwait Finance House, 57.5% and Islamic International Arab Bank, 51.1%. The low percentage of funds allocated to financing activities by some Islamic banks is due to factors such as limited business opportunities, or the policy of the banks which puts a limit on funds for financing activities. In theory, the more funds allocated for financing, the more profits they acquire. However, high financing could also expose the banks to bad debt problems.

(ii) There are four banks which give priority to investment, namely Shamil Bank of Bahrain, 26.9%; Bank Islam Malaysia, 15.6%; Dubai Islamic Bank, 11.3% and Islami Bank Bangladesh, 10.6%. The higher percentage of investment activities is due to the fact that governments of the countries in which these banks operate issue securities based on Islamic principles, thus creating an investment avenue for Islamic banks. For instance, Bank Islam Malaysia can invest in *Syariah*-compliant government securities. Similarly for Islamic banks in Dubai and Bahrain. In other countries, Islamic securities are still not widespread, and hence opportunities to invest through the purchase of *Syariah*-compliant securities are somewhat limited.

(iii) Most of the Islamic banks have a low percentage of cash in their funds, with the exception of two banks. Bank Islam Malaysia and Shamil Bank of Bahrain maintain high liquidity of about 42.2% and 28.2% of the total assets, respectively. Cash reserves held by other Islamic banks are in the range of 5% to 10%. Bank Muamalat Indonesia has the lowest cash holding, that is 1.6% of total assets, followed by Albaraka Turk, Turkey with

4%. If there are no restrictions on the inflow and outflow of funds in a country, Islamic banks with surplus funds may be able to undertake investments in international markets centred in Bahrain or at the Labuan International Financial Exchange which has already listed securities and bonds issued based on *Syariah*.

(iv) In general, the proportion of fixed assets held by Islamic banks is not more than 2% of the total assets. Kuwait Finance House has the highest percentage of fixed assets, 4.6% of total assets, followed by Islami Bank Bangladesh with 4.5%. Heavy concentration in fixed assets represents a loss to the bank. This is because the larger the value of fixed assets, the bigger the annual depreciation charge that must be deducted from the bank's net income.

(v) There is no significant differences in the percentage of "other assets" held by Islamic banks, except for Bank Muamalat Indonesia where the percentage of other assets to total assets is 58.6%. As for other Islamic banks, this percentage is not that high and most of the assets held are in the form of transactions among subsidiary companies. However, Islami Bank Bangladesh recorded the lowest percentage of other assets, that is 0.3%. This is followed by Bank Islam Malaysia at 3.2% and Shamil Bank of Bahrain at 4.9%.

The type of investment undertaken can influence returns or income received by an Islamic bank. The short-term and long-term trend of income also depends largely on the investment made. The types of investment include investment in subsidiaries and associated companies, Islamic securities, real estate and company shares. The types of investment and the amount of funds allocated for each type of investment vary among banks. Table 6–10 shows the types of investment undertaken by Islamic banks.

TABLE 6–10   Investment Undertaken by Islamic Banks (%)

Type	A	B	C	D	E	F	G	H
Securities	99.6	40.0	100	27.0	60.4	96.8	39.6	100
Subsidiaries & associated companies	0.4	29.7	–	73.0	23.0	–	15.9	–
Real estate	–	–	–	–	16.6	3.2	44.5	–
Others	–	30.0	–	–	–	–	–	–
Total	**100**	**100**	**100**	**100**	**100**	**100**	**100**	**100**
Investment out of total assets (%)	**15.6**	**22.0**	**10.6**	**0.5**	**16.9**	**16.0**	**11.3**	**4.3**

Note: List of banks is as in Table 6–4.

Table 6–10 shows that there are several similarities and differences in terms of the amount and distribution of investment made by Islamic banks in selected countries. Some of the main features are as follows:

(i) Only four banks concentrate on investment activities. They are Shamil Bank of Bahrain, Kuwait Finance House, Albaraka Turk and Bank Islam Malaysia, which allocated 22%, 16.9%, 16% and 15.6% of their funds respectively for investment activities. However, the type of investment differs among them. For example, both Islami Bank Bangladesh and Islamic International Arab Bank invested 100% in securities. On the other hand, 99.6% and 96.8% of Bank Islam Malaysia's and Albaraka Turk's investment activities were in securities, while for the other banks such investment was in the range of 40% to 60%. Investment in securities include investment in central government and state government securities, treasury bills, stocks and shares, bonds and unit trusts.

(ii) The second preferred area of investment is investment in subsidiaries and associated companies. Bank Muamalat Indonesia had 73% of this form of investment in 2007.

(iii) Real estate is the least preferred form of investment for most Islamic banks, except for Dubai Islamic Bank. The percentage of such investment made by Kuwait Finance House and Albaraka Turk, Turkey was very low.

SOCIAL AND WELFARE ACTIVITIES

Most Islamic banks have a high sense of corporate social responsibility. The issue lies in how much and how far this responsibility is actually implemented, and whether this information should be made public by the Islamic banks. The Accounting and Auditing Organization for Islamic Financial Institutions (AAOIFI), an organization responsible for preparing and issuing accounting standards of Islamic banks, has released standards relating to the account presentation and account statement of Islamic banks. AAOIFI does not provide any standards on matters relating to social responsibility. Nonetheless, the organization is currently developing a governance standard on corporate social responsibility. It does, however, provide standards that deal with the determination of *zakat* base, measurement of items to be included in the *zakat* base and disclosure of *zakat* in the financial statement of Islamic banks. In this case, *zakat* is regarded as a social rather than religious responsibility. AAOIFI has also recommended that the statement related to *qard hassan* loans be provided if a bank issues loans of this kind. Based on the latest financial statements, only Islamic International Arab Bank, Jordan prepared financial statement on this matter. Shamil of Bank Bahrain, Islami Bank Bangladesh, Kuwait Finance House, Albaraka Turk and Dubai Islamic Bank have not prepared financial statement on *qard hassan* loans as suggested by AAOIFI. Bank Muamalat Indonesia did, however, provide a statement on *qard hassan* loans which was presented in the form of notes to the account.

Factors such as the absence of *zakat* collecting activities, the low amount of *qard hassan* loans given out and the absence of laws or written regulations requiring Islamic banks to carry out social activities may have induced Islamic banks not to comply with standards related to *zakat* and *qard hassan* loans. For example, the establishment laws of Jordan Islamic Bank clearly state the bank's social role, which is to enhance ties and cooperation among society and among community members through:

(i) Granting benevolent loans to the needy in order to enable the recipients to be independent or meet certain financial obligations.

(ii) Creating and administering funds or specific savings for a variety of beneficial social purposes.

(iii) Other miscellaneous social activities which are subjected to the general objectives mentioned above.

In line with the regulations set, Jordan Islamic Bank has carried out various social activities and has listed them in its annual financial statements. Contributions and donations that the bank granted to mosques, the Holy Quran memorization prizes, *zakat* committees and other charitable associations amounted to JOD201,500 in 2007. (Jordan's official currency is the Dinar or JOD.) A total of JOD8.7 million of *qard hassan* loans were granted during 2007 from which 19,112 people benefited. In terms of financing to craftsmen and small-scale industries, the bank had financed 71 projects by the end of 2007 amounting to JOD1.6 million. The bank also patronized the mutual insurance fund where the compensation paid from this fund amounted to JOD385,000 in 2007. The total number of recipients who had benefited from this fund at the end of 2007 was 81,371 and the outstanding balance was JOD17.86 million. Jordan Islamic Bank also supports other miscellaneous social activities including education aid, humanitarian relief within and outside the country, and assistance to other welfare organizations.

Likewise, Islami Bank Bangladesh has shown tremendous commitment towards its social role since its inception. This is in accordance with the objectives of its establishment. To consolidate its social activities, Islami Bank Bangladesh has set up an organization called Islami Bank Foundation. This Foundation has apportioned financial aid to those in need through various programmes such as income generating programmes, healthcare and medicare programmes, humanitarian help programmes, educational programmes, relief and rehabilitation programmes and *dakwah* (religious outreach) programmes. This Foundation has established six modern hospitals, two service centres and five vocational training institutes. In addition, the bank has also implemented programmes to develop human resources by providing them with skills in specific areas so as to improve their economic condition and quality of life. A special institute that provides religious and moral education has also been established.

The social programmes carried out by this bank have also been taken up by other Islamic banks in Bangladesh. For example, the major activities of Social Investment Bank Limited which was established in 1995 are directed towards the welfare of the society in Bangladesh. This bank works towards developing various sectors in Bangladesh, including modernizing the management of social organizations such as mosques, colleges, *wakaf* institutes and other welfare organizations, as well as developing the properties that had been created through the processes of *wakaf*, charity and donation to bring about higher and more effective returns. In relation to this, Social Investment Bank has introduced a cash *wakaf* certificate where income from these funds is used to implement activities allowed by *Syariah* (www.siblbd.com). Apart from that, the bank also makes available a social savings fund which is to provide assistance to the poor and needy. Sources of the funds include the bank's annual profit as well as public contributions.

The social activities of Bank Muamalat Indonesia are carried out through Baitulmaal Muamalat which has developed a variety of programmes such as B-Community, B-Care, B-Smart and B-BMT. Through the B-Community programme, efforts are channelled towards developing self-sufficiency in communities and promoting community welfare. The B-Care programme involves distribution of aid to victims of natural disasters such as floods and fires as well as to those suffering human tragedy including wars, famines and diseases. Baitulmaal Muamalat distributed a total of Rp9.6 billion in relief aids to natural disaster victims in Indonesia in 2007 (Indonesia's official currency is the Rupiah or Rp). Educational aid in the form of scholarship grants (a full-year tuition fee) to students of private and state universities is distributed through the B-Smart programme. The recipients of this aid are given the opportunity to participate in the various social activities conducted by Bank Muamalat Indonesia. As at the end of 2007, Baitulmaal Muamalat has granted a total of 1,600 scholarships to the tsunami orphans of Aceh. The B-BMT programme is a micro-financing programme designed to enhance the development of micro businesses. Aid is normally given in the form of working capital and work facilities. Bank Muamalat Indonesia also provides service for the mobilization and distribution of *zakat*. *Zakat* amounting to Rp12 billion has been mobilized by the bank (Bank Muamalat Indonesia, 2007).

Dubai Islamic Bank also implements a range of social activities which benefit various sectors of Islamic societies and groups in the United Arab Emirates. The bank provides a *zakat* savings fund where funds are obtained from shareholders' profit. This *zakat* fund, known as *sandouq al-zakat*, is placed in a dedicated account and transacted separately. The bank also receives *zakat* money from other parties or customers who appoint the bank to pay *zakat* from their money and to use the money for charity and other welfare purposes in accordance with *Syariah*. The funds from the *zakat* savings are mostly given to orphans, welfare organizations, students and those in need, either within or outside of the Emirates. Another social activity conducted by Dubai Islamic Bank is the provision of interest-free loans, or *qard hassan* for marriage, medical treatment and debt repayment. In 2007, a total of 1,928 *qard hassan* loans totalling Dh18.48 million were issued. (The currency in Dubai is called dirham or Dh). Apart from this, the bank on its own initiative had conducted research and inquiry on the methods of slaughter of animals whose meat is imported into Dubai. On discovering that most of the animals were slaughtered through electrocution, the bank, with the cooperation of Dubai Co-operative Society held negotiations with major companies in Europe for the slaughter of animals to be done according to the Islamic method. Representatives from both the bank and the cooperative society were sent to conduct as well as to monitor the slaughtering at these slaughter houses.

ACCOUNTING POLICIES

Islamic banks must comply with Islamic business principles in all their transactions. Instead of interests, Islamic banks use four main mechanisms in mobilizing their funds. These mechanisms are profit-loss sharing, sale and purchase, fixed charges or commission and free service. As such, many Muslim scholars are of the view that Islamic banks should have methods of measuring, recording and reporting of transactions that are different from those of conventional banks. In general, the preparation and presentation of financial statements of conventional banks are based on accounting systems of the West which place importance on the economic interest of a particular transaction as well as the information required by users of the financial statement. However, the principal objective of the financial statement of the Islamic bank is not only to report the financial position of the bank, but also to provide information which customers and users of the statement need in order to assess the bank's compliance with the precepts of *Syariah*.

The task of ensuring that the Islamic bank does not violate *Syariah* rules is done by the Syariah Supervisory Board. The Board will issue a report as to whether the bank has complied with *Syariah* principles or otherwise and this account is published in the annual report of the bank.

A pure Islamic bank has yet to exist as the majority of Islamic banks are still using Western accounting systems to record business transactions and generate financial information. There are, however, some banks which have created their own accounting standards. The initial step to create accounting standards for Islamic banks was taken by Islamic Development Bank during its annual meeting in 1987. It received strong support from other Islamic banks. The outcome of the meeting was the establishment of a Steering Committee with the aim of recommending the appropriate and suitable accounting standards for Islamic banks. In 1988, the Steering Committee presented its report but not all members accepted the recommendations made by this committee. As a result, a new committee was set up to review and improve on the recommendations made by the earlier Steering Committee. Although the accounting standards put forward by this new committee were endorsed and accepted, the committee did not propose the method of implementation. It was because of the absence of a concrete implementation rule or guide that Islamic banks subsequently created their own accounting policy. They took into account views of the Syariah Committee as well as external auditors in developing their accounting policies. The accounting policy is also dependent on the banking regulations and laws of the country where the Islamic bank operates.

When choosing which policy to adopt, the majority of Islamic banks would use the policies already adopted by other pioneer Islamic banks as a benchmark. However, banks which belong to the same parent company or are subsidiaries, would normally adopt the accounting policies of the parent company. There are reporting variations among Islamic banks in preparing their financial statements. These differences occur not only among Islamic banks in different countries, but also among Islamic banks in the same country. For example, El Gharb Islamic Bank of Sudan does not report its accounting policy while Tadamon Islamic Bank of Sudan does.

It was as a result of the recommendations made regarding the need to have a common standard of accounting for Islamic banks during a meeting of Islamic Development Bank in Jeddah, that the Accounting and Auditing Organization for Islamic Financial Institutions (AAOIFI) was formed in 1991. Having uniform accounting standards for Islamic banks is crucial because the objective of reporting in Islamic banking differs substantially from that of conventional banking. While the accounting objective of the conventional bank is to aid the decision making of users of the financial statement, the accounting objective of the Islamic bank is to enable users to assess the bank's compliance with *Syariah* laws. Since its inception, AAOIFI has successfully produced several standards related to accounting and other financial transactions of Islamic banks. These consist of 23 accounting standards, 5 auditing standards, 6 governance standards, two codes of ethics for accountants and auditors in Islamic financial institutions and 30 *Syariah* standards. The standards of financial accounting issued by AAOIFI concentrate mostly on transactions in Islamic financial institutions based on *Syariah* principles. The standards developed by AAOIFI are comprehensive and include matters related to the basics of financial statement preparation, income recognition and expenses, methods of recording investments undertaken, allocation of doubtful debts, record of fixed assets and depreciation, distribution of profit between the banks and the depositors, payment of *zakat* and responsibility on all expenses issued.

The Basis of Financial Statement Preparation

Although AAOIFI has prepared accounting standards for Islamic banks, they are not legally bound to comply with these standards. However, some countries require Islamic banks to comply with standards and legislation imposed by the regulatory authority of those countries. For example, Bank Islam Malaysia and Bank Muamalat Malaysia prepare their financial statements in accordance with the provisions issued by the Malaysian Accounting Standards Board, provisions of the *Companies Act 1965* and approved accounting standards in Malaysia, Bank Negara Malaysia Guidelines and *Syariah* requirements. Both banks do not make any reference to the accounting standards issued by AAOIFI. Islami Bank Bangladesh asserts that the basis for preparing the financial statements is subject to the formats and provisions as prescribed under the *Banking Company Act 1991*, the *International Financial Reporting Standards* adopted as *Bangladesh Accounting Standards*, the *Companies Act 1994*, the *Securities and Exchange Rules 1987*, *Dhaka and Chittagong Stock Exchange's Listing Regulations* and other laws and rules applicable in Bangladesh, and AAOIFI standards. Bank Muamalat Indonesia reports that its financial statement preparation is in conformity with the *Statement of Financial Accounting Standards No. 59 "Accounting for Sharia Banks"*, the *Accounting Guidelines for Indonesian Sharia Banks* and other principles issued by the Indonesian Institute of Accountants as well as other standards imposed by Bank Indonesia and the Capital Market Supervisory Agency. As for Kuwait Finance House, the preparation of its financial statement is in accordance with the International Financial Reporting Standards. Meanwhile, Islamic banks in Turkey keep their accounting records and prepare their unconsolidated financial statements in accordance with the accounting and valuation standards described in the *Turkish Accounting Standards* and *Turkish Financial Reporting Standards*. Similarly, in preparation of its financial statements, Dubai Islamic Bank follows the standards issued by the International Accounting Standards Board and other policies issued by the United Arab Emirates.

Islamic banks which comply with AAOIFI standards are mostly those originating from the Middle East such as Shamil Bank of Bahrain, Albaraka Islamic Bank of Bahrain, Islamic International Arab Bank and Qatar Islamic Bank. These banks have clearly stated that their financial statement preparations are in accordance with the AAOIFI standards. They also follow the additional standards imposed in their respective countries. These observations highlight that the acceptance of accounting standards established by AAOIFI is relatively low which may be due to the voluntary nature of AAOIFI itself. There is a high possibility for the standardization of annual reporting among Islamic banks if the functions of AAOIFI are assumed by the Islamic Financial Services Board.

Revenue Recognition

Revenue recognition is the record of revenue when an exchange transaction has taken place or when the earning process has been completed. The principle of revenue recognition states that revenue is recognized either when it is earned or when it is realized. The timing of revenue recognition warrants careful observation because it is critical to the measurement of net income. Generally, revenues are recognized at the time of sale or provisioning of service. Not all Islamic banks describe their revenue recognition policy in their annual reports. Those who do are Bank Islam Malaysia, Shamil Bank of Bahrain, Albaraka Islamic Bank, Kuwait Finance House and Dubai Islamic Bank. Nonetheless, the methods of recognizing revenue vary among them. Islami Bank Bangladesh, on the other hand, does not provide any explanation as to the method used in revenue recognition. AAOIFI has issued a guide on revenue recognition and has suggested that revenues are realized when all the following conditions are satisfied (AAOIFI, 2000, p. 61):

- The bank has the right to receive revenue which means that the earning process should be complete. The point at which the earning process is complete differs between types or sources of revenues. For example, the earning process for revenue from services is complete when the bank delivers the service. Similarly, the earning process for revenue from the sale of goods is complete upon their delivery, while the process for revenue earned from allowing others to use the bank's assets (leasing) is complete through the passing of time.

- There exists an obligation on the part of another party to remit a fixed or a determinable amount to the bank.

- The amount of revenue should be known and collectible with reasonable degree of certainty, if not already collected.

There are similarities in the revenue recognition policies of Bank Islam Malaysia and Bank Muamalat Malaysia. For both banks, revenues are recognized on an accrual basis. Revenues from financing of customers are recognized based on the constant rate of return method while income from dealings and investment securities is recognized based on an effective yield basis. When an account is classified as non-performing, revenue will not be recognized until it is realized on a cash basis. The account is classified as non-performing if repayments are in arrears for more than a period of six months. This policy is in accordance with the guidelines provided by Bank Negara Malaysia. Islamic banks in Malaysia follow the MASBi-1 standards which are the accounting standards for Islamic banks set by the Malaysian Accounting Standards Board.

Shamil Bank of Bahrain in its 2007 annual report described in detail its revenue recognition policy as follows (Shamil Bank, 2007, p. 50):

- **Profit participation and management fees**

  Income from profit participation and management fees charged to funds managed by the bank is recognized on the basis of the bank's entitlement to receive such revenue from restricted and unrestricted investment accounts as stipulated in the *mudharabah* agreement, except when the bank temporarily waives its entitlement.

- **Profits from *murabahah* and *istisna* transactions**

  The profits acquired through *murabahah* and *istisna* transactions are recognized by proportionately allocating the attributable profits over the period of transaction where each financial period carries its portion of profits irrespective of whether or not cash is received. Profit is not accrued on *murabahah* and *istisna* transactions if the repayment instalments are overdue for more than 90 days, unless the director considers the accrual as justified.

- **Income from assets for rent**

  Income from rented assets is proportionately allocated over the rental period so as to provide a constant rate of return throughout the rental or lease term.

- **Income from *mudharabah* contracts**

  Income from *mudharabah* contracts is recognized when the *mudarib* declares profits.

- **Profits from *musyarakah* contracts**

  In the event that a *musyarakah* contract exceeds more than one financial period, the bank's share of the profit is recognized when the partial or final settlement takes place. Losses are recognized to the extent that such losses are deducted from the bank's share of *musyarakah* capital. However, with regard to diminishing *musyarakah* transactions, profits and losses are recognized after considering the decline in the bank's share of the *musyarakah* capital and consequently, its proportionate share of the profit or losses.

- **Dividend income**

  Dividend income will be recognized when the right to receive payment is established.

- **Fees and commissions**

  Fees and commissions are recognized as income when payment is received. Commissions on letters of credit and letters of guarantee are recognized as income over the period of transaction. Fees for structuring and arranging financing transactions for and on behalf of other parties are recognized after the bank has fulfilled its obligations in relation to the related transactions.

  Among Islamic banks that describe their revenue recognition method in detail are Dubai Islamic Bank and Albaraka Islamic Bank, Bahrain. The following are examples of the methods practised by Dubai Islamic Bank (Dubai Islamic Bank, 2007).

- *Murabahah*

  If the income is quantifiable and contractually determined at the beginning of a contract, then this income is recognized on a time-apportioned basis over the period of the contract based on the principal amount outstanding.

- *Istisna*

  Istisna's revenue and the associated profit margin (the difference between cash price of *al-masnoo* to the customer and the total *istisna* cost to the bank) are computed based on a time-apportioned basis.

- *Ijarah*

  Ijarah income is recognized based on a time-apportioned basis over the lease term.

- *Musyarakah*

  Income is computed based on the reducing balance on a time-apportioned basis that reflects the effective yield on the asset.

- *Mudharabah*

  Income and losses on *mudharabah* financing are recognized on an accrual basis if they can be reliably estimated. Otherwise, income is recognized on distribution by the *mudarib*. Losses are charged to income on their declaration by the *mudarib*.

- **Fees and commission income**

  Income from fees and commission is recognized when earned.

- **Rental income**

  Rental income is recognized based on an accrual basis.

- **Dividend**

  Dividends from investments in equities are recognized when the right to receive the dividends is established.

- *Sukuk*

  Income is accounted for on a time-apportioned basis over the term of the *sukuk*.

- **Sale of property**

  Revenue on sale of property is recognised on the basis of the full accrual method as and when all the following conditions are met:

  - A sale is consummated and contracts are signed;

  - The buyer's initial investment, to the date of the financial statements, is adequate to demonstrate a commitment to pay for the property; and

- The bank has transferred to the buyer the usual risks and rewards of ownership in a transaction that is in substance a sale and does not have a substantial continuing involvement with the property.

Revenue on sale of apartments is recognized on the basis of percentage completion as and when all of the following conditions are met:

- A sale is consummated and contracts are signed;

- The buyer's investment, to the date of the financial statements, is adequate to demonstrate a commitment to pay for the property;

- Construction is beyond a preliminary stage, that is, commencement of design work or construction contract or site accessibility, etc.;

- The buyer is committed;

- The buyer is unable to obtain a refund for non-delivery of the unit;

- The likelihood of the bank being unable to fulfil its contractual obligations is remote; and

- The aggregate sale proceeds and costs can be reasonably estimated.

Apart from the standards issued by international accounting organizations or by organizations which have authority in particular countries, some Islamic banks have to comply with the revenue recognition method of financial authorities which regulate and supervise the banks. For example, the revenue recognition method issued by the Central Bank of Iran is as follows:

1. *Hire purchase*: Income from hire purchase transactions is recognized when payment is received.

2. *Instalment sale*: The income is credited into the receivable income account and is recognized when the term is due.

3. *Civil partnership*: Income is recognized at the end of the contract term.

4. *Mudharabah*: Income is recognized at the end of the contract term.

5. *Futures transaction*: Income from both cash sales and credit sales is recognized with the latter as instalment sale.

6. *Jo'alah*: Income is recognized on a cash basis.

7. *Debt purchase*: Income is recognized on an accrual basis.

8. *Masaqat and mozaraah*: Income is recognized on a cash basis.

9. *Gharz-al-hassanah*: Commission is recognized on an accrual basis.

10. *Direct investment*: Income from the sale of shares is recognized when the sale is completed while dividends are recognized when received.

The Central Bank of Iran also established the following method for income and other expenditure streams:

(i) Income obtained from operations performed in conformance to past banking laws is recognized on an accrual basis.

(ii) Profit and commission for on-going transactions are recognized on a cash basis.

(iii) Commission for the maintenance of government accounts, bonuses for bonds and profits obtained through reserves are recognized on a cash method on the basis of the resolution of the Council for Money and Credit.

(iv) Interests received from agents and foreign banks are recognized as income based on an accrual method. Interests received by current accounts from agents of foreign banks, secured loans issued by Hamburg branches and capital provided by Hong Kong branches are recognized as income on a cash basis. Commissions from foreign exchange operations, administration fees to Iran-Egypt Development Bank and commissions from the sale of mortgage notes or bills of exchange and trade bills are recognized on the cash method.

(v) Profit paid to investment accounts, gifts paid to the *gharz-al-hassanah* account and interests paid to foreign currency fixed deposits are recognized as expenditure on an accrual method. Interests paid to foreign agents due to debit balance and the commissions paid are recognized as expenditure on a cash method.

In addition to the standards issued by international accounting organizations, some Islamic banks such as Jordan Islamic Bank are also required to comply with the laws of their establishment. For Jordan Islamic Bank, the law outline the revenue recognition methods for the bank, which are provided in *Section 18* and *Section 19* as follows:

Section 18:

Profit or loss associated with joint financing and investment activities must be recorded in separate accounts and must be presented separately from the income and expenditure associated with activities and services received by the bank. The same treatments apply to investment income and expenditure for specific purposes, whereby an account must be maintained for each project.

Section 19:

In accounting for the profit related to its financing and investment activities, the bank is not allowed to use accounting methods based on estimated or expected profits. On the other hand, the accounting must be subject to the profits which are recognized according to the financing method provided by the bank and which conforms to the following regulations:

(i) In the *mudharabah* method, profit must be recognized on the basis of the latest solution of the account which is executed between the bank and the party utilizing the fund. The solution must be based on the actual amount of money received and the recognition of the income. The solution must also be approved and received in full. Yearly profits must be credited into the account in that particular year, whereby solution is implemented regardless of whether the project is fully or only partly completed.

(ii) In the diminishing participation method, profit or income must be recognized on the basis of net income received by the project up until the end of the financial year, even if the income is not received in the form of cash. In such a situation, the recognized income will be regarded as money which is supposed to be acquired, or receivables.

(iii) In the method of purchasing for another party at an agreed mark-up profit, the profit will be recognized on the basis of the completion of the subsequent contract as well as on the difference between the actual cost and the price agreed by the party instructing the purchase.

(iv) All expenditure and costs related to the various operations of financing must be matched with each particular operation itself and cannot be incurred on or regarded as general expenditure issued by the bank.

Investment

Investment is one of the methods used by Islamic banks to generate revenue. There are four types of investment that Islamic banks can undertake, namely, purchase of negotiable securities such as shares, bonds, government issue notes and negotiable deposit certificates; investment in subsidiary and associated companies; investment in properties or real estates; and lastly, other investments. The policy chosen to record the investment undertaken will influence the investment value reported in the financial statement. If the investment value increases and this value is not reported, then the reported value of the company will be lower than the actual value. Similarly, if the recent value of the investment is lower than the value at the time the investment is made and this reduction is not reported, this will have the effect of overvaluing the true or actual value of the company. This investment process is not clearly detailed by AAOIFI; it only states that investment must be recorded at cost less the provision for any permanent diminution in value. The explanation on investment made by Bank Islam Malaysia is almost similar to those of Bank Muamalat Malaysia. Bank Islam Malaysia, in its 2008 annual report, offered the following explanation on the accounting policy in investment (Bank Islam Malaysia, 2008, p. 92):

- Securities are classified as held-for trading if they are acquired or incurred principally for the purpose of selling or repurchasing in the near term or if they are part of a portfolio of identified securities that are managed together and for which there is evidence of a recent actual pattern of short-term profit-taking. These securities are stated at fair value and any gain or loss arising from a change in the fair value will be recognized in the income statement.

- Securities available-for-sale are securities that are not classified as held-for-trading or held-to-maturity. These securities are measured at fair value. Investments in equity instruments that do not have a quoted market price in an active market and whose fair value cannot be reliably measured are stated at cost.

- Securities held-to-maturity are securities that have fixed or determinable payments and fixed maturity and the bank has the positive intention and ability to hold to maturity. These securities are measured at amortized cost using the effective profit method. Gain or loss is recognized in the income statement when the securities are derecognized or impaired, as well as the amortization of premium and accretion of discounts.

Investment policy differs between banks. For instance, Kuwait Finance House regards securities as investments which are ready to be sold and are evaluated at cost. Dubai Islamic Bank, on the other hand, provides an explanation of fair values for different types of investment activities in its notes to the accounts. If an investment is traded in an organized financial market, the fair value is simply the quoted market price at the close of business on the date of the balance sheet. For the unquoted investments, the fair value is the market value of similar investments. Meanwhile, for investment in properties, the fair value is determined periodically based on the valuations of independent professional valuators.

Shamil Bank of Bahrain describes in detail the value assigned to each investment made, as follows (Shamil Bank, 2007):

- **Investments in leasing**

  Investments in leasing (*ijarah*) are stated at cost and are reduced according to the bank's depreciation policy for property and equipment or lease term, whichever is the lower.

- **Investments in *sukuk***

  Investments in *sukuk* are carried at amortized cost, less provision for impairment in value. The resulting difference is recognized in the consolidated statement of income.

- **Investments held for trading**

  These investments are initially recognized at cost and subsequently re-measured at their fair value.

- **Investments in property**

  Investments in real estate are initially recognized at cost and subsequently re-measured at fair value.

- **Investments available for sale**

  Investments available for sale are re-measured at fair value.

- **Investments in associated companies**

  Investments in associated companies are carried in the balance sheet at cost plus post-acquisition changes in the bank's share of net assets of the associate.

- *Mudharabah* **investments**

  Mudharabah investments are initially recorded at cost and subsequently re-measured at fair value.

Provision for Doubtful Debts

Doubtful or bad debts are unavoidable in the banking industry. Although *Syariah* makes it mandatory for Muslims to pay their debts, in practice Islamic banks are haunted by bad debts. For this, AAOIFI has suggested that Islamic banks present four matters related to doubtful debts, as follows (AAOIFI, 2000, p. 91):

(i) Provision charged to income statement during the period.

(ii) Receivables written off during the period.

(iii) Receivables collected during the period which were previously written off.

(iv) The balance of the allowance for doubtful receivables as of the beginning and end of the period.

Islamic banks in Malaysia and Indonesia, Kuwait Finance House, Dubai Islamic Bank, Albaraka Turk and Islamic International Arab Bank are among those that disclose their provision for doubtful debt policies. Although Islami Bank Bangladesh and Shamil Bank of Bahrain do not specify any policy regarding this matter, they do provide a certain sum as provision for doubtful debts. Generally, there are two types of provisions created by Islamic banks, namely general and specific provisions. General provision is based on a percentage of the loan portfolio and covers possible losses which are not specifically identified. Specific provision is made for doubtful loans which have been individually reviewed and specifically identified as bad and doubtful. The following are examples of policies related to the provisions of doubtful debts as practised by Bank Muamalat Malaysia (Bank Muamalat, 2007, p. 64):

- Specific allowances are made for doubtful debts which have been reviewed individually and specifically identified as substandard, doubtful or bad.

- General allowances are also provided based on a percentage of the financing portfolio to sustain losses which cannot be identified specifically. These percentages are reviewed on an annual basis and adjustments, if necessary, are made to the overall general allowances. General allowance is also made for certain high-risk accounts.

- Any uncollectible financing or part of it which is classified as bad is written off after taking into consideration the realizable value of collateral, if any, when the management is of the opinion that there is no prospect of recovery.

- Additional allowances for doubtful debts are provided when the recoverable amount is lower than the net book value of financing (outstanding amount of financing, net of specific allowances) and long outstanding non-performing financing on the following basis:

- ■ Assigning 50% of the force sale value of the properties held as collateral for non-performing financing which is outstanding for more than five years but less than seven years; and

- ■ No value will be assigned for the collateral of non-performing financing which is outstanding for seven years and above.

- Any allowance made during the year is charged to the income statement.

- During the year, the bank has adopted a more stringent classification policy on non-performing financing, whereby financing is classified as non-performing and sub-standard when repayments are in arrears for more than three months from the first day of defaults or after maturity date.

- The bank has also adopted a more stringent basis for specific allowances on non-performing financing by making 20% specific allowance on non-performing financing which are more than 5 months in arrears, 50% for non-performing financing in arrears of 8 months and 100% for non-performing financing in arrears of 11 months and above.

Fixed Assets and Depreciation

Fixed assets are assets bought for the generation of revenue. These fixed assets are usually in the form of buildings, motor vehicles, office equipment and management information system. AAOIFI does not provide detailed guidelines on policy related to fixed assets. There is no guideline pertaining to the assigning of value except for matters related to depreciation. The fixed assets are presented as notes to the account. Among the banks which report their policies on fixed asset accounting are Bank Islam Malaysia, Shamil Bank of Bahrain, Islami Bank Bangladesh, Bank Muamalat

Indonesia, Albaraka Turk, Islamic International Arab Bank, Kuwait Finance House and Dubai Islamic Bank. The policy related to fixed assets practised by Bank Islam Malaysia is as follows (Bank Islam Malaysia, 2008, p. 93):

- All items of property and equipment are stated at cost less accumulated depreciation and impairment losses, if any.

- Property and equipment which are no longer in active use and are held for disposal are stated at the carrying amount at the date when the assets are retired from active use, less impairment losses, if any.

- Costs include expenditures that are directly attributable to the acquisition of the asset and any other cost directly attributable to bringing the asset to working condition for its intended use, and the cost of dismantling and removing the items and restoring the site on which they are located. The costs of self-constructed assets also include the cost of materials and direct labour. Purchased software that is integral to the functionality of the related equipment is capitalized as part of that equipment. When significant parts of an item of property and equipment have different useful lives, they are accounted for as separate items (major components) of property and equipment. Gain or loss on disposal of an item of asset is the difference between the net proceeds from disposal and the net carrying amount of the asset and is recognized in "other income" in the income statements.

- The cost of replacing part of an item of an asset is included in the carrying amount of the asset only when it is probable that the future economic benefits embodied within the part will flow to the bank and the cost of the item can be measured reliably. The carrying amount of the replaced part is derecognized. The cost of the day-to-day servicing of property and equipment are recognized in the income statement as incurred.

- Management information system development costs and work-in-progress are not depreciated until the assets are ready for their intended use. The straight-line method is used to write off the costs of the other assets over the term of the estimated useful lives. The estimated useful lives for the current and comparative periods are six years for building improvement and renovations; two to six years for furniture, fixtures, fittings and equipment; and four years for motor vehicles. Depreciation methods, useful lives and residual values are reassessed at the reporting date.

- Long-term leasehold land is not amortized. Leasehold land with tenure of less than 50 years is amortized in equal instalments over the period of the respective leases. Management information system development costs and work-in-progress are not depreciated. Leasehold land that normally has an indefinite economic life and whose title is not expected to be passed to the lessee by the end of the lease term is treated as an operating lease. The payment made on entering into or acquiring a leasehold land is accounted for as prepaid lease payments. On adoption of FRS (Financial Reporting Standard) 117, *Leases,* the bank treats such a lease as an operating lease, with the unamortized carrying amount classified as prepaid lease payments in accordance with the transitional provisions in FRS 117.67A. The prepaid lease payments are amortized on a straight-line basis over the lease term.

Some Islamic banks state their fixed assets at cost less accumulated depreciation. Depreciation is computed based on the straight-line method at annual rates. Albaraka Turk states that the costs of repairs are capitalized if the expenditure increases the economic life of the asset. For Dubai Islamic Bank, depreciation is computed using the straight-line method based on the estimated useful lives of the fixed assets.

Allocation of Profit

One of the special features of Islamic banks is the application of the profit-loss sharing principle in their transactions. Unlike conventional banks, depositors of Islamic banks do not know in advance returns from their deposits. This is because most of the deposit facilities offered by Islamic banks are based on the concept of *mudharabah*. AAOIFI's guideline provides no clear suggestion on the allocation of profit. The guide merely states that Islamic bank, when conducting its task as manager of the investment funds deposited by customers, will receive returns in the form of a percentage of the profit. Islamic banks that clarify the method of profit allocation between the depositors and the bank are Kuwait Finance House, Islamic International Arab Bank and Islami Bank Bangladesh. Dubai Islamic Bank only states that allocation of profit is calculated according to the bank's own standard procedures and is approved by the bank's own Syariah Supervisory Board. Shamil Bank of Bahrain, on the other hand, gives a general description of the profit allocation between investment account holders in its annual report.

Payment of *Zakat*

The obligation to pay *zakat* is another unique feature of Islamic banks. AAOIFI has recommended that payment of *zakat* be stated when a particular bank is responsible for the payment of *zakat* on behalf of its owners. In addition, if the bank provides services for mobilizing and distributing *zakat*, then the report must be presented in a separate statement. Most Islamic banks state their policies on payment of *zakat* except for those in Turkey. Islami Bank Bangladesh does not mention any policy on *zakat*, but does implement payment of *zakat* and it is regarded as one of its operational expenses. This method is also practised by several banks in Sudan.

According to Bank Islam Malaysia, its *zakat* payment is in accordance with *Syariah* rules and is as approved by the Syariah Supervisory Board. Most banks in the Middle East assert that *zakat* is the responsibility of shareholders and not the banks. For instance, Islamic International Arab Bank and Kuwait Finance House clearly state that *zakat* must be borne by the shareholders and depositors, independently. The banks are not responsible for the collection of *zakat* on their behalf. However, Kuwait Finance House assesses the *zakat* that needs to be paid by the shareholders according to the method set by its Syariah Supervisory Board. Dubai Islamic Bank is the only bank which presents a complete description of *zakat* payment. It states that *zakat* is computed as per the articles and memorandum of association of the bank and approved by the Fatwa and Syariah Supervisory Board, on the following basis (Dubai Islamic Bank, 2007, p. 20):

- *Zakat* on shareholders' equity is deducted from their dividends and is computed on their *zakat* pool (shareholder's equity less the paid-up capital, donated land reserve and cumulative charges in fair value) plus employees' end of service benefits.

- *Zakat* on profit equalization provision is charged to this provision after computation is made.

- *Zakat* is disbursed by a committee appointed by the Board of Directors and operating as per the by-law set by the Board.

- *Zakat* on paid-up capital is not included in the *zakat* computations and is payable directly by the shareholders themselves.

Other Policies

Apart from the important policies discussed above, there are also practices that differ from one Islamic bank to another. The initiatives taken by AAOIFI to handle this matter are commendable as the organization has successfully developed standard guidelines for the preparation and presentation of financial statements of Islamic financial institutions. However, since AAOIFI is not a legislative organization, Islamic banks are not obliged to comply with or adhere to the recommendations made. As a result, there are differences in the preparation and presentation of financial statements of Islamic banks. A distinctive example is the presentation of deposit services under the *mudharabah* principle. This deposit is removed from the balance sheet by some banks as it is not regarded as a liability. In cases where financing is based on the principle of profit-loss sharing, it is the practice of some Islamic banks to jointly bear the administration expenses and other general expenditure with depositors. Therefore, profits distributed to the depositor would be based on net profit after deducting all expenses. Banks which are practising this method include Kuwait Finance House and Dubai Islamic Bank. In contrast, all administration expenditure is fully borne by the bank (shareholders) in the case of Bank Islam Malaysia and Jordan Islamic Bank.

RISK MANAGEMENT

Financial institutions are in the business of risk management and reallocation. Globalization and financial liberalization compounded by the explosion of technological capabilities have exposed banks to greater and more risks. There are three main categories of risk that banks are exposed to, namely credit risk, market risk and operational risk.

Credit risk is closely tied to default borrowing or contractual obligation. Market risk is the exposure to uncertain market conditions which reduce the value of investment or portfolio. Operational risk is the result of uncertainties regarding the actual operations of a bank including failed internal processes as well as people and system failure. In 1988, the Bank for International

Settlements (BIS), an organization established in 1930 with the original objective of facilitating the settlement of payments between banks, published a set of minimal capital requirements for banks known as Basel I which required banks to hold capital equal to 8% of their risk-weighted assets. Under this framework, credit risk and market risk can be measured to determine capital requirement sufficiency. Since 1988, many changes have taken place in the banking environment including risk management practices, supervisory approaches and the financial market landscape. Taking into consideration operational risks, apart from the credit risks and market risks that banks face, a new international standard ensuring that banks hold sufficient capital reserves was published. The new framework, Basel II, is the continuation of Basel I and has been fully implemented by all member countries as at end of 2006. Islamic banks are also expected to comply with the requirements stipulated under Basel II. There are three principal pillars in Basel II, namely:

(i) Minimum capital requirements

(ii) Supervisory committee

(iii) Market discipline

Under Basel II, the 8% capital requirement of Basel I still holds, but not the method of risk computation. In the initial framework, only credit risk and market risk were given due recognition while operational risk was regarded as part of these risks faced by banks. However, the new framework attaches importance to operational risks and thus requires banks to include operational risk measurement in calculating the minimum capital requirement level. Hence, the first pillar of the new accord requires banks to assess their market and operational risk and provide capital to cover such risk. By aligning the minimum capital requirements more closely with a bank's actual exposure to credit and operational risk, Basel II framework's explicit incentives in the form of lower capital requirements allow banks to adopt more accurate measures of risk and more effective processes of controlling their exposure to risk. The new capital framework also recognizes the necessity to exercise effective supervisory review of banks' internal assessments of their overall risks. The third pillar leverages on the ability of market discipline to motivate prudent management by promoting greater transparency through the banks' public disclosures.

Almost all Islamic banks have reported their risk management policy. Nonetheless, no uniformity in the reports could be established. For example, Jordan Islamic Bank touched only on its credit risk and market risk management. Shamil Bank of Bahrain only reported on credit risk, while Albaraka Islamic Bank of Bahrain reported on liquidity risk and profit-loss sharing risk. Dubai Islamic Bank categorized risk into credit risk, market risk, profit rate risk, currency risk and liquidity risk. Compared to Islamic banks in the Middle East, Islamic banks in Malaysia and Indonesia presented more comprehensive information regarding their risk management practices. Risk management of Bank Muamalat Indonesia includes liquidity risk, operational risk, legislation risk, reputational risk, strategic risk and compliance risk.

Bank Islam Malaysia, Bank Muamalat Malaysia, Qatar Islamic Bank, Kuwait Finance House, Albaraka Turk and Islamic International Arab Bank are among those Islamic banks that publish the types of risks and their associated risk management practice as well as their risk management structure. This enables users of the financial statement to compare the banks' risk management with that of others. The following explains the risk management practices adopted by Bank Islam Malaysia (Bank Islam Malaysia, 2008).

Market risk. Market risk is the loss arising from adverse movements in market variables such as rate of return risk, foreign exchange rate risk, displaced commercial risk, equity investment risk and commodity risk.

Credit risk. Credit risk arises from loss of revenue and capital as a result of the inability to meet the terms of a contract by the customer of counter parties through financing, dealing and investment activities.

Liquidity risk. Liquidity risk refers to the potential inability of the bank to meet its funding requirements arising from cash flow mismatches at a reasonable cost.

Operation risk. Operation risk is risk of loss resulting from inadequate or failure of internal processes, people, systems and external events.

***Syariah*-compliance risk.** *Syariah*-compliance risk refers to the bank's failure to comply with *Syariah* rules and principles as determined by the *Syariah* regulatory bodies of Bank Negara Malaysia, the Securities Commission and the bank's own *Syariah* council.

Board Risk Committee. The Board Risk Committee (BRC) is responsible for effective functioning of the integrated risk management of the bank. As a committee of the Board, BRC acts within its delegated authority to decide on or recommend to the Board of Directors risk management issues. Its members comprise two independent non-executive directors and two non-independent non-executive directors. One of the independent non-executive directors acts as the committee chairman.

Some of the main functions of BRC include to review and recommend risk management strategies and policies to the Board; to review and propose the setting of the bank's risk tolerance at enterprise and strategic business unit levels; to oversee the overall management of all risks covering market risk, credit risk and operational risk; to approve risk methodologies for measuring and managing risks; to review the bank's entire risk management processes, systems and internal control; and to approve contingency plans for dealing with extreme internal and external events or disasters.

Management Risk Control Committee. The Management Risk Control Committee (MRCC) is responsible for ensuring that the policies approved by the Board are properly implemented. The committee also ensures the effective management of operational issues. Under the MRCC, there are four sub-committees, namely Asset and Liability Management Committee, Operational Risk Control Committee, Credit Risk Control Committee and Recovery Management Committee.

Risk Management Framework. The Risk Management Framework (RMF) was formulated with the aim of managing the bank's risks in a more holistic manner through philosophical and practical approaches. The methodology of the RMF is based on the concept of *solah* (pillar of Islam) which is built upon five elements, that is *niyyah* (statement of *solah*), *jama'ah* (implementation structure of *solah*), *syarat* (necessary elements of *solah*), *rukun* (essential activities of *solah*) and *qaedah* (facilities required for *solah*). All these five elements are adopted in managing the bank's risks.

SUMMARY

Modern Islamic banking system started with the operations of Mit Ghamr Savings Bank in the Nile River Valley, Egypt in the early 1960s. Since then, Islamic banks have mushroomed not only in Muslim countries but in non-Muslim or Western countries as well. Islamic banking products are now widely accepted by both Muslim and non-Muslim customers. This is evident of the capability of Islamic banks in fulfilling the modern banking needs of customers but in line with the requirements of *Syariah*. Islam is a universal religion and is founded on belief in Allah (s.w.t.), the One and Only, and guided by the holy Quran and *Hadith*. Hence, it follows that all operations of the Islamic banking system must be founded on *Syariah* principles. Nonetheless, the Islamic banking system is still in need of harmonization as there exist differences in *Syariah* practices among Islamic banks in their business transactions. These differences are translated into differences in the characteristics of the products and services offered. Basically, the financial products and services offered by Islamic banks are similar to those of the conventional banks, particularly in terms of deposit facilities, financing and other services. Almost all Islamic banks offer deposit facilities such as current account, savings account and investment account. The only difference is in terms of the added value each product offers. The same applies to financing facilities. Differences which may occur in terms of the amount of deposit made by customers and the type of financing given priority by a particular bank, are due to the differences in the economic, social and cultural factors among the Muslim countries where the banks operate. Consequently, disparities also arise in terms of financing concentration, methods in managing fund and services provided.

The most apparent differences lie in the usage of *Syariah* principles upon which a bank's modes of financing are based, and the bank's views on the types of social activities to be conducted. Although profit-loss sharing modes of financing are preferable, the practices of most Islamic banks indicate otherwise. Furthermore, a majority of financing facilities are granted to less risky sectors in the economy. Some Islamic banks are very committed with regard to social responsibility while others are found to be moving in tandem with conventional banks while not violating *Syariah*. In terms of developing a standardized financial recording and reporting model for Islamic banks, the role of the Accounting and Auditing Organization for Islamic Financial Institutions (AAOIFI) in this matter should be commended. Unfortunately, the standards recommended by AAOIFI are not legally binding, and banks can opt not to adopt or comply with these standards. As a result, most banks are more inclined to comply with recommendations of international accounting organizations or the authorities in their respective countries. Consequently, no uniformity in the financial statement presentations among the Islamic banks exists.

As with conventional banks, Islamic banks have started to place importance on risk management. The practice of risk management has become even more critical as Islamic banks are now required to comply with the Basel II framework. Risks associated with Islamic banks include credit risk, profit-sharing risk, market risk, liquidity risk and operational risk. Theoretically, if the internalization of Islamic values is high among the users of Islamic banking services, the risks involved would naturally be lower compared to conventional banking since the debtor is obligated by religion to pay back all of his debt and thus effectively reducing credit risk. Furthermore, there would not be any risk related to deposit withdrawal as customers would have deposited with the bank for religious reasons and hence would not be motivated by high returns on deposits. Operational risk, which is now given importance under Basel II, should very rarely arise because Islamic work ethics would guide the bank workers to be trustworthy, efficient and meticulous in performing their duties.

REFERENCES AND FURTHER READING

AAOIFI. *Accounting, Auditing and Governance Standards for Islamic Financial Institutions*. Bahrain: The Accounting and Auditing Organization for Islamic Financial Institutions, 2000.

AlBaraka Islamic Bank of Bahrain. *Annual Report* (various issues).

Albaraka Turk. *Annual Report* (various issues).

Aryan, Hossein. "The Impact of Islamization on the Financial System." In *Islamic Financial Markets*, edited by Rodney Wilson, 155–170. London and New York: Routledge, 1990.

Baldwin, David. "Turkey: Islamic Banking in a Secularist Context." In *Islamic Financial Markets*, edited by Rodney Wilson, 33–58. London and New York: Routledge, 1990.

Bank Asya. *Annual Report* (various issues).

Bank Islam Malaysia Berhad. *Annual Report* (various issues).

Bank Islam Malaysia Berhad. *Bank Islam, Penubuhan dan Operasi*. 2nd ed. Kuala Lumpur, 1989.

Bank Melli Iran. *Annual Report* (various issues).

Bank Muamalat Indonesia. *Annual Report* (various issues).

Bank Muamalat Malaysia Berhad. *Annual Report* (various issues).

Bank Syariah Mandiri. *Annual Report* (various issues).

Dubai Islamic Bank. *Annual Report* (various issues). United Arab Emirates.

El Gharb Islamic Bank of Sudan. *Annual Report* (various issues).

Faysal Islamic Bank of Bahrain. *Annual Report* (various issues).

Haron, Sudin. *Principles and Operations of Islamic Banking*. Selangor Darul Ehsan (Malaysia): Berita Publishing, 1996.

Islami Bank Bangladesh Limited. *Annual Report* (various issues).

Islamic Bank of Bahrain. *Annual Report* (various issues).

Islamic International Arab Bank. *Annual Report* (various issues).

Jordan Islamic Bank. *Annual Report* (various issues).

Karim, R.A.A. "Standard Setting for the Financial Reporting of Religious Business Organizations: The Case of Islamic Banks." *Accounting and Business Research*. Vol. 20, No. 80 (1990): 299–305.

Kuwait Finance House. *Annual Report* (various issues).

Muslim Commercial Bank. *Annual Report* (various issues).

Qatar Islamic Bank. *Annual Report* (various issues).

Shallah, Ramadan. "Jordan: The Experience of the Jordan Islamic Bank." In *Islamic Financial Markets*, edited by Rodney Wilson, 100–128. London and New York: Routledge, 1990.

Shamil Bank of Bahrain. *Annual Report* (various issues).

Turkiye Finans. *Annual Report* (various issues).

www.bis.org.

CHAPTER 7

ISLAMIC FINANCIAL MARKETS

This chapter discusses the development of the Islamic financial markets, the financial instruments which have been created and how they are transacted. The discussion also covers the Islamic financial markets in Malaysia and the authorities involved because the Malaysian Islamic financial markets are at the forefront in terms of growth as well as breadth and depth.

INTRODUCTION

In the early stages of their establishment, the focus of Islamic banks was on providing various deposit and financing facilities which were *riba*-free. The overwhelming support from Muslim depositors resulted in an extraordinary liquidity problem for Islamic banks. In many cases, the banks' funds could not be mobilized and remained idle because of limited investment opportunities since they are restricted from channelling these funds into interest-based financial instruments. Consequently, Islamic banks were unable to invest the excess funds and reap returns from their investment. In the conventional system, however, a mechanism that allows surplus banks to loan out their excess funds to deficit banks exist. Various financial instruments are also available to the surplus banks to invest any excess funds they have.

In light of the problems facing Islamic banks, the global Islamic banking system viewed that having its own financial markets was essential for further growth. In principle, the financial market is the meeting place of two parties with mutual needs – one party requires funds to support its financial needs, and the other has unused surplus funds which it intends to invest for the purpose of attaining returns or income. Realizing the existing problems, intellectuals directly involved in Islamic banking system began to put their thoughts into how an Islamic financial market could be created and the form of mechanism required. Islamic financial instruments also needed to be developed as alternatives to the conventional ones. These financial instruments must, however, possess the following features of conventional financial instruments:

(i)   They must be negotiable, that is, it must be easy to transfer the ownership of the instruments from one holder to another.

(ii) They must be liquid, that is, they may be easily sold when cash is required.

(iii) They must carry minimum risk.

(iv) They must be easily valued and priced.

Due to the fact that Islamic financial markets are at a developing stage, these new concepts have raised many theoretical and practical questions. The issue of religious rules (*hukum*) also sometimes causes confusion and continuous debate not only among the local intellectuals but also between countries.

TYPES OF FINANCIAL MARKET

Conventional financial market is made up of four components, namely capital market, money market, futures market and mortgage market. The capital market trades in instruments with an original maturity of more than one year. Money market deals in short-term financial instruments whose maturity period is one year or less. The forward and future market involves a contract between two parties for future delivery of currencies, securities or commodities. Mortgage market covers real estate financing (e.g. financing of homes, buildings and other properties). Although these are the common financial market components frequently discussed in text books, another financial instrument with a unique transaction mechanism is becoming increasingly popular in wealth mobilization. This mechanism is referred to as unit trust. Unit trusts are open-ended investments and they offer access to a wide range of securities.

The four components of the financial market need not necessarily exist in all countries of the world. With the exception of developed countries, the existence of these components depends to a large extent on a country's level of economic development.

Capital Market

Capital market is the place where long-term financial instruments with maturity exceeding one year are issued and traded. The principal goal of establishing this market is to channel savings into long-term productive investments. Participants in this market comprise those from the government and private sectors. In the conventional market, the financial instruments issued and traded are those issued by the government as well as by the private sectors. The government is defined as the authorities comprising the federal government, state governments, local authorities and government agencies. These authorities would in certain instances use the capital market either to obtain funds to finance administration and development expenses, or to invest any surplus funds. The private sector comprises giant companies, medium and small companies, as well as individuals.

The financial instruments in the capital market may be categorized into equity instruments and debt instruments. Equity instruments are in the form of share certificates, either common or preferred stocks. Debt instruments are made up of bonds which may be classed into common bonds and convertible bonds. The main difference between stocks and bonds lies in their payment of returns (either in the form of dividend or interest) to the owner or holder. For a person who holds shares of a company, there is no guarantee that he shall receive annual dividends since the company has no legal obligation to pay dividends to shareholders. Payment of dividends depends only on profits and it is the Board of Directors who determines whether or not to pay dividends to stockholders. On the other hand, when bonds are issued, the company is bound by law to pay annual interest in accordance with the terms made at the time of the issuance. If the company fails to pay interest as promised, it may face legal actions from the bondholders. Furthermore, this clearly suggests that the company is facing financial problems.

In Malaysia, any company doing business or wishing to do business in the country must be registered with the Companies Commission of Malaysia under the *Companies Act 1965*. The owner and the company are two separate entities. The relationship between the owner of the company and the company itself depends on the amount and types of shares held. Although shareholders are legally the rightful owners of the company, it does not mean that they are responsible for all actions undertaken by the company. Shareholders are also not responsible for the company's debts. However, in case of liability claim on the company, the amount is limited to the value and total shares owned.

The difference between common stock and preferred stock rests on dividend payment. Unlike common stock, the payment of dividends for preferred stock is usually in the form of a fixed percentage and it takes priority over common stock dividends. For common stock, dividends paid depend entirely on the discretion of the Board of Directors. In addition, preferred stockholders have a claim prior to common stockholders on the company's assets. Preferred stock is of two types, namely cumulative and non-cumulative. Cumulative stock accords the holders a continuous claim on the dividends. Hence, any unpaid dividends will be accumulated until the company resumes paying them. As such, cumulative stockholders are entitled to all past and present dividends. On the contrary, non-cumulative preferred stockholders only receive dividend in the current year. Non-cumulative preferred stock does not confer any claims on missed dividends.

The central point in the issuance and transaction of stock is the concept of limited liability, whereby the stockholder's financial liabilty is limited to the amount he has invested in the event that the business incurs a loss. He is not personally liable for the company's debt other than the value of his investment. This concept of limited liability is actually related to the *mudharabah* principle in Islam, whereby the enterpreneur is neither held responsible for the loss incurred by the business nor is he required to replace the owner's capital should such a loss incurred under the condition that the loss is not due to his carelessness or negligence. However, issues of relevance between the owner and the company such as in the context of conventional company legislation are not mentioned anywhere in the original source of Islamic *fiqh* (jurisprudence) and were never discussed by Muslim scholars and *ulama* (Usmani, 1992). Nevertheless, Muslim scholars believe that the concept of limited liability is closely related to the concept of "juridical person" or separate entity. Given that *Syariah* accepts the concept of juridical person, it is thus permissible for Islamic banks to deal with stocks and shares.

Since stocks represent a financial claim or is a title of ownership, these certificates do not constitute money. Hence, the negotiation and transfer of ownership pertain only to the object of the certificate and not the certificate itself which is regarded from the legal point of view as a proof of the claim. Under *Syariah*, common ownership is permissible and therefore it is legal to undertake sales, pawning or donation. During the process of buying and selling stocks, what changes is only the ownership right, and it is this exchange of value that is paid using cash or other modes of payment.

In contrast to common stock, preferred stock cannot be bought by Muslims and Islamic banks. This is because preferred stock is associated with a pre-determined fixed rate of return which is prohibited by *Syariah*. However, as an alternative, Muslim scholars suggested that preferred stocks may be issued by using the concept of a preference dividend based on a pre-determined profit ratio. Since what is specified is only the profit ratio and not a fixed payment, the preferred stocks based on this concept do not contradict *Syariah* (Mannan, 1990). This simply means that preferred stockholders do not know the amount of annual dividends to be received and dividends are based on the profits made by the company. Hence, large profits are translated into high dividends for stockholders.

This view was researched and reviewed by the Syariah Advisory Council of the Securities Commission of Malaysia. The Council, in its 20th meeting on 14 July 1999, put forward a resolution that non-cumulative preferred shares be allowed by *Syariah* by applying the concept of *tanazul* (to drop claims to rights). The application of this concept is based on the agreement of the common stockholders during the general meeting to commit *tanazul* for the issuance of preferred stocks. Subsequently at every general meeting, the common stockholders would also commit *tanazul* in order to grant dividends to preferred stockholders based on the percentage of net profit obtained by the company. This means that the percentage of return to preferred stockholders is based on profit and not the face value of the preferred stocks. The amount of returns received by individual investor is in turn based on the amount of stocks held. Due to the fact that the issuance and distribution mode of returns are based on profit, the *mudharabah* principle is the most appropriate *Syariah* principle to be used as the basis for stock issuance. Besides the requirement to comply with positive laws and other regulations as determined by monetary authorities, there are other matters that must be adhered to for the issuance of stocks to be *Syariah*-compliant. Similar to any ordinary public offering, a prospectus describing the financial and non-financial aspects of the company will have to be provided to potential investors. Among the important information that should be stated are:

(i) Investors must be aware that the contract is governed by the principle of *mudharabah.*

(ii) The method of distributing returns to investors must be clearly stated in the contract. Aspects such as profit ratio, when dividends will be paid and mode of payment must be stated.

(iii) The purpose of the stock issuance must be clear. One aspect that is still constraining the application of stocks in the Islamic capital market is the issue of reselling stocks bought. Before the money invested by the stockholder can be utilized by the issuing company, the purpose of the proceeds must be clearly stated in the contract.

The *ulama* are of the view that for as long as no investment has been undertaken, a stock cannot be resold at a higher price during the period after it is issued and bought. The transactions within this period is subject to the *Syariah* rules of disposition of money and thus it should be sold at its face value. Thus, the prospectus should specify as to when the stocks are permissible for transactions. Under current practice, the permissible date is usually concurrent with the date the stock is listed on the stock market.

Another issue that has stirred much debate among Muslim scholars is stock market speculation. Islam forbids speculation because it involves gambling or *maisir*. But the issue of speculation in the stock market has not met with any resolution due to the difficulty in determining its position. Stockholders' returns from their investment in stocks are of two types, capital gains and dividends. Capital gain is profit made as a result of selling stocks for more than the original purchase price. Dividends, on the other hand, are the cash distribution of earnings to the stockholder. Naturally, several questions pertaining to the Islamic capital market and the trading of stocks arise: Is it allowable by *Syariah* for investors participating in the Islamic capital market to sell today the stocks bought yesterday? Is the buying and selling of stocks considered gambling? Or is one really buying or selling a certain right over the company?

Although scholars associate speculation with gambling, this view is not reciprocated by the Syariah Advisory Council of the Securities Commission of Malaysia. At its 10th general meeting on 16–17 October 1997, this Council ruled that speculation may be allowed. Although speculation was never discussed by Muslim jurists, the *bai muzayadah* principle may be associated with this practice. However, *Syariah* does not allow cheating and manipulation in the stock market. In addition, there are *fatwa* which have listed stocks that are either deemed as permissible or prohibited for Muslim investors. In Malaysia, the Syariah Advisory Council of the Securities Commission publishes a list of *Syariah*-compliant stocks. As at end of November 2008, a total of 855 *Syariah*-compliant securities listed on the main board, second board and MESDAQ market were approved by the Syariah Advisory Council of the Securities Commission of Malaysia. This represents 85% of the total securities listed. *Syariah*-compliant securities as defined by the Council include ordinary shares, warrants as well as transferable subscription rights.

The three main elements that make stocks non-permissible are *riba*, gambling and prohibited products or related products. But even so, investment is permitted in activities that have tolerable level of mixed contributions from permissible and non-permissible activities where the non-permissible activities represent only a small percentage of the activities and do not exceed the benchmarks established by the Council. For example, the Council has established four benchmarks for determining the tolerable level of mixed contributions from permissible and non-permissible activities as follows (www.sc.com.my):

 (i) The 5% benchmark is used to assess the level of mixed contributions from activities that are clearly prohibited such as *riba*, gambling, liquor and pork.

 (ii) The 10% benchmark is employed to assess the level of mixed contributions from the activities that involve the element of *umum balwa* (common plight and difficult to avoid) such as interest income from fixed deposits in conventional banks. This benchmark is also used for tobacco-related activities.

(iii) The 20% benchmark is applied to assess the level of contribution from mixed rental payment from non-compliant *Syariah* activities including rental payment from premises that are involved in gambling, sale of liquor, etc.

(iv) The 25% benchmark is used to assess the level of mixed contributions from the activities that are generally permissible according to *Syariah* and have an element of *maslahah* (public interest), but there are other elements that may affect the *Syariah* status of these activities. Examples of such activities include hotel and resort operations, share trading, stockbroking and others; these activities may also involve other activities that are deemed as non-permissible according to *Syariah*.

In contrast to stocks, conventional bonds are prohibited as they represent interest-based funding. There are various types of bonds in the conventional capital market which are normally issued by the corporate sectors to obtain funds, namely mortgage bonds, debenture bonds and subordinate debentures. Mortgage bonds are normally issued with maturities of between 20 and 40 years. They give the bondholders first claim on some or all of the issuing company's assets in the event of default. The maturity period of debenture bonds is typically up to 25 years. Unlike mortgage bonds, these bonds are secured by assets and in terms of priority they are ranked after mortgage bonds. Subordinate debentures are also known as convertible bonds because they are issued as loans and the issuing company pays a fixed annual interest rate to the bondholders. Upon maturity, the holders have the choice to convert them into common stocks. Therefore, until such conversion they are considered long-term debts and the issuing company is contractually obligated to pay interest and principal payments.

In the early stages of Islamic banking in Malaysia, there were not many financial instruments in the form of debt certificates issued by the authorities or the government and corporate bodies which could be subscribed to by Islamic banks. However, the government of Malaysia through its central bank, Bank Negara Malaysia, issued debt certificates that may be subscribed or bought by Islamic banks under the *qard hassan* principle. The certificate, known as Government Investment Certificate, was issued to provide an opportunity to Bank Islam Malaysia to invest its surplus funds. The bondholder was given gift or *hibah* every year-end at a pre-determined rate. This commitment of the government in issuing bonds which are *Syariah*-compliant continues to this day. As at end of September 2008, the size of Islamic bonds issued in Malaysia was RM37.66 billion which represented 44.9% of total bonds issued in the country. Meanwhile, the amount of *sukuk* outstanding for the same period was RM146 billion.

One suggestion made by Muslim scholars which has yet to be widely practised by Islamic banks is the issuance of an "asset-based *mudharabah*" instrument in place of debenture bonds. This instrument represents monetary claim against funds under the management of the Islamic bank on a fiduciary basis. The operations and arrangements of this instrument are similar to mutual funds or unit trust. There are two types of *mudharabah* instruments suggested, namely unrestricted *mudharabah* and restricted *mudharabah*. Under unrestricted *mudharabah*, the Islamic bank acts as the *mudarib* and is authorized to use full discretion in managing the affairs of the funds. The restricted *mudharabah*, on the other hand, has specifications as to the period, place, purpose and type of business allowed. The bank is only allowed to perform functions that are prescribed in the prospectus or *mudharabah* agreement. The following are the suggested features of a *mudharabah* bond (Pervez, 1996):

(i) Asset valuation is undertaken at the end of each prescribed year. A positive price movement over the previous asset-valuation date reflects return on investment which is declared on each asset valuation date. Net profit after payment of all *mudharabah* costs is distributed between the instrument holders and the bank. The bank's management fee is a fixed percentage of the profit as agreed in the contract. The bank may, however, on its sole discretion reduce but not enhance its fee by voluntarily forgoing part thereof.

(ii) In the event of a net loss, the net asset value is reduced and the bank cannot impose managemant fee for the period. If the loss is as a result of gross negligence or violation of the terms of the contract, then the bank has the responsibility to compensate for the loss.

(iii) The creditors do not have any recourse to other assets of the instruments holders should their claims exceed the total assets of the *mudharabah*.

(iv) Although the bank's management fee based on a fixed percentage of net profit is permittted, imposing a fixed amount of payment is not.

(v) In line with the contract, reserves, as a percentage of net profits, can be built to meet future contingencies and unforeseen losses.

At maturity of the contract, the amount held in reserves after meeting all costs and claims is distributed to holders of the bond.

Jordan is among the earliest countries to introduce asset-based *mudharabah* bonds. As stipulated in *Law No. 13 of 1978*, Jordan Islamic Bank is allowed to issue financial instruments called *muqaradah* bond. This Law defines the bond as follows:

> *Documents having a uniform value, issued by the bank in the names of the persons who subscribe thereof by paying their face value on the basis of participation by the holders of these bonds in the annual profits realized, in accordance with the terms of each separate issue of such bonds.*

Based on the above interpretation, the most important element of the *muqaradah* bond is that its issuance and returns to the holders are based on the profit-sharing principle. Although Jordan Islamic Bank was allowed to issue such bonds, the instruments were issued by the bank only in 1997. Instead, it was first undertaken by the Jordanian government, though on a limited scale. The enactment of the *Muqaradah Bond Act 1981* by the Jordanian government paved the way for the Ministry of Awqaf to develop *wakaf* assets. Among the authorities which have been allowed to issue bonds under this Act are the Ministry of Awqaf, public institutions with financial independence and municipalities. One important aspect related to the issuance of *muqaradah* bonds provided by law is that the Jordanian government guarantees the settlement of the face value of the bonds. This guarantee is in line with the *fatwa* issued by the Jordanian Fatwa Committee that government's guarantee (the government as the third party) is permissible and does not contradict *Syariah*. At the end of 2007, the *muqaradah* bonds were valued at JOD218.5 million whilst at the end of 2006 it was JOD166.7 million (Jordan Islamic Bank, 2007). The issuance process depends mainly on which projects the bank regards as economically potential. After identifying the financial needs of a project which it intends to venture into, Jordan Islamic Bank would offer the bonds to the public by allowing them to purchase the bonds based on a fixed face value. Annual profit would only be distributed based on the profit obtained from the project and the principal money would be returned upon its completion.

Apart from Jordan, Pakistan was also interested in issuing *Syariah*-based bonds when it converted its whole economic system to an Islamic system in 1977. For that purpose, two new laws were formulated, called *Modaraba Companies and Modaraba (Flotation and Control) 1980* and *Modaraba Companies and Modaraba Rules 1981*. The aim of these laws is to provide the necessary framework for the flotation of *mudaraba* instruments and permit management companies, banks and other financial institutions to register themselves as *mudaraba* companies and to enable them to issue financial instruments of this type in Pakistan. This financial instrument bears similarities to *muqaradah* bonds issued in Jordan, that is, bonds with restrictions and without restrictions. An additional feature of the bonds in Pakistan is that they can either be for a limited period or for perpetuity. These Islamic bonds are traded on the Karachi Stock Market. Besides *mudharabah* bonds, another type of Islamic financial instrument recommended by the Council of Islamic Ideology, Pakistan, is the Participation Term Certificates (PTCs). The following are the salient features of PTCs (Qureshi, 1990):

1. PTCs are for a specified period not exceeding ten years excluding the grace period.

2. The broad principles governing the legal aspects of PTCs are laid down by the government by making suitable amendments in the prevailing *Company Act*.

3. As the PTC finance is provided for a specific period, it is secured by a legal mortgage on fixed assets of the company and a floating charge on the current assets owned by the company.

4. For the purpose of profit allocation to PTC holders, the investment ranks pari-passu with equity. Profit sharing is based on mutual agreement.

5. Pre-tax profits before appropriations are used in determining return to the PTC holders.

6. Profits payable to the PTC holders are income tax-deductible expenses.

7. The share of profits paid to PTC holders is deducted prior to shareholders' claim on the company's profits.

8. In the event of a loss, the first recourse shall be to free the reserves including the credit balance in the profit and loss accounts of the issuer and the balance of the loss will be shared between the PTC holders and other providers of funds in proportion to their funds.

9. Proceeds of the PTC must be used exclusively for implementing the project as stated when the PTC was issued to potential investors. PTC issuers must conduct the business with diligence and efficiency and to use all expertise and wisdom when operating the business ventured into.

10. For purpose of providing protection to the PTC holders, a trustee must be appointed and given the authority to obtain information from the company, to visit the plant and to inspect machinery of the company as well as to have access to all their business records.

11. Options may be given to PTC holders to convert a certain portion of their outstanding certificates to ordinary shares.

12. A rights option may also be given to ordinary shareholders to subscribe to any new issuance of PTCs.

From the above features, one can see many similarities between PTCs and conventional bonds. For instance, PTCs are secured by mortgage and floating charges and this feature is similar to mortgage bonds. Furthermore, the option for the holders to convert their certificates to common or ordinary shares is a feature of subordinate debentures. Although this instrument is acceptable in Pakistan, some Muslim scholars are doubtful as to the permissibility of it (Ariff and Mannan, 1990). This is because its legality from the *Syariah* viewpoint has yet to be established. Nevertheless, PTCs and *mudharabah* bonds have been issued in Pakistan although they have not been well received. For example, the face value (nominal) of investments in securities undertaken by banks in Pakistan at the end of 2008 was PKR1,000,357.2 million and of this amount, investment in PTCs was only PKR35,175.1 million or 3.5% of the overall investment. Meanwhile, investment in *mudharabah* bonds was PKR30,265.8 million or 3% of total investment. Islamic bonds or more commonly known as *sukuk,* which are based on the *mudharabah* concept have not been fully developed by other Islamic countries and banks alike throughout the world. Islamic Development Bank, despite being the pillar of financial management based on *Syariah,* has not been in the forefront in issuing *sukuk mudharabah.* The bank, however, has introduced two asset-based *mudharabah* instrument schemes known as Islamic Banks' Portfolio (IBP) and Unit Investment Fund (UIF). IBP is a pool of funds contributed by institutions and individual investors for the purpose of financing trade, undertaking leasing and for equity participation in corporations of Islamic countries. UIF, on the other hand, is largely used to finance leasing assets and for instalment sales. Since their establishment and until 2006, IBP valued at US$4.4 billion and UIF at US$1.8 billion were managed by Islamic Development Bank.

This situation does not mean that no other efforts have been taken to develop Islamic bonds. Malaysia, for instance, is quite advanced in developing Islamic bonds. Islamic bonds are issued by both the government and private sector. Since the issuance of Islamic bonds based on *musyarakah* by Shell MDS Sdn Bhd in 1990, their popularity has been on the rise from year to year. In

2001, the issuance of Islamic bonds in Malaysia surpassed that of conventional bonds. As at end of June 2008, the Malaysian bond market reached a size of more than RM500 billion with corporate bonds representing 51% or RM258 billion of total outstanding bonds. Throughout 2008, a total of 44 Islamic bonds or *sukuk* with an issuance value of RM3,234 million were approved by Securities Commission of Malaysia (www.sc.com.my).

Besides Malaysia, Bahrain also plays an important role in the issuance of Islamic bonds. Islamic bonds issued in Bahrain are based on the principles of *salam* and *ijarah*. The history of Islamic bonds in Bahrain started in 2001 when *salam sukuk* was first issued. This monthly issuance valued at US$25 million each was offered for sale by Bahrain Monetary Agency (BMA). As at end of November 2008, BMA had administered new issuance of *salam sukuk* worth BD6 billion. Apart from *salam sukuk*, BMA also issues *ijarah sukuk*. The first *ijarah sukuk* was issued in September 2001 with a value of US$100 million and a maturity of five years. In addition, on 20 July 2004, BMA issued *ijarah sukuk* in Bahraini currency (dinar or BD) totalling BD40 million (US$106 million) with a maturity of ten years. Up until November 2008, new issuances of *ijarah sukuk* totalling BD5 billion were issued and traded on the Bahrain Stock Market.

The presence of the Islamic International Finance Market (IIFM) is also expected to act as impetus for the issuance of Islamic bonds worldwide. As an international body which among its major tasks is to endorse the issuance of Islamic bonds and ensure they are indeed *Syariah*-compliant, the service of IIFM is highly required by companies intending to issue Islamic bonds and would like their bonds to be subscribed by the international community. As at the end of July 2008, IIFM had endorsed six issuances of Islamic bonds as follows (http://www.iifm.net):

(i) US$600 million – Malaysia Global *Sukuk*

(ii) US$400 million – Solidarity Trust Services Limited Trust Certificates

(iii) US$700 million – Qatar Global *Sukuk*

(iv) US$250 million – Bahrain Monetary Agency International *Sukuk*

 (v) US$100 million – Tabreed Finance Corporation Trust Certificates

(vi) US$120 million – Durrat Al-Bahrain Sukuk Company B.S.C.

Currently, principles such as *ijarah, istisna, salam, murabahah* and *bai bithaman ajil* are used widely in structuring Islamic bonds. However, there is a lack of consensus among the *ulama* as to the fact that the discounting method implemented in transactions in the bond secondary market is *Syariah*-compliant. For instance, the principle of *bai al-dayn* which is widely used in Malaysia is strongly opposed by the *ulama* in the Middle East on the basis that only debt certificates of the same value may be transacted.

Money Market

The most important function of the money market is to provide an efficient means for economic units in the economy to adjust their liquidity positions. Financial instruments in this market have three crucial features, namely low default risk, short term to maturity and high marketability. In the conventional money market, the most widely traded financial instruments are treasury bills, negotiable certificates of deposits, banker's acceptance and repurchase agreements.

Treasury bills are bills issued by the treasury department of a country. The proceeds of these bills are used to finance government operating expenditures. The bills are sold to investors on a disounted basis (lower than face value). The income obtained by investors is the difference between the face value and the purchase price of the bills. Treasury bills are issued with maturities of three months, six months, nine months and one year. Negotiable certificates of deposits are another type of time deposit facilities offered by financial institutions, particularly commercial banks, with a minimum amount of savings for each certificate (e.g. RM50,000). The certificate usually has a maturity period of not more than one year, and the interest rate offered by the bank is pre-determined at the initial stage of the savings period. The certificate is then resold at any time, whether at the issuing bank or at the secondary market.

Banker's acceptance arises most often in connection with international trade and is commonly issued to facilitate import-export transactions. It is known as a bill of exchange drawn on and accepted by banks. Upon acceptance, that is, when the banker's acceptance is endorsed by the bank, the bank assumes responsibility for ultimate payment to the holder of the draft. With this, the financial instrument becomes negotiable and can be traded on the secondary market. Banker's acceptance transactions are implemented based on the discounting method, where purchase is made at a value which is lower than the value of the certificate on maturity. On the maturity date, the bank pays the holder of the banker's acceptance the face value of the certificate. A repurchase agreement is normally issued by the banks and other financial institutions such as discount houses and merchant banks. This agreement consists of the sale of a short-term security by the bank to investors in return for cash, and pledges to repurchase the instrument from the investor at some later date at a pre-determined price which constitutes the face value plus interest payment. The agreement gives the buyer the right to retain interest earnings based on the period of execution of the repurchase.

Financial instruments for the Islamic money market have not really expanded to Muslim countries. Nevertheless, Malaysia, followed suit by Indonesia, have started to pave the way by providing *Syariah*-based financial instruments for negotiation in the money market. In 1994, Malaysia established an Islamic inter-bank money market which consisted of three chief components, namely inter-bank trading in Islamic financial instruments, Islamic inter-bank investments and inter-bank cheque clearance system. However, in 1999 when consolidation occurred in the cheque clearance system, RENTAS (Real Time Electronic Transfer of Funds and Securities), the Islamic inter-bank cheque clearance system ceased to be regarded as a component of the Islamic inter-bank money market. Currently, the Islamic inter-bank money market is made up of two components only, namely inter-bank trading of Islamic financial instruments and *mudharabah* inter-bank investments.

Inter-bank trading is a market where banks would trade among one another all the *Syariah*-based financial instruments. These financial instruments comprise Government Investment Issue (GII), Bank Negara Negotiable Notes (BNNN), Islamic Accepted Bills (IAB) and Islamic Negotiable Instruments (INI). Financial instruments of this type were introduced as a mechanism whereby the deficit bank (investee) obtains investment from a surplus bank (investor bank) based on *mudharabah*. The period of investment is normally from overnight to 12 months. The rate of return is usually based on the rate of gross profit before distribution for investments of one year. At the time of the negotiation, the investor bank will not know the amount of return it will receive; it will only know at the end of the investment period. On 2 February 1996, Bank Negara introduced a minimum benchmark rate for these investment certificates which is based on the prevailing rate of the Government Investment Issues plus a spread of 0.5%. The purpose of imposing this benchmark rate is to ensure that only banks with reasonable rates of return may participate in the Islamic money market.

Besides the financial instruments mentioned above, Bank Negara also provides Islamic inter-bank deposit facilities based on the *wadiah* principle. This facility is intended to serve as a method to absorb any surplus liquidity in the Islamic banking system. Apart from Malaysia, Indonesia has also taken similar steps in providing financial instruments for the Islamic money market system and making available inter-bank deposit based on the *wadiah* principle and inter-bank investment certificates based on the *mudharabah* principle.

Forward and Future Markets

The goal of the forward market and future market is to enable participants in the markets to offset their price risk in future transactions which involve money, security or commodity. The seller and buyer in both markets are allowed to establish their terms of the exchange prior to future delivery date. Unlike forward market in which contracts between seller and buyer are not standardized, contracts in the future market are. Additionally, future contracts are made between parties involved in the transactions and the futures exchange, and not with each other.

Forward market is allowed by *Syariah*, as supported by the fact that there are a number of *Syariah* principles which are of relevance to forward transactions, namely *salam, istijrar* and *istisna* (also known as *bai salam, bai istijrar* and *bai istisna*, respectively). However, there is divergence of opinion regarding the types of goods that may be transacted in the forward market. For instance, Islamic banks in Jordan, Egypt and Sudan are prohibited from engaging in forward currency trading. Currency trading can only be executed at spot rate (sometimes called immediate rate or other rates), whereas both spot and forward transactions are available at Islamic banks in other countries. Futures market, meanwhile, is the least developed component of the Islamic capital market because it is very much at a controversial stage. The legitimacy of future market is inconclusive among Muslim scholars. Some scholars have asserted that futures market is not permissible because it involves the sale of goods not in possession of the goods. Others have strong opposite opinions on the matter. Kamali (1997), a modern scholar, was of the opinion that futures contracts may be allowable because it does not involve gambling, *riba* and uncertainties. In fact, there is no clear prohibition in the Quran and *Hadith* against futures sales. However, ElGari (1998) questioned the usability of this financial instrument. He believed that if the *salam* principle was applied on future sale transactions, then payment should be made at the time the contract was signed and not in the future. Nevertheless, the Syariah Advisory Council of the Securities Commission of Malaysia, at its 11the meeting on 26 November 1997, resolved that the futures contract involving crude palm oil was allowable and in accordance with *Syariah*.

With forward markets for commodities allowed by *Syariah*, there is a high possibility for the securitization of debts that emerge from these transactions. In fact some Muslim countries have already created bills to be traded in the capital market and money market based on forward trading. For example, banker's acceptance is a financial instrument created based on forward trading. However, there is divergence of opinion pertaining to the legitimacy of debt securitization that derives from such instrument. In Malaysia, transactions based on the *bai ad-dayn* concept is widely enforced, but this concept is rejected by scholars in the Middle East. Consequently, this has limited the use of this instrument and questioned its applicability in the market.

The most widely traded financial derivatives in the forward and future markets as well as the capital market of the conventional system are warrants and options. Warrants are a type of security which gives its holder the right to buy common stocks directly from a company at a potentially advantageous price. This right is usually issued in combination with long-term debts such as bonds or debentures. Options, on the other hand, allow the holder to enter into contracts to buy or sell shares, commodities or currencies at a pre-determined price called the strike price until some future date. There are two types of options, namely call option and put option. In a call option, the holder is given the right to buy, while a put option gives the holder the right to sell a security or a futures contract at a strike price. The company, on the other hand, has the responsibility to sell or buy the options at the pre-determined price. However, the holder of the warrants and options may at any time sell his right on the stock exchange or any secondary market at a market determined price.

There is considerable debate among Muslim scholars about the legality of warrants and options which has yet to be resolved by *Syariah*. *Syariah* permits the use of options. For instance, in the case of *murabahah* and *ijarah*, options are sometimes given to the buyer or tenant in the event that the goods contract defaults. ElGari (2004) was of the opinion that call option is lawful and is called *arboon*. This view is supported by Kamali (2002). In Malaysia, warrants and options are permitted so long as they originate from shares which are allowed by *Syariah*. The legitimacy of warrants and options lies in the fact that the holder is entitled to exercise his right just as the owner of a property has the right to dispose of his property in the open market. In this case, warrants and options are regarded as *mal* and the owner of the *mal* may resell it.

Mortgage Market

Mortgage market refers to the market that provides finance for real estate. Real estate loans are normally issued by various types of financial institutions. Commercial banks, savings and loan institutions and cooperatives are institutions in the forefront in providing this type of property loan. Interest-based loans impose various terms and conditions including matters related to interest rate and method of repayment. Repayment varies and depends to a large extent on the lending institution. Some institutions charge fixed monthly instalments until maturity, while others charge either a small initial instalment with progressive payment until full repayment is made or repayment based on the amount of interest incurred. There are also loans which require the borrower to settle all interest incurred but pay instalment on the principal and interest at some future date.

As with conventional banks, Islamic banks adopt various methods with respect to matters related to real estate financing. Repayment depends on the *Syariah* principle applied by each bank. For instance, an Islamic bank buys a property at the original price and sells it to its customer at a higher price. The customer is required to pay a certain portion of the profit the bank earned from the higher sale price before paying the original purchase price of the property. Some banks require that the customer pay the profit together with the original cost of the real estate during the initial stage of financing. Others adopt a repayment method whereby the customer makes small initial payments followed subsequently by higher repayments towards the end of the financing period. The amount of instalment depends largely on the agreement between the bank and its clients. Although Islamic banks do not face any real issues or problems in providing such real estate financing, the securitization concept must be in placed or established so that it does not become immobilized.

In the conventional system, there are two types of mortgage-backed securities instruments, namely pass-through mortgage securities and mortgage-backed bonds. Pass-through mortgage securities refer to securities that "pass through" all payments of principal and interest on pools of mortgages to holders of security in the pool. For example, let us assume a financial institution has a real estate loan of RM100 million (inclusive of principal and interest) for which a RM100 million bond is issued against this property. Thus, when the borrower pays for the loan plus interest, the financial institution would immediately channel that payment to the bondholder based on the value of the bond held. For instance, if a person holds 1% of the bond value, he is entitled to receive 1% of the total principal and interest payment. Mortgage-backed bonds are similar to corporate bonds which have a fixed maturity date and interest payment except that these bonds have specific mortgages as collateral. The bondholders would receive interest payment on the due date and principal payment upon maturity. Collaterals on these bonds are the real estate loans issued by the financial institution to the real estate owners.

Islamic mortgage market is still undeveloped. Currently, no Islamic financial institution has used real estate financing in *sukuk* issuance. However, Malaysia has taken precedence over the development of Islamic mortgage market. The use of Islamic mortgage bonds is administered through the National Mortgage Corporation or Syarikat Cagamas Berhad (Cagamas), a subsidiary company of Bank Negara Malaysia. Cagamas was established in 1986 with the objective of financing the purchase of housing loans and other consumer receivables from financial institutions and issuing bonds to purchase the loans. These Cagamas bonds would then become the main driver of growth and catalyst for the development of a secondary mortgage market. There are four types of bonds issued by Cagamas: (i) Fixed Rate Bonds which have tenures of one and a half years to seven years with semi-annual interest payments; (ii) Floating Rate Bonds which have tenures of up to seven years and an adjustable interest rate pegged to the Kuala Lumpur Inter-bank Offer Rates (KLIBOR); (iii) Short-term Notes which have maturities between 1 month to 12 months and only pay the face value at maturity; and (iv) *Sanadat Mudharabah Cagamas* which are Islamic bonds based on the profit-sharing principle. Bondholders receive dividends semi-annually based on a pre-determined profit-loss ratio.

Funds collected through the issuance of conventional financial instruments are used to purchase housing loans. The *Sanadat Mudharabah Cagamas* are used to purchase Islamic home financing debts. Since 2001, Cagamas has also started to acquire Islamic hire purchase debts. Although Cagamas purchases Islamic home financing debts and Islamic hire purchase debts from financial institutions, the acquisition made is purchase with recourse. This means that when the bank sells the debts to Cagamas, it agrees to reimburse Cagamas for losses resulting from the purchased loans such as replacing any bad debts. Cagamas has also set several conditions in its debt purchase transactions. As at the end of 2007, total Islamic home financing debts purchased by Cagamas was RM12.6 million, while Islamic leasing debts purchased amounted to RM3,408.6 million (www.cagamas.com.my).

Although Cagamas, in principle, has paved the way for the implementation of the securitization process for Islamic home financing debt and Islamic hire purchase debt, this process could be developed further by allowing Islamic financial institutions to issue their own bonds. Apart from financial institutions, other organizations could also be authorized to manage the issuance and trading process of these Islamic mortgage bonds. *Syariah* principles such as *wakalah* could possibly be used to implement and develop the Islamic mortgage market.

Unit Trust Market

The unit trust market is another branch of the financial market which can be explored and operated more actively in accordance with *Syariah*. Unit trust funds are essentially collective investment schemes structured to allow investors with similar investment objectives and risk tolerance to pool their savings in a common fund. The pool will then be managed by an investment company and invested in a diversified portfolio of authorized investment on behalf of the investors in accordance with the investment objectives of the trust funds. The investment scheme of the unit trust fund involves a tripartite relationship between the fund manager, trustee and investor who are legally bound by the terms and conditions specified in the Trust Deed. The fund managers are professionals who are highly skilled in investment and are responsible for the management and operations of the unit trust funds. The pooled funds are invested in any or a combination of investments such as shares, money market instruments, futures contracts, commodities, bonds, private debt securities and others. If the accumulated funds are invested mainly in shares traded on the stock exchange, then the funds are known as equity funds. Assets of the trust funds are owned by the trustee, not the fund manager. Investors normally do not have any rights on the assets purchased by the managers; instead their investment returns are in proportion to the numbers of units owned.

The method of fund mobilization based on the unit trust scheme first started in the United Kingdom in 1931. In Malaysia, a unit trust was first established by a company called Malayan Unit Trusts Limited in August 1959. In 1963, this company was bought over by the South-East Asia Development Corporation which had two subsidiaries, namely Singapore Unit Trusts Limited which operated in Singapore and Asia Unit Trusts Berhad which had operations in Malaysia (Bank Negara Malaysia, 1984). The industry was initially regulated by Bank Negara Malaysia but since 1993, the principle legislative body governing the establishment, operation and administration of unit trust is the Securities Commission of Malaysia. The governing legislatures for the unit trust industry are the *Trusts Act 1949* and the *Companies Act 1965*.

There are two types of unit trusts, open-ended and closed-ended unit trusts. With an open-ended fund, there is no fixed pool of money. The total amount of money available for investment and the number of units in existence increase or decrease depending on the subscription and redemption of units in the fund. Investors of the unit trust may at any time redeem on demand their units at market price, either directly from the manager or through appointed agents. Closed-ended fund, on the other hand, has a fixed size and are incorporated companies whose businesses are to buy and sell shares on the stock exchange. No new shares are issued after the subscription period ends. Closed-ended fund shares are listed and traded through the stock exchange and prices of these shares are determined by market forces. Investors normally receive two types of returns, namely capital profit from the price increase of the unit trust, and annual dividends, if any, obtained at the end of the financial term.

The development of the unit trust industry in Malaysia gained momentum and unit trusts became a household product with the establishment of Perbadanan Nasional Berhad which manages the Amanah Saham Nasional scheme in April 1981. A variety of unit trust schemes were launched by this corporation and subsequently by other finance corporations. As at 31 December 2008, there were 39 corporations managing unit trust schemes. The total funds approved were 521 and the approved fund size was 473.939 billion units, while units in circulation were 208.342 billion. The total account for the trust units was 12,274,908, with the asset value of funds totalling RM169,414 billion (www.sc.com.my).

Since managing unit trust does not involve any elements of *riba*, it is therefore relatively easy to put into operation a trust scheme that complies with *Syariah* principles. Currently, a great number of fund management companies are involved in managing trust funds. These companies are not only operating actively in Muslim countries but also in Western countries such as the United States and the United Kingdom. In Malaysia, the successful launch of two unit trust funds in 1993 by Arab Malaysia Unit Trust Berhad created the impetus for other fund management companies to follow suit. This is evidence by the increasing number of *Syariah*-compliant unit trust funds available today. For instance, all the unit trusts managed by Perbadanan Nasional Berhad conform to *Syariah*.

When a *Syariah*-compliant unit trust scheme is launched, a number of conditions must be complied with. Among them, the investment undertaken must be in companies that are not involved in activities which encompass the elements of *riba, maisir* and *gharar*. The companies must not also be involved in the supply, manufacture or service of things prohibited by Islam such as alcohol, gambling and non-*halal* food products. A Syariah Monitoring Board must be established to monitor and endorse that the investment undertaken does not involve Islamic prohibitions. A process of cleansing or purification shall be carried out on the returns of the Islamic unit trust should any part of it raises doubts.

As at 31 December 2008, there were not less than 149 *Syariah*-compliant funds in Malaysia which represented more than 25% of the total unit trust funds. Two models which may be applied in managing Islamic unit trust funds are *mudharabah* and *wakalah*. If the *mudharabah* model is applied, the fund manager would act as the *mudarib* and profits obtained from the investment would be shared with the investor. On the other hand, if the *wakalah* principle is used, the manager would only act as a representative and would receive administrative fees for his efforts. The type of principle used is normally stated in the prospectus. Under normal conditions, the contents of the *Syariah*-compliant fund prospectus are not much different from that of the conventional fund prospectus. This is because conditions imposed by the Securities Commission of Malaysia for both Islamic and conventional trust funds are fairly analogous except for statements with respect to managing of the funds, appointment of the Syariah Monitoring Board members and profit distribution method.

ISLAMIC FINANCIAL MARKET PRACTICES IN MALAYSIA

The practices of Islamic financial market largely depend on the financial instruments available. However, the scope of discussion in this section is limited to the practices of the issuance and trading of the main financial instruments in the Malaysian financial market. One important aspect of the financial market that needs a great deal of attention is the supervision and regulation of each component of the financial market. For instance, in Malaysia, the entire financial market was initially under the supervision of Bank Negara

Malaysia. However, when the Securities Commission of Malaysia was established on 1 March 1993, the supervisory and regulatory role was transferred to the Securities Commission of Malaysia. Financial instruments are limited to particular groups only. Normally, individual and retail clients do not have the opportunity to use these financial instruments to meet their financing needs due to the requirements imposed for using such facilities. The requirements or conditions imposed in turn depend largely on the financial market regulator. For instance, the issuance of financial instruments in the capital market necessitates the fulfilment of certain preconditions set by the Securities Commission of Malaysia which may be viewed on its website, www.sc.com.my. This section will discuss major Islamic financial instruments which are actively traded on the market. Among the financial instruments which will be discussed are:

a. Government Investment Issue

b. Bank Negara Negotiable Note

c. Short-term Trade Bill

d. Islamic Negotiable Deposit Instrument

e. *Mudharabah* Inter-bank Investment

f. Bonds based on *bai bithaman ajil* and *murabahah* principles

g. Bonds without coupon value

h. Bonds based on the *ijarah* principle

i. Bonds based on Cagamas *mudharabah*

Government Investment Issue

Government Investment Issue (GII) is a long-term non-interest bearing government security issued by the Malaysian government to fund the government's development expenditure. It is also one of the most actively traded Islamic financial instruments on the secondary market. The GII was first issued in 1983 by the government to enable Bank Islam Malaysia to channel its surplus fund to an income-generating investment. This initial issuance was based on the *qard hassan* principle, where investors would provide interest-free loans to the government and at maturity the investors would receive *hibah* or gift from the government based on certain percentages. However, GII was not a tradeable instrument as *qard hassan* principle did not permit trading on the secondary market. In order to allow the instrument to be traded on the secondary market, the underlying concept was changed to *bai al-inah* principle, from June 2001. Under this principle, Bank Negara Malaysia on behalf of the government will sell government-owned assets and subsequently buy back the assets at its nominal value plus profit through a tender process. The nominal value will be settled at maturity while the profit rate will be distributed semi-annually. Profit rate is based on the weighted average yield of the successful bids of the auction.

The task of issuing GII is given to Bank Negara Malaysia through its Department of Investment Operations and Financial Market. At certain times Bank Negara Malaysia will invite financial institutions to subscribe to GII. Each certificate is valued at RM1 million while the minimum purchase amount is also RM1 million. The purchase of this financial instrument is limited to members of the financial market, namely commercial banks with Islamic banking branches, Islamic banks, merchant banks and discount houses. Transaction of this financial instrument is based on scriptless trading, where the sale and purchase is recorded by the Department of Investment Operations and Financial Market. When purchasing GII, financial institutions are also required to make other payments such as commission and stamp duty. Similarly, when GII matures, Bank Negara Malaysia would pay the holders the agreed price. This instrument is normally traded on the secondary market using the *bai al-dayn* principle. The selling price is usually pre-determined by the seller as well as the buyer. In March 2005, the Malaysian Government issued the first profit-based GII worth RM2 billion. This five-year coupon-bearing paper pays half-yearly profit to investors. A significant development was achieved on 17 June 2005 when the *Government Funding Act 1983* (previously known as the *Government Investment Act 1983*) was amended whereby the issuance limit of the GII was increased from RM15 billion to RM30 billion. The outstanding amount of GII issued as at 18 February 2008 was RM46 billion. The issuance of GII was RM18 billion and RM10 billion in 2008 and 2007, respectively.

Bank Negara Negotiable Note

Bank Negara Negotiable Note (BNNN) is a short-term Islamic financial instrument issued by Bank Negara Malaysia to financial institutions involved in the money market. These notes are a type of deposit notes based on the *bai al-inah* principle. Bank Negara Malaysia would offer its assets (usually in the form of a collection of shares listed on Bursa Malaysia) to be purchased by way of tender by financial institutions that have been listed by the central bank as members of the financial market. At the same time, the central bank agrees to repurchase the notes at RM1 million per note. This financial instrument was first issued by the central bank in 1999.

The timing and amount of negotiable notes to be issued depend on the central bank. Institutions that wish to subscribe to the notes are required to submit their respective tenders to the Department of Investment Operations and Financial Market before the closing date. As with Government Investment Issue, the issuance of these notes is also based on scriptless transaction. For this type of notes only sales information such as the name of the buyer and total amount of purchase, needs to be registered. The buyers would then pay in cash the agreed tender price to the central bank. These notes are tradable on the secondary market based on the *bai al-dayn* principle.

The potential seller would make an announcement of his intention at the secondary market, and the sales value depends on factors such as the time span involved in the transaction and the maturity period of the notes. At the end of the maturity period, the central bank would pay holders the face value of the notes. Bank Negara Negotiable Notes issued for 2001, 2002 and 2003 were RM1 billion, RM2 billion and RM1 billion, respectively. The outstanding amount as at the end of 2003 was RM3 billion. In 2001, 2002 and 2003, the notes traded on the money market totalled RM1.2 billion, RM2.2 billion and RM8.8 billion, respectively. In order to further spur the trading activities of the notes, financial institutions that are appointed as principal dealers are allowed to list the sale or purchase price. Market participants may conduct their business transactions based on the price offered by the principal dealers.

In 2006, the BNNN was replaced by Bank Negara Monetary Note (BNMN) pursuant to the amendments of the *Central Bank of Malaysia Act 1958*. As such, all maturing issues of BNNN will be replaced with BNMN on a gradual basis. The maximum maturity of BNMN has been lengthened from one to three years and may be issued either on a discounted or coupon-bearing basis. As at 18 February 2008, the outstanding amount of BNMN in the markets stood at RM500 million.

Short-term Trade Bill

Islamic short-term trade bill was first introduced in Malaysia in 1992. This financial instrument is similar to banker's acceptance in the conventional banking system and is based on the concept of *murabahah* and *bai al-dayn*. These bills are another money market instrument aimed at encouraging and promoting both foreign and domestic trade by providing traders with an attractive Islamic financial products for either purchase or sale purposes. However, these short-term trade bills can be drawn to finance domestic purchases or imports and domestic sales or exports of goods or items that are not prohibited in Islam.

For imports or domestic purchases, financing provided by the Islamic bank is based on the *murabahah* principle. Under this concept, the bank appoints the customer as the purchasing agent who then purchases the required goods from the seller on behalf of the bank. The bank pays the seller for the goods and then resell them to the customer on deferred payment of up to 200 days. Upon maturity, the customer shall pay the cost of goods plus profit margin as agreed by both parties. The bill represents the customer's promise to pay the bank the rate stipulated in the bill upon maturity. If the bank is willing to accept the responsibility as the recipient of the bill, then the result would be what is termed Islamic Accepted Bills. If the bank decides to sell the bill to a third party, then the concept of *bai al-dayn* or debt sale will apply. Normally, the sales are based on the discounted *bai al-dayn* method. At maturity, if the bill has been sold to a third party, the bank which accepts the responsibility (or the bank which undertakes to endorse acceptance) will make payment to the legal bill holders. At the same time, the client will issue payment to the bank to fulfil his responsibility as stated in the bill. The seller or exporter will prepare export documents under the sale contract or letter of credit. The documents are then presented to the bank for purchase. The seller will then draw another bill of exchange on the bank. This mode of financing enables the seller to obtain instant cash for managing his working capital by selling the debt to the bank.

This sale transaction involves a securitization process, whereby the bank purchases the customer's right to the debt, which is normally securitized in the form of an accepted bill. The sale is based on the *bai al-dayn* principle and the bill is sold to the customer at a discount from the face value. The bill may be traded on the secondary market and the price of the bill is determined by using a certain formula, that is, by taking into account the face value, annual rate of profit and number of days remaining to maturity.

At maturity, the bank would issue payment to the bill holder and collect back the payment from the gains of the letters of credit in the original transaction. These short-term trade bills may also be redeemed before the end of the maturity period. The amount required to be paid for this early redemption depends on factors such as face value, the redemption rate which has been mutually agreed upon and number of days remaining to maturity. The Islamic Accepted Bill is an actively traded financial instrument on the secondary market. In 2008, a total of RM7,020 million of these bills were traded as compared to RM5,183 million in 2007. This is evidence that *Syariah*-based short-term trade bills are increasingly becoming a popular financial instrument among businessmen in dealing with international business transactions.

Islamic Negotiable Instrument of Deposit

Islamic negotiable instrument of deposit is a type of deposit facility provided by Islamic banks for their clients. This instrument was first issued in the year 2000. *Bai bithaman ajil* is the original principle used. However, this instrument can also be issued based on the *mudharabah* and *bai al-inah* principles. The minimum amount for each certificate of deposit is normally RM50,000. These negotiable certificates of deposit can be traded on the secondary market. The selling price is usually determined by several factors, namely the face value of the certificate, maturity period and profit rate given by the bank if the *mudharabah* principle is used. The tender method would be used if the certificates are based on the *bai al-inah* principle.

The issuance process of this instrument is subject to the approval of Bank Negara Malaysia. The issuance process is normally executed by the treasury department of a financial institution, and the branch only acts as a link between the client and the treasury department at the headquarters. At maturity, the headquarters would pay the holder the principal plus return. The clients can sell the instrument before maturity on the secondary market or to the issuing bank. The use of this type of financial instrument has not reached its maximum capacity in the money market. A major issuance of this financial instrument in Malaysia was the RM200 million Active Commodities Islamic Negotiable Instruments of Deposit by AmIslamic Bank in August 2008.

Mudharabah Inter-bank Investment

The *Mudharabah* Inter-bank Investment was initiated by Bank Negara Malaysia in 1994, when the Islamic money market was first introduced in the Malaysian Islamic banking system. This instrument is the mechanism whereby the deficit financial institution can obtain investment from the surplus financial institution on a *mudharabah* or profit-sharing basis. Some of the features of this instrument are as follows:

(i) Investment time span is from overnight to 12 months.

(ii) Minimum amount of each investment is RM50,000.

(iii) Rate of return is based on the rate of gross profit before distribution for an investment of one year of the investee bank.

(iv) The profit-sharing ratio is negotiable between both the investor and investee.

(v) At the time of negotiation, the return is unknown to the investor bank since the actual return will only be crystallized at the end of the investment period. (However, Bank Negara Malaysia maintained that as of February 1996, the minimum rate of return would be based on the return provided by the Government Investment Issue plus 0.5%.)

The formula for calculating the profit element to be paid to the provider of the fund or investor is as follows:

$$Y = \frac{P \times R \times T \, (K)}{36500}$$

Where:

    Y = Amount of profit to be paid to the investor
    P = Principal investment
    R = Rate of profit before distribution for a one-year investment of the investee bank
    T = Total number of days invested
    K = Profit-sharing ratio

This instrument is actively traded on the Islamic inter-bank money market. The total money market transactions under the *Mudharabah* Inter-bank Investments was RM256.1 billion in 2006. Throughout 2007 and 2008, a total of RM271 billion and RM224 billion of this instrument was traded, respectively.

Bonds Based on *Bai Bithaman Ajil* and *Murabahah* Principles

Bonds based on the *bai bithaman ajil* principle (also commonly known as BaIDS or *Bai bithaman ajil* Islamic Debt Securities) are among the early Islamic financial instruments introduced in the capital market in Malaysia. This method can be used by those requiring funds to purchase new fixed assets. Among the earliest issuances by government-owned companies using this method was the RM2.2 billion issuance by KLIA Berhad for financing the construction of the Kuala Lumpur International Airport in 1996 (Osman, 2001). This issuance was secured by the government of Malaysia. In the private sector, Houlon Corporation issued *bai bithaman ajil* bonds valued at RM150 million under two issuances. The first issuance was on 3 September 1997 and valued at RM120 million with a tenure of seven years. The second issuance worth RM30 million was made on 3 January 1998 and matured on 2 January 2005. The value of *bai bithaman ajil* bonds issued in the market was RM1,350 million, RM820 million and RM2,590 million in 2008, 2007 and 2006, respectively.

The issuance process and cycle of bonds based on the *murabahah* principle (also commonly known as MUNIF or *Murabahah* Underwritten Notes Issuance Facility) are quite similar to those of *bai bithaman ajil* bonds. The difference between BaIDS and MUNIF lies in their maturity period. The maturity period of *murabahah* bonds is shorter, normally not more than five years. Moccis Trading Sdn Bhd was among the earliest to issue a MUNIF bond. It was valued at RM50 million and issued on 29 March 1996. This bond had a tenure of five years. Another issuer of MUNIF bonds was Teledata Sdn Bhd which issued bonds valued at RM30 million on 5 April 1996. The bond's maturity date was 4 April 2001. The total issuance value of MUNIF bonds in the market as at end of 2007 was RM400 million. The basic process for bond issuance based on the *bai bithaman ajil* principle is shown in Figure 7–1.

FIGURE 7–1 Process of Issuance and Cycle of *Bai Bithaman Ajil* Bonds

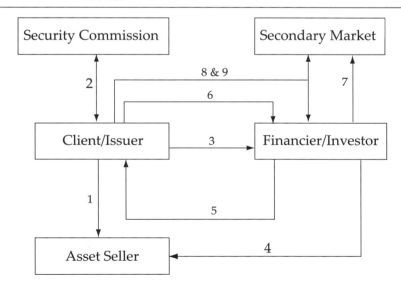

Figure 7–1 shows the issuance process of a *bai bithaman ajil* bond. The flow is as follows:

1. The applicant (the bond issuer) will discuss and identify the assets intended to be purchased from the seller of goods and then sets the conditions for the purchase.

2. The issuer will apply for approval to issue bonds from the Securities Commission of Malaysia. There are a number of requirements and conditions which must be fulfilled before approval can be granted. Bond issuance can only be executed after approval is obtained.

3. The issuer will discuss with and submit requests to the financier or investor. Discussion and agreement on the financing conditions include issuance expenditure and the pre-determined returns to the investor.

4. The financier or investor will undertake the purchase on behalf of the issuer, and payment will be made according to the agreed terms between the issuer and the seller of the goods. At times, the client may be appointed to represent the issuer and purchase the asset himself.

5. The financier will sell the goods to the issuer on a deferred payment basis, that is, at the purchase price plus margin of profit.

6. The issuer evidences the deferred payments by issuing bonds. These bonds may be based on the principal instalment along with a profit element, which means that only one type of certificate or note is issued. Alternatively, the bondholders will receive two types of payments. If the bondholder desires to take profit periodically, secondary notes maturing every six months or every one year will be issued depending on the agreement. He will receive the principal payment at maturity. The value of a note or certificate that represents the capital component

is called primary note, whereas the profit portion is known as secondary note.

7. The financier upon receiving the bonds may resell them on the secondary market based on the *bai al-dayn* principle.

8. When profit payment to the bondholder is due (e.g. after six months), the issuer will make profit payments to the holders of the secondary notes.

9. On maturity, the issuer will fulfil all responsibilities involved based on the principal value of the bonds.

Bonds Without Coupon Value Based on *Murabahah* and *Bai al-Inah* Principles

In the conventional banking system, bond without coupon value or zero coupon bond is a type of financial instrument whereby the issuer pays only the face value of the bond at maturity. This means the investor buys the zero coupon bonds at a deep discount from the face value. Normally, the bonds are traded on the secondary market and the discount price is determined through a bidding process. This process is allowable in *Syariah* and the principle related to it is called *bai muzayadah.* The Syariah Advisory Council of the Securities Commission of Malaysia approved the use of this method at its 10th general meeting in 1997. This mode of financing is what the country's financial industry needs (Hussain, 1997). The industry is in dire need of a benchmark for corporate bonds, that is, a benchmark for the current value of an asset and the profit level. Khazanah Nasional, a government corporation that manages the assets of the Malaysian government, was found to be a suitable institution to issue this Islamic benchmark bond. Consequently, in September 1997 Khazanah Nasional issued the first Islamic bond, known as Khazanah Bonds, with a face value of RM1 billion using the *murabahah* method, and a maturity period of three years. The outstanding amount of Khazanah Bonds as at 18 February 2009 stood at RM3,350 million. The basic issuance process of this type of bond is shown in Figure 7–2.

FIGURE 7–2 Issuance Process and Cycle of *Murabahah* Bonds Without Coupon Value

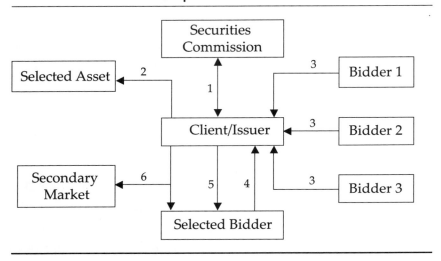

Figure 7–2 shows the issuance process of bonds without coupon value based on the *murabahah* principle. The steps involved in the flow are as described below:

1. The issuer will apply for approval to issue bonds from the Securities Commission of Malaysia. A number of requirements and conditions must be fulfilled and information provided before approval can be granted.

2. The issuer will identify the pool of assets to be sold to the financier. The repurchase value of the asset will be determined and the payment of the repurchase price will be made by the issuer on a particular date in the future (bond maturity date).

3. A number of financiers (bidders) will be invited to present purchase offers on the identified assets, and payment must be made at the beginning of the duration.

4. The bidder with the best offer price is selected, and the selected bidder will undertake two agreements with the issuer. The first agreement involves the cash sale by the bond issuer based on the purchase price offered by the selected bidder. The second agreement involves the resale which is based on the *murabahah* principle by the financier to the issuer. The selling price comprises a cost and profit element.

5. The original owner of the asset or the issuer will issue *murabahah* notes or bonds to the financier. To enable these notes to be negotiable on the secondary market, they may be broken up into several certificates with smaller face values according to the amount agreed upon.

6. At maturity, the issuer will pay the financier or bondholders the face value of the bond.

The above process describes the situation where the *'aqd* resale of assets is done by the financier for the issuer or the original owner of the asset. Thus, the principle of this second sale is known as *murabahah*, which is a sale involving cost and profit elements. On the other hand, if the original asset owner executes the sale and then promises to purchase it at a higher price, then the principle used is *bai al-inah* and the bonds involved are known as bonds without coupon value based on the *bai al-inah* principle. In this situation, the two *'aqd* involved are, first, sale by the issuer based on the offer price by the financier, and secondly the pre-determined repurchase price as agreed upon at the time the offer was made to the financier.

Bonds based on the *bai al-inah* concept can also be issued through the normal process which involves only one financier without administering any tender, or issued based on the *bai muzayadah* principle. The issuance process for *bai al-inah* bond is shown in Figure 7–3. The steps involved are as described below:

1. The issuer will apply to the Securities Commission of Malaysia for approval to issue bonds. A number of requirements and conditions must be fulfilled and information provided before the approval can be granted.

2. The issuer will identify the pool of assets to be sold to the financier. The sale involves cash payment.

3. At the same time, the issuer will inform the financier about his willingness to repurchase the asset at an agreed price and the method of payment. The repurchase price includes the original price plus the financier's profit. Payment is usually done in instalments and the resale process is executed by the buyer.

4. As documentary evidence of the arrangement is entered between the issuer and financier, the issuer will issue bonds to the financier. The bonds can be issued either by using primary notes and secondary notes, or simply notes that have both the elements of cost and profit.

5. The investor may sell the bonds on the secondary market or hold them to maturity.

6. The issuer will amortize the notes at maturity.

FIGURE 7–3 Process of Issuance and Cycle of *Bai al-Inah* Bonds

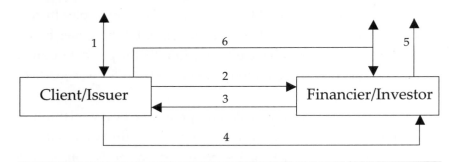

Bai al-inah bonds were first used by Bank Negara Malaysia when the second series of the Malaysia Savings Bond worth RM377 million was issued. The Merdeka Savings Bond was first issued in January 2004 by Bank Negara Malaysia. The April 2008 issuance of three-year Merdeka Savings Bond amounted to RM2 billion. The bonds will be issued in two series in 2009. Similarly, the *bai al-inah* principle was adopted by the profit-based Government Investment Issue in 2001. Bank Negara Negotiable Notes are also issued based on this principle.

Bonds Based on the *Ijarah* Principle

Bonds based on the *ijarah* principle were among the earliest types of bonds to be discussed and suggested as a mode of Islamic financing by Muslim intellectuals. The following are some of the situations where bonds based on the *ijarah* principle may be used:

(i) The financier purchases and then leases out the asset required by the client for a rental fee. The client or lessee makes periodic rental payment to the financier or lessor. This responsibility towards the asset owner can be securitized with the rental payment value based on either monthly, quarterly, semi annual or yearly payments until the end of the rental period. The notes or bonds created based on this rental value may be kept by the asset owner or resold on the secondary market.

(ii) *Ijarah* bonds may also be issued when the issuer requires funds for his working capital. In such a situation, the issuer will identify his assets such as buildings or factories and sell them to the financier. The financier will buy the assets in cash and then rent them out to the issuer who shall make periodic payments as agreed between both parties. Rent payment may be securitized, where the agreement to pay monthly rentals will be made in the form of notes and submitted to the financier. These notes or bonds may be kept or resold on the secondary market by the financier.

(iii) The third situation involving the *ijarah* principle is the creation of a special intermediary body known as special purpose vehicle (SPV). The SPV will act as the bond issuer and issues certificates to investors at a pre-determined profit. The SPV will then enter into an agreement to purchase the assets and lease them to the lessee. The lessee is obliged to make periodic rental payment to the SPV which in turn will use these proceeds to pay the financier.

In Malaysia, the first *ijarah* bond was issued by Segari Energy Ventures Sdn Bhd on 30 September 1997 valued at RM521.5 million. Repayment to the holder was made four times, RM116 million on 31 March 2002, RM124.5 million on 31 March 2003, RM157 million on 31 March 2004 and RM124 million on 31 March 2005. The total value of *ijarah* bonds issued in the market was RM6,259 million and RM8,417 million in 2008 and 2007, respectively. The biggest issuer in 2008 was Dewa Ringgit Sukuk Limited which issued RM3,500 million worth of *ijarah* bond. Figure 7–4 shows the process of issuance and the cycle of *ijarah* bonds where the issuer needs to acquire assets.

The process of issuance and the cycle of *ijarah* bonds to fulfil the requirements for fixed assets purchase by a business organization may be described as follows:

1. The applicant (the bond issuer) will discuss and identify the asset intended to be purchased from the seller and will determine the conditions for the purchase of the commodity.

2. The issuer will apply from the Securities Commission of Malaysia approval to issue bonds. The approval is subject to a number of conditions and requirements as set out by the Securities Commission of Malaysia.

FIGURE 7–4 Issuance and Circulation Process of *Ijarah* Bonds for Fixed Assets

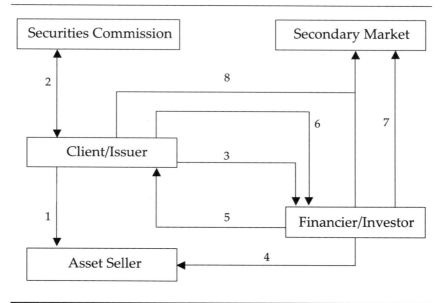

3. The issuer will discuss with and submit requests to the financier or investor. Agreement on the conditions for financing includes issuance expenditure and the pre-determined profit to be paid to the investors.

4. The financier or investor makes the purchase and payment according to the initial agreement made between the issuer and the seller of the asset.

5. The financier will then rent the asset to the issuer according to the rental price and other conditions agreed upon.

6. As documentary evidence of the arrangement is entered into by both parties, the issuer shall issue the bonds. These bonds may be based on monthly, quarterly or semi annual rental payments as agreed.

7. After receiving the bonds, the financier may resell them on the secondary market based on the *bai al-dayn* principle.

8. At maturity, the issuer will amortize payments to the financier holding the notes or the other parties concerned in the event that the notes have been sold in the market.

An almost similar process is followed if the issuer requires financing for circulating capital. In this situation, the issuer has to identify either an individual asset or combined assets to be sold to the financier. After the assets have been purchased by the financier for cash, the financier will subsequently rent the asset to the issuer. The issuer will then issue bonds of equivalent value to the rentals which will be paid to the financier either monthly, quarterly or semi annually.

The amount of rental payments depends on several factors such as the type of asset, pre-determined return and the agreed rentals. An extension of the *ijarah* principle is the *ijarah wa-iqtina*. Under this principle, rental payments would be higher because at the end of the rental period, the tenant would purchase the asset at a pre-determined price. In addition to this, another principle that is used in Malaysia is the *ijarah muntahiah bit-tamlik* principle whereby ownership of the commodity is automatically transferred to the tenant at the end of the rental period. Rental transaction occurs between the commodity owner and the tenant while the latter is responsible for bond issuance. The bonds issued present documentary evidence to amortize indemnities arising from the rental of the asset concerned. However, there are situations where a company or organization is established specifically to act as the intermediary between the financier and the tenant of the said asset or commodity. This organization is called special purpose vehicle (SPV) or special purpose company. The establishment of such an organization is sometimes required when transactions involve the government or a global market, or when a relatively large amount of assets are involved. At times its establishment becomes necessary in order to fulfil legislative requirements. For instance, when the government of Malaysia issued bonds with a five-year maturity period valued at US$600 million in July 2002, Malaysian Global Sukuk Inc. was established as the special purpose vehicle. Bond issuance using special purpose vehicle under normal circumstances is as shown in Figure 7–5.

FIGURE 7–5 Issuance and Cycle of *Ijarah* Bonds Using Special Purpose Vehicle

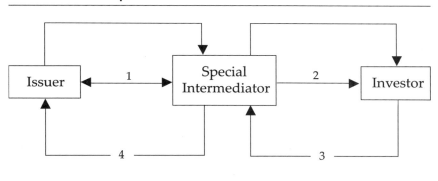

The SPV involved in this process is established either as a subsidiary company by the party intending to issue the bond or a financial institution possessing efficiency and expertise in handling the business of bond issuance and administration. The steps involved are as follows:

1. The customer enters into an agreement to sell an asset or a combination of assets to the SPV according to conditions mutually agreed upon. The seller will also agree to rent the asset sold. The conditions which need to be taken into account include the selling price, method of payment, rental payment, rental period and options at the end of the rental period (option to purchase the asset, or direct transfer of ownership to the tenant or permanent ownership rights to the SPV).

2. The SPV will take on the task of issuing the bonds and invite investors to undertake the investment. Bonds will be issued based on the assets purchased by the SPV. The investors shall have shared ownership of the asset and the SPV will also later undertake the task of distributing profit to the investors.

3. The investors pay in cash when purchasing issued bonds.

4. The SPV will pay the purchase price to the seller after deducting expenditure.

5. The SPV receives periodic rental payments from the seller on the due dates.

6. The SPV will channel the rental payments to investors (i.e. bondholders) in the form of profit on particular dates in line with the receipt of rental payments.

When the government of Malaysia made the decision to issue Islamic global bonds for the first time, various parties and several processes were involved. The issuance of this bond worth US$600 million involved a principal manager, The Hongkong and Shanghai Banking Corporation. Other managers comprised ABC Islamic Bank, Maybank International, Abu Dhabi Islamic Bank, Bank Islam Malaysia, Dubai Islamic Bank, Islamic Development Bank and Standard Chartered Bank. The bonds were listed on the Luxemburg Stock Exchange and Labuan International Financial Exchange. The first step involved was to establish a special purpose vehicle or SPV. The SPV was established by the Ministry of Finance under the name Malaysia Global Sukuk Inc. in Labuan, which acted as the issuer. Malaysia Global Sukuk appointed several parties to take on the role of trustees, administrators handling payments and collection of rentals, and the task of registering the issued bonds. Various documents had to be prepared involving the relationship between the seller and buyer of assets, tenant and rent provider, and *sukuk* issuer and purchaser. Some of the important documents were issuer's declaration of trust, trust certificate or *sukuk*, sale and purchase agreement of the asset, seller's declaration of trust, master *ijarah* agreement and service agency agreement. The bond issuance process is shown in Figure 7–6.

FIGURE 7–6 Process of Issuance and Cycle of the US$600 Malaysia Global Sukuk Bonds

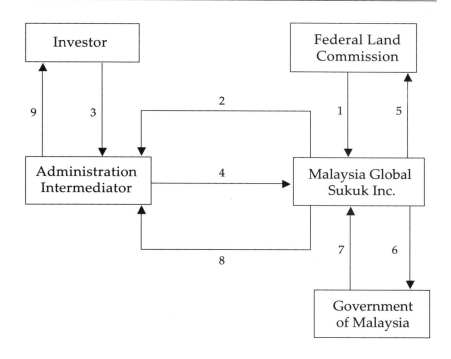

The steps may be summarized as follows:

1. Malaysia Global Sukuk negotiates with the Federal Land Commission to sell land and buildings owned by the government of Malaysia. In this case the assets involved are the Selayang Hospital, Tengku Ampuan Rahimah Hospital in Kelang, the Government Complex and Housing Complex

at Jalan Duta. The sale and purchase agreement is signed, and in this situation the property involved is termed as trust property.

2. Malaysia Global Sukuk appoints a party who is responsible for the issuance and administration of the *sukuk* (bonds). This party will play an intermediary role between Malaysia Global Sukuk and the bond purchasers.

3. The financial intermediary, on behalf of Malaysia Global Sukuk, handles the bond issuance and receives collections from the investors. The *sukuk* buyer or holder has ownership rights of the trust property. The *sukuk* holder pays the face value for the *sukuk* as agreed upon.

4. The financial intermediary channels to Malaysia Global Sukuk the acquired cash after deducting all the administration charges.

5. Malaysia Global Sukuk issues payment to the Federal Land Commission based on the purchase price of the asset. In this case ownership is not transferred to Malaysia Global Sukuk, but as a trustee it has the right of claim on the trust property. Thus, Malaysia Global Sukuk has the right on all realized privileges in future transactions.

6. Malaysia Global Sukuk undertakes a rental agreement with the government of Malaysia and this agreement includes matters related to maintenance, rental payments, amount and method of payment. In this case, the basis for the rental rate is LIBOR (London Inter-bank Offered Rate) plus the profit ratio.

7. The government of Malaysia makes rental payments to Malaysia Global Sukuk on the stipulated dates.

8. From the proceeds of rentals, Malaysia Global Sukuk pays dividends to the *sukuk* holders. The face value of the *sukuk* is amortized at the end of the maturity period.

9. The financial intermediary channels the rental payments made by Malaysia Global Sukuk to the investors.

Bonds Based on Cagamas *Mudharabah*

Cagamas Berhad, established in 1986, started issuing Islamic bonds called Cagamas *Sanadat Mudharabah* on 25 March 1994. Proceeds from the sale of these bonds were used to purchase Islamic home financing. As of 11 December 2001, Cagamas started to purchase Islamic hire purchase financing and leases. As at 18 February 2009, the outstanding value of Cagamas *Sanadat Mudharabah* was RM50 million. The issuance of Cagamas *Sanadat Mudharabah* bond is shown in Figure 7–7.

FIGURE 7–7 Issuance and Cycle of Cagamas *Sanadat Mudharabah*

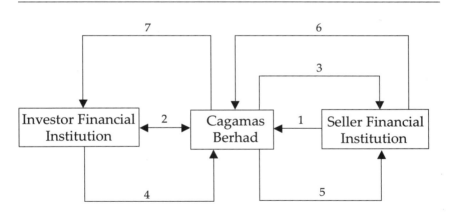

The steps in the issuance process and the cycle of Cagamas *Sanadat Mudharabah* bonds are as follows:

1. The qualified financial institution as listed by Cagamas will inform Cagamas of its intention to sell and will quote the

highest rate of return to Cagamas, together with the estimated sales value and the sales term.

2. Cagamas will appraise the selling price offered with potential buyers (financial institutions) and the buyers will inform Cagamas the rate of return that they expect.

3. Cagamas will subsequently inform the seller the required rate of return. If the rate is lower than the offered rate, then the sale shall proceed. On the other hand, if the required rate is higher than the offer rate, then the seller may either revise the offer rate or cancel the sale altogether. If the offer to Cagamas is higher than the required rate, then Cagamas will provide an initial purchase contract that endorses matters such as value, terms, difference between rates, date of purchase and service fees calculation.

4. On the day that the decision of the tender is to be made known, the seller may still cancel the sale if the buyer's required rate of return is higher than the rate offered. On the other hand, the sale will proceed if the seller agrees to the buyer's price. The buyer must settle the purchase price with Cagamas.

5. Cagamas will transfer the sales proceeds to the seller.

6. When the payments are due from the borrower, the seller will make these payments to Cagamas.

7. Cagamas will pay the buyer an amount as agreed in the *mudharabah* contract between Cagamas and the buyer.

ORGANIZATIONS ASSOCIATED WITH ISLAMIC FINANCIAL MARKET

The early history of the Malaysian financial market development may be looked at from two different angles, that is either from the perspective of the development of financial institutions or from the perspective of the development of existing financial instruments in the financial market. The first formal financial institutions in Malaysia began when Chartered Merchantile Bank of India, London and China (later named Merchantile Bank) established its branch in Penang in 1856, which was subsequently followed by the establishment of a Chartered Bank branch in 1875. These banks were set up to fulfil the banking needs of the mining and farming industries. The services provided included trade financing, working capital and money delivery between London, India and China. Local commercial bank, Kwong Yik (Selangor) Banking Corporation, was not set up until July 1913 (Bank Negara Malaysia, 1984). The development of the financial and banking system in Malaysia had passed through several phases with each phase having different features and significance. The early era of development was followed by the era of Japanese occupation, the pre-independence era, the post-independence era, the pre-New Economic Policy era, the era of the New Economic Policy, the post-New Economic Policy era, the pre-economic crisis era and the post-economic crisis era. Starting with branches of foreign commercial banks and followed by the establishment of local commercial banks, the Malaysian banking industry in 2007 consisted of 21 commercial banks, 11 Islamic banks and 14 investment banks (Bank Negara Malaysia, 2007).

Since all trading transactions involve currency, it is thus necessary to briefly describe the development of money as a medium of exchange and the institutions responsible for currency issuance and circulation. In Malaysia, the use of money as a medium of exchange began during the reign of Muzaffar Shah (1445–1459), the fourth sultan of the Malacca Sultanate. When Malacca fell to the Portuguese and then the Dutch, these colonists began to introduce their own currencies (Bank Negara Malaysia, 1984). When the British occupied Tanah Melayu (the Malay peninsula), they also introduced their currency. The first organization established to issue currency was the Board of Commissioners of Currency of

Straits Settlements of Penang, Malacca and Singapore, which was established under the *Ordinance VIII of 1897*. The Board continued its function of issuing currency notes until 1967 when its currency issuance function was taken over by Bank Negara Malaysia or the Central Bank of Malaysia.

Bank Negara Malaysia (its original name was Bank Negara Tanah Melayu or Central Bank of Malaya and was changed to Bank Negara Malaysia when Malaysia was established in 1965) as the single regulator of the banking system in Malaysia was established on 26 January 1959, in line with the independence of Malaya in 1957. Since its establishment, Bank Negara Malaysia has experienced several changes particularly with respect to its objectives and functions. For instance, originally Bank Negara Malaysia also acted as the supervisory body for the capital market in Malaysia, but this responsibility was transferred to the Securities Commission in 1993. Nevertheless, Bank Negara Malaysia maintains its function as the regulatory body in the money market. This bank is also responsible for the management of government securities and acts as a banker and financial advisor to the government.

In contrast to the history of currency, the development of the Malaysian capital market was pioneered by foreigners. For instance, share trading in the country was introduced by the shareholders of agricultural corporations such as Guthrie & Co Ltd (1821), Fraser & Co Ltd (1873), Malakof Plantation Co Ltd (1879), Inch Kenneth Rubber Ltd (1902) and Sime Darby & Co Ltd (1910). Most of the shares of these companies were listed on the London Stock Market (Securities Commission, 2004). The first informal securities organization in Malaysia was the Singapore Stockbrokers' Association, which was established on 23 June 1930. In 1937, this association was re-registered as the Malayan Stockbrokers' Association, but it did not trade public shares. In 1960, the public trading of shares began with the formation of the Malayan Stock Exchange which was later renamed the Stock Exchange of Malaysia in 1964. With the secession of Singapore from Malaysia in 1965, it became known as the Stock Exchange of Malaysia and Singapore. When the currency interchangeability between Malaysia and Singapore ceased in 1973, the Stock Exchange of Malaysia and Singapore was separated into Kuala Lumpur Stock Exchange Board and Stock Exchange of Singapore. In 1976, the operations of Kuala Lumpur Stock Exchange Berhad was taken over by the Kuala Lumpur Stock Exchange, which was incorporated on 14 December of the same year as a company limited by guarantee. The Kuala Lumpur Stock Exchange Board was renamed the Kuala Lumpur Stock Exchange in 1994. In 2004, the Kuala Lumpur Stock Exchange became a demutualized exchange and was converted to a company limited by its shares, called Bursa Malaysia.

Before 1993, the capital market in Malaysia was regulated by multiple institutions and agencies including the Ministry of Finance, Kuala Lumpur Stock Exchange Board, Registrar of Companies, Bank Negara Malaysia, Capital Issues Committee and Foreign Investment Committee. The two main legislations governing securities regulations involved in the monitoring and supervision of security-related matters were *Companies Act 1965* and *Securities Industry Act 1973*. The latter was replaced with *Securities Industry Act 1983*.

Over time, the involvement of multiple agencies presented some difficulties and complications as each had its own guidelines and conditions for approval. Moreover, the many rules laid down by each agency, when taken together, translated into a lengthy and complex process. In 1988, a task force was set up to study the development of the capital market in Malaysia. Based on this report, a recommendation for the establishment of a securities commission was made. In August 1991, a committee was set up to advise the Ministry of Finance on the formal structure of the proposed new commission. A report was presented to the Ministry of Finance in February 1992. In August of the same year, the Cabinet approved the working paper on the establishment of the Securities Commission and two other bills, the *Securities Commission Bill* and the *Futures*

Industry Bill. All the related bills were passed by Parliament at the end of 1992, and the Securities Commission was officially established on 1 March 1993 with the coming into effect of the *Securities Commission Act 1993*, which also marked the dissolution of the Capital Issuance Committee and the Panel of Take-overs and Mergers. With the establishment of the Securities Commission, the corporate debt market became jointly regulated by Bank Negara Malaysia and the Securities Commission. The duplication of authority between the two agencies was later identified and amendments to the *Banking and Financial Institutions Act 1989* and the *Securities Commission Act* were made to address this issue. With these amendments in place, the Securities Commission became the sole regulatory body in the corporate bond market in Malaysia in July 2001.

Securities Commission

Securities Commission of Malaysia (SCM) was officially established on 1 March 1993 under the *Securities Commission Act 1993* to fulfil the demands and recommendations for a single regulatory authority which is responsible for the systematic development of the capital market as well as broader issues including investor protection. In line with its objectives, SCM sets its mission statement as such:

> *To promote and maintain fair, efficient, secure and transparent securities and futures markets and to facilitate the orderly development of an innovative and competitive capital market (www.sc.com.my).*

Since the main focus of SCM is on matters related to regulation, its regulatory functions are as follows (www.sc.com.my):

1. Acting as registering authority for prospectuses of corporations other than unlisted recreation clubs.

2. Acting as approving authority for corporate bond issues.

3. Regulating all matters relating to securities and futures contracts.

4. Regulating the take-overs and mergers of companies.

5. Regulating all matters relating to unit trust schemes.

6. Licensing and supervising all licensed persons.

7. Encouraging self-regulation.

8. Ensuring proper conduct of market institutions and licensed persons.

In order to facilitate SCM in the implementation of its responsibilities, its organizational structure is broken down into several levels. At the pinnacle of the organizational structure are the 9 members of the Securities Commission. These members are appointed by the Minister of Finance and comprise prominent figures in the industry. As members of the Securities Commission, they are responsible for setting policies related to the regulation and direction of the capital market in Malaysia. The implementation of all the policies comes under the jurisdiction of the SCM management which is divided into two levels, senior managers and managers. Senior management comprises directors and managers who lead the divisions in SCM such as Market Supervision, Enforcement, Corporate Resources, Strategy and Development, Issues and Investments. Each department under these divisions is headed by a head of department. The Department of Islamic Capital Market is placed under the Strategy and Development Division.

In 2001, SCM published the Capital Market Master Plan which presents a strategic roadmap for the development of the capital market in Malaysia. This ten-year comprehensive plan charts the strategic positioning and future direction of the Malaysian capital market for the next 10 years, with the following vision (Securities Commission, 2004):

1. To be internationally competitive in all core areas necessary to support Malaysia's basic capital and investment needs, as well as its longer term economic objectives.

2. To be a highly efficient conduit for the mobilization and allocation of funds.

3. To be supported by a strong and facilitative regulatory framework that enables the capital market to perform its functions effectively and provide a high degree of confidence to its users.

The master plan outlined 6 major objectives, 24 strategic initiatives and 152 recom-mendations. The major objectives specified are as follows:

1. To be the preferred fund-raising centre for Malaysian companies.

2. To promote an effective investment management industry and a more conducive environment for investors.

3. To enhance the competitive standing and efficiency of market institutions.

4. To develop a strong and competitive environment for intermediation services.

5. To ensure a stronger and more facilitative regulatory regime.

6. To establish Malaysia as an international Islamic capital market centre.

The master plan also contains 13 recommendations for action forwarded by SCM to enhance the international competitiveness position of Malaysia as an Islamic capital market. The action recommendations are:

1. To actively pursue more dynamic efforts to introduce competitive and innovative Islamic financial products and services.

2. To facilitate efforts to introduce and promote a wider range of Islamic collective investment schemes.

3. To further liberalize investment restrictions for the *takaful* industry in order to facilitate greater mobilization of *takaful* funds into the Islamic capital market.

4. To pursue efforts to mobilize untapped Islamic assets through securitization.

5. To enhance efforts to increase the pool of Islamic capital market expertise through training and education.

6. To establish a single Syariah advisory council for the Islamic finance sector.

7. To establish a facilitative tax and legal framework for the Islamic capital market.

8. To pursue efforts to develop an appropriate financial reporting framework for the Islamic capital market in collaboration with the Malaysian Accounting Standards Board.

9. To pursue more efforts to enhance the awareness of Malaysia as an Islamic capital market at the domestic and international levels.

10. To establish strategic alliances between Malaysia and other Islamic capital markets.

11. To get the government and government-related entities to consider issuing Islamic debt securities in the global market.

12. To pursue the listing of Malaysian Islamic equity funds in the international market.

13. To provide incentives to encourage the entry of foreign intermediators and professionals with expertise in Islamic capital market-related businesses.

In May 2007, the *Capital Markets and Securities Act 2007* was passed by the Malaysian Parliament and came into force in September of that year. The Act marked a major milestone in SCM's efforts to strengthen the capital market's regulatory framework in Malaysia. Among the key features of the Act are greater investor protection through the enhancement of SCM's power to take civil and administrative actions; and the introduction of a single licensing regime as opposed to multiple separate licenses.

SCM has conducted various activities towards the development of a comprehensive Islamic capital market in Malaysia as well as in the international market. SCM has also put forth guidelines for the issuance of Islamic securities. The guidelines cover aspects such as the need to appoint an advisor in the securities issuance process, the documents required when submitting the application for approval, those qualified to issue Islamic bonds, appointment of *Syariah* advisors, rating requirements, underwriting requirements, form of issuance and other requirements.

SUMMARY

The role of financial markets is to bring together buyers and users of funds. In the absence of a financial market, surplus units are unable to channel their money to productive investments, and deficit units are unable to obtain financing to meet their financial needs. This was indeed a problem faced by Islamic banks during their early years of establishment. Even after more than 30 years of their establishment, this problem still looms over the Islamic banking industry as most countries do not yet have in place Islamic financial markets. Since financial instruments associated with *riba* are not permitted by *Syariah*, it follows that alternative financial instruments that are permissible must be developed. In view of this problem, the Islamic banking industry has on many occasions considered and proposed to have its own financial markets. The deliberation lingers on till today.

In certain countries, the governments have shown tremendous support and commitment to the establishment of a complete Islamic financial system. On-going efforts are taking place towards this end. The financial market consists of four major components and each component has been given due attention. In the money market, Islamic banks have been efficiently adjusting their liquidity positions through a variety of Islamic financial instruments that are now available. In addition, agencies such as the central banks and financial authorities are participating actively in the Islamic money market through the issuance of negotiable certificates of deposit in order to resolve liquidity problems faced by Islamic financial institutions. With respect to the Islamic capital market, Islamic financial instruments containing features of equity and debt instruments have already been developed. The trading of stocks on the exchange is permissible so long as it does not involve stocks that are associated with businesses prohibited by Islam. For debt instruments, Islamic bonds or *sukuk* have yet to be fully developed. Nevertheless, *sukuk* based on the *bai bithaman ajil, ijarah, salam* and *murabahah* principles are widely used and issued in a number of Muslim countries. As for the mortgage markets and forward markets, although these markets are still in an infancy state, instruments are already being developed for them. However, the instruments are not extensively used in countries practising Islamic banking system mainly due to the divergence of opinion among *ulama* and *Syariah* experts on the legality and applicability of certain transactions and principles.

Malaysia has taken progressive steps in the establishment of an institution with the main focus of developing the Islamic financial markets. In Malaysia, financial instruments for all four components of the financial markets have been successfully developed.

Furthermore, Malaysia has set up several agencies which are directly involved in regulating and supervising the financial markets. For instance, the capital market is regulated and supervised by the Securities Commission of Malaysia. In its Capital Market Master Plan, the Securities Commission of Malaysia has detailed plans and made recommendations for the development of the Islamic capital market. It is envisaged that by the year 2010, Malaysia would have in place a comprehensive and viable Islamic financial system. Apart from the Securities Commission of Malaysia, Bank Negara Malaysia is very much responsible for matters pertaining to the money market financial instruments, while Cagamas Berhad plays an important role in the mortgage market.

REFERENCES AND FURTHER READING

Affin-UOB Research. "Islamic Capital Market: Its Pillars of Faith." *Investors Digest* (February): 26–32, 2004.

Ariff, Mohammad and Muhammad Abdul Mannan. *Developing A System of Islamic Financial Instruments*. Jeddah: IRTI, Islamic Development Bank, 1990.

Bahrain Monetary Agency. *Islamic Finance Review*, Issue 6 (July 2004).

Bank Islam Malaysia Berhad. *2008 Annual Report*. Kuala Lumpur.

Bank Negara Malaysia. *Money and Banking in Malaysia*. Silver Anniversary Edition 1959–1984. Kuala Lumpur: Economics Department, 1984.

Bank Negara Malaysia. *2007 Annual Report*. Kuala Lumpur

ElGari, Mohamed A. "Short term Financial Instruments based on Salam Contracts". In *Islamis Financial Instruments for Public*

Sector Resource Mobilization, edited by   Ausaf Ahmad and Tariqullah Khan, 249–266. Jeddah (Saudi Arabia): IRTI, Islamic Development Bank, 1998.

ElGari, Mohamed A. "The Qard Hassan Bank". Paper presented at the International Seminar on Nonbank Financial Institutions: Islamic Alternatives, Kuala Lumpur, March 2004.

Hussain, Abdul Rashid. "Islamic Benchmark Bonds." Working paper presented at the Islamic Capital Market International Conference, Kuala Lumpur, 15–16 July 1997.

Jordan Islamic Bank. *Annual Report* (various issues).

Kamali, Mohd Hashim. "The Futures Contract: A *Syariah* Perspective." Working paper presented at the Islamic Capital Market International Conference, Kuala Lumpur, 15–16 July 1997.

Kamali, Mohd Hashim. *Islamic Commercial Law: An Analysis of Futures and Options.* Kuala Lumpur: Ilmiah Publishers, 2002.

Mannan, Muhammad Abdul. "An Appraisal of Existing Financial Instruments and Market Operations from an Islamic Perspective." In *Developing a System of Financial Instruments,* edited by Mohammad Ariff and Muhammad Abdul Mannan, 75–104. Jeddah (Saudi Arabia): IRTI, Islamic Development Bank, 1990.

Muamalah Financial Consulting Sdn Bhd. Islamic Bonds and Islamic Capital Market Course, Kuala Lumpur, 6 April 2004.

Osman, Mashitah. "Islamic Bond Market: State of Play in Malaysia." Working paper presented at the Islamic Private Debt Securities Seminar, Kuala Lumpur, 24–25 September 2001.

Pervez, Imtiaz Ahmad. "The Financial Instruments Used by Islamic Banks." *New Horizon,* No. 46/47 (1996): 19–21.

Qureshi, D.M. "The Role of Shariah Board Financial Instruments in a Muslim Country." In *Developing a System of Financial Instruments*, edited by Mohammad Ariff and Muhammad Abdul Mannan, 49–67. Jeddah (Saudi Arabia): IRTI, Islamic Development Bank, 1990.

Rosly, Saiful Azhar and Mahmood M. Sanusi. "The Application of Bay' al-Inah and Bay' al-Dayn in Malaysian Islamic Bond: An Islamic Analysis." *International Journal of Islamic Financial Services*, Vol 1 No. 2 (July–September 1999).

Securities Commission of Malaysia. *Annual Report* (various issues).

Securities Commission of Malaysia. *Resolution of the Securities Commission Shariah Advisory Board*, 2002.

Securities Commission of Malaysia. *Capital Market Development in Malaysia: History and Perspectives*. Kuala Lumpur, 2004.

Usmani, Mohammad Taqi. "The Principle of Limited Liability From the Shariah Viewpoint." A paper presented at the 7th Expert-level Meeting on Islamic Banking, Kuala Lumpur, 27–29 July 1992.

www.bma.gov.bh

www.bnm.gov.my

www.cagamas.com.my

www.sc.com.my

CHAPTER 8

ISLAMIC INSURANCE SYSTEM

Insurance is one of the important elements of a country's financial system. However, the conventional insurance system which has been in existence for about 3,000 years is not compatible with the religious belief of Muslims due to the presence of elements of riba or interest, gharar or uncertainties, and maisir or gambling. To meet the needs of Muslims, takaful, a form of Islamic insurance which complies with Islamic principles was introduced. This chapter discusses in detail the basic concepts of takaful and its practice. For comparison purposes, the operations of conventional insurance will also be described.

INTRODUCTION

The *Oxford Dictionary* describes insurance as "an agreement that a company makes to provide compensation for loss, damage, or injury to a person or organization in return for a payment or a series of payment (called premium) made in advance". In legal terms, insurance is a contract by which the insured pays a specified amount of money known as premium to another party, the insurer, who in return agrees to compensate or indemnify the insured for specific future losses as listed in the contract.

The original concept of insurance involves a cooperative system which is based on collective agreement among a group of people to jointly indemnify each other against loss that may befall any one of them. Reimbursements are made from the fund to which each participant within the group has contributed a certain amount of money or premiums. The Islamic banking system was established because of the presence of *riba* in the conventional banking system. In the same light, Muslims are prohibited from transacting in the conventional insurance system since conventional insurance does not conform to the *Syariah* principles as it embodies the three elements of *gharar, maisir* and *riba*.

Gharar is the element of "uncertainty" that exists in life insurance policies and general insurance policies. The "uncertainty" factor is the main feature in the contract or *mu'qud'alaih*, while in Islam this point must be something which is clear and certain. Uncertainty is present in conventional insurance because the value and timing of compensation cannot be determined and known at the time the contract is made. For example, in conventional insurance, the policyholder agrees to pay a premium to the insurance company, and in return the company guarantees to pay compensation in the event of a loss or catastrophe. However, the policyholder is not notified of the method, source nor the amount of money that the company would pay him. Under the Islamic insurance concept, all parties to the contract need to know exactly how much they must contribute and how much compensation they will receive. In addition, *gharar* also exists when injustice or bias arises in the agreement made by both parties. This situation occurs in both life and general policies of the conventional insurance system. For example, life insurance policyholders would lose their premiums if they terminate their participating policies before they are eligible for the cash surrender value. Similarly for general policyholders, the insurance company would be at an advantage in the event of a policy cancellation within a short-term period.

Maisir or gambling is an extension of the "uncertainty" concept. For example, a person buys a life insurance policy with the hope that his family or beneficiaries would receive a certain amount of money upon his death. The policy undertaker, however, has knowledge neither of the source of the money that would be paid to his beneficiaries nor of how it would be obtained. The element of *riba* exists in the conventional insurance system because the insurance company guarantees to pay fixed returns on the money contributed by the policyholder.

Given the presence of these prohibited elements in the conventional insurance system, Muslim *ummah*, particularly those involved in business, are truly in need of a system which is *Syariah*-compliant to cover them from losses incurred due to unforeseen disasters, catastrophes or tragedies. According to Muslim intellectuals, this concept of mutual help and cooperation is indeed encouraged in Islam. This concept could be made the foundation for the implementation of the Islamic concept of insurance where elements such as collective responsibility, unity and mutual interest form the core elements.

BACKGROUND OF THE CONVENTIONAL INSURANCE SYSTEM

The word "insurance" was first used in 1651. Insurance means the act or the system of guarantee of life or property based on premium payments. The practice of paying premium as cover for loss had existed since 1635, although it only involved cover for loss of property and not for life. The word originates from "insure" or "ensure" and was taken from *enseurer*, an old

French word that means "to convince" or "to promise on oath". After 1376, the word *insuren* or *ensuren* was used to convey the meaning "to give consent" or "to provide assurance" (Barnhart, 1988). In general, the conventional insurance system today is of two types, personal insurance and social insurance. Personal insurance is basically a voluntary insurance scheme provided to individuals to cover them against any disaster or loss. Although at times personal insurance schemes are offered by the government, more often this type of insurance is provided by private companies. One of the main features of this type of insurance is voluntary involvement and risk transfer based on the contract of agreement undertaken between the insurance company and the individuals participating in the insurance schemes. In contrast with personal insurance schemes, social insurance is a compulsory scheme which is usually administered by the government. Benefits of the social insurance scheme are normally determined by legislation and emphasis is placed on the concept of social sufficiency. An example of a social insurance programme in Malaysia is the Social Security Organisation or SOCSO and in the United States, the Social Security System.

Personal insurance may be categorized into two types, private insurance and property insurance. Private insurance provides cover against losses related to life and health, while property and liability insurance is cover for losses on property as a result of a disaster or catastrophe. A method, similar to this concept of mutual assistance and shared responsibility in society, existed around 2500 BC in the Egyptian society. Under this method, every member of society would contribute funds to help the less fortunate, including financing burial expenses or financing cost of medical care for those suffering from serious illnesses. This concept was also adopted by the Greeks and Romans.

The basic concept of insurance for property came into existence around 3000 BC (Vaughan and Vaughan, 1999). During this period, Chinese merchants practised risk-sharing techniques in transporting their goods. When travelling across treacherous waters, the merchants would redistribute their goods across many ships in order to limit the loss due to ship capsizing. In the event of a capsize, the loss incurred would not be centred on certain parties only, but instead it would be shared by many parties and was therefore made manageable.

Besides this practice, the concept of risk transfer was also recorded in the *Code of Hammurabi* (around 1800 BC). According to this *Code*, if a trader or merchant receives a loan to purchase goods, he is required to pay the lender an additional sum in exchange for the lender's guarantee to cancel the loan should the goods be stolen. A similar system was applied by the Phoenicians and Greeks in their seaborne commerce. The borrower was given the option to pay high interest rate on the loan received in exchange for the creditor's guarantee to cancel the loan if the ship or cargo vanished at sea or was stolen. This contract was known as *bottomry contract* if ships were used as a guaranty and *respondentia contract* if cargo was presented as the guaranty.

Marine insurance is the first insurance of modern times to be introduced. The use of this insurance started in Italy in the 13th century and spread to other European countries and later to England. Unlike the *bottomry contract* which was associated with loans, this method involved free trade. Ship owners and traders who wished for protection would list the name of the ship, its cargo or load, the destination and other important information on a piece of paper and would display such information to the public. The party who was willing to bear the risk would write his name under the paragraph that outlined the types and amount of risks and other terms of agreement. The practice of writing under the paragraph or *writing under* later led to the creation of the term *underwriter*.

Fire insurance as known today originated in 1591 in Germany. However, the Great Fire of London of 1666 demonstrated the urgent need for fire insurance and was the major contributor to the development of this type of insurance. In the aftermath of this disaster, a medical doctor by the name of Nicholas Barbon who was involved in redeveloping the city of London after the great fire, opened an office to insure houses and buildings. Casualty insurance, meanwhile, was said to have been introduced in 1848 when the English Parliament approved the establishment of a company to sell insurance for the protection of train passengers.

The history of life insurance began on 18 June 1536 when a group of guaranteed sponsors in London issued a life insurance policy to a man. The period of coverage was for a year at a value of £400. The man died within that period and the guaranteed sponsors paid up as per the agreement. The first insurance company was established in 1699 in London, called the Society for the Assurance of Widows and Orphans.

As in most countries in the world, insurance service in Malaysia is divided into two, namely life insurance and general insurance. Life insurance involves life coverage and coverage for other unforeseen disasters which cause the loss of income due to permanent disability as well as physical impairment. General insurance, on the other hand, involves coverage for loss of property resulting from fire, theft and other disasters.

There is no information available as to when insurance was first introduced in Malaysia (formerly Malaya). However, branches of insurance companies belonging to England, America and other countries dominated the insurance business in the big towns of Malaya (Bank Negara Malaysia, 1989). If the development of trade involving tin and rubber were to be taken as a basis of the origins of the insurance business, then the late 1800s and early 1900s may be regarded as the beginning of the insurance business in Malaysia. In fact, the first branch of a foreign commercial bank was set up in Malaya in 1909. Local insurance companies were first established in the 1950s. In 1963, there were 6 insurance companies and by the end of 2007 as many as 126 licences had been issued. Out of the total licences issued, 41 companies were direct insurers, 7 were professional reinsurances, 34 were insurance brokers, 37 were adjusters (valuators) and 7 were financial advisors. In the direct insurance business, 9 companies conducted life insurance business, 26 companies conducted general insurance business, while 7 conducted both life and general insurance by the end of 2007. The number of registered agents was 78,587 for life insurance and 39,165 for general insurance. Total assets of insurance companies were RM122,550.3 million, with RM102,601.3 million belonging to life insurance and RM19,949 million to general insurance as at end of 2007. The number of new policies issued for 2007 alone was 1,337,312, worth a total of RM186,327.2 million. This made the total number of policies issued up until 2007 to be 10,909,194 with an insured value of RM723,000.7 million. The amount of claims paid in 2007 was RM4,606.3 million (Bank Negara Malaysia, 2007a).

Before 1961, the operations of insurance companies in Malaysia were governed under the *Life Assurance Companies Ordinance 1948* and *Fire Insurance Companies Ordinance 1948*. Due to the emergence of certain unhealthy practices in the insurance industry, the government introduced a new legislation known as the *Life Assurance Act 1961* which was later amended to become *Insurance Act 1963*. As the insurance industry continued to expand, more effective supervision and regulation of the industry was required. Recognizing this, the function of regulating and supervising the insurance industry was transferred to the Central Bank of Malaysia commencing 1 April 1988 with the appointment of the Governor of the Central Bank as the Director General of Insurance.

Prior to 1988, the insurance industry was under the purview of the Treasury. Insurance laws were further consolidated when the *Insurance Act 1963* was amended and replaced with the *Insurance Act 1996*. Under this Act, a range of regulations and authority were provided to the Central Bank of Malaysia to approve the appointment of director and chief executive officer, selling or buying of big share capital interests, establishment of offices and subsidiary companies, and appointment of auditors and valuators. Apart from the Act, insurance companies are also regulated under the *Insurance*

Regulations 1966. Since its inception, several amendments have been made to the regulations, especially when changes were required in the insurance industry during the economic crisis between 1997 and 1998.

The arrival of the new century brought a range of challenges to the industry, particularly, globalization. However, by international standard, the insurance industry in Malaysia can be considered relatively small. Some of the challenges identified are as follows (Bank Negara Malaysia, 2001):

(i) Increasing competition from traditional companies in line with the global trend towards mergers and consolidation that creates international insurers which are much bigger in size, more skilled and more centred on core competency areas.

(ii) Competition from new companies such as asset managers, captive insurers (general insurance), independent financial advisors and internet companies. By not depending on middlemen in the insurance business, these companies are able to improve their product range and performance as well as bringing down costs.

(iii) Self-adjustment and adaptation to suit technological advancement which in principle has changed the way businesses are administered.

(iv) Meeting the needs of more sophisticated and knowledgable consumers.

In light of future challenges, it is hoped that the insurance industry in Malaysia would be able to achieve the following goals:

(i) Be the long-term savings initiator which is resilient and effective in order to support economic growth.

(ii) Possess a strong financial position in facing market fluctuations and competition pressure.

ISLAMIC INSURANCE SYSTEM 431

(iii) Adopt international business best practices and management.

(iv) Be in tune with the latest phase of innovation with a wide range of products at competitive prices for consumers.

(v) Conduct business through distribution channels of wide scope and variety for the convenience of consumers.

(vi) Display high standards of professionalism and ethics.

(vii) Be more productive and cost effective.

Bank Negara Malaysia has presented various recommendations towards the achievement of the above goals. The recommendations would be achieved in three phases as follows:

(i) Building the capacity of domestic insurers.

(ii) Promoting mergers and reinforcing incentives to improve performance.

(iii) Motivating innovations through liberalization and progressiveness.

One of the recommendations in the first phase is to allow qualified insurance companies to sell *takaful* products. This implies that the *takaful* system is set to play a major role in the insurance industry in Malaysia.

HISTORY AND DEVELOPMENT OF THE ISLAMIC INSURANCE SYSTEM

Islamic insurance system is known as *takaful*. Thus, in the discussion of Islamic insurance the term *takaful* is used. *Takaful* is a system created to provide protection against disasters similar to the protection provided by the conventional insurance system.

Since the conventional insurance system cannot serve the Islamic *ummah*, *takaful* becomes the alternative. In essence, *takaful* is an extension of the concept of mutual assistance as well as the concept of blood money as practised by the Arabs before Islam was established. It is believed that the concepts of compensation and group responsibility are accepted by Islam and the Prophet (p.b.u.h.). Muslim intellectuals and jurists are of the opinion that the concept of joint responsibility in the *aqila* system as practised by the *Muhajirin* (Muslims from Mecca) and *Ansar* (Muslims in Medina) laid the foundation for *takaful*. It is also believed that *takaful* was first introduced when Muslim Arabs expanding their trade to India, South East Asia and other Asian countries, mutually agreed to contribute to a fund to cover members in the group who incurred mishaps or robberies along the numerous voyages. (Long distance journeys are normally associated with huge losses arising from a multitude of misfortunes such as disasters or robberies.)

This early *takaful* practice bore some similarities to the marine loans practised by the Greeks. Marine loan was said to be the foundation for the concept of modern conventional insurance. Under the marine loan concept, money was loaned to shipowners and was repayable only upon safe completion of a voyage. High interest rate, which was paid for successful voyages, was not only regarded as cost of capital, but also as risk of capital loss. Although this practice of conventional insurance system is unacceptable in Islam, Muslim jurists do not prohibit the concept of insurance itself. The reason is that the core of *takaful* is the element of cooperation which is absolutely encouraged in Islam.

Alongside the prolific establishment of Islamic banks, *takaful* institutions were created to provide insurance cover to Muslims. The first *takaful* company was established in 1979 in Sudan. In the same year, Arabic Insurance Company was established, followed by the establishment of Dar al-Mal al-Islami in Geneva in 1981. In 1983, Luxembourg Islamic Takaful Company and Bahrain

Islamic Takaful Company were created. As with Islamic banks, *takaful* companies have expanded their operations to include both Muslim and Western countries. For instance, a *takaful* company, called First Takaful USA, was set up in the United States. At the end of 2007, there were more than 130 *takaful* companies operating worldwide with 59 operators based in the Gulf Cooperation Council countries of Bahrain (15), Kuwait (11), Qatar (5), Saudi Arabia (22) and the United Arab Emirates (4). Apart from these countries, *takaful* companies have also been established in Iran (17 *takaful* operators), Sudan (15 *takaful* operators), Egypt (6 *takaful* operators), Jordan (3 *takaful* operators), Bangladesh (6 *takaful* operators), Pakistan (4 *takaful* operators) and Sri Lanka (2 *takaful* operators). In the South East Asian region, *takaful* companies are already operating in Malaysia, Brunei, Singapore, Indonesia and Thailand.

In Malaysia, a special task force was set up in 1982 by the government to study the viability of establishing a *takaful* company. Following the recommendations of this task force, the *Takaful Act* was enacted in 1984. Subsequently, the first *takaful* operator, Syarikat Takaful Malaysia Berhad, was established in November 1984 and commenced operations in July 1985. The monopoly status enjoyed by Syarikat Takaful Malaysia for almost ten years came to a halt when in 1994 the government decided to introduce competition to the industry by issuing licence to MNI Takaful Sdn Bhd to offer insurance products founded on *Syariah*.

The rapid development of the *takaful* system in Malaysia motivated and inspired neighbouring Muslim countries to implement the system. Brunei Darussalam, for instance, allowed the establishment of Takaful IBB Berhad in 1993. This was followed by the establishment of Insurance Islam TAIB Sdn Bhd and Takaful Bank Pembangunan Islam Sdn Bhd. In Indonesia, Syarikat Takaful Indonesia which came into existence as a result of a joint effort between Syarikat Takaful Malaysia Berhad and its Indonesian counterpart, began operations in August 1994.

From only 5 *takaful* operators in 2002, the numbers have now reached 38 operators in the country. Thailand is another emerging *takaful* market with three companies providing Islamic insurance, namely Dhipaya Insurance, Finansa Life Assurance and Kamol Insurance. Meanwhile there are three companies providing *takaful* cover in Singapore, that is HSBC Insurance, NTUC Income and United Overseas Insurance.

On 28 October 1995, the ASEAN Takaful Group (ATG) was established as an informal body to foster and enhance greater mutual cooperation among ASEAN (Association of South East Asian Nations) *takaful* operators in terms of exchange of information and re*takaful* business. In 2003, ATG amended its constitution to accommodate memberships from outside the ASEAN region and changed its name to Asia Takaful Group. Recently, it was registered as a company limited by guarantee and renamed Global Takaful Group. In order to realize the re*takaful* business, ATG Retakaful Pact was established and began operations on 1 October 1996. On 17 May 1997, Asean Retakaful International Ltd (ARIL) was incorporated and registered under the *Offshore Insurance Act 1990*. ARIL began its operations as an offshore entity in Labuan in September 1997 with an authorized capital of US$50 million and paid-up capital of US$4 million, all of which were contributed by Syarikat Takaful Malaysia. The establishment of ARIL is aimed at enhancing cooperation in addition to subsidizing re*takaful* requirements among *takaful* operators in ASEAN. In addition, it is hoped that the re*takaful* facility would be used by other *takaful* operators outside of ASEAN.

At the international level, at the D-8 (Group of eight Developing Muslim countries) Summit held in Istanbul in June 1997, the D-8 member countries (Bangladesh, Indonesia, Iran, Malaysia, Egypt, Nigeria, Pakistan, Turkey), agreed for Malaysia to host the meeting of the task force associated with finance, banking and privatization. Bank Negara Malaysia was asked to look into the possible areas of cooperation which Malaysia could offer to the Organization of

Islamic Countries (OIC). In fulfilling this responsibility, two aspects related to *takaful* offered by Malaysia were information exchange and training. Malaysia yet again played a significant role in the expansion of the *takaful* system at the international level when in 1999 a Malaysian *takaful* company assisted in the establishment of a *takaful* company in Sri Lanka.

In line with the challenges of the new century, Bank Negara Malaysia has also outlined a number of strategies to expedite the development of the *takaful* business. Among the strategies are:

(i) To increase the number of *takaful* operators.

(ii) To improve the framework for the supervision of *takaful*.

It is expected that Bank Negara Malaysia would be issuing new *takaful* licences. The consequent increase in the number of *takaful* operators is to help speed up the achievement of the following goals:

(i) To expedite the development of *takaful* businesses in line with the more developed Islamic banking system.

(ii) To promote market competition in pricing, product innovation, customer service and operation efficiency.

(iii) To increase *Syariah*-based re*takaful* programmes among *takaful* operators.

(iv) To highlight ASEAN Retakaful International Ltd as the foremost re*takaful* operator in the region.

(v) To make Malaysia the centre of *takaful* expertise.

The supervision framework meanwhile aims to create a healthy *takaful* industry, and the main aspects emphasized are as follows:

(i) To review the *Takaful Act 1994* and related legislation in order to address existing weaknesses.

(ii) To progressively increase the statutory minimum paid-up capital of the *takaful* operators, in line with their capacities to develop and undertake higher risks. The increase in basic capital for the *takaful* operators would improve their capacities to compete more effectively in the domestic market and subsequently at the international level.

(iii) To introduce accounting standards for *takaful* business and drafting of a *Model Account Bill* for *takaful* operators.

(iv) To monitor and improve on the uniform code of ethics and market practice for *takaful* operators.

As at the end of 2008, there were eight *takaful* operators in Malaysia, namely Syarikat Takaful Malaysia Berhad (established on 29 November 1984), Etiqa Takaful Berhad or formerly known as Takaful Nasional Sdn Bhd (established on 20 September 1993), Takaful Ikhlas Sdn Bhd (established on 21 April 2003), CIMB Aviva Takaful Berhad or formerly known as Commerce Takaful Berhad (established on 7 April 2006), Hong Leong Tokio Marine Takaful (established on 19 June 2006), Prudential BSN Takaful Berhad (established on 8 August 2006), HSBC Amanah Takaful Sdn Bhd (established on 11 August 2006) and MAA Takaful Berhad (established on 1 July 2007). Total assets of these *takaful* operators were RM8,815.8 million as at the end of December 2007 with market penetration of 7.2%. Out of the total assets, RM7,442.7 million were from family *takaful* and RM1,373.1 from general *takaful*. Throughout 2007, a total of RM2,557.8 million of new contribution income was made. For the year ending 2007, the net benefits and claims payments for family *takaful* was RM534.2 million, while for general *takaful* it was RM218.5 million. Hence, *takaful* assets and net contributions recorded an average growth rate of 27% and 19% respectively from 2003 to 2007 (Bank Negara Malaysia, 2007b).

PHILOSOPHY, PRINCIPLE AND OPERATIONAL CONCEPT OF *TAKAFUL*

The word "takaful" originates from the Arabic word *kafalah* meaning "mutually guaranteeing" or "mutually caring for one another". The verb *kafalah* means to protect or look after someone's interest or to provide a guarantee to someone. When *"ta"* is added to the word, it conveys the idea of two parties who provide mutual guarantee to one another.

When the task force on the "Study for the Establishment of an Islamic Insurance Company in Malaysia" presented its report consisting of recommendations to establish Islamic insurance companies to the Prime Minister of Malaysia in 1984, the suggested philosophy was as follows:

> The philosophy of Islamic insurance places importance on sincerity of intention to assist one another. Thus, the financial contribution for this purpose is based on the spirit of *tabarru'* (donation). In line with this spirit and the principles of mutual responsibility, cooperation and protection and conforming to the qualities of selflessness and not being driven towards mere acquisition of profit, the Task Force has decided that the Islamic insurance philosophy is to be as follows:
>
> > *The internalization of the spirit of mutual responsibility, cooperation and protection in activities of the society towards the prosperity of the ummah and the unity of society.*

Although the modern *takaful* system was just introduced in 1979, the concepts of mutual assistance and cooperation had actually been advocated since the early years of Islam. Muslim jurists and *ulama* are of the view that the concept of insurance is implementable due to the following factors:

(i) The policyholders cooperate among themselves for the common good.

(ii) Every policyholder pays an amount required as contribution to help those in need of assistance.

(iii) Losses are divided and liabilities are spread according to a community pooling system.

(iv) The element of uncertainty is eliminated in respect of subscription and compensation.

(v) No one member of the system shall derive benefits at the expense of others.

THE *TAKAFUL* PRINCIPLE

According to the task force for the establishment of *takaful* companies in Malaysia, there are three core principles in *takaful*, namely:

(i) mutual responsibility,

(ii) mutual cooperation and

(iii) mutual protection.

The quality of being mutually responsible is advocated in Islam. Muslims are not only responsible towards the Creator, Allah (s.w.t.), but also towards other creations. In the context of *takaful*, the feeling of responsibility towards one another is the foundation of solidarity of Islamic community. The principles are illustrated through the following *hadiths* compiled in Sahih Bukhari and Sahih Muslim.

> *The attitude of believer and the feeling of brotherhood to one another is like that of a single body. When one member of the body is hurt, it will have an effect on the whole body. Situation of the believers, as regards*

their being merciful and kind and showing love among themselves, resembles one body, so that if any part of the body is not well, then the whole body is affected.

The relationship between one believer and another (in a community) is like that of a building where one part of the building strengthens the other parts. A believer to another believer is like a building where each part enforces the others.

Each of you has a responsibility and each of you is responsible towards those under your responsibility. Each one of you is a person of responsibility, and each one of you is responsible for those under your responsibility.

The second principle by which *takaful* operations is bound is mutual cooperation. This quality of cooperation among the *ummah* is also advocated in Islam. The principle of cooperation is established through the Quran and *Sunnah*. For example, verse 2 of *Surah al-Maidah* and verse 177 of *Surah al-Baqarah* touch on the matter of cooperation.

...Help ye one another in righteousness and piety, but do not help one another in sin and rancour...

It is not righteousness that you turn your faces towards East or West, but righteousness is whoever believes in Allah and the Last Day, and the Angels, and the Book, and the Messengers; and spending out of his wealth for His love towards kin, and orphans and the poor and the wayfarer and those who ask and the freeing of slaves and those in debt; to be steadfast in prayer and practice regular charity; to fulfil the contract which you have made; and to be firm and patient in pain or suffering and adversity and throughout all periods of panic. Such are the people of truth, the God-fearing.

The *Sunnah* has also established the principle of cooperation as illustrated in the compilation of *Hadith* narrated by Abu Dawood:

Whosoever fulfils the intention of a brother, Allah will fulfil his intentions.   (Yasir Qadhi, 2008)

The third principle is the principle of mutual protection from disasters. Disaster and prosperity are both sent by Allah (s.w.t.), and the advocation to help one another is found in the following *Hadith* narrated by Ibnu Majah:

Indeed a believer who can give security and protection to the life and property of mankind.   (Al-Khattab, 2007)

However, in line with current developments, the implementation of the *takaful* system today is based on several principles, that is, principles grouped under the *Syariah* principles and general principles in Islam. For example, while the original principle of *takaful* was based on the concept of collaboration or *ta'awun*, today it is managed based on the *al-takjiri* principle. Hence, just as the conventional insurance system is based on the commercial concept and operated by big companies, the *takaful* system is also operated by business companies whose goal is to mobilize funds for the purpose of making profit.

In *takaful* operation, this principle involving commerce is important because the fund contributed by *takaful* participants need to be mobilized for growth purposes. If the accumulated fund remains idle, there is a big possibility that the fund could soon become depleted and eventually lead to the dissolution of the cooperative agreement. Thus, for the sake of the economic development of the *ummah* and Islam, the accumulated fund would have to be multiplied through business or other economic activities.

The implementation of the *takaful* system involves two parties, namely the party who manages the operation and administration of the fund, and the party who participates in it. The party who manages the *takaful* company may choose which concept or model to apply. In general, *takaful* operations are confined to the principles of *takjiri*, *mudharabah*, *wakalah* and *tabarru*.

Takjiri

Takjiri is an Arabic word meaning commerce. Given that the operation of *takaful* is based on the concept of commerce, *takaful* operators must hence observe Islamic business practices. Business areas prohibited by *Syariah* cannot be ventured into. Further, the fund contributed by *takaful* participants cannot be invested in *riba*-based financial institutions. Islamic business ethics and morals must be strictly adhered to and no elements of exploitation must exist between *takaful* operators and the participants. The concept of justice and fairness must also be observed. Management of *takaful* companies must also avoid the tendency for mere profit acquisition. In brief, all the Islamic principles and philosophy must be conformed to at all times. Systematic management methods and cautious investment would reduce risk of loss, resulting in the business rendering profit to both parties, that is, the operator and participants.

Mudharabah

Under this concept, the *takaful* operator acts as the *mudarib* or entrepreneur who is appointed by the *takaful* participants. The *takaful* participants, on the other hand, act as *shaib-ul-maal* or investors or fund contributors. Participants appoint the *takaful* operator to mobilize their fund in businesses which are not prohibited by *Syariah* and the profit obtained is shared by both parties according to a mutually agreed ratio. In this *takaful* system, claims by a participant depend on the types of cover he participates in. Contributions need to be made monthly, or yearly, or in one lump sum. These contributions are known as *ra's-ul-mal'*.

Wakalah

Under the *wakalah* or representative concept, the *takaful* operator acts as the administrator of the fund and manages the fund in trust on behalf of the participants. The *takaful* operator earns a fee for services rendered using the *ujr* principle and has no right to receive profit from the fund. All acquired profit is given back to the *takaful* participants.

Tabarru

Tabarru is an Arabic word which means to donate, to contribute or to give to charity. The *tabarru* principle is the essence of the Islamic *takaful* system. In the *takaful* system, participants make two kinds of payment, namely payment for their personal savings and a donation or contribution which would aid other participants who are faced with difficulty or disasters. It is this donation that would be used by the *takaful* company in making payments to fellow participants who suffer from a defined loss.

Operational Concept

There are four concepts or models of cover operation offered by *takaful* operators, namely the non-profit concept, *mudharabah* concept, *wakalah* concept and combination concept (Abu Bakar, 2004).

The Non-Profit Concept

This concept involves a group of individuals in a community who mutually agree to provide sincere contribution to members of the community faced with disaster or misfortune. The contributions paid by the participants are in the form of donation or commonly known as *tabarru*. This earnest contribution may be done systematically within a set period of time, or only administered at the time that a member faces a misfortune. *Takaful* using this method can also be conducted in a modern and organized way. If this *takaful* is managed by an organization, then the *wakalah* concept would still be applied. This means that the operator would act as the representative who manages the fund and receives payment for services rendered. However, the participants will not receive any return on the pool of fund which they have contributed. An example of a company using this method is the Al Sheikhan Takaful Company in Sudan.

The *Mudharabah* Concept

The *mudharabah* concept refers to the cooperative risk-sharing between the operator and participants. The operator is appointed as the entrepreneur who mobilizes the fund in economic activities, and profits obtained from underwritings would be shared by both the operator and participants. As with other models, the participants are required to contribute to two types of accounts, the general account and the *tabarru* account. Under this concept, the operator does not impose any service charge or management charge for the services rendered or tasks handled when operating the *takaful*. Management or administration charge is imposed on the shareholders' fund. In Malaysia, this concept is used by Syarikat Takaful Malaysia.

The *Wakalah* Concept

Under the *wakalah* concept, the operator acts as the agent who manages the contributions and mobilizes the participants' fund. A service fee is imposed by the operator for the services rendered and the operator or agent does not share in any surplus of the fund. All risks related to the business undertaken would be borne by the participants. A service fee would also be imposed by the operator on the profit from the investment of the participants' fund. The *takaful* operator offers services such as general *takaful* and family *takaful*. In Malaysia, this concept is practised by Takaful Ikhlas.

The Combination Concept

The combination concept is based on the merging of the *wakalah* and *mudharabah* principles. The *takaful* operator acts as the representative who manages participants' fund and a service fee is imposed for the services rendered. Profit obtained from the investment undertaken using participants' fund would be shared between the operator and participants. Hence, the *wakalah* model is used for underwriting activities while the *mudharabah* model is used for investment activities.

TYPES OF *TAKAFUL* COVER

As explained earlier in the chapter, the history of conventional insurance cover began when several members of a community with mutual interest came together to protect their community from possible disasters, which if occurred would result in loss of property or lives. In the event that the latter occurs, it is important that the interests and welfare of the heirs or beneficiaries of the deceased (or insured) be taken care of. It is for this reason that conventional insurance companies provide two types of coverage, namely coverage for mishaps that could befall individuals, and coverage for loss incurred on property. Individuals are covered by way of life insurance, and property is covered through a general insurance scheme. *Takaful* offers similar types of coverage. However, for individual coverage it is referred to as family *takaful* rather than life insurance. Property coverage is termed as general *takaful*. Let us now examine these two types of coverage.

Family *Takaful*

Family *takaful* is a scheme involving collaboration between a number of individuals in a community with the goal of helping one another in the event of a disaster that may be inflicted upon any one of them. In general, there are three types of *takaful* family cover:

(i) Ordinary collaboration

(ii) Collaboration with savings

(iii) Collaboration based on specific groups

In ordinary collaboration, a group of people reciprocally guaranteeing each other agrees to contribute a premium to the *takaful* fund. The contribution is in the form of a donation to the fund of the group. In the event any member is inflicted with a mishap or disaster, the *takaful* operator will make payment from the pool fund to the contributor or his beneficiaries subject to the stipulated terms of agreement.

In the "collaboration with savings" type of cover, apart from mutually helping one another in the group, participants also deposit savings which is withdrawn later at the end of a certain time frame. This type of contribution hence involves two kinds of payment, namely payment for the purpose of personal savings, and payment for sincere contribution or donation to other members of the group in the event of a mishap or disaster.

In "collaboration based on specific groups", participants consist of those from community groups that wish to create a pact based either on the same ethnicity, organization or the same district. In cases like this, the terms would be formulated such that optimum benefit would be enjoyed by the particular group alone. Contributions may be made jointly, that is by the organization and the individual involved.

Syarikat Takaful Malaysia offers family *takaful* products as follows (www.takaful-malaysia.com.my):

• Family Takaful Plan

• Dana Saham Takaful Plan

• Ma'asyi Takaful Plan

- Workers' Fund Takaful Plan

- Mortgage Takaful Plan

- Personal Accident Takaful Scheme

- Takaful myMedicare

- Hawa Takaful Plan

- Rawat Takaful Plan

- Sihat Takaful Plan

- Takaful myMedicare1

- Siswa Takaful Plan

- Waqaf Takaful Plan

For group family *takaful*, Syarikat Takaful Malaysia offers the following products:

- Group Rawat Takaful Plan

- Group Personal Takaful Plan

- Group Family Takaful Plan (credit)

Takaful Ikhlas has the following family *takaful* plans (www.takaful-ikhlas.com.my):

- Ikhlas Savings Takaful

- Ikhlas Education Takaful

- Ikhlas Education Takaful Classic

- Ikhlas Lifestyle Takaful

- Ikhlas Capital Investment-Linked Takaful

- Ikhlas Premier Investment-Linked Takaful

- Ikhlas Wanita Takaful

General *Takaful*

General *takaful* is a short-term contract which provides protection against material loss or damage to assets belonging to participants, arising from a catastrophe or misfortune. This means that a group of individuals collaborate to contribute to a fund for the coverage of losses inflicted upon properties of members in the collaborative group. General *takaful* may be grouped according to types of insurance, namely fire *takaful* scheme, accident *takaful* scheme, marine *takaful* scheme and engineering *takaful* scheme. As an example, Syarikat Takaful Malaysia offers general *takaful* services as follows (www.takaful-malaysia.com.my):

- *Fire Takaful Scheme*: Coverage is provided for buildings, machineries, household content and stocks as a result of fire, lightning or domestic gas explosion. Coverage is also provided for losses resulting from disasters such as riots, strikes, earthquakes, floods, storms and other natural disasters which are beyond human control.

- *Motor Takaful Scheme*: Coverage is given to vehicle owners for losses or damages caused by theft or accident concerning their vehicles.

- *Employer Liability Takaful Scheme*: Coverage is provided to employers for losses which have to be borne resulting from compensations which they have to pay out to the public, employees or others due to negligence on their part.

- *Machinery Breakdown Takaful Scheme*: Coverage is provided to machinery owners, in particular factory operators, for losses due to loss of income resulting from damage of machinery, explosions, etc.

- *Marine Cargo Takaful Scheme*: Coverage is provided to owners of goods, whether buyer or seller, for damage or loss of goods while in the process of delivery whether by land, air or sea.

- *Houseowner's and Householder's Takaful Scheme*:   Coverage is provided to owners and tenants who undertake coverage for loss or damage of their household belongings and home (the structure).

IMPLEMENTATION METHOD OF *TAKAFUL* SYSTEM

There are several operational concepts which may be implemented by *takaful* operators, for both family *takaful* and general *takaful*. The concept selected by an operator would depend on the *Syariah* principle it intends to apply. This section will only discuss the implementation method of the *takaful* system found in Malaysia. The discussion will include methods practised by Syarikat Takaful Malaysia, Etiqa Takaful and Takaful Ikhlas. The implementation methods of general *takaful* will be presented, followed by those of family *takaful*.

Implementation of General *Takaful*

General *takaful* involves coverage for properties. This facility is offered by all *takaful* operators in Malaysia. However, slight variations exist in the method of implementation. For instance, Syarikat Takaful Malaysia uses the *mudharabah* and *tabarru* principles in its operation of general *takaful*. Depending on the scheme taken up, the participant would contribute an amount of money in accordance with the terms involved and sign a mutual agreement of *mudharabah* with the company. At the same time, the participant agrees to donate a portion of his money to other participants who are hit by disasters. The flow of general *takaful* operations is as shown in Figure 8–1.

FIGURE 8–1 Method of Operation of General *Takaful*, Syarikat Takaful Malaysia

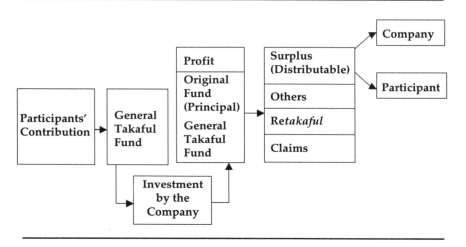

As shown in Figure 8–1, all of the participants' contributions would be put in the General Takaful Fund. The money in the fund would be invested by the company, and the profit attained would be placed back into the fund. At the end of the stipulated period, surplus or profit from the fund would be distributed back to the participants. Before distribution, deductions would first be made for matters such as payment of claims, re*takaful* and reserves. The company would not impose any fee for management, but would instead receive its share through profit-sharing of the surplus made from the investments.

The principles used by Etiqa Takaful in the operations of general *takaful* are *tabarru, wakalah* and *mudharabah*. The *tabarru* principle is used when participants agree to mutually help one another. The *wakalah* principle is applied between the participants and the operator, that is, Etiqa Takaful, whereby the company receives payment for the tasks performed. The *mudharabah* principle applied between the participants and the operator entails an agreement on the part of the participants to share the profit on any surplus from the fund which is past its term but is not yet collected by participants.

An example of the *mudharabah* text placed in the certificate is as follows:

> *If after the expiry of the takaful there is net surplus from the General Takaful Fund, it will be shared between the participant and the company in the ratio of 50:50 provided that the participant had not submitted any claims or received any benefits during the period that the takaful was in force.*

The operation flow of the general *takaful* scheme of Etiqa Takaful Berhad is illustrated in Figure 8–2.

FIGURE 8–2   Method of Operation of General *Takaful*, Etiqa Takaful

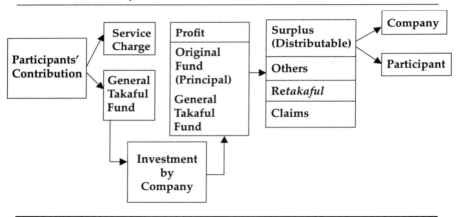

Figure 8–2 shows that participants' contributions are deposited into the General Takaful Fund; at the same time the company imposes a service charge on the participants. The money from the fund is invested by the company. As with Syarikat Takaful Malaysia, the profit is added to the fund and the accumulated fund is then used for payments such as payment on claims and re*takaful*. Sharing of profits is based on the agreed ratio and made on the underwriting surplus and investment income.

The operational flow of Takaful Ikhlas differs slightly from that of Etiqa Takaful as shown in Figure 8–3. (Etiqa Takaful imposes a service charge at the initial stage, that is when the participant starts to pay premium.)

FIGURE 8–3   Method of Operation of General *Takaful*, Takaful Ikhlas

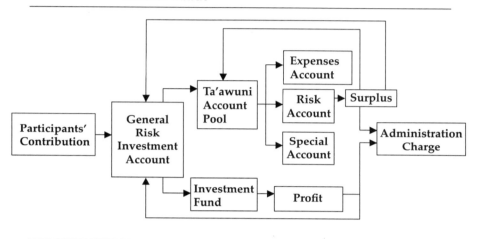

Figure 8–3 shows that participants contribute to the General Risk Investment Account (GRIA). The GRIA is divided into two types of funds, namely Ta'awuni Account Pool and Investment Fund. The Ta'awuni Account Pool (*tawaani* means collaboration or cooperation) is subdivided into three types of accounts or funds, Expenses Account, Risk Account and Special Account. Expenses Account contains front-end and back-end charges imposed on participants. Front-end charges are fees charged at the time of the initial purchase of the policy or contract renewal and are commissions paid to agents or representatives. Back-end charges are payments imposed on participants such as claims processing charges, policy renewal charges and fees for other transactions. Risk Account is based on the *tabarru* principle and is used for mutual coverage of participants. Payment into this account is based on a one-year coverage, re*takaful* charges and reserves. Any surplus in this account will be allocated to the GRIA. This special account is also founded on the *tabarru* concept and its purpose is to function as

a supporting fund to the Risk Account and to provide coverage for participants. If funds in this account are insufficient to compensate or indemnify participants, the company (shareholders) will issue a loan to subsidize the deficit.

Funds in the investment account would also be invested by the company. If there is any surplus or profit, the company will impose a service charge and the surplus will be deposited back into the GRIA.

Implementation of Family *Takaful*

There are three main objectives held by those who participate in the family *takaful* scheme. First, to provide financial coverage for their beneficiaries in the event of premature death. Secondly, to have a form of savings for future use or for old age. Thirdly, to be financially prepared in the case of an accident which results in long-term disability or in the case of a chronic disease. Thus, the *takaful* operator will normally offer a scheme which provides cover to achieve such objectives. Although family *takaful* is divided into two major categories, namely family *takaful* and group family *takaful*, the discussion here is limited to the implementation of family *takaful*.

Participants who undertake family *takaful* coverage with Syarikat Takaful Malaysia make a contribution, which is credited into the Participant's Account (PA) and Participant's Special Account (PSA). The operation flow of the family *takaful* offered by Syarikat Takaful Malaysia is shown in Figure 8–4.

FIGURE 8–4   Implementation of Family *Takaful*, Syarikat Takaful
Malaysia

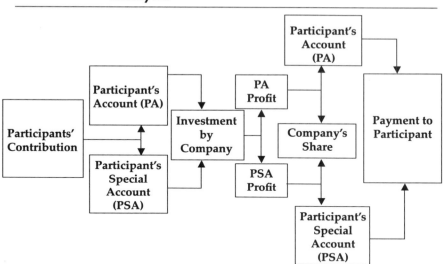

As can be seen from Figure 8–4, funds accumulated in the PA and PSA will be invested by the company based on the principle of *mudharabah*. The profit obtained will then be shared according to the ratio agreed at the beginning of the contract. The PA is treated in accordance with the principle of *mudharabah* whereas the PSA is treated on the basis of *tabarru*. The participants' share of profit will be credited into the related account. Profit from investment of the PA and PSA will be credited into their respective accounts. The surplus from both accounts will be repaid accordingly to the participants. In the event of the premature death of a participant, beneficiaries are entitled to claim the policy value from the PA fund as well as the accumulated amount from the PSA. On the other hand, if there is no claim made during the policy period, the participant can claim from the PA fund along with any surplus allocated to him in his PSA. If the participant withdraws before the maturity date of the policy, he can only claim the balance in his PA fund.

The operation concept of Etiqa Takaful does not differ much from that of Syarikat Takaful Malaysia. Participants' contribution is also credited into the PA and PSA. The PA has elements of savings while the PSA is maintained based on the *tabarru* concept. However, there is a slight difference with respect to allocation of profit. While Syarikat Takaful Malaysia apportions profit based on gross profit, that is returns from investments, Etiqa Takaful imposes a service charge on profit acquired from investments using PSA funds. Distribution of profit will only be done after the service charge has been made to the operator.

Takaful Ikhlas, on the other hand, models its *takaful* business on the *wakalah* concept whereby the participants appoint it to manage all aspects of the *takaful* business transactions. As with other *takaful* operators, participants' contribution for mutual coverage against disasters is conducted through the *tabarru* concept. Equally, the family *takaful* product provided by Takaful Ikhlas is classified into two groups, namely coverage with savings and savings alone. There is not much difference between these two types of coverage, except that participants' contribution for coverage with savings is deposited into the Personal Investment Account, while participants who choose the scheme for coverage alone would have their contributions credited into the Personal Risk Investment Account. The operation of the Takaful Ikhlas scheme with savings is shown in Figure 8–5.

FIGURE 8–5   Operation Method of Family *Takaful*, Takaful Ikhlas

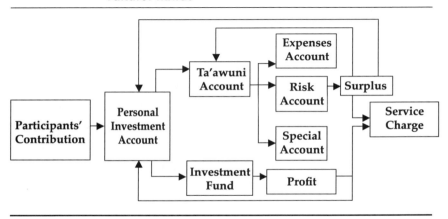

As can be seen from Figure 8–5, participants' contribution is placed in the Personal Investment Account. The funds collected are then apportioned into two accounts, the Ta'awuni Account and the Investment Account. The Ta'awuni Account is further split into three, Expenses Account, Risk Account and Special Account. Expenses Account consists of service charges collected by the company for the operation of the *takaful* business. Risk Account consists of donations rendered for mutual coverage and Special Account is set up to subsidize deficits in the Risk Account. The total amount of deposits made by participants in the investment fund will be invested by the company and the profit obtained will be subjected to management fees or charges. The surplus would be channelled into the participants' Personal Investment Account.

Similarly with the participants' Risk Account, any surplus in this account would also be invested. The profit obtained would be subjected to management fees or charges and the surplus will be allocated to the Personal Investment Account. Payment to participants would be made either at maturity or when a participant is faced with a mishap. Payment issued at maturity is done by using the participant's savings in his personal account and profit in the Risk Account. Payment before maturity as a result of a mishap is done by using the participant's savings in the Personal Investment Account and surplus in the Risk Account.

SUMMARY

The insurance system came into existence due to the natural desire of humans to help one another in their community. The history of insurance began around 3000 BC when Chinese traders practised risk-sharing techniques in transporting their goods when travelling across treacherous water. Apart from that, during 2500 BC the Egyptians also practised a system of mutual assistance. Help was rendered in the event that any member of their community faced difficulty as a result of death or financing the high cost of medical treatment. The *Code of Hammurabi* introduced in 1800 BC outlined the aspects of compensation to those who suffered losses as a result of disasters.

The 13th century saw the beginning of modern insurance when marine insurance was introduced in Italy, followed by life insurance in 1536. Fire insurance was introduced in 1591 in Germany, and the Great Fire of London of 1666 was said to have opened the eyes of the people in Britain to the need for such an insurance cover. Insurance coverage for accidents started in 1848 when a company sold insurance cover to train passengers. No precise information is available as to when insurance was first introduced in Malaysia. However, the development of the tin and rubber industry during the late 1980s and early 1900s was said to be the early period of the insurance system in the country. By the end of 2007, as many as 126 insurance licences had been issued to companies operating in the conventional insurance system in Malaysia.

However, features associated with conventional insurance are incompatible with Islamic principles. According to the *ulama*, conventional insurance does not conform to the rules and requirements of *Syariah* as it embodies three main elements, namely *gharar* (uncertainty), *maisir* (gambling) and *riba* (interest) which are prohibited in Islam. Since Muslims are also subject to possible disasters, a suitable system to cover them from unexpected disasters and catastrophes is essential. The demand for Islam to have its own insurance system became even more pressing when Islamic banks were established throughout the world simply because the banks needed to have some form of cover for the risk associated with unpaid financing. Consequently, most Islamic banks are shareholders of *takaful* companies. For instance, Syarikat Takaful was established by Bank Islam Malaysia Berhad.

Islamic insurance, or better known as *takaful*, had its beginnings in the early years of Islam under the *aqila* system. The modern *takaful* system began in 1979 when a *takaful* company started its operations in Sudan. In Malaysia, the *takaful* system was introduced in 1984 with the establishment of Syarikat Takaful Malaysia. Today, besides Syarikat Takaful Malaysia, there are seven other *takaful* companies operating in Malaysia. The concepts used by these companies in their operations are not uniform. Some use the *mudharabah* and *tabarru* concepts while others use the *wakalah* concept. As with the development of the Islamic banking system, the progress and rapidity of the development of the *takaful* system in Malaysia is to a large extent influenced by government involvement. Compared to other Islamic countries, the Malaysian government is highly committed to the advancement of the *takaful* industry. Through Bank Negara Malaysia, detailed and well-organized plans have been made towards making the domestic *takaful* industry a reputable and exemplary model for other countries. Although the *takaful* industry is still in its infancy compared to the conventional industry, it now offers products similar to those of the conventional insurance system.

REFERENCES AND FURTHER READING

Abu Bakar, Md Azmi Abu Bakar. *The Development of Takaful in the Global Perspectives*. Working paper presented at the seminar *Takaful* for Non-*Takaful* Practitioners, Islamic Banking and Finance Institute Malaysia, Kuala Lumpur, 19–20 July 2004.

Al-Khattab, Nasiruddin. *Sunan Ibn Majah*. Beirut (Lebanon): Darussalam, 2007.

Badan Petugas Penubuhan Syarikat Insurans Secara Islam Di Malaysia. *Laporan Penubuhan Syarikat Takaful*, Prime Minister's Office, Kuala Lumpur, 1984.

Bank Islam Research and Training Institute. *Takaful (Islamic Insurance), Concept & Operational System.* Kuala Lumpur: BIMB Research and Training Institute, 1996.

Bank Negara Malaysia. *Annual Report 1989.*

Bank Negara Malaysia. *Annual Report 2001.*

Bank Negara Malaysia. *Annual Insurance Statistics 2007(a).*

Bank Negara Malaysia. *Annual Takaful Statistics 2007(b).*

Barnhart, Robert K. *The Barnhart Dictionary of Etymology.* USA: The H.W. Wilson Company, 1988.

Muslehuddin, Muhammad. *Insurance and Islamic Law.* New Delhi (India): Markazi Maktaba Islami, 1982.

New Encyclopedia Britannica, The. Vol. 9. Chicago (Illinois, USA): Encyclopedia Britannica Inc., 1983.

Oxford English Dictionary, The. 2nd ed. Vol. VII. Oxford: Clarendon Press, 1991.

Vaughan, Emmet J. and Therese Vaughan. *Fundamentals of Risk and Insurance.* 8th ed. New York (USA): John Wiley & Sons, 1999.

www.maybank2u.com.my

www.takaful-ikhlas.com.my

www.takaful-malaysia.com.my

www.takafulnasional.com.my

Yasir Qadhi, Abu Ammar. *Sunan Abu Dawood.* Beirut (Lebanon): Darussalam, 2008.

Yusuf, Mohd Fadzli. *Takaful Sistem Insurans Islam.* Kuala Lumpur: Utusan Publications & Distributors Sdn Bhd, 1996.

CHAPTER 9

ORGANIZATIONS RELATED TO THE ISLAMIC BANKING SYSTEM

This chapter discusses the role and development of important organizations related to the Islamic banking system. The organizations and associations that will be described encompass those which provide general or specific services in particular aspects to Islamic financial institutions throughout the world and, in some cases, to selected countries.

INTRODUCTION

There were two major organizations which played a significant role in the early phase of modern Islamic banking system in most Muslim countries. They were the Islamic Development Bank (IDB) and the International Association of Islamic Banks (IAIB).

IDB and IAIB were established as a result of resolutions made at the Second Islamic Conference of Foreign Ministers of the Organization of Islamic Conference (OIC) in Karachi, Pakistan in December 1970. The Foreign Ministers expressed the view that a study should be conducted towards the establishment of an international Islamic trading and development bank as well as the establishment of a federation of Islamic banks. The task of conducting the study was assigned to a panel of experts from 18 Muslim countries who in their report recommended that a financial institution based on a participation scheme be established. The panel further proposed three types of institutions.

The first type of institution proposed was an international Islamic bank. Its functions were to include:

- Financing the intra-trade activities among Muslim countries.

- Providing funding to development and investment institutions.

- Being responsible for the transfer, settlement or resolution of conflict between the central institution and Islamic banks in Muslim countries. This task was to be the beginning towards an integrated Islamic economic system.

- Establishing central institutions in Muslim countries. These institutions would offer short-term and long-term financing for trading and developmental needs of associated countries.

- Supporting the efforts of the central institutions in Muslim countries in achieving their objectives within the framework allowed by Islam.

- Administering and utilizing *zakat* money.

- Managing the surplus funds of central institutions.

The second institution proposed was a specialized agency to be called Investment and Development Body of Islamic Countries. The functions of the agency were to include the following:

- To undertake investments of the financial capital on behalf of Muslim countries.

- To harmonize investment projects and development projects of Muslim countries.

- To identify suitable areas for investment and conduct studies in those areas.

- To offer advisory service and technical assistance on projects assigned as regional investment in Muslim countries.

The third institution proposed was the Association of Islamic Banks which was to act as a consultative body in the area of Islamic banking and economy. This association was supposed to be responsible for providing technical advice and assistance to countries wishing to set up their own Islamic banks. Apart from assigning experts to these Muslim countries, the association was expected to disseminate knowledge related to Islamic banking and finance. It was also to act as a liaison body in the exchange of knowledge and experience in the field of Islamic banking among the member countries.

The proposal forwarded by the panel of experts were not immediately accepted by the Foreign Ministers. Instead, at the third conference in March 1973 in Libya, the Foreign Ministers decided to review the proposal. In addition, the ministers decided to set up the Department of Economy and Finance at the OIC Secretariat for the purpose of conducting studies and providing advice in the area of economy, particularly on the establishment of Islamic banks. The task of reviewing and formulating the draft constitution, laws and regulations related to the establishment of Islamic banks was undertaken by a group of experts from oil producing countries which were approved by the Foreign Ministers of OIC in August 1974 in Jeddah, Saudi Arabia. The establishment of IDB became a reality in October 1975, with its headquarters in Jeddah.

Unlike IDB whose establishment was sponsored by Muslim countries, the establishment of the International Association of Islamic Banks (IAIB) was a private initiative. It was Saudi Prince Mohamed al-Faisal al-Saud who provided the impetus for the establishment of this association, in addition to being the main motivator in the setting up of Islamic banks in most Muslim countries. The establishment of this association became a reality on 20 August 1977 with Prince Mohamed al-Faisal as the chairman. In the same year, the association received recognition at the ninth Islamic Conference of Foreign Ministers of the OIC and was bestowed the OIC observer status. Until 1997, IAIB played a leading role in undertaking and facilitating research and development activities in Islamic banking. The following were among the objectives of the association:

- To promote the concept, philosophy and principles of Islamic banking.

- To reconcile conceptual and operational problems as well as standardize both the operational and application aspects of *Syariah*.

- To create areas of cooperation among members.

- To provide assistance in human capital development.

- To encourage the establishment of Islamic banks and to provide technical assistance and expertise.

- To represent, mediate and act as arbiter for and between Islamic banks.

- To coordinate exchange of data among Islamic banks and maintain a databank of all Islamic financial institutions.

- To develop Islamic inter-bank markets and to promote the flow of funds between Islamic banks.

To achieve the above objectives, the organizational structure of IAIB was categorized into four main bodies, namely General Secretariat, Syariah Board, General Assembly and Board of Directors. The General Assembly consisted of one representative from each member and this body appointed members of the Board of

Directors. The General Secretariat administered the daily functions of IAIB, and was headed by the Secretary General. Meanwhile, the functions of members were monitored by the Syariah Board. Members of this Board comprised heads of Syariah Boards of Islamic banks which were members of the association, as well as Muslim jurists who were members by invitation. This Board was also responsible for supervising and regulating the operations of members to ensure that they did not deviate from Syariah. The Board also formulated *fatwa* and directives to be adhered to by members. Although the objectives of the association were noble and it brought benefits to the Islamic banking industry as well as the Muslim *ummah* as a whole, this initiative was dissolved in 1997.

Its successor, the General Council of Islamic Banks and Financial Institutions was established in Bahrain. This was followed by the formation of other associations to promote the establishment of a sound Islamic banking system. These associations consist of the Islamic Financial Services Board centred in Kuala Lumpur and the International Islamic Financial Market centred in Bahrain. In Malaysia, an organization known as the Association of Islamic Banking Institution Malaysia has been set up to promote and represent the common interest of its members who are financial institutions offering Islamic financial products and services. In the education sector, the Institute of Islamic Banking and Finance Malaysia was created to promote education and training in Islamic banking.

ISLAMIC DEVELOPMENT BANK

The Islamic Development Bank (IDB) was officially inaugurated on 15 Syawal 1395 *Hijrah* corresponding to 20 October 1975, with its headquarters in Jeddah, Saudi Arabia. The principal establishment of IDB may be likened to that of the World Bank. However, the establishment of IDB is to provide assistance to Muslim countries (almost all Muslim countries are IDB shareholders) and its assistance is based on the *Syariah* principles. Among the objectives for the establishment of IDB is to foster economic development and social progress of group members as well as reinforce the cooperative relationship among OIC member countries. This bank is also responsible for the mobilization of financial resources in existing member countries or between member countries. In addition, it has been envisaged that IDB will have the capacity to raise the level of savings and investment as well as increase the inflow of funds for developmental purpose in member countries. These objectives were formulated with the aspiration that the economic development and social advancement of member countries could be fostered in conformity with *Syariah* principles. Some of the functions of IDB are:

- To participate in equity capital for productive projects and enterprises in member countries.

- To undertake investments either in the form of equity participation or other methods of financing for infrastructure development in member countries.

- To provide financing to private parties or the public for the implementation of projects, enterprises or other programmes in member countries.

- To establish and operate special funds for specific purposes.

- To set up and manage trust funds.

- To accept deposits and mobilize funds through *Syariah* compatible modes.

- To assist in the promotion of trade among members particularly in capital goods.

- To appropriately invest surplus funds which are not needed in its operations.

- To provide technical assistance to member countries.

- To provide training facilities to personnel involved in development activities in member countries.

- To conduct research and development in Islamic economics, banking and finance.

- To enhance economic cooperation and coordination among member countries in collaboration with development partners.

- To carry out other activities that can assist in meeting its objectives.

- To operate in accordance with the principles of *Syariah*.

In its 2007–2008 annual report, these functions were summarized as follows (*Islamic Development Bank, Annual Report, 2007–2008*, Appendix VI):

> *The main function of IDB is to provide various forms of development assistance for poverty alleviation through human development, forgoing economic cooperation by promoting trade and investment among member countries, and enhancing the role of Islamic finance in the social and economic development of member countries. It establishes special funds for specific purposes including a fund for assistance to Muslim communities in non-member countries, in addition to setting up trust funds.*

> *In addition, IDB mobilizes financial resources using Shari'ah-compliant modes and provides technical assistance to member countries, including provision of training facilities for personnel engaged in development activities in member countries.*

In the early part of its establishment, the bank had only 22 members, but its membership had increased to 47 by the end of 1994. As at end of 2008, the number of members had increased to 56. One of the main prerequisites for membership is that the prospective member country must be a member of the OIC and must be willing to accept the terms stipulated by the IDB Board of Governors. In the early part of its establishment, the authorized capital for the bank was Islamic dinar (ID) six thousand million. Islamic dinar is the accounting unit used by IDB, where one unit of ID is equivalent to one unit of Special Drawing Rights of the International Monetary Fund. In 2007, total authorized capital was ID30 billion, and the subscribed capital was ID15 billion. Members' funds increased to ID5.3 billion and paid-up capital increased by 9.1% to ID3.07 million. Other components of members' funds were ID22.7 million in capital reserve, ID1,523.9 million in general reserve and ID538.1 million in fair value reserve as at end of 2007.

The bank's headquarters is located in Jeddah, Saudi Arabia while two of its regional offices, one in Rabat, Morocco, and the other in Kuala Lumpur, were opened in 1994 and 1995, respectively. In 1997, IDB opened a representative office in Almaty, Kazakhstan which serves as a link between IDB member countries and the Central Asian Republics. The fourth regional office was established in Dakar, Senegal in 2007. In addition, the bank also has field representatives in 14 member countries, namely Indonesia, Iran, Uzbekistan, Libya, Pakistan, Senegal, Sudan, Sierra Leone, Guinea, Guinea Bissau, Mauritania, Nigeria, Bangladesh and Azerbaijan. The official language of the bank is Arabic, though English and French are also used as supplementary working languages. Apart from the capital funds contributed by its members, IDB also receives financial resources in other forms to finance its operations. These financial resources are normally derived from financing activities, shareholding in companies and the placement of liquid cash in commodity trading. Further, the recording and presentation of the funds' financial statement are not consolidated into IDB's financial statement. There are also schemes in which IDB acts as *mudarib* or entrepreneur, undertaking trade ventures using funds from other parties and imposing operational fees on these ventures.

In order to supplement its subscribed capital, IDB has developed several *Syariah*-compatible schemes and financial instruments.

These include the Investment Deposit Scheme, IDB Unit Investment Fund, Islamic Banks' Portfolio for Investment and Development, Export Financing Scheme, BADEA Export Financing Scheme and Special Assistance Grants. (BADEA is the Arab Bank for Economic Development in Africa.)

The Investment Deposit Scheme which was first introduced in 1980 is a short-term investment facility provided to investors participating in foreign trade financing operations. The mode of financing used is based on the *murabahah* principle. Deposits accepted are only those in the form of the Islamic dinar, American dollar and Saudi riyal currencies. At the end of 2007, the fund raised from the scheme during the year was ID35.3 million. It was used to finance operations under the IDB general *murabahah* financing.

The Special Assistance Grants scheme was introduced in early 1998 in pursuant to the Board of Governors' *Resolution BG/3–1417*. Through this resolution, funds amounting to ID1 billion were created which included the transfer of assets of the former Special Assistance Account established by IDB. With the establishment of the Waqf Fund, all assets and liabilities of the Special Assistance Account created in 1979 were consolidated into this new fund including the three activities which were formerly under the Special Assistance Account, namely Special Assistance, Special Account for Least Developed Member Countries and Special Reserve. The Special Reserve Account was replaced by the Waqf Fund. At the end of the 2007 financial year, the net funds accumulated totalled ID939.9 million, made up of US$79.8 million in the Special Assistance Account, US$230.7 million in the Special Account for Least Developed Member Countries and US$1,195.7 million in the Waqf Fund.

In addition to the funds above, IDB set up other funds called IDB Infrastructure Fund and Awqaf Properties Investment Fund (APIF). Funds accumulated either through share capital contributed by members or through special schemes, are utilized by IDB to implement activities in accordance with its establishment goals.

The activities conducted by the bank may be categorized into three main groups, namely:

(i) Project financing, technical assistance and *waqf* fund operations (Special Assistance)

(ii) Trade financing operations

(iii) Specialized fund and affiliated institutions

Project Financing, Technical Assistance and Waqf Fund Operations (Special Assistance)

Originally the method of financing used by IDB was simply based on loans issued by way of holding equities in the projects concerned. Nevertheless, the bank's method of financing has expanded over the years to include leasing which was introduced in 1977, profit sharing in 1978, instalment sales in 1985 and *istisna* in March 1996.

Apart from direct financing, IDB also channels its financing through the National Development Financing Institutions (NDFI) which provides funding to small and medium-sized enterprises as well as to the private and public sectors. As with direct financing, the facilities channelled through NDFI also take the form of leasing, instalment sales or *istisna* or a combination of these methods. This type of financing is referred to as line of financing.

Technical assistance financing provided by IDB is closely related to project financing and aims to assist member countries identify potential projects. The assistance includes provision for the preparation of feasibility studies, detailed design and engineering works, provision for consultancy services and preparation of tender documents. Further, assistance is rendered in the provision of research and training equipment. IDB also helps to conduct sectoral studies and monitor projects being implemented. Priority for such technical assistance is given to the least developed member countries.

The *waqf* concept refers to provision of aid to those in need. The Waqf Fund was established in 1979 to provide aid to Muslim communities in non-member countries with emphasis on education and health. The fund also aims at alleviating the suffering of Muslims in member and non-member countries who have been badly affected by natural disasters such as droughts, floods and earthquakes. The fund is also used to finance expenses of activities which do not bring any profit to the bank. Currently, the income generated from the Waqf Fund is used for social development programmes such as financing the following activities:

- Special assistance programmes, particularly for Muslim communities in non-IDB member countries.

- Islamic Research and Training Institute (IRTI).

- Scholarship programmes.

- Technical assistance programmes.

- International Centre for Biosaline Agirculture.

The total project financing and technical assistance provided by IDB in the financial year 2007 and for the period from 1976 to 2007 are shown in Table 9–1.

Based on Table 9–1, total financing provided by IDB throughout the financial year ending 2007 was about ID1,737.8 million (US$2,663.6 million), which included 183 approved activities of which 110 represented project financing and 73 were technical assistance. The overall total project financing and technical assistance (not including amortized financing) for the period 1976–2007 was ID14.8 billion (US$20.6 billion), whereby 98.8% or ID14.7 billion (US$20.4 billion) was for project financing with technical assistance accounting for the remaining ID174 million (US$232.2 million). Since 1976 till end of 2007, a total of 2,338 projects received financial assistance from IDB of which 1,732 represented projects under project financing, while 663 were technical assistance projects.

TABLE 9–1 IDB Project Financing and Technical Assistance (in ID million)

Type of financing	2007			1976–2007		
	No.	Amount	%	No.	Amount	%
Project financing:						
Loan	39	239.2	13.8	732	3,361.2	22.6
Equity	24	207.7	11.9	213	1,299.1	8.8
Leasing	22	623.9	35.9	330	4,473.6	30.1
Instalment sale	8	222.5	12.8	231	2,154.8	14.5
Profit-sharing/ Musharaka	2	48.1	2.8	11	148.2	1.0
Istisna	12	288.1	16.6	126	2,339.5	15.8
Combined lines of financing	3	97.5	5.6	32	351.8	2.4
Others	0	0	0	57	542.5	3.7
Subtotal	110	1,727	99.4	1,732	14,670.8	98.9
Technical assistance	73	10.9	0.6	663	174.0	1.1
Grand total	183	1,737.9	100	2,395	14,844.8	100

Source: Islamic Development Bank, *Annual Report*, 2007–2008.

Notes:

(i) Total financing for the 1976–2007 period is not inclusive of financing already amortized or cancelled.

(ii) Financing issued in 2007 includes financing through the Special Account for Least Developed Member Countries.

(iii) "Others" refers to investment in *sukuk* and in financial institutions.

Projects participated in by IDB encompass a range of sectors, including social (education and health), agriculture, public utilities, transport and communications, industry, mining and Islamic financial services. The breakdown of projects for the 2007 financial year is as follows: 6 projects in the agriculture and agro-industry, 7 projects in the industry and mining sector, 21 transport and communications projects, 24 projects related to public utilities, 51 social services projects and 38 projects in the financial services sector.

Table 9–2 shows the distribution of IDB funding according to sectors for the year ending March 2007 as well as the period since the establishment of IDB until 2007. Loans are normally issued for projects which have socio-economic impact. Such projects encompass infrastructure development, such as road transport, ports, airports, irrigation, land development, schools, hospitals, low-cost housing, rural development and others. The repayment period for loans under the IDB Ordinary Capital resources is from 15 to 25 years with a grace period of 3 to 7 years. Total project financing from this fund amounted to ID1,372 million (US$2,087 million) in 2007. The repayment period for loans from the Special Account for Least Developed Member Countries is 25 to 30 years including a grace period of 10 years. IDB imposes a service fee based on actual expenses provided not exceeding 2.5% per year for ordinary loans and 0.75% for loans under the Special Account for Least developed Member Countries. The maximum loan amount from the Ordinary Capital resources is US$10 million, while from the Special Account for Least Developed Member Countries is between US$0.5 million and US$3 million. However, in special cases the loan extended to least developed member countries may be increased to US$5 million.

TABLE 9–2 Distribution According to Sectors: IDB Project
Financing and Technical Assistance (in ID million)

Sector	2007			1976–2007		
	No.	Amount	%	No.	Amount	%
Agriculture and agro-industry	6	30.2	2.2	329	1,176.6	10.3
Industry and mining	7	89.6	6.5	152	1,231.0	10.7
Transport and communications	21	407.1	29.7	332	2,565.6	22.4
Public utilities	24	463.2	33.8	334	3,432.8	29.9
Social services	51	226.9	16.5	567	2,385.8	20.8
Financial services	38	155.3	11.3	300	678.6	5.9
Grand total	147	1,372.3	100	2,014	11,470.4	100

Source: Islamic Development Bank, *Annual Report*, 2007–2008.

Under equity financing, IDB also participates in the share capital of new proposed or existing enterprises. This equity participation is of two forms, that is, either direct equity holding (IDB undertakes direct investment in the business organization concerned) or through financing done via NDFI. Whichever method is chosen, the investment made by IDB must not exceed one third of the project's total paid-up capital.

Leasing facility usually involves the purchase of capital equipment or other fixed assets with IDB retaining the ownership right of the leased assets thoughout the leasing period. The leasing period may extend up to 20 years with a gestation period of up to 5 years. This facility is usually provided to member countries categorized as medium income and high income countries. Today, the profit margin is set at 5.1% with the option for a floating rate.

The maximum amount of financing provided through leasing is ID80 million per project.

Under the instalment sale concept, IDB will purchase equipment and resell them to clients at a higher price. The repayment period extends up to 20 years. The main difference between this method and leasing is that ownership of asset is transferred to the purchaser on delivery. Meanwhile, in the case of leasing, ownership of asset is transferred at the end of the leasing period. Here, IDB imposes mark-up of 5.1%, and the maximum value of a sale is ID80 million.

The profit-sharing concept involves the pooling of funds between two or more parties for the financing of a project, with each party sharing the profit or loss according to a mutually agreed contract. The *istisna* concept which was first introduced in 1998 refers to the method whereby the seller agrees to make available or to sell to the purchaser a commodity of a specified type on an agreed date. This mode of financing is used to promote and enhance intra-trade among member countries, finance infrastructural projects implemented by private sectors such as electric generators and transformers and the like. *Istisna* is normally used when the instalment sale mode of financing is not suitable. Similar to the instalment sale, the repayment period extends up to 20 years with a grace period of 5 years. The mark-up used is also similar to that in instalment sale mode of financing, that is, 5.1%, and the maximum amount of financing is ID80 million.

Financing through NDFI is provided by IDB to encourage the development of small- and medium-sized industries of the private sector. The modes of financing adopted include instalment sale, *istisna* and leasing. This mode of financing was originally extended directly to the NDFIs, but from 1999 it was extended to the governments of the member countries who would then channel it to the respective NDFIs. Loans extended to governments of the member countries are limited to a ceiling of ID7 million per project and are given as interest-free loans. Nonetheless, beneficiary of the loans must pay IDB an administrative fee of not more than 2.5%

per annum. Repayment period is between 15 to 20 years inclusive of a grace period of 3 to 7 years. However, softer conditions are also provided for particular types of projects in least developed member countries whereby repayment period may be extended up to 30 years including a grace period of 10 years. A service fee for administration expenses is set at a maximum of 0.75% per annum.

Technical assistance is provided by IDB for conducting feasibility studies; the preparation of technical designs and tender documents; preparation of sectoral plans, construction programme and institutional support for capacity building as well as consultancy services for the supervision of projects during their implementation stage. Financing is in the form of a grant or an interest-free loan. The maximum value of the grant is ID300,000 while the repayment period for the interest-free loan must not exceed 16 years including a grace period of 4 years with a service fee not more than 1.5% per annum. The grant issued is taken from the IDB Waqf Fund.

For financing of foreign trade, the *murabahah* concept is applied where IDB purchases the requested commodity and then resells it to the beneficiary. The maximum period for import financing is 30 months while it is 120 months for export financing. For both import and export financing, the mark-up calculation is based on the 12-month LIBOR (London Inter-bank Offered Rate) quoted on the LIBOR IO (Interest Only) page of Reuters (a global information company) on the date of each disbursement, plus a gross spread. This gross spread is subject to several factors such as risk, tenure, commodity being financed and market conditions. A 30% rebate of the gross spread is given for payments made on or before the due dates.

As discussed earlier in this chapter, the Waqf Fund is used for a variety of activities. Among the activities are special assistance especially for Muslim communities in IDB non-member countries, Islamic Research and Training Institutes, scholarship programmes, technical cooperation programmes, special fund for least developed countries, financing of technical assistance, free-of-charge financing and the Adahi Project. The discussion that follows will only cover the use of the Waqf Fund for the purpose of Special Assistance Programme, Scholarship Programme, Technical Cooperation Programme, OIC-Vaccine and Illiteracy Eradication Programme.

Special Assistance Programme was first introduced in 1979. The primary goal is to promote socio-economic development and the uplift of Muslim *ummah* in non-member countries. Development is implemented specifically in the areas of education and health. It also aims to alleviate the sufferings of communities inflicted by disasters in both member and non-member countries. When the fund was first introduced, IDB Board of Governors made the resolution that this special assistance account may only be used in the following areas:

(i) Training and research for member countries towards the reorientation of their economic, finance and banking activities in line with *Syariah* law;

(ii) Rehabilitation aid for victims of natural disasters and/or conflicts;

(iii) Aid to member countries to expand and enhance the Islamic *syiar*.

Ever since this programme was implemented, assistance provided to Muslims in non-member countries had concentrated on developing the socio-economic development of Muslim communities, particularly in the education, social and health areas including emergency and relief operations. In 2007, IDB financed 62 special assistance projects worth US$25.7 million, of which US$11.1 million was approved for 23 projects in member countries and US$14.6 million for 39 projects in non-member countries. The activities of the Special Assistance Programme received funding from the IDB Waqf Fund. Since its launch, a total of 1,185 projects under the Special Assistance Programme worth US$640.8 million had been financed by IDB. Out of this amount, US$417.6

million was allocated for 465 operations in member countries and US$232.2 million was approved for 729 projects in non-member countries.

The IDB scholarship programme was introduced in 1983, and up until 2007 IDB had introduced three types of scholarships as follows:

- Scholarships for Muslim communities in non-member countries.

- IDB merit scholarships for high technology.

- Masters of Science scholarships in science and technology for the least developed member countries of IDB.

The Scholarship Programme for the Muslim communities in non-member countries was launched in 1404 H (1983–1984). Its aim is to provide educational opportunities to the academically meritorious and financially needy Muslims from non-IDB member countries to pursue undergraduate study in fields such as medicine, dentistry, agriculture, management, business and others. The scholarships are awarded as grants or interest-free loans (*qard hassan*) which students are required to repay after graduation and gainful employment to the Waqf Fund set up by IDB. The repaid fund would then be used to provide scholarships to other deserving students from the same communities. The total amount of scholarship awarded since its inception and up until 2007 was US$67 million. A total of 7,877 scholarships had been given out up to 2007 of which 5,237 recipients had completed their studies and 2,640 are at various stages of their studies. The bank has so far extended scholarships to 48 countries including 10 member countries.

The Merit Scholarship Programme for High Technology was introduced in 1411 H (1991–1992) and implemented the year after. This programme aims to develop technically qualified human resources in IDB member countries and also to advance research in science and technology. Some significant changes took place in 2003. The number of yearly scholarships awarded was increased from 20 to 35, and the recipients of the programme were broadened to include scholars from institutions in emerging high technology countries in Asia and other member countries. Furthermore, focus was shifted purely to doctorate degrees. These scholarships are usually awarded to doctoral candidates for a period of three years and up to a year for post-doctoral candidates. From its establishment until 2007, a total of US$15 million had been spent, involving 392 recipients from 254 institutions from 46 member countries.

The Masters of Science Scholarship Programme in Science and Technology was launched in 1998 with the objective of assisting the least developed member countries of IDB in the development of human capital in the areas of science and technology. This programme has offered scholarships to 19 of the least developed member countries including Afghanistan, Benin, Burkina Faso, Chad, Comoros, Djibouti, Gambia, Guinea, Guinea-Bissau, Maldives, Mali, Mauritania, Mozambique, Niger, Sierra Leone, Somalia, Togo, Uganda and Yemen. A total of 205 scholarships worth US$1 million have been awarded since its launch. Students have been placed in various institutions in member countries such as Egypt, Mali, Malaysia, Morocco, Pakistan, Senegal, Turkey and Uganda.

The Technical Cooperation Programme which was initiated in 1404 H (1983–1984) was established with the following objectives:

- To mobilize the technical capabilities of member countries by promoting and enhancing collaboration among them.

- To promote cooperation and the exchange of relevant experience, information and technologies in line with the development need of the member countries.

- To reduce delay in project implementation by lessening managerial, technical and institutional constraints.

During 2007, 108 operations involving a total amount of US$2.8 million were approved under this programme. The programme entails three types of activities, namely recruitment of experts, on-the-job training and seminars and workshops.

To date, 1,510 operations worth US$33.7 million have been approved whereby US$4.7 million was for recruitment of experts, US$11.8 million was for on-the-job training activities and US$17.2 million was for seminars and workshops. In December 1999, the Board of Executive Directors approved two technical grants worth US$3.5 million and US$5.6 million respectively for two special programmes, namely Eradication of Illiteracy in The Islamic World, and Self-sufficiency in Human Vaccine Production. The recipient countries of the illiteracy eradication programme aid were Bangladesh, Chad, Djibouti, Gambia, Jordan, Mauritania, Morocco, Sierra Leone, Sudan and Yemen. Meanwhile, for the vaccine grant, aids were issued to Algeria, Egypt, Iran and Tunisia.

Trade Financing Operations

Trade finance activity was one of the initial activities conducted by IDB. The activity was conducted either through direct funding from IDB's own funds or through special funds established by IDB. Several trade financing schemes were implemented by IDB with the names of the schemes based on the name of the fund financing the scheme. In line with the goal to enhance trade financing activities, IDB introduced the Two-Step Murabahah Financing. Under this mode of financing, IDB acted in two ways. First, IDB provided financing to financial institutions to finance its own trade activity. Secondly, IDB accepted the funds provided by the financial institutions to finance its own trade operations. At the end of the 2007 financial year, the trade financing schemes that had been implemented by IDB were as follows:

- Import Trade Financing Operations
- Export Financing Scheme
- Islamic Banks' Portfolio for Investment and Development
- IDB Unit Investment Fund

The Import Trade Financing Operations (ITFO) scheme was introduced in 1977. The funds for ITFO mainly come from IDB's own resources and from the Two-Step Murabahah Financing scheme. The ITFO scheme has the following goals:

- To finance the import financing needs of member countries.

- To promote and encourage intra-trade among member countries.

- To supplement the activities of IDB by providing *Syariah*-compliant trade financing.

The ITFO scheme normally provides short-term financing. The method involves the purchasing of commodities and reselling them against deferred payment (*bay-al-murabaha*) at cost price and reasonable rate of profit to member countries. In 2006, a total of 67 operations worth US$2.6 billion were approved. Funds under this scheme are generally extended for the import of commodities such as crude oil and petroleum products, raw and chemical materials, fertilizers, iron and steel items, spare parts, pulp paper and natural rubber. From the date of its inception until 2006, ITFO had approved 1,420 operations worth US$23.5 billion.

The Export Financing Scheme is a special fund established by IDB under *Article 22* of its *Articles of Agreement*. This fund was originally established under the name "Long-term Trade Financing Scheme" in 1985 with the objective of promoting the exports of traditional and non-traditional commodities of member countries. The scheme has its own membership, capital, resources and budget. Its accounts are maintained separately. The scheme provides financing to the non-conventional commodity exports of member countries with a repayment period of between six months and five years. For consumer commodities, the maximum repayment period is 24 months. For the export of raw materials and capital commodities, the maximum repayment period is three years and five years, respectively. During 2006, a total of 17 operations worth US$378.1 million were approved. Up until 2006, a total of 217 projects worth US$1.7 billion had been approved.

The BADEA Export Financing Scheme was the outcome of a memorandum of understanding signed on 23 February 1998 between IDB and the Arab Bank for Economic Development in Africa (BADEA) based in Khartoum, Sudan. BADEA has approved an allocation of US$50 million to finance foreign trade between the Arab and African countries. This funds are used specifically to finance exports of Arab countries that are members of the Arab League to African countries that are members of the Organization of African Unity but do not belong to the Arab League. Between 1998 and 2006, the BADEA Export Financing Scheme extended financing to 12 operations worth US$163.6 million. Out of this amount, US$39.1 million was approved in 2003. Most of the funds were used by African countries to import capital commodities from Arab countries.

The Islamic Banks' Portfolio for Investment and Development also allocates a major portion of its funds to finance trading activities. In 2006, a total of 8 projects worth US$202.8 million involving Bangladesh, Lebanon, Egypt, Pakistan, Saudi Arabia, Tunisia and Turkey were financed through this scheme. Up until 2006, 186 trade financing projects worth US$3,039.1 million had been approved.

IDB Unit Investment Fund also uses a portion of its resources to finance trading activities either as direct financing or through syndication. During 2007, one project valued at US$15 million was approved, making it a total of 111 trade financing projects worth US$921.3 million approved altogether.

The year 2006 was the last year IDB undertook trade financing activities. In 2007, all trade related activities of IDB such as ITFO, BADEA Scheme and Islamic Banks' Portfolio for Investment and Development were taken over by the International Islamic Trade Finance Corporation (ITFC). The establishment of ITFC was approved at the 30th meeting of the IDB Board of Governors in June 2005 and commenced operations in 2007. Among the main objectives of ITFC are to promote and finance intra-trade among member countries and upgrade the export capabilities of member countries.

Since the year 2000, other funds of the bank have been used to finance trade operations. The funds involved include Islamic Corporation for the Development of the Private Sector, Awqaf Properties Investment Fund and the Treasury Department trade financing. Up to the end of 2007, sums of US$40.1 million, US$51.3 million and US$548.7 million were disbursed through Awqaf Properties Investment Fund, Islamic Corporation for the Development of the Private Sector and the Treasury Department, respectively. The number of projects under trade finance which was approved by IDB in 2007 as well as the corresponding amount approved since the implementation of these schemes, are shown in Table 9–3.

TABLE 9–3 IDB Trade Finance Total

Type of scheme	2007			Overall		
	No.	Amount (US$ million)	%	No.	Amount (US$ million)	%
Import Trade Financing	67	2,602.5	99.4	1,420	23,512.3	80.7
Export Financing	–	–	–	217	1,669.9	5.7
Islamic Banks' Portfolio	–	–	–	186	3,039.1	10.4
Unit Investment Fund	1	15	0.6	111	921.3	3.2
Total	68	2,617.5	100	1,934	29,142.6	

Source: Islamic Development Bank, *Annual Report*, 2007–2008.

Activities of Specialized Funds and Affiliated Institutions

In line with its current development and challenges, IDB has sought new methods or has coordinated its activities in line with the changes that are taking place in the organization. Today, IDB is a parent organization that has many corporate entities whose legislation and financial operations are independent and separate from IDB. The bank has also established many funds with the goal of making itself the catalyst or mobilizer of resources that would aid the bank in implementing additional tasks such as providing training and conducting research related to Islamic finance and banking. Among the entities and funds managed by IDB are:

- IDB Unit Investment Fund

- IDB Infrastructure Fund

- Islamic Solidarity Fund for Development

- Islamic Corporation for Insurance of Investments and Export Credits

- Islamic Corporation for the Development of the Private Sector

- Islamic Research and Training Institute

- IDB Sacrificial Meat Utilization Project of the Kingdom of Saudi Arabia – Adahi Project

- Awqaf Properties Investment Fund

- World Waqf Foundation

- International Centre for Biosaline Agriculture, Dubai

- The OIC Networks Sdn Bhd, Malaysia

The IDB Unit Investment Fund is a trust fund established in December 1989 under *Article 23* of the *Articles of Agreement* of IDB. The aim of the fund is to participate in the economic development of member countries through the pooling of savings of institutional and individual investors. The fund is listed on the Bahrain Stock Exchange. At the end of 2007, the initial issue which was US$100 million was raised to US$325 million and held by 20 investors from 11 countries. These accumulated funds are mobilized by way of direct financing, mutual financing and syndicated financing. The financing principles used include the *murabahah*, *istisna*, instalment sale, and resale and leasing principles. Since its inception, the fund has financed 111 projects worth US$921.3 million. At the 2007 Board of Executive Directors meeting, the Board agreed to transfer the Unit Investment Fund to IDB's member group, the Islamic Corporation for the Development of the Private Sector.

The IDB Infrastructure Fund (IFF) was established in 1999 and is based in Bahrain. The fund specifically focuses on infrastructure development in IDB member countries. As such, funds are invested in infrastructure projects and infrastructure-related industries in member countries. As at end of 2007, this fund had invested US$584 million in 11 projects covering nine member countries.

In May 2007, IDB launched the Islamic Solidarity Fund for Development (ISFD) with the prime aim of alleviating poverty, enhancing capacity building, eliminating illiteracy, and eradicating diseases and epidemics in the organization's member countries. The fund is established on the basis of voluntary contributions from all member countries. The fund is in the form of *waqf* and commenced operations in early 2008. IDB has contributed US$1 billion towards the capital of the fund with another US$1.6 billion contributions coming from its 30 member countries.

The Islamic Corporation for Insurance of Investments and Export Credit (ICIEC) was established on 1 August 1994 and began operations in July 1995 with an authorized capital of ID150 million (US$240 million) which is made up of 150,000 shares of ID1,000 each. IDB has subscribed US$160 million of the authorized capital while US$77 million is subscribed by the 37 OIC member countries. The goals of this *Syariah*-based organization are:

- To provide export credit insurance and re-insurance coverage on non-payment export receivables from commercial and non-commercial risks.

- To provide investment insurance and re-insurance against country risk.

Between 1996 and January 2008, ICIEC's total business insured was US$3.7 billion. During the 2006–2007 financial year, the total number of policies issued was 75 with its current commitments of US$1,467 million. For the same financial year, ICIEC's business insured amounted to US$859 million.

The Islamic Corporation for the Development of the Private Sector (ICD) was established in November 1999 as an independent international organization with an authorized capital of US$1 billion. Out of this authorized capital, US$500 million has been made available for subscription with IDB subscribing 50%, member countries 30% and public financial institutions in member countries 20%. The ICD provides a variety of financial products including direct financing, asset management, structured financing and advisory services. The corporation utilizes modes of financing that are in accordance with Islamic concept of financing such as equity participation and term financing such as *murabahah*, leasing, instalment sale and *istisna*. Since its establishment, ICD has approved a total of 121 projects worth US$680.5 million. At the end of 2007, 23 members had participated in this programme. The main objectives of ICD are:

- To identify opportunities available in the private sector that could function as engines of growth.

- To provide a wide range of *Syariah*-based financial products and services.

- To encourage the development of and expand the access to the Islamic capital market.

The Islamic Research and Training Institute (IRTI) was established in 1981 with the mandate to undertake research and training activities in the areas of Islamic economics, finance and banking. This institute also provides training facilities for the work force involved in economic development activities in member countries. The functions of the institute are as follows:

- To organize and conduct basic and applied research with the aim of developing models and methods for the application of *Syariah* in the areas of economics, finance and banking.

- To provide training and develop professionals in Islamic economics in order to fulfil the research and training requirements of *Syariah*-observing institutions in member countries.

- To train personnel in member countries who are involved in development activities.

- To establish centres which collect, organize and disseminate information that is related to its activities.

- To carry out activities that may be relevant or conducive to the attainment of its purpose.

In 1982, the government of Saudi Arabia appointed IDB to manage its project on the utilization of hajj meat. The prime goal of this project is to assist pilgrims to fulfil one of the important rites of animal sacrifice and at the same time to utilize and distribute the sacrificial meat to the poor and needy Muslims in member and non-member countries. In 2007 IDB slaughtered a total of 732,855 animals. The sacrificial meat was distributed in Mecca and transported via air, sea and land to several destinations in 27 countries.

Awqaf Properties Investment Fund (APIF) was established in pursuant to the decision made during the Sixth Awqaf Ministerial Meeting held in Jakarta on 29 October 1997. The fund had an initial subscribed capital of US$51 million and the capital base was increased to US$59 million in 2007. Since its establishment, APIF has approved 28 projects worth US$529 million in Indonesia, Kuwait, Malaysia, Saudi Arabia and the United Arab Emirates.

World Waqf Foundation was established in September 2001 (1422 H). IDB has contributed US$25 million to the foundation. The minimum value for individual contribution is at least US$1 million. The objectives of the foundation are:

- To further enhance IDB's efforts in the development of *waqf* funds.

- To support *waqf* towards increasing the social and economic development of Muslim communities and eradicating poverty.

- To fulfil the aspirations of welfare and philanthropic organizations for the establishment of an international *waqf* organization.

- To manage *waqf* properties entrusted to the foundation for safe-keeping and investment, and spend the income in accordance with the requirements of *Syariah*.

The International Centre for Biosaline Agriculture (ICBA) which is based in Dubai commenced operations in June 1999. The objective of ICBA is to develop irrigated agriculture technology that uses water of moderate to high salinity. The centre is expected to develop plant technologies that produce crops using various levels of saline water. Since its establishment, IDB and other donors have contributed a total of US$29.6 million for ICBA's activities. Throughout 2007, the centre conducted three technical programmes; 21 production and management systems programme; and 7 joint programmes under the communication, networking and information management programme. The centre also held seven courses and four workshops and seminars.

The OIC Information Systems Networks (OICIS-Net) is a project which was initiated in pursuance of the Meeting of Heads of Islamic Countries in Kuwait in 1987. The OICIS-NET is a joint venture with IDB holding 51% of the shares in the company. The main activities of this company are information services, e-commerce, internet connectivity and consultancy services. This project aims to improve the exchange and sharing of information resources among the member countries. The pilot project took off in nine member countries, namely Egypt, Indonesia, Kuwait, Malaysia, Morocco, Oman, Pakistan, Senegal and Turkey. A range of components are found in the information network, including network institution development, data base development, systems and standards, information service, telecommunications and training of personnel in information and communication technology. In the endeavour to develop this data base, priority has been given to the trade, corporate and agriculture sectors.

ACCOUNTING AND AUDITING ORGANIZATION FOR ISLAMIC FINANCIAL INSTITUTIONS

The Accounting and Auditing Organization for Islamic Financial Institutions (AAOIFI) is a non-profit organization established in Bahrain on 1 Safar 1410 corresponding to 27 March 1991. This organization, which was formerly known as Financial Accounting Organization for Islamic Banks and Financial Institutions (FAOIBFI) aims to develop accounting, auditing, governance, ethics and *Syariah* standards for the Islamic financial institutions. The chief motivator for the establishment was Dr. Rifaat Ahmed Abdel Karim. He was also AAOIFI's first Secretary General. The current Secretary General is Dr. Mohamad Nedal Alchaar.

The AAOIFI's organizational structure consists of six divisions, namely General Assembly, Board of Trustees, Accounting and Auditing Standards Board, Syariah Board, Executive Committee and Secretariat General. The General Assembly is the highest authority. It is responsible for the formulation of policies of the organization. Membership consists of four categories, namely founding members, associate members, regulatory and supervisory authorities and observer members. Founding members include the Islamic Development Bank (Saudi Arabia), Dar Al Mal Al Islami (Switzerland), al-Rajhi Banking and Investment Corporation (Saudi Arabia), Albaraka Banking (Bahrain), Kuwait Finance House (Kuwait) and Bukhari Capital (Malaysia). At the end of 2008, AAOIFI's membership included more than 160 institutional members from 40 countries.

The Board of Trustees consists of 20 part-time members appointed by the General Assembly every five years. Members of the Board remain in office until new members are appointed to replace them. Appointment of members are based on geographical location and from among the following:

- Regulatory and supervisory authorities

- Islamic financial institutions

- Accounting and auditing institutions related to Islamic financial institutions

- *Syariah fiqh* scholars

- Users of financial statements of Islamic financial institutions

The trustees have the authority to appoint the AAOIFI board members and terminate their membership in accordance with statutory provisions, to arrange sources of finance for the organization and invest these financial resources, to appoint two of its members to sit on the Executive Committee and to appoint the Secretary General. Although the Board has wide ranging authority, the trustees do not have the right or power to interfere in the other boards of AAOIFI.

The AAOIFI's Accounting and Auditing Standards Board is composed of 20 part-time members appointed by the Board of Trustees for a five-year term. This Board meets at least twice a year. Members are from among the following:

- Regulatory and supervisory authorities

- Islamic financial institutions

- Accounting and auditing institutions related to Islamic financial institutions

- Syariah Supervisory Boards

- Users of financial statements of Islamic financial institutions

- University professors in the field of accounting and finance

- Certified accountants

The duties and responsibilities of the Board are as follows (www.aaoifi.com/aasb):

- To prepare, adopt and interpret accounting, auditing and regulatory statements, standards and guidelines for Islamic financial institutions.

- To prepare and adopt code of ethics and educational standards related to the activities of Islamic financial institutions.

- To review with the intention of making additions, deletions or amendments to any accounting and auditing statements, standards and guidelines prepared by the Accounting and Auditing Standards Board. This is relevant to the enhancement and development of the activities of Islamic financial institutions. Moreover, it is to fulfil the needs of the users of financial statements of Islamic financial institutions.

- To prepare and adopt the due process for the preparation of standards, regulations and by-laws of the Accounting and Auditing Standards Board.

As with other boards, the Syariah Board consists of not more than 20 members each serving a four-year term. These *Syariah* experts are representatives of the Syariah Supervisory Boards of the Islamic financial institutions that are AAOIFI members, and the *Syariah* members in the central banks. Among the roles and functions of the Board are (www.aaoifi.com/sharia-board):

- To achieve harmonization and convergence in the concepts and application of the *fatwa* issued by the Syariah Boards of Islamic financial institutions in order to avoid contradiction or inconsistency on the *fatwa* issued.

- To assist in the development of *Syariah*-approved instruments and thus facilitating Islamic financial institutions in managing developments in the areas of finance, investment and other banking services.

- To study any enquiries raised by the Islamic financial institutions to the Syariah Boards and to take action, either by giving *Syariah* opinion on matters requiring collective *ijtihad* (reasoning), or settling divergent points of view or acting as an arbitrator.

- To review and study standards issued by AAOIFI in accounting, auditing, code of ethics and related statements to ensure that they conform to *Syariah* regulations and principles.

The Executive Committee consists of six members, namely the Secretary General, the Chairman of the Accounting and Auditing Standards Board, the Chairman of the Syariah Board and three members from the Board of Trustees. This committee is charged with the responsibility of reviewing work plans, annual budgets, financial statements and auditor's reports. The committee also acts as the body that approves work and finance regulations of AAOIFI. The Secretary General is the prime pillar in the daily administration of the organization. He is tasked with implementing the plan approved by both the Supervisory Committee (the supreme authority of the organization) and by the Financial Accounting Standards Board for Islamic Banks and Financial Institutions.

Since its establishment, AAOIFI had put into operation three major issuances, namely Accounting, Auditing and Regulatory Standards for Islamic Financial Institutions, Syariah Standards, and Statement on the Purpose and Calculation of the Capital Adequacy Ratio for Islamic Banks (www.aaoifi.com). The organization has also issued 68 standards in Islamic finance.

GENERAL COUNCIL FOR ISLAMIC BANKS AND FINANCIAL INSTITUTIONS

Incorporated in Manama, Bahrain, the General Council for Islamic Banks and Financial Institutions (CIBAFI) was established in May 2001. Currently, most of its members are from the United Arab Emirates, Kuwait and Malaysia. Membership of the council is comprised of 130 Islamic banks and financial institutions from 40 countries including Islamic commercial banks, merchant banks and financial institutions with Islamic window, Islamic funds and *takaful* companies.

CIBAFI is an international non-profit organization with the core mandate to enhance the image and ability of its members to serve customers through the practice of ethical investment, professionalism and transparency. This role is accomplished through the following (www.cibafi.org):

- Preparing a database or directory of banks and financial institutions that comply with Islamic ethics.

- Participating in the development of Islamic banking and finance by encouraging research and development and organizing conferences in this area.

- Improving and promoting the understanding of Islamic finance and banking and enhancing its existence locally and globally.

- Participating in the development of human resources by providing its members training and consultancy services as well as technical assistance.

The council comprises the General Assembly, Board of Directors, Executive Committee and General Secretariat. Members of the General Assembly consist of ordinary and observer members. Meetings are held once a year to draft and decide on policies or general specifications which are to be complied with and implemented by the council. The Board of Directors, on the other hand, decides on activities to be implemented by the council. These activities would in turn be monitored and supervised by the Executive Committee. The General Secretary, meanwhile, is the principal manager of all activities planned.

To further strengthen its presence, the council is enhancing its efforts to educate government personnel and the general public worldwide on the principles of Islamic banking. As an organization that prepares and provides information, CIBAFI is actively involved in publishing a number of research studies including Islamic Finance in the Gulf Cooperation Council, Islamic Finance Directory 2007, CIBAFI Performance Indicators, Islamic Finance Directory 2006, Islamic Finance Directory 2005 and IFSI First Global Report. It also acts as a centre for conducting comparative studies related to legislation and other fields. Presently, CIBAFI is working with the Islamic Development Bank and Islamic Financial Services Board to introduce a central *Syariah* council for issuing *fatwa* which would assist in dealing with different interpretations of *Syariah*-compliant standards and practices between jurisdictions across the globe.

INTERNATIONAL ISLAMIC FINANCIAL MARKET

The International Islamic Financial Market (IIFM) is a non-profit organization which was established as a result of the effort initiated by the Central Bank of Malaysia and Labuan Offshore Financial Services Authority (LOFSA) which asserted the importance of having an Islamic market to mobilize Islamic financial instruments. This initiative proposed by Malaysia was collectively shared by a number of countries as well as organizations including the Islamic Development Bank, Central Bank of Bahrain, Bank Indonesia (Indonesia's central bank), Bank of Sudan (Sudan's central bank) and Brunei's Ministry of Finance. As a result, an agreement was signed in Paris on 13 November 2001, whereby all the parties involved recognized and acknowledged the shortcomings in the Islamic financial system. Some of the shortcomings identified are:

- The absence of an international Islamic financial market.

- The lack of development of the Islamic capital market.

- Insufficient number of market participants and *Syariah*-compliant financial instruments.

- The lack of uniformity and consistency in *Syariah* interpretations of ambiguous and doubtful issues.

- The absence of a proper mechanism for the creation of an Islamic financial market.

- The absence of global acceptance of the accounting standards and practices of Islamic financial products.

- The absence of a secondary market for the transaction of *Syariah*-compliant financial instruments.

To overcome the above shortcomings, the six founding members agreed to set up a body with the vision of becoming a prominent institution which promotes the active and well-regulated trading of Islamic financial products and instruments internationally. The mission of IIFM is to promote the emergence and integration of the Islamic financial market into a mainstream global market. Initially, it was suggested that the organization be based in Labuan, Malaysia, but it was eventually incorporated in Bahrain on 1 April 2002. The Royal Decree for the establishment of this organization was gazetted on 11 August 2002, followed by its registration on 25 November 2002. Among the objectives of this organization are (www.iifm.net):

- To promote and enhance the development of international financial markets in accordance with *Syariah* principles.

- To promote active participation of both Islamic and non-Islamic financial institutions in the secondary market.

- To coordinate and act as a one-stop centre for *Syariah* harmonization of interpretations and views in the global financial market.

- To increase the framework of cooperation among Islamic financial institutions all over the world.

- To issue market guidelines, best practices procedures and assist in the formulation of standards for the Islamic financial market.

Membership of IIFM totals 43 and is categorized into five groups, namely founder member, full member, member, associate member and observer member. Founder members are required to pay an annual fee of US$35,000 and are the permanent members of the Board of Directors. Full members comprise central banks and monetary authorities, and full membership commands an annual fee of US$25,000. Four board seats are reserved for full members. The member category is given to Islamic financial institutions. They are required to pay an annual fee of US$20,000, and members are allowed to fill five board seats. Associate members comprise other financial institutions which are interested in Islamic financial services and their annual fee is US$5,000. Meanwhile, the annual fee for observer members is US$2,000. Both associate members and observer members have no voting rights in the general meetings.

Although this organization has various functions, major activities conducted currently cover only four areas, namely *Syariah* endorsement, standardization and harmonization, market listing and trading, and issuance of guides. In terms of its organizational structure, IIFM consists of the Board of Directors (16), Syariah Supervisory Advisory Panel (8), Executive Committee (7) and IIFM Management.

In principle, the Board of Directors is responsible for policies approval. The Board also has the authority to approve the admission of new members and to appoint IIFM officers. The Syariah Advisory Panel's responsibilities are to approve the application and mechanism of transactions of a particular financial product and instrument, to work closely with AAOIFI Syariah Board and to provide guidelines for harmonization and uniformity in decision making, and to review issues presented by the Board of Directors and the Executive Committee.

Since its establishment, IIFM has endorsed several global financial instruments including the Malaysia Global Sukuk worth US$600 million on 26 June 2002, Islamic Development Bank Sukuk worth US$400 million on 3 August 2003, Qatar Global Sukuk worth US$700 million on 8 September 2003 and Bahrain International Sukuk worth US$250 million in 2004. In 2004, the organization endorsed the US$100 million Tabreed Financial Corporation Sukuk. The Malaysia Global Sukuk and Qatar Global Sukuk are based on the *ijarah* concept, while Islamic Development Bank Sukuk is based on the *ijarah, murabahah* and *istisna* concepts (www.iifm.net). The global corporate *sukuk* issued by Tabreed Financial Corporation is a combination of *ijarah istisna* and *ijarah mawsufah fi al dhimmah* or forward leasing contracts.

Following its relaunch in August 2006, IIFM has embarked on a more focused and market-driven approach to position the organization as a major player in the global Islamic banking and finance industry. The new revised business plan of IIFM places greater emphasis on the standardization of Islamic financial instruments and contracts, cross border trading and infrastructure development. Previously, importance was placed more on *Syariah* endorsement on the legality and permissibility of financial instruments issued by financial institutions. Nonetheless, development of the global primary and secondary capital market, development of a short-term financial market and the creation of a market for Islamic financial instruments still remain key areas for IIFM. In order to ensure that standardized documents and products developed by IIFM are accepted and adopted by Islamic financial institutions around the world, the organization engages the industry and *Syariah* scholars in discussions through several of its working groups. Working groups that IIFM currently manages include Documentary Convergence Working Group, IIFM/ISDA Islamic Finance Working Group and IIFM/ICMA Shariah Compliant Repo Core Working Group.

In October 2008, IIFM launched the Master Agreement for Treasury Placement (MATP) which is the first ever standardized agreement for commodity *murabahah* transactions. The MATP comprises a stand-alone Master Murabaha Agreement, Master Agency Agreement and commodity purchase Letter of Understanding. Prior to this, financial institutions had to use 20 different documents when dealing with commodity *murabahah* transactions. It is envisaged that the development of such standardized agreement will translate into huge cost and resource savings for financial institutions. Currently, IIFM is in the midst of finalizing two more standard documents, namely the Master Agreement for Islamic Hedging (*Ta'Ahut*) and the *Syariah*-compliant Repurchase Agreement (Repo). The former document when completed shall be the standard document used for privately negotiated *Syariah*-compliant hedging transactions. It is being jointly developed by IIFM and the International Swaps and Derivatives Association (ISDA). The latter document is a collaborative effort between IIFM and the International Capital Market Association (ICMA) with main concentration on the development of recommendations, standard documentations, standard language and guidance for secondary market transactions and standardized practices in trading of *sukuk* as well as other Islamic financial instruments. IIFM and ICMA have also agreed to develop the Global Master Repurchase (Repo) Agreement and a handbook on the best practice recommendations for *sukuk* primary issuance.

ISLAMIC FINANCIAL SERVICES BOARD

The Islamic Financial Services Board (IFSB) was established on 3 November 2002 and began operations in March 2003. The Board was established in Malaysia under the *Islamic Financial Services Board Act 2002* which bestowed on IFSB the immunities and privileges normally granted to international organizations and diplomatic missions. This organization is similar to other international standard-setting bodies which have vested interest in the establishment and promotion of financial system best practices, including the Basel Committee on Banking Supervision, operating under the auspices of the Bank for International Settlements, International Organization of Securities Commissions and International Association of Insurance Supervisors. The goal of IFSB is to be an organization that unifies financial authorities, especially authorities in countries having Islamic banking systems, in order to ensure the soundness and stability of the system.

Consequently, the critical task of IFSB is to issue standards, guiding principles and technical notes for Islamic financial institutions. There are three categories of membership, namely full membership comprising supervisory authorities of each sovereign country, associate membership comprising monetary authority or financial supervisory or regulatory organizations, and observer membership comprising Islamic financial institutions throughout the world. In 2008, there were 21 full members, 21 associate members and 136 observer members (www.ifsb.org).

Since its establishment, IFSB has published seven prudential standards and guiding principles for the Islamic financial services industry as follows (www.iifm.net):

- Capital Adequacy Requirement for Sukuk Securitisation and Real Estate Investment.

- Guiding Principles on Governance for Islamic Collective Investment Scheme.

- IFSB-5: Guidance on Key Elements in the Supervisory Review Process of Institutions Offering Islamic Financial Services (excluding Islamic Insurance (*Takaful*) Institutions and Islamic Mutual Funds).

- IFSB-4: Disclosures to Promote Transparency and Market Discipline for Institutions Offering Islamic Financial Services (excluding Islamic Insurance (*Takaful*) Institutions and Islamic Mutual Funds).

- IFSB-3: Guiding Principles on Corporate Governance for Institutions Offering Only Islamic Financial Services (excluding Islamic Insurance (*Takaful*) Institutions and Islamic Mutual Funds).

- IFSB-2: Capital Adequacy Standard for Institutions (other than Insurance Institutions) Offering only Islamic Financial Services.

- IFSB-1: Guiding Principles of Risk Management for Institutions (other than Insurance Institutions) Offering only Islamic Financial Services.

The standards prepared follow a lengthy and stringent procedure as outlined in the Guidelines and Procedures for the Preparation of Standards/Guidelines established by IIFM. The preparation of standards also calls for the issuance of exposure drafts for public consultation which involves the organization of workshops and public hearings when the occasion necessitate. In 2008, IFSB published two industry guidelines which are:

- Guidance Note in Connection with the Capital Adequacy Standard: Recognition of Ratings by External Assessment Institutions on *Syariah*-compliant Financial Instruments.

- Technical Note on Issues in Strengthening Liquidity Management of Institutions Offering Islamic Financial Services: The Development of Islamic Money Market.

In addition to these documents, the organization had issued the Compilation Guide on Prudential and Structural Islamic Finance Indicators in the previous year. With the issuance of the Compilation Guide, a standard methodology for data compilation and dissemination among institutions offering Islamic financial services is now available to both market players and supervisory authorities. In order to promote awareness on issues related to the regulation and supervision of Islamic financial institutions as well as create awareness of Islamic finance in non-Muslim countries, IFSB has been actively involved in organizing international conferences, seminars, workshops and dialogues around the world.

ASSOCIATION OF ISLAMIC BANKING INSTITUTIONS MALAYSIA

The Association of Islamic Banking Institutions Malaysia (AIBIM) is an organization registered with the Malaysian Registrar of Societies. The association was established on 12 July 1995 with the prime objective of enhancing and promoting the establishment of sound Islamic banking systems and practices in Malaysia. This endeavour is accomplished in cooperation and consultation with Bank Negara Malaysia and other regulatory bodies in Malaysia.

AIBIM also functions as an organization that promotes and represents the interests of members consistent with the laws of Malaysia. The association also provides and promotes education and training in order to upgrade Islamic banking expertise in Malaysia. In pursuing the prescribed objectives, AIBIM establishes networks with other similar associations, locally and abroad. In addition, the association awards recognition to individuals and organizations with outstanding contributions towards the development of Islamic banking practices in Malaysia. The awards bestowed are the Islamic Finance Figure and the Excellent Performance Award.

Membership of the association is of two categories, ordinary membership and associate membership. Ordinary membership is open to all Islamic banks, commercial banks, merchant banks, financial companies and other financial institutions providing Islamic banking services as approved by the Finance Minister of Malaysia. Associate members comprise those considered qualified and accepted by the AIBIM Council. These members, however, are not eligible to represent the AIBIM Council and do not have any voting rights at the general meetings. The management of the association lies with 11 elected members and 3 co-opted ordinary members. The elected members will appoint from among themselves those who will hold management positions such as that of president, vice president, honourable secretary and honourable treasurer. The daily management of the association is handled by the executive secretary (www.aibim.com.my).

ISLAMIC BANKING AND FINANCE INSTITUTE MALAYSIA

The BIMB Institute of Research and Training Sdn Bhd (BIRT), a subsidiary of Bank Islam Malaysia Berhad, was the first institution established with the main objective of promoting human capital development in Islamic banking and providing understanding of the Islamic banking system. This institute was incorporated under the *Companies Act 1965* on 13 April 1995, and began operations on 1 August 1995. Apart from organizing various seminars and short training programmes, the institute also offers academic programmes at the diploma level through an education institution known as the Islamic Banking and Finance College. Among the diplomas offered are Diploma in Accounting, Diploma in Islamic Banking, Diploma in Marketing and Diploma in *Takaful*.

In line with the blueprint outlined in the Financial Sector Master Plan launched in early 2001, the Malaysian government proposed that an institution wholly owned by the Islamic finance and banking industry be established (Bank Negara Malaysia, 2001). Thus, BIRT was acquired by the industry and changed its name to Islamic Banking and Finance Institute Malaysia Sdn Bhd (IBFIM). The launching of this new institute was officiated by Tun Daim Zainuddin, then the Malaysia's Finance Minister, on 19 February 2001. The shareholders of IBFIM comprise Bank Negara Malaysia and 12 financial institutions that offer Islamic banking products.

IBFIM's vision is to become a leading international human capital and business developer in Islamic finance. In the area of training and education, IBFIM provides two main programmes, training programme and structured programme. Under its training programmes, IBFIM is actively involved in organizing in-house and public seminars, workshops and conferences in the area of Islamic finance and management. The structured programmes consist of certificate courses, skill-based courses in Islamic finance and advanced programmes with international exposure. Currently, IBFIM offers three types of certification programmes, namely Islamic Certified Credit Professional, Islamic Financial Planner and Shariah Scholars Induction Programme.

In the area of *Syariah* advisory and audit services, the activities conducted include advisory services in the area of Islamic banking and finance, *takaful*, unit trusts, mutual trusts, asset management, *sukuk*, Islamic real estate investment trusts or REITs, leasing and information technology. IBFIM also provides services such as the screening of *Syariah*-compliant stocks and securities, the development of *Syariah*-approved financial institutions as well as *Syariah* audit services. The business advisory and development area entails research related to the development and structuring of *Syariah*-based products, models of *Syariah*-based operations, *Syariah* accounting standards, risk management and *Syariah* asset and liability management (www.ibfim.com.).

SUMMARY

Islamic financial institutions developed rapidly in the 1970s. As their number increased substantially, it became apparent that a special organization was needed to act as a liaison or arbitrator in resolving issues of mutual interest to the Islamic financial services industry. The Jeddah-based Islamic Development Bank (IDB) is one of the main catalysts in the establishment of Islamic banks worldwide. This bank which was established in 1975, is the leading institution in mobilizing wealth of Muslim countries through cooperation among them as well as in raising the economic level of least developed Muslim countries. Projects implemented by IDB are intended to not only benefit its member countries but also Muslim communities in both Muslim and non-Muslim countries. The bank runs four categories of programmes, namely project financing, technical assistance and *waqf* fund operations, trade finance operations and activities of specialized funds and its affiliated institutions.

Apart from IDB, several organizations whose members are Islamic financial institutions have also been set up with the objective of protecting the interest of its members and implementing activities of mutual benefits. The first organization of this kind to be established was the International Association of Islamic Banks. This organization was unfortunately dissolved in 1997 after 30 years in operation. In its place, the General Council for Islamic Banks and Financial Institutions was launched in Bahrain. However, the council has yet to make its presence felt in the industry as its activities are limited to organizing seminars and conferences. At the national level, associations such as the Association of Islamic Banking Institutions Malaysia was established to protect the mutual interest of its members that are local Islamic financial institutions. The association is also committed to promoting and enhancing the development of Islamic banking.

In order to complement these organizations, institutions whose membership comprise the central banks and monetary authorities were established. For instance, the Accounting and Auditing Organization for Islamic Financial Institutions (AAOIFI), which is based in Bahrain, was established specifically for handling matters related to accounting and auditing standards of Islamic financial institutions. Islamic Financial Services Board (IFSB) centred in Kuala Lumpur was established to ensure the soundness and stability of Islamic finance through regulating and supervising the industry. The International Islamic Financial Market (IIFM), based in Bahrain, is responsible for the promotion and development of Islamic financial instruments in the secondary market.

With respect to education and training, a number of organizations at both the national and international levels such as the Islamic Banking and Finance Institute Malaysia and the Jeddah-based Islamic Research and Training Institute, have been established for the purpose of creating human capital in Islamic banking.

REFERENCES AND FURTHER READING

Bank Negara Malaysia. *Financial Sector Master Plan*. Kuala Lumpur, 2001.

Islamic Development Bank. *Annual Report* (various years). Jeddah (Saudi Arabia).

Musa Kamal, Rahayu. "Standardization: The Password to Progress." *Islamic Finance News*, August/September 2008: 28–30.

www.aibim.com.my

www.banking-business-review.com

www.ibfim.com

www.ifsb.org

www.iifm.net

www.isdb.org

www.islamicfinanceonline.com/gcibfi

www.Lariba.com

www.mcca.com.au

GLOSSARY

A'mal
Plural for *mal* (work) necessary in a partnership, or terms stated at the time of establishment of the partnership.

'Abd
Worker; *'abd ma'dhun* is a worker who has been the authority to perform a task on behalf of his employer.

Ahad
The term used for a *hadith* narrated by only one narrator or coming from only one source.

Ahkam al-muamalat al-Islamiah
Islamic *muamalah* rules.

Ahkam
Regulations or instructions, rules. Singular: *hukm*

Ahliyah
Legislative capacity.

Ahliyat al-ada'
Legislative capacity to perform a certain responsibility.

Ahsan al-hadith
The best spoken words.

Ajal
Period of time; period in which delivery is deferred.

Akhlaq
Behaviour, actions and work ethics.

Al-adillat-al-ijtihadiyyah
Views or opinions acquired through thorough thinking and perseverance in resolving problems at hand. In *Syariah*, it refers to *ijma* and *qiyas*.

Al-adillat-al-qatiyyah
Views or opinions which are absolute, whose truth cannot be disputed. In *Syariah*, this refers to the Quran and *hadith*.

Al-amin
Reliable, honest, trustworthy.

Al-arabun
See *urbun*.

Al-bai bithaman ajil
See *bai bithaman ajil.*

Al-Bayan
Explanation.

Al-Burhan
View.

Al-Dikra
Provider of reminders, or source of nobility.

Al-Furqan
That which discerns between the truth and faslehood or between authentic and corrupted.

Al-Haqq
The truth.

Al-hawala
Transference of debt from one person to another. Also termed *al-hiwalah.* One of the *Syariah* principles in Islamic Banking System (normally termed *hiwalah*).

Al-Hikmah
Wisdom.

Al-hiwalah
See *Al-hawala.*

Al-Hakim
That which/who judges or executes rules.

Al-ijarah
See *ijara.*

Al-ijarah thumma al-bai
Rent or lease which provides and option to purchase by the tenant or lessee. It is one of the *Syariah* principles used by the Islamic Banking System in Malaysia.

Al-kafalah
Guarantee. It is a guarantee made by a person to the owner of an item who places the item with a third party. In the event that the owner submits any claims on the item, the guarantor is required to fulfil it. It is one of the *Syariah* principles used by the Islamic Banking System in Malaysia (commonly called *kafala*).

Al-khair
Good deeds; good.

Al-Mau'izah
Advisor or criticizer.

Al-Mofaviza
  General partnership (it is
  a form of partnership in
  musyarakah).

Al-mudharabah
  See *mudharabah*.

Al-muhaimin
  Guardian; protector.

Al-murabahah
  See *murabahah*.

Al-musyarakah
  See *musyarakah*.

Al-Naimah
  Blessing.

Al-Nur
  Light.

Al-qardhul hasan
  See *qard hasan*.

Al-Qayyim
  Guardian; protector.

Al-Rahmah
  Forgiveness.

Al-rahn
  See *rahn*.

Al-Ruh
  The life of life.

Al-Shifa
  Healer.

Al-Tadhkirah
  Remembrance or mindful of
  Allah.

Al-Tanzil
  A form of guidance that
  descend from elevated sources
  such as revelation (*wahyu*) from
  Allah the Most High.

Al-ujr
  A commission or fee charged
  on a service provided. It is one
  of the *Syariah* principles used
  by the Islamic Banking System
  in Malaysia.

Al-urbun
  See *urbun*.

Al-wadiah yad dhamanah
  Deposit on Trust with security
  or guarantee, where the trustee
  guarantees to return the items
  involved on demand. It is one
  of the *Syariah* principles used
  by the Islamic Banking System
  in Malaysia.

Al-wakalah mal
  An agency contract between
  two parties where one party
  act on behalf of the other a
  specified in the contract.

Al-wakala al mutlaqa
  Absolute Agency.

'Amal
Work or action.

Amil
See mudarib; also termed *amel*.

Amwal
Plural for *mal* (wealth). Wealth released as capital in a partnership.

Ansar
Muslims in Madinah that provides assistance to those who flee from persecution in Mecca during the Meccan period.

Aqa'id
See aqidah.

'Aqd
Agreement or contract.

Aqidah
The form of faith and belief of Muslims in Allah s.w.t. Also termed *aqa'id*.

Aqilah
Persons having family ties or cooperative connections and who assist in unintended killings. They are, together with the killers, held responsible by law to indemnify "blood money".

Arboon
See arbun.

Ardh
Land. The majority of jurists have the opinion that land owner does not qualify to receive rights to profit compared to other factors like wealth, labour and credit capability.

Arkan
Elements or qualities of an action, the absence of which results in the action being invalid.

Arsh
Compensation due to inflicting injury.

As-salam
Sales and purchase concept where the price is paid in advance for an item which will be delivered later.

Asbab al-nuzul
The reason for the sending down (of a Quranic verse).

Athaman mutlaqah
Absolute currency. It refers to the use of dinar and dirham.

Awqaf
  Property transferred
  voluntarily for trust keeping,
  to be utilized for the welfare of
  the public.

Ayah
  Guidance signs or a
  communication from Allah
  s.w.t. Singular form: *ayat*.
  It refers to the verses of the
  Quran.

Ayn
  Tangible goods or property
  with physical form.

Aziz
  The term used for a *hadith* with
  only one narrator, where the
  individual is highly reliable
  and is accepted as a narrator of
  hadith.

Bai'
  A general term which is used to
  mean sale and other exchange
  transactions or contracts.

Bai al-dayn
  Sale of Debt. It is applied
  to debt financing where its
  existence is based on trade
  documents. It is one of the
  Syariah principles used by the
  Islamic Banking System in
  Malaysia.

Bai' al-Inah
  A sales contract which
  involves the processes of
  sale and repurchase between
  two contracting parties. For
  example a seller will sell
  an item by credit and then
  repurchase it by cash at a lower
  price compared to the original
  selling price. This system is
  adopted by the Islamic banking
  system in Malaysia.

Bai' al-istijrar
  A sales contract which involves
  repeated delivery of goods at a
  pre-agreed price and payment
  mode. It is also commonly
  known as *istijrar*.

Bai' al-istisna
  Order sales (*see istisna*).

Bai' al-muzayadah
  Sales undertaken by a certain
  party in the open market by
  tender, where the sale will be
  executed to the party offering
  the higher price.

Bai al-urbun
  Sale with advanced payment or
  down payment.

Bai' al-wafa'
  A sales conditional contract,
  where the seller pays back

the selling price to the buyer
and the buyer returns the
purchased goods.

Bai' bithaman ajil
Increment on the cost with
deferred payment, or deferred
payment sale, also referred to
as *bay' mujjal* or *bai muazzal*.

Bai' muazzal
See *bai' bithaman aji*. This
method is used by Islamic
banks in Bangladesh in their
real estate financing.

Bai'-salam
Salam sale where the buyer
makes an immediate payment
and the seller defers the
delivery of the goods to a
certain period in the future.
Also termed *baiul-salam*.

Bay' bi'l-nasiah
Sale by credit.

Bay' mujjal
See *bai bithaman ajil*.

Buda'ah
The item submitted to another
party to be traded without
involving any reward or profit
sharing.

Da'if
Weak. It is a term used for a
hadith which is not strong and
which will be rejected if it is
one that touches on religious
command or prohibition. It
may be taken as a guide if it is
in the form of advice, fable or
good behaviour. *See sakim*.

Dar al-harb
Country or region that has
the potential to be at war with
Islam.

Dar al-Islam
Country or region under
Islamic rule and applying
Islamic law.

Dar al-sulh
Country or region that has an
agreement with Muslims.

Darb
Efforts put in on the face of the
earth.

Dayn/dain
Loan, debt, or receivables.

Dayn mu'ajjal
Debt increment due to
extension of loan period.

Dhaman
Compensation or obligation.

Dhaman al-'amal
Responsibility that exists in a partnership based on expertise, where one of the partners is responsible in implementing a contract or in completing a task agreed upon by the other partner.

Dhaman al-thaman
Responsibility that exists in a partnership based on credit strength, where every partner is jointly or individually responsible in paying the price of the goods bought by credit.

Din
Obedience, compliance; practice; conform.

F'il
Action or doing.

Far
See *furu*.

Fard
A term for *hadith* which is narrated by one narrator at each level, or which is narrated by narrators in the same district only.

Fasidun
People who cause destruction or woe.

Fasiqun
Those who rebel.

Faskh
Cancellation or dissolution.

Fatwa
A ruling issued by authorities in Islam.

Furu
Branch. Singular: *far*.

Ghaib
A term for *hadith* which comes from only one source, that is, whether from the Companions or those who lived after them.

Gharim
The debtor who fails to pay debts from outstanding obligations.

Hadith/hadis
Information, narration, story, reports or records of the *sunnah* of the Prophet Muhammad p.b.u.h.

Hamish jiddiyyah

Initial payment or deposit paid by a buyer who intends to buy a certain item.

Haram

Shariah ruling that prohibits or consider something forbidden. One of the *ahkam* in Islam.

Hasan

Good, reasonable or appropriate. A term used for *hadith* which can be adopted.

Hizim

Binding; a contract which is binding.

Hibah

Gift.

Hila

Plural form: *hiyal*. It is a type of juristic instrument which is created to accomplish something which is in principle conflicting with *Syariah*. This application is only found in the Hanafi and Shafii *mazhab*. Hanbali and Maliki *mazhab* do not object to its use.

Hiwalah

See *al-hiwalah*.

Hiyal

See *hila*. It is a concept amongst those in the Hanafi *mazhab*, whereby an established partnership is not limited and possesses rights or contributions that are equal and balanced amongst partners.

I'ktikadat

Rule, stipulation.

Ibadah

Action with respect to worshipping Allah.

Ibahah

Truth.

Ibra'

The process of cancelling one's own rights. For example, a person has the right to claim payment of debts owed to him by a debtor, but he cancels that right by cancelling the debt concerned.

Ijara

Rent or lease. Also called *al-ijarah*. It is an agreement where a property owner will rent or lease out the property to a tenant or lessee for a stipulated period. In return, the tenant or lessee will provide rental or lease payment according to the predetermined amount and time. It is one of the *Syariah* principles in the Islamic banking system.

Ijara wa-iqtina
Hire purchase contract or lease purchase contract, whereby at the end of the lease period the ownership right of the lease asset will be transferred to the tenant.

Ijma
Mutual agreement, opinion or collaborative stand. It is one of the sources of *Syariah*.

Ijtihad
The practice or method of problem solving, or the process of mental perseverance undertaken with full concentration and commitment to solve a particular issue, especially that related to religion.

Ikala
Reciprocation or replacement. Also termed as *iqala*, i.e. cancellation of contract on mutual agreement.

Ilahi
See *kudsi*.

Illa
Reasoning created through the same process. Plural: *'ilal*.

Ilm al-ma'ani
Knowledge of rhetoric or the art of effective usage of words or flowery language.

Ilm al-tajwid
Knowledge of Quran recital.

Inan
Limited investment partnership.

Inan syarikat mal
Limited financial partnership, financial participation.

Intiha'
Termination, end, dissolution or cancellation of a partnership.

Iqala
See *ikala*.

Isnad
Links of a *hadith*.

Isqat
Elimination or cancellation of rights.

Istikhraj
Conclusion drawn by method of analogy. *See istinbat.*

Istinbat
To search and draw on a hidden meaning by the process of *ijtihad*. Also termed as *istikhraj*.

Istisna
Contract for the manufacture or production of particular goods.

Istijrar
See bai al-istijrar.

'Iwadh
Compensation, replacement value.

Ja'iz
An action whether executed or disregarded, results in neither reward nor sin. Also termed as *mubah*.

Jami
Something gathered or accumulated together. Also termed as *musannaf*.

Jihalah
Unknown or uncertainties in a contract which may cause disputes in the future.

Jins
From the same type, genus or group.

Jo'alah
Service charge, i.e. a guarantee where the party requiring a service will pay a certain amount of charges to the party providing the service. This is one of the *Syariah* principles used in the Islamic banking system in Iran.

Kafil
Person who guarantees.

Kafirun
Person whose faith is not within Islam.

Kalam-Allah
Words of Allah S.W.T.

Khiyar
Option or right. Plural: *khiyarat*.

Khiyar al-'ayb
Option or right given to the buyer or tenant to revoke on discovering defects on the goods intended to be purchased or rented.

Khiyar al-ru'ya
Option or right given to the buyer or tenant to revoke after inspecting the goods intended to be purchased or rented.

Khiyar al-shart
   Option or right given to the
   buyer or tenant subject to
   specific conditions.

Khiyar al-wasf
   Option or right given to the
   buyer or tenant based on the
   quality of the goods involved.

Kudsi
   The term used for the *hadith*
   which contains Allah's
   revelation. This type of *hadith* is
   taken from Allah's Messenger's
   sunnah and is termed *nabawi*
   hadith. Other terms used are
   ilahi or *rabbani hadith*.

Lazim
   Ties, bond.

Ma'lul
   See *mu'allal*.

Mahfuz
   Stuck in the mind. The term
   used for *hadith* in the category
   of *hadith* which can be adopted.
   Its status is higher than that of
   hadith of the *shadhdh* category.

Mahjoor
   Person prohibited by law
   to undertake contracts or
   businesses.

Majmul
   Brief.

Makbul
   Accepted. The term for
   the *hadith* which fulfils all
   conditions for it to be adopted.
   Hadith of this category are also
   normally grouped as *sahih* or
   hasan hadith.

Makruh
   Action which is not encouraged
   but neither is it forbidden, and
   doing it will not result in sin or
   abhorrence. One of the *ahkam* in
   Islam.

Maktu
   The term for the *hadith* whose
   origin of *isnad* is linked
   directly to the people after the
   Companions.

Mandub
   See *sunna*.

Maniha
   To accord the right to utilize an
   asset for a certain period to a
   person who is in need of it.

Mansukh
   See *nasikh*.

Mardud

Rejected. The term used for
hadith which is classified as
not adoptable. This *hadith*
comes from weak or unknown
narrators, and what is narrated
differs from the narration of
others who are reliable. *See
munkar, matruk, matruh,* and
mawdu.

Marfu

The term for *hadith* whose
origin of *isnad* is linked directly
to Allah's Messenger p.b.u.h.

Maruf

Acceptable. The term for
hadith classified as that which
can be adopted. It is however
considered weak and is verified
by other *hadith* of the same
standing with it.

Marufat

Good.

Masaqat

A contract whereby the owner
of trees would hand over
his trees to another party to
manage it, and the profit would
be distributed according to an
agreed upon ratio. Also termed
as *mosaqat.* It is one of the
Syariah principles used by the
Islamic Banking System of Iran.

Masnun

See sunna.

Matn

Content of *hadith.*

Matruh

Disposed of. The term for *hadith*
which cannot be adopted. The
hadith come from narrators
known to be untruthful or
who openly misbehaved and
told lies. *See mardud, munkar,
matruh,* and *mawdu.*

Mawdu

Imaginary, made up. The
term for *hadith* which cannot
be adopted. The *hadith* are
made up on purpose and are
regarded the most dangerous
and of lowest status. *See
mardud, munkar, matruk, and
matruh.*

Mawkuf

The term for *hadith* whose
origin of *isnad* is linked directly
to the Companions of Allah's
Messenger p.b.u.h.

Milk mushtarak

Joint ownership.

Modaraba

See mudarabah.

Modarabah
  See *mudarabah*.

Mosaqat
  See *masaqat*.

Mozara'ah
  A contract where a landowner assigns his land to be worked on by another party for a certain period, and the profit will be divided according to a mutually agreed upon ratio. It is one of the *Syariah* principles used by the Islamic Banking System of Iran.

Mozare
  The landowner in the *mozara'ah* contract.

Mozarebeh
  See *mudarabah*.

Mu'allah
  Suspended, hanging. The term used for the *hadith* where one or two or all the names of the narrators are not mentioned in the *isnad*.

Mu'allal
  The term used for *hadith* which has weaknesses or defects in its *isnad* or *matn*. Also termed as *ma'lul*.

Muamalat
  Business or commercial transactions or activities involving contracting parties.

Mu'ayyan
  Specification of goods through weights and measures for the purpose of transaction or sale.

Mubham
  Vague or unclear.

Mudarabah
  Partnership. Also termed as *modarabah, al-mudharabah,* and *modaraba*. Also known as *qirad* and *muqaradah*. The concept is applied where the investor who allocates capital to entrepreneur to undertake a business will not interfere in the business or enterprise. Profit is shared according to a pre-agreed upon ratio whilst loss is borne by the investor. One of the *Syariah* principles in Islamic Banking System.

Mudarib
  Entrepreneur who undertakes business on someone else's capital. Also called *amil* and *rabb al-mal*.

Mufawada

The concept used by the Hanafi *mazhab* for equal partnership in terms of capital issued between the partners and in other matters.

Muhajirun

The people of Makkah who perform the *hijrah* to Medina with Prophet Muhammed p.b.u.h.

Muhaqalah

The sale of food product which is not yet harvested. (This type of sale is not allowed in Islam.)

Muhkamaat

Clear and concise in meaning.

Mujtahid

Persons with expertise in Islamic law and other branches of the religion.

Mukhabarah

Contract regarding sharing of agriculture produce, where the landowner places an order for the produce at a selected area. (This kind of contract is forbidden.) Also termed as musaqah, which refers to transactions with Jews at Khaibar.

Munafa'a

Usufruct or utility.

Munfasil

The term for *hadith* with broken links in the *isnad*. **See** *munkati*.

Munkar

Disregarded. The term for *hadith* which cannot be adopted. Narrated by only one narrator and differs from the narration of others with credibility. **See** *mardud, matruk, matruh,* and *mawdu.*

Munkarat

Vice or evil doings.

Munkati

The term used by Imam Shafii and al-Tabrani for *hadith* with broken *isnad*.

Muqaradah

See mudarabah and qirad.

Muqasah

Amortization of debt through contra transactions.

Murabahah

Increment over cost or cost plus mark up, also termed as *al-murabahah*. It is one of the *Syariah* principles used by the Islamic Banking System.

Mursal

The term used for the *hadith* where the narrators after the time of the Companions quoted the words of the Prophet directly, without mentioning the names of the Companions.

Musannaf

See *jami*.

Mushrika

See *musyarakah*

Mushrikoon

Opposers of Islam during the time of Allah's Messenger p.b.u.h.

Musnad

Authority. Also termed as *sanad*.

Mustahabb

See *sunna*.

Musyarakah

Joint venture. Also termed as *al-musyarakah*, and *mushrika*. A concept where several investors cum entrepreneurs provide capital for a business venture. The investors participate in the management. Profit is to be shared according to a pre-agreed upon ratio and loss is to be shared according to capital contribution ratio. It is one of the *Syariah* principles used in the Islamic Banking System.

Mutasyaabihaat

Vague, and the actual meaning cannot be determined.

Mutawatir

The term for *hadith* narrated by many narrators with no dispute amongst them.

Muttasil marfu

The term for the *hadith* where the *isnad* is not broken and is linked directly to Allah's Messenger P.B.U.H.

Muttasil mawkuf

The term for the *hadith* where the *isnad* is not broken and linked directly to the Companions.

Muzayadah

See *bai al-muzayadah*.

Nabat al-bi'ra

To dig a well that releases water.

Nabawi

The term for *hadith* taken from the *sunnah* of Allah's Messenger p.b.u.h. It contains Allah's revelation. Also termed *hadith kudsi*.

Nasa'a
See *nasiah*.

Nasiah
Delay, defer or wait. Taken from the word *nasa'a*.

Nasikh
Cancellation. Also termed as *mansukh*.

Qard
Loan.

Qard al-hasanah
See *qard hasan*.

Qard hasan
Loan for welfare or goodwill. Also termed as *qard al-hasanah, al-qardhul hasan* and *qarz-e-hasna*. It is one of the *Syariah* principles in the Islamic Banking System.

Qard-e-hasna
See *qard hasan*.

Qirad
Trust financing, profit sharing of trustees, and equity sharing. Also termed as *mudarabah* or *muqaradah*.

Qiyas
Juristic instrument in the form of comparison by analogy. It is one of the sources of *Syariah*.

Qal
Speech.

Rabb al-mal
See *mudarib*.

Rabbani
See *kudsi*.

Rabia
Hill or high land.

Rahn
Pawn or security. Also termed as *ar-rahn*. It is one of the *Syariah* principles in the Islamic Banking System in Malaysia.

Riba
Interest or interest rate.

Riba al-buyu
See *riba al-fadl*.

Riba al-duyun
See *riba al-jahiliyya*.

Riba al-fadl
Riba that emerges from trade and sale transactions involving ribawi commodities. Also known as sales *riba*. Also

termed as *riba al-hadith, riba al-sunnah, riba al-buyu, riba ghyr al-mubashir* and *riba al-khafi*.

Riba al-hadith
See *riba al-fadl*

Riba al-jahiliyya
Riba which existed before Islam became established. It emerged as a result of extension of debt period and is commonly called debt *riba*. Also termed as *riba Al-Quran, riba al-nasiah, riba al-duyun, riba al-mubashir* and *riba al-jali*.

Riba al-jali
See *riba al-jahiliyya*.

Riba al-khafi
See *riba al-fadl*.

Riba al-mubashir
See *riba al-jahiliyya*.

Riba al-nasiah
See *riba al-jahiliyya*.

Riba al-qaradah
Riba which emerges due to the creditor asking for additional payment because of the lengthening of the normal debt period.

Riba Al-Quran
See *riba al-jahiliyya*.

Riba al-sunnah
See *riba al-fadl*.

Riba ghyr al-mubashir
See *riba al-fadl*.

Ruhul-kudus
Holy spirit.

Saddadah-dhara'i
Barrier to the use of a certain method. It is a principle formed by the Maliki *mazhab* to bar the use of methods allowed by *Syariah* to attain objectives which are by origin *haram*.

Sahib al-mal
Fund owner of investor.

Sahih
The term for *hadith* which can be adopted.

Sakim
Not significant. The term for *hadith* which is not strong and which will be rejected if it is one that touches on religious commands and prohibitions. It may however be used as a guide if it is in the form of advice or narration of good behaviour.

Salam

   See bai' salam.

Samsarah

   Broker, agent or business that attains commission.

Sanad

   See musnad.

Sandauq al-zakat

   Zakat funds.

Shadhdh

   The term for *hadith* that comes from only one reliable source, and the contents differ somewhat from what is narrated by other narrators.

Shirkatul meelk

   See syarikat mulk.

Shurut

   Conditions or terms.

Sukuk

   Certificate of proof of debt or proof of investment.

Sunan

   See sunnah.

Sunna

   Action which is promoted but not obligated. One of the *ahkam* in Islam. Also termed as *masnun*, *mandub* or *mustahabb*.

Sunnah

   Ways, rules or behaviour in life. In the context of *Syariah*, it refers to behaviour, action, reaction, tacit approval and utterances of Allah's Messenger p.b.u.h. in various situations in life. Plural: *sunan*.

Sunnat al-awwalin

   The ways or examples of people in the past.

Sura

   Noble or pure. Singular: *surat*. It refers to the verses of the Quran.

Surat

   See sura.

Syahadah ad-dayn

   Debt certificate

Syar

   Path or way leading to water. *See syariah* and *syara'a.*

Syariah

   Path or way. Also termed as *syar*. Commonly known as Islamic law.

Syarika
Partnership. *See musyarakah.*

Syarikat 'aqd
Joint partnership. It involves joint partnership in capital issuance as well as in the management of the venture concerned.

Syarikat a'mal
Workforce or manpower partnership. In this case, experience and expertise of partners are important criteria in establishing the partnership.

Syarikat mal
Financial partnership. In this case, cash is an important criteria in establishing the partnership.

Syarikat mulk
Asset partnership. Also termed as *shirkatul meelk*. It only involves partnership in ownership on an asset and does not involve any joint enterprise in the development of the asset.

Syarikat wujuh
Credit partnership. In this case, partnership is based on credit.

Taqrir
Implicit truth.

Ujr
See *al-ujr.*

Ummat Al Islam
The Islamic community as a whole or the Muslim ummah.

Uqud
Akad, promise, pledge or responsibility.

Urbun
Also termed *arboon*. It is a type of deposit or initial payment as part payment of goods or services intended to be purchased and which will not be void if the transaction is discontinued. (According to the Hanbali *mazhab* it will be void.)

Usul
Roots or origin or primary source.

Usul al-fiqh
Knowledge of the origins of Islamic law or Islamic Jurisprudence.

Wadiah
Trust. Also termed *al-wadiah*. It is trust that is entrusted by a property owner to another party who will keep the property and returns it

on demand. It is one of the *Syariah* principles in the Islamic Banking System.

Wahy matluww
Revelation that is read.

Wajib
See *fard*.

Wakalah
See *al-wakalah*.

Warik
A type of currency in the beginning era of Islam. It originated from silver which was molten down to form dirham.

Yastinbitun
See *istinbat*.

Zalimun
Persons who commit injustice, vice or wrongdoings.

INDEX